'Psychoanalytic Investigations in Philosophy is humanistic interdisciplinary writing at its finest. The diverse essays, compiled and edited by Dorit Lemberger, herself a model of the interdisciplinary, dazzle in their brilliance and clarity. There are philosophical studies of psychoanalytic themes and approaches, psychoanalytic studies of literature, and several essays in which philosophy, psychoanalysis, and interpretation inform each other and coalesce. Each author is trained, informed, and experienced. A treasure!'

Edward L. Greenstein, *former head of the Interdisciplinary Graduate Program in Hermeneutics and Cultural Studies, Bar-Ilan University*

'This book forms a beautiful tapestry, presenting the creative fruits of thought that were formed during elaborate theoretical explorations and are now neatly packed and formulated for the reader's enjoyment. It is a major contribution to those who are interested in psychoanalysis not only as a clinical practice, but also as an intellectual discipline that can be carefully interwoven along with philosophical, linguistic, and other disciplines, thus forming a rich and inspiring variety of models for hermeneutic, interdisciplinary thought.'

Noga Ariel-Galor, Ph.D., *Tel-Aviv University and Haifa University*

Psychoanalytic Investigations in Philosophy

This pioneering volume explores and exemplifies the relevance of psychoanalysis to contemporary philosophical problems. The novelty of the book's viewpoint is the consideration of psychoanalysis as an existentialist mode of thinking that deals with current existential problems such as loneliness, uncertainty, struggling with personal tragedies, and rehabilitation.

Each chapter presents classic aspects of psychoanalytic theory based on Greek tragedies, as well as their similarities with interdisciplinary aspects in other areas of study such as modern literature, hermeneutics, and philosophy of language. To deepen each subject, each chapter also applies an interdisciplinary methodology that illuminates previously hidden insights arising from the fusion of psychoanalysis and philosophy. Featuring contributions from well-known scholars like Professor Avi Sagi and Professor Dov Schwartz, as well as more up-and-coming writers, the book suggests possible implications of philosophical, hermeneutical, and literary theories to the perception of post-modern issues concerning agency and the subjective emotional world.

Psychoanalytic Investigations in Philosophy is of great interest to scholars of psychoanalysis and hermeneutic philosophy, as well as teachers and academics who want to explore new teaching methods in various disciplines, and general-interest readers who wish to expand their horizons around concepts that can be applied to better understand themselves and the age in which we live.

Dorit Lemberger, Ph.D., is a senior lecturer at Bar-Ilan University, in the department of Hermeneutics and Cultural studies that includes a Psychoanalysis and Hermeneutics track. She is an advisor of many doctorate students who write interdisciplinary research using Wittgenstein's philosophy and pragmatic thinkers to enlighten linguistic usage in Hebrew literary texts and Psychoanalytic writings. Dr. Lemberger is an associate editor of *Hebrew Studies* Journal.

Philosophy & Psychoanalysis Book Series
Series Editor: Jon Mills

Philosophy & Psychoanalysis is dedicated to current developments and cutting-edge research in the philosophical sciences, phenomenology, hermeneutics, existentialism, logic, semiotics, cultural studies, social criticism, and the humanities that engage and enrich psychoanalytic thought through philosophical rigor. With the philosophical turn in psychoanalysis comes a new era of theoretical research that revisits past paradigms while invigorating new approaches to theoretical, historical, contemporary, and applied psychoanalysis. No subject or discipline is immune from psychoanalytic reflection within a philosophical context including psychology, sociology, anthropology, politics, the arts, religion, science, culture, physics, and the nature of morality. Philosophical approaches to psychoanalysis may stimulate new areas of knowledge that have conceptual and applied value beyond the consulting room reflective of greater society at large. In the spirit of pluralism, *Philosophy & Psychoanalysis* is open to any theoretical school in philosophy and psychoanalysis that offers novel, scholarly, and important insights in the way we come to understand our world.

Titles in this series:

Integration and Difference: Constructing a Mythical Dialectic
by Grant Maxwell

Enriching Psychoanalysis: Integrating Concepts from Contemporary Science and Philosophy
Edited by John Turtz and Gerald J. Gargiulo

Psyche, Culture, World: Excursions in Existentialism and Psychoanalytic Philosophy
by Jon Mills

The Emergent Container in Psychoanalysis: Experiencing Absence and Future
by Ana Martinez Acobi

Archetypal Ontology: New Directions in Analytical Psychology
by Jon Mills and Erik Goodwyn

Psychoanalytic Investigations in Philosophy

An Interdisciplinary Exploration of Current Existential Challenges

Edited by Dorit Lemberger

Taylor & Francis Group

LONDON AND NEW YORK

Designed cover image: © Getty

First published 2023
by Routledge
4 Park Square, Milton Park, Abingdon, Oxon OX14 4RN

and by Routledge
605 Third Avenue, New York, NY 10158

Routledge is an imprint of the Taylor & Francis Group, an informa business

© 2023 selection and editorial matter, Dorit Lemberger; individual chapters, the contributors

The right of Dorit Lemberger to be identified as the author of the editorial material, and of the authors for their individual chapters, has been asserted in accordance with sections 77 and 78 of the Copyright, Designs and Patents Act 1988.

All rights reserved. No part of this book may be reprinted or reproduced or utilised in any form or by any electronic, mechanical, or other means, now known or hereafter invented, including photocopying and recording, or in any information storage or retrieval system, without permission in writing from the publishers.

Trademark notice: Product or corporate names may be trademarks or registered trademarks, and are used only for identification and explanation without intent to infringe.

British Library Cataloguing-in-Publication Data
A catalogue record for this book is available from the British Library

ISBN: 978-1-032-35374-6 (hbk)
ISBN: 978-1-032-35373-9 (pbk)
ISBN: 978-1-003-32658-8 (ebk)

DOI: 10.4324/9781003326588

Typeset in Times New Roman
by MPS Limited, Dehradun

Contents

Prologue: "As If I Could See the Darkness": What Does It Mean to Investigate Psychoanalysis from a Wittgensteinian Point of View?   ix

1 Rollo May and R. Joseph Soloveitchik: Psychotherapy and Philosophy   1
DOV SCHWARTZ

2 From Fear to Creativity: Melanie Klein's Interpretation of Literary Fiction as Conceptual Investigations   33
DORIT LEMBERGER

3 Psychoanalysis and Obsessive-Compulsive Disorder: A Wittgensteinian-Existential Perspective   56
NIR SOFFER-DUDEK

4 "Look into the Depths within Yourself and Find the Outside World": The Contribution of Rudolf Steiner's Monistic Philosophy to Psychoanalytic Conceptualization   76
TALI SELLA

5 Malfunctions in the Symbolic Space: A Psychoanalytic-Semiotic View   93
SHARON STRASBURG

6 "Bring Words back from their Metaphysical to their Everyday Use" – Meaning in Life through Ordinary Language Use 113
YAEL MISHANI-UVAL

7 Language Game and Separations: A Psychoanalytic-Philosophical View about the Infinity of the Separation Experience 133
OPHIRA SCHORR LEVY

8 Unhappy-Certainty 152
ALICE MAYA KEINAN

9 "Tragic Knots" Following Acquired Chronic Medical Conditions: A Relational Perspective in Psychotherapy in Medical Settings 174
ORIN SEGAL

10 Language Games and Private Language, Wizards and Witches: How a Child with Autism Builds their Emotional World – A Psychoanalytic, Philosophical, and Literary View 198
IRIT HAGAI

11 Self-Constructive vs. Self-Destructive Mechanisms in the Writings of Anorexics 218
RUTH KAPLAN ZARCHI

12 The Land of Shadows and Intuition: Bion's and Wittgenstein's Return to Plato's Cave 241
RONNIE CARMELI

13 Shades of Loneliness: A Psychoanalytic Study of Samuel Beckett's *Rockaby* 263
TSIKY COHEN

Index 284

Prologue: "As If I Could See the Darkness": What Does It Mean to Investigate Psychoanalysis from a Wittgensteinian Point of View?

Wittgenstein articulated the central problem facing researchers in the social sciences and the humanities: How can an emotion or an emotional object be recognized by an individual who feels it in the first person? Further, can such an object be described in a way recognizable both to the individual who feels it and by another person?

> If someone observes his own grief, which senses does he use to observe it? With a special sense—one that *feels* grief? Then does he feel it *differently* when he is observing it? And what is the grief that he is observing—one which is there only while being observed? "Observing" does not produce what is observed. (That is a conceptual statement.) Again: I do not "observe" *that* which comes into being only through observation. The object of observation is something else.[1]

Wittgenstein's response is general: We are engaging in a conceptual investigation. We must understand the way in which we conceptualize in order to answer the above questions on the nature of an emotional object and how it may be depicted.

This problem also lies at the core of psychoanalytic research, and in particular at the core of those studies that incorporate literary analysis. The psychoanalysts whose research will be discussed in this book all share a focus on conceptual investigation, following Wittgenstein, even if some did not know Wittgenstein at all (Freud, Klein) and others were only barely familiar with his investigations (Meltzer, Britton). The essays examined do not focus on case descriptions, but rather on the way in which psychoanalytic concepts advance thinking about a person's psyche and its development by means of an interdisciplinary conceptual study.

(A detailed outline of the essays will be added later, following the review.)

---

1 Ludwig Wittgenstein, Philosophical Investigations Part II (PPF), 4th ed., ed. P. M. S. Hacker and J. Schulte, trans. G. E. M. Anscombe, P. M. S. Hacker, and J. Schulte (Chichester: Wiley-Blackwell, 2009), 67.

Chapter 1

Rollo May and R. Joseph Soloveitchik

Psychotherapy and Philosophy

Dov Schwartz

R. Joseph B. Soloveitchik held that Jewish thought had, for centuries, disregarded the actual foundations of life and the study of human existence, consequently failing to contend adequately with theological questions. The reason is that, in his view, the revealed sources do turn to the deep layers of being and of the personality. And yet, despite the pessimistic tone he adopted as a starting point in his discussions of the loneliness, alienation, and estrangement of human existence, he did not confront this distress as insoluble and his later writings – dating to the mid-1960s and 1970s – are considerably optimistic.

What was the source of the knowledge displayed by Soloveitchik regarding the foundations of concrete existence? At the time of his studies at Berlin University in the 1920s, the dominant discourse had been Heideggerian. Soloveitchik was unquestionably influenced by basic Heideggerian concepts such as thrownness, authentic existence, and anxiety. Soloveitchik's endeavor, however, which is adapted to his religious and preaching surroundings, clearly presents and articulates existential dimensions. He does not offer a profound analysis of existential conditions but he does present brilliant interpretations of texts and fascinating homiletical messages, weaving into them translucent descriptions of existential circumstances.

I will attempt to trace the sources of several patterns that appeared in R. Soloveitchik's late thought, such as the threat that the mathematical sciences pose to the study of concrete existence, the persistence of loneliness despite social involvement and integration, loneliness as singularity, and modes of repression. These patterns originate in existentialist thought and are clearly formulated as basic assumptions of existential therapy. Soloveitchik relied on these sources while incorporating halakhic and religious aspects into his discussions. I will first comment on the methodology in Soloveitchik's relevant works and then proceed to examine the sources of loneliness and existence in his thought.

On the Method

Soloveitchik showed interest in trends within phenomenological and existential psychotherapy that entered the United States mainly in the 1950s and 1960s.[1] He also gave a series of lectures at the National Institute of Mental Health in New York, some of which were published during his lifetime (*The Lonely Man of Faith*), and others included in his posthumously published works (for example, in the anthology *Out of the Whirlwind*). Rollo May was a key figure in this therapeutic trend. Although representatives of this trend are not explicitly mentioned in Soloveitchik's writings since he cites mainly philosophers and theologians, their imprint is evident in his language and style.

Existence

One of the most crucial events in phenomenological and existential psychotherapy was the publication of a collection titled *Existence: A New Dimension in Psychiatry and Psychology*. The collection, published in 1958, was edited by Rollo May, Ernest Angel, and Henry Ellenberger and comprised a selection of up-to-date European research literature, including articles by psychotherapists such as Eugene Minkovski and Ludwig Binswanger. The book powerfully exposed the deep link between existentialist psychotherapy and the eponymous philosophy. May's two introductions to this book – "The Origins and Significance of the Existential Movement in Psychology" and "Contributions of Existential Psychotherapy" – clearly and systematically presented the new trend in psychology for the first time relying on, for example, Kierkegaard, Nietzsche, Heidegger, and Sartre, no less and perhaps even more than on the professional literature on the subject. His previous books too, such as *The Meaning of Anxiety* (1950) or *Man's Search for Himself* (1953), included philosophical analysis as a basis of therapeutic approaches. I will point to May's traces in Soloveitchik's writings from the mid-1960s onward.

May's introductions to *Existence: A New Dimension in Psychiatry and Psychology* represent the methods and achievements of phenomenological and existential psychotherapy. From many perspectives, these introductions sum up the psychotherapeutic literature by relying, as noted, on philosophical literature. May's influence on Soloveitchik, therefore, does not convey the authority of one specific thinker, however important, but rather the hallmark of a philosophical trend that grew out of psychotherapeutic practice. May's thought also conveys the contributions of Erich Fromm, Ludwig Binswanger, Roland Kuhn, Eugene Minkovski, Frederik J. J. Buytendijk, Victor Frankl, and others. In recent decades, this trend was popularized in the books of Irwin D. Yalom.

From the start, phenomenological and existential psychotherapy adopted an apologetic stance. Its advocates contended with the claim that their

---

1 See, for example, Herbert Spiegelberg, *Phenomenology in Psychology and Psychiatry: A Historical Introduction* (Evanston, IL: Northwestern University Press, 1972).

approach was not scientific and protested against the contempt shown to them by psychoanalysts and experimental psychologists. They, therefore, relied especially on Martin Heidegger, who was perceived as a reputable philosopher, while showing reservations about attempts to associate them with, for example, Jean-Paul Sartre, who was perceived as extreme and as a productive writer of fiction with dubious philosophical credentials. These psychotherapists called for relating to the patient as other and to psychotherapy as conveying an intersubjective relationship. The challenge to the scientific norm that makes scientific truth contingent on the scientists' distance from the topic of their research made this psychotherapeutic trend scientifically questionable. One of its founders, Ludwig Binswanger, writes:

> For as soon as I objectify my fellow man, as soon as I objectify his subjectivity, he is no longer my fellow man; and as soon as I subjectify an organism or make a natural object into a responsible subject, it is no longer an organism in a sense intended by medical science.[2]

May unequivocally states, "The fact that the therapist participates in a real way in the relationship and is an inseparable part of the 'field' does not, thus, impair the soundness of the scientific observations."[3] Directing the psychotherapists' attention to the roots of being and existence included the relationship with the other, a move that made the trend more vulnerable.

I will claim below that the standing of phenomenological and existential psychotherapy imprinted Soloveitchik's thought. I intend to examine the ways this trend was absorbed by Soloveitchik, who was generally aware of developments in the field.

Channels of Influence

Soloveitchik's thought was primarily religious thought. Some of his writings also relate to religion generally but, at the core, they focus on Jewish thought. He was highly influenced by phenomenological and existential psychotherapy but was apparently troubled by the fact that it was not religious. Faith was missing from these texts, contrary to, for example, the writings of Christian existentialism or the thought of philosophers as Franz Rosenzweig and Martin Buber. My claim is that Soloveitchik was inspired by May's writings both terminologically and substantially. He poured into

---

2 Ludwig Binswanger, *Being-in-the-World: Selected Papers*, trans. Jacob Needleman (New York: Basic Books, 1963), 210.
3 Rollo May, *Existence: A New Dimension in Psychiatry and Psychology* (New York: Basic Books, 1959), 27 (henceforth *Existence*). For this principle, May relied on Kierkegaard's thought. All quotes from this book in the discussion below are from May's introductions.

May's thought the divine element that had been missing from it. The most significant influence of May and his group on Soloveitchik was the description of existentialist thought as one involved in a struggle for its very existence. Striving to expose the depth of being and delving into the foundations of actual existence is viewed as opposed to the spirit of modern Western culture, which is ruled by science. This description appears mainly in *The Lonely Man of Faith* but is also felt in his other writings.

Soloveitchik absorbed existential psychotherapy dialectically. The constructs of thought are built on different perspectives, each one presenting another element as the focus of existence. For example, the external phenomena of existence are primary, immediate, and amenable to modification and change and, therefore, can be treated by therapists who are not existential. Depth phenomena, by contrast, are the result of analysis and, therefore, are not immediate. On the one hand, then, they are basic and fundamental but, on the other, one cannot begin with them. Likewise, loneliness is primary and dialogue is a level to be reached through a subjective relationship. At times, however, in order to disclose the characteristics of loneliness, one must begin with dialogue and, through it, reach existence. Soloveitchik copied the dialectical model of thinking from psychotherapists and adopted this style himself. When dealing with the covenant of fate and the covenant of destiny, for instance, he began with the covenant of fate, which is the surface dimension but is the link for reaching the covenant of destiny, which is the depth dimension.

Nevertheless, Soloveitchik did not pretend to deal with psychotherapy per se and certainly not to innovate or shed new light on the field. He was neither a Western philosopher nor a therapist – he was a preacher and a Jewish thinker. Therefore, he relied on the specialists' analyses to situate his modes of reading Scripture and interpreting Halakhah and Aggadah.

Furthermore, it merits note that many Orthodox thinkers have tended to rely on articles and works that summarized philosophical views. Even when these thinkers had gained some acquaintance with these views in their professional training, they did not return to a detailed study of them after their establishment as spiritual leaders, confining themselves instead to summaries published in books and in the press. This description applies to important rabbis such as Abraham Yitzhak Hacohen Kook, Yitzhak Hutner, Menachem Mendel Schneerson (the Lubavitcher Rebbe), as well as to Soloveitchik. Highly inspired individuals can be creative even when relying on hearsay.

Loneliness

Loneliness is a favored topic in phenomenological and existential psychotherapy. In his late writings, Soloveitchik too dealt with this topic, and particularly before and close to the death of his wife Tonya (1967) after a long struggle with cancer. May discussed loneliness quite at length in *Man's Search for Himself* and in *Existence*, viewing it as the foundation of human alienation in modernity. In a later work, he also claimed that one of the factors leading to pathological sexual relations is the individual's attempt to overcome loneliness through them.[4] Soloveitchik, as shown below, developed various notions of loneliness out of May's discussions on the concept, and adapted them to his thought.

Being Misunderstood as a Reason for Loneliness

I will argue that the conceptual move Soloveitchik presents in *The Lonely Man of Faith* rests on May's approach. Soloveitchik's sources – epistemic idealism (the subject of his dissertation) and phenomenology of religion, particularly Max Scheler – can indeed be traced back to the time of his studies at Berlin University. It is a plausible assumption, however, that he used these sources according to the thought construct he found in May's psychotherapy.

I begin my discussion with the conflict between the two figures in *The Lonely Man of Faith*. This essay describes Adam the first ("majestic man") as conquering by means of mathematical abstractions whereas Adam the second ("covenantal man") is described as seeking to understand his own unique existence and communicate with the other. I have described at length the background of Adam the first in epistemic idealism and in the conventionalist perception of science.[5] Majestic man conquers nature by mathematizing it. Mathematical constructs built in detachment from reality are the tool through which majestic man rules over nature. By contrast, the sources of Adam the second are in existentialist literature. The man of faith seeks to understand nature as given and know the foundations of his own existence:

> He does not mathematize phenomena or conceptualize things. He encounters the universe in all its colorfulness, splendor, and grandeur, and studies it with the naïveté, awe, and admiration of the child who seeks the unusual and wonderful in every ordinary thing and event. While Adam the first is dynamic and creative, transforming sensory data into thought constructs, Adam the second is receptive and beholds the world in its original dimensions. He looks for the image of God not in the mathematical formula or the natural relational law but in every

---

4 Rollo May, *Love and Will* (New York: Norton, 1969), 54.
5 Dov Schwartz, *The Philosophy of Rabbi Joseph B. Soloveitchik*, vol. 1, trans. Batya Stein (Leiden/Boston: Brill, 2007).

beam of light, in every bud and blossom, in the morning breeze and the stillness of a starlit evening.[6]

The mathematization of nature, then, is not only the scientist's control tool but also a form of worship. Adam the first senses that he is fulfilling the divine command when ruling over the world by using mathematical science. And indeed, already from the start of this essay, Soloveitchik describes how the man of faith feels misunderstood by majestic man. The result is distress:

> He looks upon himself as a stranger in modern society, which is technically minded, self-centered, and self-loving, almost in a sickly narcissistic fashion, scoring honor upon honor,[7] piling up victory upon victory, reaching for the distant galaxies, and seeing in the here-and-now sensible world the only manifestation of being.[8]

Soloveitchik created a kind of conflict between science, which relies on mathematical abstractions, and the man of faith. Clearly discernible in the tone of the writing is that the man of faith feels that majestic man not only misunderstands him but also views him with contempt. He is a stranger in a society whose language, the language of science, he does not speak.

May noted that existential psychotherapy emerged in Europe quite spontaneously in several unconnected places. He was extremely disturbed by the opposition this movement evoked in the United States, and Soloveitchik was apparently greatly influenced by May's explanations of the reasons for the rejection. May cited three causes for it, all somehow taking exception to the scientific qualifications of the new trend. One is opposition to innovation, which reverses accepted conceptions. The second is the presentation of the new movement as unscientific because it includes philosophical considerations in its approach.[9] The third source is the following:

> The *third* source of resistance, and to my mind the most crucial of all, is the tendency in this country to be preoccupied with technique and to

---

6 Joseph B. Soloveitchik, *The Lonely Man of Faith* (Northvale, NJ/London: Jason Aronson, 1965), 23.
7 Soloveitchik clarifies the matter of honor as power and control over nature in *The Lonely Man of Faith*, Part II.
8 Soloveitchik, *Lonely Man of Faith*, 6.
9 May took a critical view of the extensive authority of science and presented a balanced perception of it as an alternative: "Science may be used as a rigid, dogmatic faith by which one escapes emotional insecurity and doubt, *or* it may be an open-minded search for new truth. Indeed, since faith in science has been more acceptable in intelligent circles in our society and therefore is less apt to be questioned, it may well be that in our day this faith more frequently plays the role of a compulsive escape from uncertainties than does religion" (Rollo May, *Man's Search for Himself* [New York: Norton, 1953], 193).

be impatient with endeavors to search below such considerations to find the foundations upon which all techniques must be based. This tendency can be well explained in terms of our American social background, particularly our frontier history, and it can be well justified as our optimistic, activistic concern for helping and changing people.[10]

May pointed to the experimental dimension of American psychology. In the name of Gordon Allport, he noted that the American way is "pragmatic" and behaviorism suits it.[11] This approach, he noted elsewhere, uses action as a substitute for consciousness. The American view is "to assume that the more one is acting, the more one is alive."[12] One may plausibly assume that the pragmatism of William James and John Dewey contributed to this stance, although May viewed this approach as significantly close to existentialism. The ceaseless flow and the American pace of life lead, in his view, to a blurring of being due to the emphasis on constant change and becoming.[13] The growth of existential psychotherapy in Europe sharpened the contrast between the two cultures.

May addressed the opposition to existential psychotherapy in other writings, and explicitly noted the contempt of professionals who insisted on questioning its scientific credentials not only due to reasons focusing on technical aspects. This time, May pointed to the mathematization of science as the main cause:

> It is difficult enough to give definitions of "being" and Dasein, but our task is made doubly difficult by the fact that these terms and their connotations encounter much resistance. Some readers may feel that these words are only a new form of "mysticism" (used in its disparaging and quite inaccurate sense of "misty") and have nothing to do with science. But this attitude obviously dodges the whole issue by disparaging it. It is interesting that the term "mystic" is used in this derogatory sense to mean anything we cannot segmentize and count. The odd belief prevails in our culture that a thing or experience is not real if we cannot make it mathematical, and somehow it must be real if we can reduce it to numbers. But this means making an abstraction out of it—mathematics is the abstraction par excellence, which is indeed its glory and the reason for

---

10 *Existence*, 9.
11 See John Burnham, ed., *After Freud Left: A Century of Psychoanalysis in America* (Chicago/London: The University of Chicago Press, 2012).
12 May, *Man's Search for Himself*, 117.
13 *Existence*, 9.

its great usefulness. Modern Western man thus finds himself in the strange situation, after reducing something to an abstraction, of having then to persuade himself it is real. This has much to do with the sense of isolation and loneliness which is endemic in the modern Western world; for the only experience we ourselves believe in as real is that which precisely is not.[14]

Indirectly, May is particularly critical in this passage of the conventionalist view of science, which claims that the sensorial phenomenon and its abstract mathematical representation are not really connected. There is no true connection between, for example, the doe's run, and the speed or acceleration formula representing it. Soloveitchik did endorse the conventionalist approach but, according to May, reality is above all sensorial. How can the abstract become concrete after that abstract is the stripping of the real? May, therefore, was also indirectly critical of post-Kantian scientific idealism. Already in *Man's Search for Himself*, he had refuted opponents to the concept of the self and their claim that it cannot be reduced to "mathematical equations."[15]

Soloveitchik pointed to the encounter between the man of faith and majestic man, who acts through mathematical abstractions, as a cause of loneliness. His distress was in a way greater than May's because he characterized majestic man through Hermann Cohen's terms, defining scientific objects as objective reality (in his dissertation, Soloveitchik used Cohen's term *Wirklichkeit*). The sciences are merely "the mathematical natural sciences." Soloveitchik endorsed the weaving of several principles from May's approach:

1 A confrontation between the mathematical scientist and the person interested in concrete existence.
2 The mathematical scientist as the representative of the cultural mindset.
3 For the person interested in concrete existence, the confrontation leads to a sense of loneliness.
4 Loneliness is also alienation because abstraction detaches us from God.

Seemingly, Soloveitchik adopts May's description but replaces the latter's "mysticism" with faith. While May presents mysticism as a derogatory and derisive term, Soloveitchik presents faith as a personal moment that differs from mathematical thought. He writes:

> The biblical dialectic stems from the fact that Adam the first, majestic man of dominion and success, and Adam the second, the lonely man of

---

14 Ibid., 39–40.
15 May, *Man's Search for Himself*, 90.

faith, obedience, and defeat, are not two different people locked in an external confrontation as an "I" opposite a "thou," but one person who is involved in self-confrontation. "I," Adam the first, confronts the "I," Adam the second. In every one of us abide two *personae*—the creative, majestic Adam the first, and the submissive, humble Adam the second.[16]

According to *The Lonely Man of Faith*, the struggle between the two types takes place not only in Western society in general but also within the personality. The scientific and experiential types represent two moments of the personality, each one drawing the individual in a different direction. The scientific moment attempts to conquer even the religious experience, entirely disregarding its unique, tormenting, and anxious aspects. The actual concrete person fluctuates between the two types. Soloveitchik, then, went far beyond May and turned this into a complex struggle. His terminology, however, and even more so the process he described, conveys May's influence.

Loneliness in a Social Setting

May claimed that loneliness links up with self-alienation. The modern individual's fear of social loneliness leads to a fear of aloneness, which prevents understanding of solitude's positive aspects. For May, the sense of loneliness and the sense of emptiness come together and both can be viewed as expressions of anxiety.[17] May argued that loneliness is a reaction to anxiety-provoking events:

> Perhaps the reader can recall the anxiety which swept over us like a tidal wave when the first atom bomb exploded over Hiroshima, when we sensed our grave danger—sensed, that is, that we might be the last generation—but did not know in which direction to turn. At that moment, the reaction of great numbers of people was, strangely enough, a sudden, deep loneliness.[18]

Loneliness is an expression of the disorientation of modern humans and, as such, a threat to their existence. May tried to expose the causes of this situation: "Modern Western man, trained though four centuries of emphasis on rationality, uniformity, and mechanics, has consistently endeavored, with unfortunate success, to repress the aspects of himself which do not fit these

---

16 Soloveitchik, *Lonely Man of Faith*, 84–85.
17 May, *Man's Search for Himself*, 26–27.
18 Ibid., 27.

uniform and mechanical standards."[19] As a response to loneliness, modern individuals strive for social acceptance. They adapt themselves to social demands but, in the course of these efforts, deny their own selves and their real existence since humans can develop "meaningful relations" with their social surroundings only through their existential resources.[20] This, precisely, is the root of the alienation in loneliness. Individuals deny existential anxiety instead of embracing it and develop superficial ties to escape loneliness.

According to May's preliminary discussion, loneliness is above all a state of consciousness that reacts to the events. Loneliness is an expression of basic states such as existential anxiety and alienation. May did not see loneliness as an independent state of depth. Alienation and anxiety lead to emptiness and disorientation, and in fact to loneliness. At the same time, loneliness is the inability to develop significant relationships with the other. Intersubjective communication is possible if individuals will only acknowledge the characteristics of their existence.

Soloveitchik went beyond this presentation of loneliness as an "external" reaction rooted in depth dimensions. He developed the concept of loneliness according to his preferred model, which draws a distinction between surface and depth states – for example, fear versus anxiety and pain versus suffering. The depth state is a given and is not necessarily affected by external events. It characterizes humans as beings with defined characteristics, of which external emotional states are only local and temporary expressions.

Another distinction is that between loneliness as a temporary or prolonged detachment and absence from the society, a state of being "alone," and loneliness as a fundamental depth characteristic. In Soloveitchik's terms, the distinction is between "loneliness" and "aloneness."[21] At the opening of the first chapter of *The Lonely Man of Faith*, he writes:

> Let me emphasize, however, that by stating "I am lonely" I do not intend to convey to you the impression that I am alone. I, thank God, do enjoy the love and friendship of many. I meet people, talk, preach, argue, reason; I am surrounded by comrades and acquaintances. And yet, companionship and friendship do not alleviate the passional experience of loneliness which trails me constantly. I am lonely because at times I feel rejected and thrust away by everybody, not excluding my most intimate friends.[22]

---

19 Ibid., 33.
20 Ibid.
21 Soloveitchik, *Lonely Man of Faith*, 3.
22 Ibid.

In *The Lonely Man of Faith,* we find two factors leading to the distress of "passional" loneliness:

1. Loneliness as a replacement of the intelligible scientific world with a transcendent one. Loneliness is a special mode of faith in the *Deus absconditus.*
2. Loneliness as untransferable. Human existence is so particular and personal that, by definition, cannot be shared with the other.

I discuss below the roots of the perception of loneliness as singularity. At this stage, I consider the thought pattern adopted by Soloveitchik whereby the loneliness of singularity is also a feature of a lonely person who integrates into a vibrant society. Loneliness as the absence of company is, as noted, an "external" and superficial state, contrasting with loneliness as an existential characteristic, a mode of the relationship between existence and reality. This depth of loneliness prevails even when an individual is socially integrated.

Both models of loneliness, the surface one and the depth one, appear implicitly in May's work as well a few years after *Man Search for Himself*. Loneliness is by then identical to alienation and thus a kind of fundamental dimension of existence:

> There is also plenty of evidence that the sense of isolation, the alienation of one's self from the world, is suffered not only by people in pathological conditions but by countless "normal" persons as well in our day. Riesman[23] presents a good deal of sociopsychological data in his study *The Lonely Crowd* to demonstrate that the isolated, lonely, alienated character type is characteristic not only of neurotic patients but of people as a whole in our society and that the trends in that direction have been increasing over the past couple of decades. He makes the significant point that these people have only a *technical* communication with their world; his "outer-directed" persons (the type characteristic of our day) relate to everything from its technical, external side. ...

> [This person] is a stranger in his world, a stranger to other people whom he seeks or pretends to love; he moves about in a state of homelessness, vagueness and haze as though he had no direct sense connection with his world but were in a foreign country where he does not know the language and has no hope of learning it but is always doomed to wander in quiet despair, incommunicado, homeless, and a stranger.

---

23 David Riesman, with Nathan Glazer and Reuel Denney, *The Lonely Crowd: A Study of the Changing American Character* (New Haven: Yale University Press, 1950).

> Nor is the problem of this loss of world simply one of lack of interpersonal relations or lack of communication with one's fellows. Its roots reach below the social levels to an alienation from the natural world as well. It is a particular experience of isolation which has been called "epistemological loneliness."[24]

May describes people active in social settings but living a lonely existence because they are alienated from their society. The cause of their alienation is antithetical to that noted by Soloveitchik. For Soloveitchik, the sense of loneliness and alienation results from him turning to the deep layer of existence while those surrounding him confine themselves to the surface one. By contrast, for May, alienation follows from the individual's surface consciousness of his surroundings. For both of them, however, loneliness as a layer of existence is a cause of distress. For May, distress is expressed in pathology whereas for Soloveitchik it is a factor in the turn to the divinity, and, more precisely, a factor that compels divine intervention. Soloveitchik describes May's model – the lonely man within the social setting – in the following colorful terms:

> Who knows what kind of loneliness is more agonizing: the one which befalls man when he casts his glance at the mute cosmos, at its dark spaces and monotonous drama, or the one that besets man exchanging glances with his fellow man in silence? Who knows whether the first astronaut who will land on the moon, confronted with a strange, weird, and grisly panorama, will feel a greater loneliness than Mr. X, moving along jubilantly with the crowd and exchanging greetings on New Year's Eve at a public square?[25]

The principle of loneliness within a social setting appears in May's analysis, and Soloveitchik takes it into an entirely different direction.

To return to May on loneliness – he notes that the lonely person is homeless and a stranger. The source for this approach, as noted, is Heidegger,[26] who argues that homelessness conveys:

1. Alienation. Homelessness is not merely detachment. For Heidegger, homelessness conveys alienation from the world. The world is not a person's home, in the routine bourgeois meaning of the term.

---

24 Existence, 56–57.
25 Soloveitchik, *Lonely Man of Faith*, 38.
26 See Dov Schwartz, *The Philosophy of Rabbi Joseph B. Soloveitchik*, vol. 3, trans. Edward Lewin (Boston: Academic Studies Press, 2019), ch. 12.

2 Lack of authenticity. Heidegger identified the "home" state as serenity and self-affirmation. A person is aware of being outside the home. For Heidegger, to be at home means to be yourself, since the home conveys authenticity.
3 Anxiety. To be outside the home causes anxiety. Anxiety follows from meaninglessness, from being "not at home (*unheimlich*)."[27]

In his article "The Synagogue as an Institution and as an Idea," which I have discussed elsewhere,[28] Soloveitchik explicitly states, "Let me start immediately with two postulates. First, man is in exile. Man is a homeless being. Second, exiled man, or homeless man, must pray; he has a strong need to pray; through prayer he redeems himself from his loneliness."[29] The hallmark of May's style, stating that a lonely person is homeless and homelessness reflects alienation, is etched in Soloveitchik's remarks.

According to Paul Tillich's approach, Soloveitchik held that the role of religious existentialism is to find religious solutions to existential problems. The existential problems are formulated in a "psychological and empirical" style but the solutions are formulated in "theological and Biblical" terms.[30] God, then, is revealed as homeless, as it were, so that humans may build the Temple to house him, and the entire people of Israel is exposed as homeless in its exile, with the synagogue as its home. Prayer, then, redeems the homeless lonely person, that is, it provides rescue from the experience of existential loneliness. The community of prayer redeems the community of loneliness in the sense of providing a home to the homeless.

Alienation from Nature

One motif that Soloveitchik uses in opposite directions in various works is the fusion with, or alienation from, nature.[31] Phenomenological literature has dealt with the natural roots of humans and with their stance vis-à-vis nature,[32] and again, psychotherapists have offered specific and eloquent versions of the philosophical discussions. In *Man's Search for Himself*, May

---

27 Martin Heidegger, *Being and Time*, vol. 1, trans. John Macquarrie and Edward Robinson (New York: Harper and Row, 1962), 233.
28 Schwartz, *The Philosophy of Rabbi Joseph B. Soloveitchik*, vol. 3, ch. 12.
29 Joseph B. Soloveitchik, "The Synagogue as an Institution and as an Idea," in *Rabbi Joseph H. Lookstein Memorial Volume*, ed. Leo Landman (New York: Ktav, 1980), 324.
30 Soloveitchik, *Lonely Man of Faith*, 8.
31 Avi Sagi, *Albert Camus and the Philosophy of the Absurd*, trans. Batya Stein (Amsterdam/New York: Rodopi, 2002), 5–24.
32 One example is the very influential work of Max Scheler, *Die Stellung des Menschen im Kosmos* (Darmstadt: Reichl, 1928).

concretely defined the link between the self and the connection to nature. Humans are part of nature not only in the sense of their chemical structure but also in the sense of life's functionality (hunger and fulfillment, sleep and wakefulness, and so forth).[33] He wrote:

> People who have lost their sense of identity as selves also tend to lose their sense of relatedness to nature. They lose not only their experience of organic connection with inanimate nature, such as trees and mountains, but they also lose some of their capacity to feel empathy for animate nature, that is animals.[34]

The distinction between human beings and nature is their consciousness of self. This consciousness is the source of their highest qualities.[35] Psychotherapeutic literature has indeed extensively discussed the pathological aspects of human estrangement from nature. Soloveitchik has also addressed this topic at length in his writings, particularly from a phenomenological perspective. The man of faith, as noted, stands in awe and admiration before living nature and Soloveitchik devotes to this question large sections of *The Emergence of Ethical Man*.

May presents the alienation of the modern individual not only from others and from human society but also from nature. One question in this context is whether human alienation led to alienation from nature or whether both are concurrent. May argued that the root of alienation is the human detachment from nature. In the past, God had been perceived as the connection between human consciousness and nature but, after "the death of God" in modernity, the warranted result is alienation between the two. "Thus, it is by no means accidental that modern man feels estranged from nature, that each consciousness stands off by itself, alone."[36] On "the separation of man as a subject from the objective world," May writes as follows:

> This alienation has expressed itself for several centuries in Western man's passion to gain power over nature, but now shows itself in an estrangement from nature and a vague, unarticulated, and half-suppressed sense of despair of gaining any real relationship with the natural world, including one's own body.[37]

---

33 May, *Man's Search for Himself*, 73.
34 Ibid., 68.
35 Ibid.
36 *Existence*, 58–59.
37 Ibid., 57.

In Heideggerian style, May held that the natural world is "the 'thrown world' to which each of us must in some way adjust."[38] In this way, the world is exposed to humans as the surroundings where they act and grow. Since the beginning of modernity, consciousness and the soul have been separated from nature. In the conventionalist approach of the philosophy of science, as noted, the separation between thought and sensation turns into a separation between subject and object. Moreover, an anthology published in 1967 titled *Readings in Existential Phenomenology* and edited by Nathaniel Lawrence and Daniel O'Connor from Williams College, Massachusetts, included articles by leading philosophers and psychotherapists such as Irwin Strauss, Eugene Minkovski, Frederik Buytendijk, and Rollo May. This anthology reflected the influence of the European current of existential psychotherapists on the American discourse. In the introduction, titled "The Primary Phenomenon: Human Existence," these thinkers described the new trend as grappling, above all, with the human alienation from nature and its intensification in modern thought.[39]

In the essay "Adam and Eve," Soloveitchik draws a distinction between "man-*natura*" and "man-*persona*." The former type merges with nature while the latter is alienated from it. According to Soloveitchik, "man-*persona*" is "metaphysical man, man who rebelled against Mother Nature and attempted to gain an individual identity of his own."[40] This is an aesthetic personality with a wondrous imagination who began alienated from nature but returned to it using his creative imagination rather than mathematical abstractions.

Again, we find that Soloveitchik adopted May's formula, meaning estrangement from nature as an expression of alienation. Soloveitchik, however, presents an experiential type who is interested in a dialogue with the divine. His "man of faith" is not lost to the point of reaching a pathological state, as May's type is, but rather one well aware of his own way of pursuing a goal and a purpose. Although he does not know how to reach it, he is aware of the questions troubling him and of his expectations from nature and from the divinity. In "Adam and Eve," Soloveitchik even hints that the type alienated from nature began as a type who merges with it but, moved by the transcendent drive to go beyond nature, became alienated from it. The religious drive enables to present the pathological as a desirable state.

Finally, it merits note that May also devoted a long discussion to the human search for self-transcendence. In a section titled "Transcending the

---

38 Ibid., 61.
39 Nathaniel Lawrence and Daniel O'Connor, eds., *Readings in Existential Phenomenology* (Englewood Cliffs, NJ: Prentice Hall, 1967), 1–11.
40 Joseph B. Soloveitchik, *Family Redeemed: Essays on Family Relationships*, ed. David Shatz & Joel Wolowelsky (New York: Toras HaRav Foundation, 2000), 9.

Immediate Situation," he clearly determines, "Existence is always in process of self-transcending."[41] In his writings, Soloveitchik frequently resorts to the self-transcendence principle.

Loneliness as Singularity

Soloveitchik, as noted, presented loneliness as singularity or, in other words, as the impossibility of transferring the existence of the subject to the other. "There is no one who exists like the 'I' ... because the *modus existentiae* of the 'I' cannot be repeated, imitated, or experienced by others."[42] Loneliness implies an existential experience of detachment and insecurity due to the "singularity and uniqueness of each existence."[43] The perception of existence as singular is found in May's discourse as well, in two meanings:

1   Autonomy, referring to the free expression of views.
2   Unique responses to existence as a whole when confronting the modes of existence in the world.

The first meaning grows from the matter that concerned May in many of his writings, which is the definition of existence:

> *Being* is a category which cannot be reduced to introjection of social and ethical norms. It is, to use Nietzsche's phrase, "beyond good and evil." To the extent that my sense of existence is authentic, it is precisely *not* what others have told me I should be, but is the one Archimedes point I have to stand on from which to judge what parents and other authorities demand. Indeed, *compulsive and rigid moralism arises in given persons precisely as the result of a lack of a sense of being.* Rigid moralism is a compensatory mechanism by which the individual persuades himself to take over the external sanctions because he has no fundamental assurance that his own choices have any sanction of their own.[44]

The singularity feature, as formulated in this passage, is not the same that Soloveitchik had intended. In May's understanding, singularity is the

---

41 *Existence*, 71.
42 Soloveitchik, *Lonely Man of Faith*, 41.
43 Joseph B. Soloveitchik, "Confrontation," *Tradition* 6.2 (1964), 14. It is unclear whether Soloveitchik is referring to singularity in the sense of inimitability, but this is unquestionably a landmark in the development of the unique concept of subjectivity in his thought.
44 *Existence*, 45 (emphasis in original).

independence of the personality, that is, freedom from social and normative pressures. Singularity, then, is subjectivity. The singular person is a subject rather than an object, but this is not singularity in the sense that the mode of existence is personal and untransferable.

Elsewhere, May presented the singularity of concrete existence as deriving from the relationship with the individual's field of action:

> *World is the structure of meaningful relationships in which a person exists and in the design of which he participates.* Thus world includes the past events which condition my existence and all the vast variety of deterministic influences which operate upon me. But it is these *as I relate to them*, am aware of them, carry them with me, molding, inevitably forming, building them in every minute of relating. For to be aware of one's world means at the same time to be designing it.
>
> World is not to be limited to the past determining events but includes also all the possibilities which open up before any person and are not simply given in the historical situation. World is thus not to be identified with "culture." It includes culture but a good deal more, such as *Eigenwelt* (the own-world which cannot be reduced merely to an introjection of the culture),[45] as well as all the individual's future possibilities.[46]

The world is determined by the person's relationships with it. Speaking about a set relationship with the world is impossible because every individual relates to the world in different modes. Furthermore, every individual has not only his own particular past but also the possibilities opening up before him. May relied on Nietzsche to note the fact that the concrete person is equivalent to the realization of her own specific possibilities: "His concept of 'will to power' implies the self-realization of the individual in the fullest sense. It requires the courageous living out of the individual's potentialities in his own particular existence."[47] More precisely, behavior patterns are not determined within a fixed state. We are constantly in process of becoming, action, and realization of possibilities in our field of existence. May's analysis clearly leads to the conclusion of individual singularity.

Soloveitchik formulated May's second meaning of singularity in more radical terms, and one example is in his eulogy for his uncle, R. Yitzhak

---

45 One of the three modes of the world according to May: Umwelt, which denotes the human connection to the natural world; Mitwelt, which denotes the connection to the human world, and, finally, Eigenwelt.
46 *Existence*, 59–60 (emphasis in the original).
47 Ibid., 30.

Zeev Soloveitchik. In the eulogy, Soloveitchik presented R. Velvel, as his uncle was known in yeshiva circles, as Moses:

> The wondrous root of the loneliness and aloneness of Moses sprouts from a great principle in Judaism. Moses was the forefather of the prophets and the master of the sages. What does this mean? Moses' standing among the prophets comes forth in his absolute and total singularity. Any attempt to imagine similarities[48] and comparisons with the rest of the prophets will distort this master's image ... separate and different from everyone. This is a specific and unique prophet, to whom comparisons with, inferences from, and associations with the rest of the prophets do not apply. His stature is inapprehensible through comparisons. His singularity was unequivocal and the difference that separated him from others—absolute. There is neither aggregation nor transition between Moses and others.[49]

Soloveitchik is obviously relying on Maimonides' claim that reaching Moses' rank is impossible. Maimonides thereby ensured the inimitability of the Torah and of Halakhah, which are the object of Moses' prophecy. Yet, Soloveitchik's description of Moses as singular and unique was generalized in *The Lonely Man of Faith*.

In *The Lonely Man of Faith*, Soloveitchik commented on "It is not good for man to be alone" (Genesis 2:18), which includes both existence ("to be") and aloneness ("alone"). "To be" is a singular depth experience that only Adam the second is aware of and is unrelated to any function or performance. "'To be' means to be the only one, singular and different and consequently lonely."[50] Soloveitchik shifted the discussion to intransitive singularity because he wished to claim that only divine grace enables the encounter between two singular individuals. Were it not for God's

---

48 Soloveitchik hints here at Maimonides' approach, claiming that every prophet uses the power of imagination but Moses does not. See, for example, Samuel Atlas, "Moses in the Philosophy of Maimonides, Spinoza and Solomon Maimon," HUCA 25 (1954): 369–400; Alvin J. Reines, "Maimonides' Concept of Mosaic Prophecy," HUCA 40 (1969): 325–361; Kalman P. Bland, "Moses and the Law according to Maimonides," in Mystics, Philosophers, and Politicians: Essays in Jewish Intellectual History in Honor of Alexander Altmann, ed. Jehuda Reinharz and Daniel Swetschinsky (Durham, NC: Duke University Press, 1982), 49–66; Dov Schwartz, "Mosaic Prophecy in the Writings of a Fourteenth-Century Jewish Neoplanist Circle," JJTP 2 (1992): 97–110; David R. Blumenthal, Philosophic Mysticism: Studies in Rational Religion (Ramat-Gan: Bar-Ilan University Press, 2006), 73–95; Menachem Kellner, Torah in the Observatory: Gersonides, Maimonides, Song of Songs (Boston: Academic Studies Press, 2010), 47–69.
49 Joseph B. Soloveitchik, "Mah Dodekh mi-Dod" [Heb], Divrei Hagut ve-Ha'arakhah (Jerusalem, WZO, 1982), 65.
50 Soloveitchik, *Lonely Man of Faith*, 40–41.

intervention, Adam the second and Eve would have failed to meet. What concerned him, therefore, was the question of intersubjective communication, with the addition of the communal dimension (I, thou, and he).[51]

Existence

My focus will now be on existence as such, meaning concrete existence. Although loneliness is perceived as a deep layer of existence, May held that the most fundamental layer is existence itself. The disregard of existence is the obstacle hindering therapeutic endeavors such as psychoanalysis. Hence, May devoted significant efforts to the definition and characterization of concrete existence. The constructs that appear in this discussion also influenced Soloveitchik.

Fact and Action

May drew a distinction between, on the one hand, fact and essence, and on the other, between fact and action. In the apologetic discourse dealing with objections to existential psychotherapy, he contrasted the European philosophical tradition in modernity, which dealt with essence, with the existentialism that deals with facts. When, for example, he relates to finitude as a factor that explains human existence and human reaction, he writes, "you and I must alone face the fact that at some unknown moment in the future we shall die. In contrast to the essentialist propositions, these latter are *existential facts*."[52] The distinction between fact and action, however, is significant for its influence on Soloveitchik's arguments and style.

May claimed that existence means processes of becoming and development on the one hand, and processes of reflection on the other. The concrete person, then, is her own latent possibilities, her potential, as well as the very awareness of her existence and the implied ethical dimension (responsibility and commitment). "A man can understand himself only as he projects himself forward. This is a corollary of the fact that the person is always becoming, always emerging into the future."[53] The individual's confrontation with the potentialities creates a condition of anxiety, whereas the understanding that the potentialities cannot be fulfilled brings with it a

---

51 On the connection to Buber's approach, see, for example, Dov Schwartz, *The Phenomenology of Existentialism: The Philosophy of Rabbi Joseph B. Soloveitchik*, vol. 2, trans. Batya Stein (Leiden/Boston: Brill, 2013), ch. 11; Nicham Ross, "Between Martin Buber and R. Joseph Dov Soloveitchik: A Response of 'The Lonely Man of Faith' to the Teaching of 'I and Thou'" [Heb], *Identities: Journal of Jewish Culture and Identity* 5 (2014): 47–74.
52 *Existence*, 13, note 13.
53 Ibid., 69.

condition of guilt.⁵⁴ More precisely: the concrete person is not potential in the Aristotelian sense, which must eventually be realized. She is potential in the sense that she has possibilities and struggles to determine which way to go, which potentiality to choose and which to develop and fulfill. May writes:

> The full meaning of the term "human being" will be clearer if the reader will keep in mind that "being" is a participle, a verb form implying that someone is in the process of *being something*. It is unfortunate that, when used as a general noun in English, the term "being" connotes a static substance, and when used as a particular noun such as *a* being, it is usually assumed to refer to an entity, say, such as a soldier to be counted as a unit. Rather, "being" should be understood, when used as a general noun, to mean *potentia*, the source of potentiality; "being" is the potentiality by which the acorn becomes the oak or each one of us becomes what he truly is.⁵⁵

May's distinction between a static and a dynamic being, or between being as a given reality and being as process, is also the source of the distinction between fact and action. Being is actually action. May differentiated action meant to blur the consciousness of self and escape from it and action as an expression of the self. Many who present themselves as active and busy are covering up anxiety.⁵⁶ This action is an escape from consciousness to being. In sum, May differentiated surface action from in-depth action.

In *Kol Dodi Dofek*, Soloveitchik rejects the metaphysical solution to the problem of evil. At the opening of this essay, he claims that the question about the cause of evil has no answer and, consequently, it is in vain we seek a solution to it. He conveyed this through a parable about attempting to understand the design of a rug by looking at it from the reverse side. In sum: humans are incapable of apprehending the divine plan. The relevant question is the question of purpose, and the only purpose is action. "What should the sufferer do to live with his suffering?"⁵⁷ Soloveitchik obviously intended Halakhah, which is mainly concerned with action. But he identified human existence as action, as opposed to metaphysics.

Furthermore, Soloveitchik also poured the distinction between fact and action into the distinction between an existence of fate and an existence of destiny. An existence of fate, which presents the person as an object, is "a

---

54 Ibid., 52.
55 Ibid., 41.
56 *Man's Search for Himself*, 117–118.
57 Joseph B. Soloveitchik, *Kol Dodi Dofek: Listen—My Beloved Knocks*, trans. David Z. Gordon (New York: Yeshiva University, 2006), 7.

factual existence, simply one line in a [long] chain of mechanical causality, devoid of significance, direction, and purpose, and subordinate to the forces of the environment into whose midst the individual is pushed, unconsulted by Providence."[58] Factuality is the first characteristic of an existence of fate. By contrast, an existence of destiny, which presents the person as a subject, is characterized as "an active existence, when man confronts the environment into which he has been cast with an understanding of his uniqueness and value, freedom and capacity; without compromising his integrity and independence in his struggle with the outside world."[59] Subjective existence is characterized by action.

Soloveitchik then proceeded to claim that the existential characteristics of the individual are reproduced in the national realm. Individual loneliness becomes national loneliness. Clearly, then, the fundamental features of the individual experience are reproduced at the national level. One significant feature of an existence of fate is loneliness.[60] Accordingly, the loneliness of the Jewish individual comes forth as antisemitism in the national sphere. The existence of destiny conferred meaning on loneliness and leveraged it for a purpose. Soloveitchik again distinguishes fact from action and writes:

> In the life of a people (as in the life of an individual), destiny signifies an existence that it has chosen of its own free will and in which it finds the full realization of its historical existence. Instead of a passive, inexorable existence into which a nation is thrust, an Existence of Destiny manifests itself as an active experience full of purposeful movement, ascension, aspirations, and fulfillment.[61]

At the national level as well, then, an existence of destiny is an existence of action, while an existence of fate is one of fact. Action conveys that the individual is a subject, whereas fact exposes the person as an object. An authentic national existence is dynamic and develops. For Soloveitchik, the realization of the national potential entails clear teleological overtones. National action is purposeful in the sense that it strives to attain goals.

---

58 Ibid., 2.
59 Ibid., 5–6. See also Avi Schweitzer (Sagi), "The Loneliness of the Man of Faith in the Philosophy of Soloveitchik," *Daat: A Journal of Jewish Philosophy and Kabbalah*, 2/3 (1978): 247–257.
60 At times, Soloveitchik reversed course, drawing inferences about the individual from the national realm. Writing about exile, he notes, "Our exile, or exile experience, is a reflection of the universal metaphysical exile awareness with which man—not only the Jew—is burdened" (Soloveitchik, "The Synagogue," 325).
61 *Kol Dodi Dofek*, 65. See also Schwartz, *The Philosophy of Rabbi Joseph B. Soloveitchik*, vol. 2, 220–224.

Personal and Collective Existence

In this case, the sources in existential psychotherapy are not the only ones. In replicating in the national realm the distinction between fact and action presents on the personal sphere, Soloveitchik relies to some extent on a group of late nineteenth-century and early twentieth-century sociologists who were active mainly in Germany (Georg Simmel, Max Weber, György Lukács, and others), and particularly on the classic distinction between *Gemeinschaft* and *Gesellschaft* drawn by Ferdinand Tönnies, one of the group's founders. This distinction stands midway between the individual and nationality since it deals with community and communitarianism. When, in *Kol Dodi Dofek*, Soloveitchik draws a distinction between – respectively – "Encampment" and "Congregation" and points to the sociological source, he indeed notes:

> Encampment and Congregation constitute two different sociological experiences, two separate groups that have nothing in common and do not support one another. An Encampment is created out of a desire for self-defense and thrives on fear. A Congregation is fashioned out of longing for the realization of an exalted moral idea and thrives on love. In the Encampment, fate's rule is unlimited, whereas destiny rules in the Congregation. The Encampment represents a phase in the development of the nation's history. The continued survival of a people is identified with the existence of the Congregation.[62]

Jacob Blidstein has already shown that the source of the split between a covenant of fate (*berit goral*) and a covenant of destiny (*berit ye'ud*) is the thought of Martin Buber.[63] But Buber himself was strongly influenced by this group of sociologists of culture as is evident in many of his articles such as "Havruta." The distinction mediating between the individual and the nation has apparently split into two types of communities: the modern association (*Gesellschaft*) as a community of fate, given that Marxist dialectic materialism detaches individuals from decisions about their fate, as shown below, and the traditional community (*Gemeinschaft*) as a community of destiny, in the sense of a partnership in a dialogical and supporting collective.[64]

---

62 *Kol Dodi Dofek*, 69.
63 Jacob Blidstein, "The Jewish People in the Thought of R. Joseph B. Soloveitchik" [Heb], in *Faith in Changing Times: On the Teachings of R. Joseph B. Soloveitchik*, ed. Avi Sagi (Jerusalem: WZO, 1996), 168–171.
64 For example, Harry Liebersohn, *Fate and Utopia in German Sociology, 1870–1923* (Cambridge, MA: MIT Press, 1988), 29–30. On the impact of the theory on Jewish thinkers, see, for example, Michael Brenner, *The Renaissance of Jewish Culture in Weimar Germany* (New Haven: Yale University Press, 1996), 40–41.

If we return to May's discussion, we find that existentialism as an idea is for him the antithesis of the modern association. He wrote:

> ... the very success of the industrial system, with its accumulation of money as a validation of personal worth entirely separate from the actual product of a man's hands, had a reciprocal depersonalizing and dehumanizing effect upon man in his relation to others and himself. It was against these dehumanizing tendencies to make man into a machine, to make him over in the image of the industrial system for which he labored, that the early existentialists fought so strongly. And they were aware that the most serious threat of all was that reason would join mechanics in sapping the individual's vitality and decisiveness. *Reason*, they predicted, *was becoming reduced to a new kind of technique.*[65]

Marxism sharply distinguishes between human action and its influences or implications. Furthermore, Marxist ideology divests the person from his individuality and turns him into a cog in a machine. May noted that the blurring of the individual facing modernity is particularly emphasized in Kierkegaard's philosophical endeavor:

> The central psychological endeavor of Kierkegaard may be summed up under the heading of the question he pursued relentlessly—how can you become an individual? The individual was being swallowed up on the rational side by Hegel's vast logical "absolute Whole," on the economic side by the increasing objectification of the person, and on the moral and spiritual side by the soft and vapid religion of his day. Europe was ill, and was to become more so, not because knowledge or techniques were lacking but because of the want of *passion, commitment.*[66]

Modern forms of association have not only alienated individuals from their own actions and deprived them of their privacy, but also present them as objects. They are active externally but not in their internal existence, meaning that they do not experience their actions as meaningful.

Soloveitchik unequivocally determines, "There is no identity without uniqueness."[67] In Soloveitchik's thought, individualism comes forth in his

---

65 *Existence,* 21–22 (emphasis in original).
66 Ibid., 24–25 (emphasis in original).
67 Soloveitchik, "Confrontation," 18.

extensive discussions about loneliness, singularity, and subjectivity. When he deals with emotional life, he emphasizes its totality, pointing out that a specific feeling cannot be detached from the full emotional spectrum.[68] Such a move not only negates existence but is also immoral. Soloveitchik also claims that action and the awareness of it is an expression of human individualism. He endorsed, as noted, the construct of fact versus action as an expression of real existence.

Repression

I return now to the focus on existence as antithetical to the spirit of Western culture. Note that a process resembling the Freudian mechanism of repression unfolded in the literature on existential therapy. This literature was strongly critical of psychoanalysis' concern with external and surface phenomena instead of with their existential foundations. May held that, in Victorian society, conceptualization, culture, rationalism, and religion had been separated and compartmentalized from concrete life. "On the surface, of course, the Victorian period appeared placid, contented, ordered; but this placidity was purchased at the price of widespread, profound, and increasingly brittle repression."[69] May argued that, parallel to the compartmentalization between these domains and existence, there is psychological compartmentalization of the personality, resulting in repression.

Compartmentalization and separation lead to the repression of "self-awareness,"[70] which leads to neuroses. In the wake of Gabriel Marcel, May claimed that the very concern with existence underwent a process of repression in Western culture. The authentic in-depth foundation threatens, as it were, the superficial values of modern society, which reacts with repression. May resolutely states: "A more serious source of resistance is one that runs through the whole of modern Western society—namely, the psychological need to avoid and, in some ways, repress, the whole concern with 'being.'"[71] He then cites Marcel in *The Philosophy of Existence*, and presents repression as a distinctly pathological move: "*Indeed I wonder if a psychoanalytic method, deeper and more discerning than any that has been evolved until now, would not reveal the morbid effects of the repression of this sense* [of existence] *and of the ignoring of this need* [to deal with it]."[72] Why did this

---

68 See Joseph B. Soloveitchik, "A Theory of Emotions," in *Out of the Whirlwind: Essays on Suffering, Mourning and the Human Condition*, ed. David Shatz, Joel B. Wolowelsky and Reuven Ziegler (New York: Toras HaRav Foundation/Ktav, 2003), 179–214. See also Schwartz, *The Phenomenology of Existentialism*, vol. 2, 280.
69 *Existence*, 22.
70 Ibid., 23.
71 Ibid., 40.
72 Ibid., (emphasis in original).

repression occur? Materialism and the functionality of existence could be behind it. May seemingly adds a powerful motive – finitude. A person chooses life, knowing it is limited. Choosing life is a result of self-awareness. Man is aware of his existence, but also equally aware of the possibility of interrupting it by committing suicide, "he is the being who is always in a dialectical relation with non-being, death."[73] Initially, then, the therapist must bring the patient to become aware of the existence layer, that is, of the basic layer that is the ground for the growth of action, thought, knowledge, and so forth.

Soloveitchik referred to existence as "the mystery of Being."[74] Existence, then, is latent and needs to be exposed. Indeed, Soloveitchik held that acquaintance with the deep-rooted existential layer is the necessary basis of personal redemption, which conveys authentic existence. He then went further and determined that knowledge of the existential layer is even more primary than knowledge of the other. When dealing with redeemed existence in *The Lonely Man of Faith*, he writes as follows:

> Even a hermit, while not having the opportunity to manifest dignity, can live a redeemed life.[75] Cathartic redemptiveness is experienced in the privacy of one's in-depth personality, and it cuts below the relationship between the "I" and the "thou" (to use an existentialist term)[76] and reaches into the very hidden strata of the isolated "I" who knows himself as a singular being. When objectified in personal and emotional categories, cathartic redemptiveness expresses itself in the feeling of axiological security. The individual intuits his existence as worthwhile, legitimate, and adequate, anchored in something stable and unchangeable.[77]

The personality's cathartic redemptiveness is described as knowledge of existence, and this knowledge implies singularity. The term that Soloveitchik uses, "the very hidden strata," hints at the repression of fundamental existence. Soloveitchik, as noted above, argued that Adam the first and Adam the second are in fact two dispositions within the same person:

> In every one of us abide two *personae*—the creative, majestic Adam the first, and the submissive, humble Adam the second. As we portrayed them typologically, their views are not commensurate; ... Yet, no matter how far-reaching the cleavage, each of us must willy-nilly identify

---

73 Ibid., 42.
74 Soloveitchik, *Lonely Man of Faith*, 24.
75 Dignity conveys power, as Soloveitchik clarifies in *The Lonely Man of Faith*.
76 Referring to the dialogical relationship.
77 *The Lonely Man of Faith*, 34–35.

himself with the whole of an all-inclusive human personality, charged with responsibility, as both a majestic and a covenantal being.[78]

Adam does not skip between dispositions, as he does not skip from a covenantal to a faith community. Both these moments are present in him. Since the opposition between them is "far-reaching," it is a plausible assumption that Adam sometimes needs to repress one disposition and allow the other to surface. The result is that Adam cannot be clearly defined. His identity is tied to "ontological loneliness."[79]

Soloveitchik hints at emotional repression in other writings as well. For example, in "Catharsis," Soloveitchik describes a state resembling repression and speaks about "inner withdrawal"[80] and "self-denial."[81] On the day of the inauguration of the Tabernacle, two of Aaron's sons, Nadav and Avihu, died devoured by fire. Aaron could not abandon the celebrations of the day and mourn for them. Instead, he had to deny his grief and largely repress it.

The notion of existence as a fundamental layer requiring an act of disclosure is fundamentally therapeutic and is clearly evident in May's work. This approach to some extent replicates the psychoanalytic mechanisms of repression. Indeed, after Freud, psychotherapeutic discussions are hardly ever entirely detached from his views.

Love

One issue that phenomenological and existential psychotherapists discussed at length is love. Love was perceived as a key to intersubjective attachments and, as such, it was related to dialogue and to the ability to create transference. Generally, Soloveitchik focused more on mourning than on love in the later stages of his thinking. Occasionally, however, he did address this issue, channeling love mainly to its functional aspects – marriage, love of parents, and so forth. In his writings from the late 1950s, he saw Eros as an aesthetic expression that must be controlled and directed in a divine direction.[82] He emphasized the selfish element in love as requiring softening so

---

78 Ibid., 84–85.
79 Ibid., 87.
80 Joseph B. Soloveitchik, "Catharsis," *Tradition* 17:2 (Spring, 1978), 47.
81 Ibid., 48.
82 See, for example, Dov Schwartz, "Aesthetics and the Limits of Reason: Major Trends in Twentieth Century Orthodox Thought" [Heb], *Daat* 73–74 (2013): 403–432; idem, *Shift in Religious-Zionism: From Unity to Plurality* [Heb] (Jerusalem: Bialik Institute, 2018), ch. 11; idem, Encounters: Chapters in Jewish Aesthetics (Ramat-Gan: Bar-Ilan University Press, 2019), ch. 4.

that love may become part of the person's general emotional setup.[83] I deal here with the psychotherapeutic models of love manifest in parenthood.

Privacy

May argued that emotions are intentional – a way of communicating and establishing relationships with people who are significant to us. Love is included in this claim.[84] Love grows from the mutual encounter between one consciousness and another. Nevertheless, May noted that the relationship with the *Eigenvelt* is a component of love:

> *Eigenvelt* cannot be omitted in the understanding of love.[85] Nietzsche and Kierkegaard continually insisted that to love presupposes that one has already become the "true individual," the "Solitary One," the one who "has comprehended the deep secret that also in loving another person one must be sufficient unto oneself."[86]

Love, then, does not imply blurring borders and sinking into the beloved. Quite the contrary, love is sustained through awareness of, and even emphasis on, the self. And indeed, a model such as this one powerfully influenced Soloveitchik's thought.

In his discussion in "Marriage," Soloveitchik argued that the individual has a non-transferable dimension he calls "numinous" in the sense that it focuses exclusively on the divine and sublime, coexisting with a transitive dimension he calls "kerygmatic" that is directed to the community and to society.[87] If the component turning to the other is the overriding one, the marriage succeeds and a healthy partnership develops. By contrast, if the non-transitive dimension is the overriding one, the only way out is divorce. In this analysis, even with love and reciprocity, the individual component does not disappear and may even be overriding.

At times, Soloveitchik presented a model of love as a withdrawal to the self. This model appears in the description of love for the father. Soloveitchik dealt with an issue discussed at great length in psychological writings – the maturation and independence of the child vis-à-vis parental influence:

> The healthy child, who is loved and supported but not coddled by his parents, will proceed in his development despite the anxiety and the

---

83 Soloveitchik, *Out of the Whirlwind*, 201–202.
84 May, *Love and Will*, 91.
85 In May's modes, love belongs to the Mitwelt. Nevertheless, he claimed that the Eigenwelt dimension is also part of love.
86 *Existence*, 65. May quotes here Søren Kierkegaard, Fear and Trembling, trans. Walter Lowrie (New York: Doubleday, 1954), 55. On individualism in Kierkegaard, see above.
87 Soloveitchik, *Family Redeemed*, 31–72.

crises that face him. And there may be no particular external sign of trauma or special rebelliousness. But when his parents consciously or unconsciously exploit him for their own ends or pleasure, or hate or reject him, so that he cannot be sure of minimal support when he tries out his new independence, the child will cling to the parents and will use his capacity for independence only in the form of negativity and stubbornness.[88]

Soloveitchik devoted significant attention to the proper parental behavior that will enable the child to grow and, as noted, he used May's model of love out of self-awareness. In the essay "Torah and *Shekhinah*," he draws a distinction between fatherly and motherly love. The mother's love is based on experiential memory – for her, the past lives in the present, vibrant as if reoccurring. By contrast, the father's memory is formal ("progressive image memory" in Soloveitchik's terminology), which is a memory that sets limits. "What one remembers does not interfere with the present; the memory does not cross the frontiers of time dimensions. The past, where the event lies, is dead; the present is alive."[89]

The mother's love, therefore, is constantly present in the life of her children. She experiences them as children even when they have already become adults and, therefore, cannot release them to pursue their adult lives. The mother always casts a shadow on the child. The mother's memory is "a nonprogressive and timeless event memory which captures and imprisons the experiences themselves and quickens bygones into new life."[90] By contrast, the father's love denotes an inner withdrawal:

> The love of father consists in helping the child to free himself from paternal authority, in moving away from him, while mother's love expresses itself in steady intensification of her emotional attachment, in surging toward her child.
>
> The Halakhah entrusted education to the father—and what is the educational gesture if not an act of granting independence to the young person and training the latter to live with dignity and responsibility and in freedom? The father was charged with this task because it fits into the framework of paternal concern. The mother was relieved of the educational duties since she instinctively resents her

---

88 May, *Man's Search for Himself*, 86–87.
89 Soloveitchik, *Family Redeemed*, 164.
90 Ibid.

child's adulthood and the independence that education is supposed to promote and foster.[91]

The father's love denotes his self-withdrawal vis-à-vis the child's maturation, while the mother's love deplores the child's independence. In this model, the mother cannot love the child while preserving the borders of privacy, whereas the father respects his child's freedom. The model of fatherly love, clearly based on self-withdrawal, conveys love while respecting the individuality of both – father and child. The father shows love toward his child but also shields his own self from being confused with or sunk into the child. Many parents who, like my own, were Holocaust survivors, tried to give their children what they had been deprived of, and in fact poured their aspirations, and through them, their personality, into the personality of the child. Soloveitchik claimed that healthy parenting requires the father's withdrawal, a model that, to some extent, resembles May's model of love while preserving the personality. Soloveitchik then turns to the love of God.

Love of God

According to the methodology that characterizes Soloveitchik's discussions, he proceeded to claim that consciousness' relationship with God also entails two concurrent aspects – one of fatherly love and one of motherly love. This conscious structure appears as a development of the classic dialectical construct of love and fear, or closeness and distance, extensively considered in phenomenological writings on religion. Soloveitchik himself relied, in many of his writings, on the dialectic of simultaneous contradictory emotions.

Soloveitchik indeed replicated the model of parental love to that of divine love and created a three-staged conscious structure:

1   Parallel between parental love and divine love God: "Every sensitive Jew knows that at times we run to the Almighty for advice and encouragement just like a confused, frustrated and disappointed child runs to its father, while at other time we cling to the *Shekhinah*, just like a child who, in utter despair, hides its head in shame in his mother's lap, finding there solace and comfort."[92]
2   Parental love is a reflection and an imitation of divine love in the same sense that earthly values are a reflection and an imitation of ideas in Plato's thought ("Platonic imagery").[93]

---

91   Ibid., 165.
92   Ibid., 166–167.
93   Ibid., 168.

3   Parental love derives from divine love ("what is transient fatherhood and motherhood if not a reflected beam of light coming to us from beyond the frontiers of the cosmos, and what is paternal or maternal concern if not an echo of the great concern of the Almighty?").[94]

The source of love, then, is divine, and love's reflection in the earthly world acts as a kind of mediating element between heaven and earth. May's *Love and Will* appeared a year after the writing of "Torah and *Shekhinah*," but it is similarly influenced by Plato in a description of love as a midpoint between the spiritual and the material.[95] May writes,

> Eros is not a god in the sense of being above man, but the power that binds all things and all men together, the power *informing* all things. I do not use in-form loosely—it means to give inward form, to seek out by the devotion of love the unique form of the beloved person or object and unite one's self with that form.[96]

According to May's reading of Plato, love is a kind of cosmic emanation uniting all objects. By contrast, Soloveitchik presents a religious reading of the Platonic approach. In this sense, parental love is a kind of "participation" in cosmic, divine love.

Summing Up

Soloveitchik adopted many models and constructs that appeared in Rollo May's works. The closeness between them seems to convey a critique of the cultural climate in the United States. Both of them reflected the contrast between European culture and their actual surroundings. This contrast stands out in light of the fact that Soloveitchik never abandoned the ideas he had absorbed in Warsaw and Berlin. Like May, Soloveitchik felt that, in his work, he exposes inner layers of existence that his predecessors had been unaware of and, moreover, that, through these layers, he discovers the contents of a new religiosity.

At least formally, the patterns that May adopted significantly contributed to the shaping of Soloveitchik's philosophical discourse. Yet, more than that, they released him from the need to engage in a detailed examination of the foundations of existence and enabled him to proceed almost immediately to the religious and halakhic realm. Soloveitchik's *oeuvre* hardly contains existentialist characteristics that had not been clearly explained in May's work.

---

94 Ibid.
95 May, *Love and Will*, 77.
96 Ibid., 78 (emphasis in original).

Soloveitchik identified with May's sources and also with his therapeutic approach, that is, with the demand to penetrate the foundations of existence in order to enable influence on the personality of the individual (for May, the patient), and May himself was actually the spokesman of phenomenological and existential psychotherapists. Whether he was indeed a direct influence is unclear, but he did give thematic expression to the new approach.

Soloveitchik, however, was mainly influenced by May's diagnoses and by the theoretical background that he provided, that is, by the philosophical and psychological theories used to evaluate the patient's pathology, and less by the therapy itself. Existential psychotherapists themselves held that it was more important to discover the foundations of existence than to create a systematic therapeutic method. The very discovery is the basis of the therapy. Soloveitchik, however, did not resort to the therapy because he held that Halakhah is the most effective therapeutic factor. He was convinced that the solutions to pathologies and to the mental anguish of alienation, loneliness, and estrangement from nature are found in halakhic behavior. The term "Halakhah" in Soloveitchik's writings reflects not only behavior but also a system of values and ideas. He, therefore, added a religious layer to May's discussions, which framed them in what he considered a suitable context. Furthermore, Soloveitchik held that Halakhah makes psychotherapy largely redundant in that it directs individuals to their real existence and leads them to confront their own selves. The hallmark of Soloveitchik's thought is the apologetic label of Halakhah's superiority, and the encounter with therapists is part of it. Hence, Soloveitchik frequently mentions the tragic standing of Halakhah, whereas May often argues that the American climate had lost the tragic dimension of concrete life.

Most of May's insights, as noted, had already been considered in philosophical, phenomenological, and existentialist literature, both in theoretical formulations and in fictional works. May himself relied extensively on existentialist philosophy, but he articulated these insights in ways that enabled access to them without recourse to abstract philosophical literature. His fluent wordings present the existentialist arguments in intelligent and user-friendly language. Soloveitchik's writings indeed show that he hardly resorted to primary sources in existentialist philosophy. In a way, his formulations are more influenced by May's smooth, flowing descriptions than by Nietzsche, Heidegger, and others. An interesting phenomenon occurred here: existential psychotherapists relied on philosophical analysis: "Martin Heidegger is generally taken as the fountainhead of present-day existential thought. His seminal work, *Being and Time*, was of radical importance in giving Binswanger and other existential psychiatrists and psychologists the deep and broad basis they sought for understanding man."[97] May's school

---

97 *Existence*, 15.

and May himself, then, relied on existentialist philosophy and developed from it not only a therapeutic school but also clear and elegant formulations of the complicated analyses of Heidegger and other philosophers.

Soloveitchik then used the therapists' formulations to build a new existentialist religious philosophy. In other words, he returned to the philosophical discourse by relying on a psychiatric and psychological articulation. Soloveitchik's discourse is indeed far from systematic and from the level of analysis endorsed by Heidegger and other philosophers. He wrote essays and sermons, not philosophical analyses, but he certainly endeavored to create a religious philosophy.

This review discussed several aspects of the influence on Soloveitchik of a discourse of the kind May engaged in as an existential psychotherapist. Obviously, there are additional aspects to this influence – such as approaches to tradition, religiosity, and time – and, in this context, I have only addressed a few basic existential features. This discussion, however, suffices to clarify the contribution of this field to Soloveitchik's style and to the flow of his existential arguments.

Thanks to Batya Stein, who translated this article from Hebrew.

Chapter 2

From Fear to Creativity
Melanie Klein's Interpretation of Literary Fiction as Conceptual Investigations

Dorit Lemberger

Introduction: Wittgenstein on Conceptual Investigation and Its Relevance for Understanding Melanie Klein's Concepts

Wittgenstein, in his complicated way, explained the centrality of concepts to any form of investigation, on the one hand, and the impossibility of defining any concept, on the other. This is because language is characterized by constant dynamism,[1] and because there is no "metalanguage" by means of which concepts can be defined in "the language itself."[2]

Language is an instrument. Its concepts are instruments .... Concepts lead us to make investigations. They are the expression of our interest and direct our interest.[3] We are not analyzing a phenomenon (e.g., thought) but a concept (e.g., that of thinking), and therefore the use of a word.[4]

Therefore, concepts should be examined in their application, and their features should be construed through their usage.[5] Our investigations emerge from the fact that certain concepts raise interest, tension, or questions, and this state of curiosity or discomfort leads to inquiry.[6]

Furthermore, Wittgenstein distinguished between his methodology and those phenomenological methodologies common in his period, which he was aware of and which he repudiated.[7] He held that even before a phenomenon

---

1 Wittgenstein, *Philosophical Investigations*, 23.
2 Wittgenstein, *Philosophical Investigations*, 121.
3 Wittgenstein, *Philosophical Investigations*, 569–70.
4 Wittgenstein, *Philosophical Investigations*, 383.
5 Wittgenstein, *Philosophical Investigations*, 43, 116.
6 Wittgenstein, *Philosophical Investigations*, 110, 132.
7 "All our forms of speech are taken from ordinary, physical language and **cannot be used in epistemology or phenomenology without casting a distorting light** on their objects. ... The very expression 'I can conceive x' is itself taken from the idioms of physics, and x ought to be a physical object. ... Things have already gone wrong if this expression is used in

is identified, thought processes occur that are embodied in language. These processes include concepts and language-games that must be clarified in order to understand a specific usage. For this reason, it is incorrect to focus on any given phenomenon, which is already a mediated product of a certain conceptualization within a certain language-game. Wittgenstein therefore rejected phenomenology as a methodology, although he recognized the existence of phenomenological problems such as the difficulty of describing an ambiguous color.[8]

Conceptual investigation is a central methodology in Wittgenstein's writings[9]; it includes, among other things, guidance for comparison between the functions of concepts in various contexts,[10] as well as comparison between concepts that seem semantically close and therefore must be distinguished from each other.[11] As mentioned, Wittgenstein refrained from defining concepts, but rather examined the way they are used in practice: "One ought to ask, not what images are or what goes on when one imagines something, but how the word 'imagination' is used. But that does not mean that I want to talk only about words. For the question of what imagination

---

phenomenology, where x must refer to a datum." Ludwig Wittgenstein, *Philosophical Remarks*, ed. Rush Rhees, trans. Raymond Hargreaves and Roger White (Oxford: Basil Blackwell, 1975), 88; emphasis mine.

8 "There is indeed no such thing as phenomenology, but there are phenomenological problems." Ludwig Wittgenstein, *Remarks on Color*, ed. G. E. M. Anscombe, trans. Linda L. McAlister and Margarete Schättle (Oxford: Basil Blackwell, 1981), 248; "But what kind of a proposition is that, that blending in white removes the coloredness from the color? As I mean it, it can't be a proposition of physics. Here the temptation to believe in a phenomenology, something midway between science and logic, is very great" (Wittgenstein, *Remarks on Color*, 3).

9 See, for example: Oskari Kuusela, "Wittgenstein's Method of Conceptual Investigation and Concept Formation in Psychology," in *A Wittgensteinian Perspective on the Use of Conceptual Analysis in Psychology*, ed. Tim Racine and Kathleen Slaney (London: Palgrave/Macmillan, 2013), 51–71.

10 "Our clear and simple language-games are not preliminary studies for a future regimentation of language as it were, first approximations, ignoring friction and air resistance. Rather, the language-games stand there as objects of comparison which, through similarities and dissimilarities, are meant to throw light on features of our language" (Wittgenstein, *Philosophical Investigations*, 130).

11 "'Seeing and imaging are different phenomena.'—The words 'seeing' and 'imaging' have different meanings. Their meanings relate to a host of important kinds of human behavior, to phenomena of human life." Ludwig Wittgenstein, *Remarks on the Philosophy of Psychology*, ed. Georg Henrik von Wright and Heikki Nyman, trans. C. G. Luckhardt and Maximilian Nyman (Oxford: Basil Blackwell, 1980), 2:629; "'Seeing and imaging are different phenomena.'—The words 'seeing' and 'imaging' are used differently. 'I see' is used differently from 'I have an image,' 'See!' differently from 'Form an image!', and 'I am trying to see it' differently from 'I am trying to form an image of it.'" Ludwig Wittgenstein, *Zettel*, ed. G. E. M. Anscombe and Georg Henrik von Wright, trans. G. E. M. Anscombe (Oxford: Basil Blackwell, 1981), 75.

essentially is, is as much about the word 'imagination' as my question."[12] Mary Warnock claimed that in this paragraph, Wittgenstein directed us to the act and not the product (the mental image).[13] Warnock emphasized that according to Wittgenstein, the description of the mental image cannot teach us about imagination, but the observation of our use of images can do so. This use is grammatical and exposes "species of thinking."[14]

At this point we should ask: What is conceptual research in psychoanalysis? Further, what is its potential contribution to an understanding of the concepts introduced by Melanie Klein? Wittgenstein's insights regarding conceptual investigation will serve as an inspiration for this chapter: It will not consist of interdisciplinary research in the accepted sense, which attempts to shed light on psychoanalytic concepts by means of a discipline external to psychoanalysis such as literature, or linguistics, etc.[15] Considerable psychoanalytic research has already been dedicated to the intersection of literature and psychoanalysis as two separate and distinct disciplines, each of which may contribute to an understanding of the other, and which may overlap.[16] A collection dedicated to the application of Klein's concepts to literary analysis mentions the three essays analyzed at length in this chapter in order to illustrate the dialogue maintained by Klein with the authors of literary works.[17] The collection's editor observed that Klein saw literary works as an expression of their authors' capacity to describe the depths of the psyche, but he did not pursue this observation further. The ultimate conclusion was that the literary

---

12 Wittgenstein, *Philosophical Investigations*, 370.
13 Mary Warnock, *Imagination* (London: Faber and Faber, 1976), 158.
14 Warnock, *Imagination*, 159.
15 A summary of this type of interdisciplinary inquiry was suggested in the following: "The interdisciplinary dialogue also often inspires theorizing within psychoanalysis itself and strengthens its creativity, innovation, as well as unconventional understandings of clinical material. *However, in contrast to clinical or conceptual research—the aim is neither primarily to contribute to a deeper or more precise understanding of clinical material nor to study concepts in detail. The focus of interdisciplinary research is the exchange of psychoanalytic knowledge with the non-psychoanalytic (scientific) world.*" Marianne Leuzinger-Bohleber and Tamara Fischmann, "What Is Conceptual Research in Psychoanalysis?," *The International Journal of Psychoanalysis* 87, no. 5 (November 2006): 1373; emphasis in original.
16 "Psychoanalysis meets literature on a number of different terrains. A piece of literature may be used to illustrate a psychoanalytic theory, or a psychoanalytic approach may be used to illuminate the work. Inevitably these two are closely related and there is often considerable overlap." David Bell, ed., *Psychoanalysis and Culture: A Kleinian Perspective* (London: Karnac, 1999), 14–15.
17 "In these papers Klein is, so to speak, having a conversation with the artist who through his ability to be in touch with primitive areas of mental life, and give them form, had discovered the very same phenomena that she encountered with her young patients. These papers deal only with the work of art itself" (Bell, *Psychoanalysis and Culture*, 15).

work "had discovered the very same phenomena that she encountered with her young patients."

In my view, this conclusion **does not** reflect the added value to be found in Klein's discussions of literary works, and thus does not reflect Klein's thoughts on the topic. Klein defined her goals in the use of literary works by focusing on the literary work as a source of inspiration for the understanding of hidden emotional processes. In the essays analyzed below, Klein pointed to three main purposes for her use of literary works: (1) The narrative reveals profound psychological insight; (2) the narrative allows us to identify the unconscious motives that are the factors which have ministered a child's behavior; and (3) the literary work allows us to redefine a central concept by shedding light on its ambiguous features.

This chapter will adopt Wittgenstein's suggestion to focus on conceptual investigation in order to analyze how Klein herself examined three of the key concepts of her thought with the help of literary works. The idea is to show that psychoanalytic language, like everyday language, can function in all sorts of ways.[18] One of these ways is the language of the imagination, and thus we may use the language of literature, which is based on imagination, to elucidate psychoanalytic concepts.

The three concepts examined in this essay had already appeared to a limited extent in the writings of Freud. In her clinical work, Klein focused on the treatment of young children; she articulated these concepts to describe the infantile life of the emotions during childhood, as well as expressions of this emotional life in maturity. Freud hardly discussed these stages, while Klein, in her observations, discovered situations that may only be explained by expanding and broadening psychoanalytic theory to apply to an infant at the beginning of life. In the present discussion, I wish to show how Klein used literary works in order to validate her clinical discoveries, and how the literary works consulted by Klein contributed to the clarification of what she saw as the ambiguity of the concepts she suggested. The concepts will be examined chronologically, according to the publication year of each essay: (1) "Infantile Anxiety-Situations Reflected in a Work of Art and in the Creative Impulse" (1929); (2) "On Identification" (1955); and (3) "Some Reflections on 'The Oresteia'" (1963). Each stage will present the concept and Klein's innovation with regard to that concept; it will then examine how the literary works discussed in each essay helped to crystallize and clarify the concept. After my explorations of the three essays, I will demonstrate how the similarities

---

18 "The paradox disappears only if we make a radical break with the idea that language always functions in one way, always serves the same purpose: to convey thoughts—which may be about houses, pains, good and evil, or whatever" (Wittgenstein, *Philosophical Investigations*, 304).

between these discussions may serve as a basis for an interdisciplinary method of literary psychoanalytical interpretation.

The First Article: The Empty Space of Infantile Anxiety

In the earliest essay in which Klein discussed a literary work, the central concept of the discussion is "infantile anxiety." Klein described an infant's development differently from Freud, and assigned special importance to infantile anxiety in describing the basic state of an infant's emotional life. In contrast to Freud, who saw instinct as the central factor that motivates people in all stages of their lives, Klein understood the central factor to be anxiety.[19] Klein's method of investigation was first and foremost based on her clinical observations, only after which she articulated her findings in terms of arguments and concepts. The essay "Infantile Anxiety-Situations Reflected in a Work of Art and in the Creative Impulse" begins with an analysis of the narrative of a Ravel opera as if it were an event in the clinic. The opera was staged at that time in Vienna, and while Klein did not see it, she indicated that she had read about it in a review in the newspaper.[20] The human characters described by Klein are a son and his mother; before we turn to the analysis, we should note that Freud hardly discussed the connection between an infant and its mother, as he himself attested.

In his essay "Female Sexuality" (1931), written at a very late stage of his thought, Freud pointed to two key matters that had not been adequately discussed in earlier writings. The first was the scarce discussion of the infant's relationship with the mother, despite its importance to a child's development until age four.[21] The second was his difficulty in trying to revivify repressed material relating to attachment to the mother during treatments.[22] In describing his focus on his female patients' relationships with their father

---

19 Janet Sayers described how the emphasis Klein placed on anxiety as a primary state leads at the second stage to attack and at the third to reparation, as we will see below in the analysis of the present essay. Janet Sayers, *Mothering Psychoanalysis* (London: Hamilton, 1991), 233–34.
20 "My account of its content is taken almost word for word from a review by Eduard Jakob in the Berliner Tageblatt." Melanie Klein, "Infantile Anxiety-Situations Reflected in a Work of Art and in the Creative Impulse," *International Journal of Psycho-Analysis* 10 (1929): 436.
21 Sigmund Freud, *The Complete Psychological Works of Sigmund Freud*, trans. and ed. James Strachey (New York: W. W. Norton, 1976), 4589–608.
22 "Everything in the sphere of this first attachment to the mother seemed to me so difficult to grasp in analysis—so grey with age and shadowy and almost impossible to revivify—that it was as if it had succumbed to an especially inexorable repression. ... The women who were in analysis with me were able to cling to the very attachment to the father in which they had taken refuge from the early phase that was in question. It does indeed appear that women analysts—as, for instance, Jeanne Lampl-de Groot and Helene Deutsch—have been able to perceive these facts more easily and clearly because they were helped in dealing with those

figure, Freud in fact admitted that he had overlooked all of the female patients who had not taken refuge from relations with their mother by connecting to the father figure. He recognized the importance of the research of female psychoanalysts who managed to reconstruct the relationship with the mother in the process of transference in treatment such as Jeanne Lampl-de Groot and Helene Deutsch. However, his discussion of the period of childhood in which the relationship with the mother is dominant as "grey with age and shadowy and almost impossible to revivify" attests to a lacuna in psychoanalytic theory and practice. The analysis below will show how Klein used literary works to fill in this lacuna.

In addition, we should emphasize the significant change initiated by Klein in the understanding of object-relations. While in Freud's writings this is a marginal topic, Klein understood object-relations as the most significant factor in emotional life, both in the earliest relations of the infant and throughout life. This is in contrast to Freud, who in his essay "The Ego and the Id" (1923) pointed to the structural organization of the emotional life, comprises the ego and the id, and the relations between them as motivating the emotional life.[23] However, as noted by David Bell, in her developmental model, Klein followed Freud in her continued emphasis on the reciprocal relations between life and death instincts[24]; this emphasis will be important to the interpretation of her essay.

The essay opens with a description of the image of a six-year-old boy, who is sitting and putting off doing his homework. All of the objects on stage, according to the reviewer, are designed in an exaggerated size in order to emphasize the child's smallness, who complains in a soprano voice of the bitterness of his fate. His mother enters, admonishes him, and punishes him, declaring, "You shall have dry bread and no sugar in your tea!" After she leaves, the child erupts in destructive anger, attacks a squirrel and a cat, breaks objects, spills ink, and more. The descriptions become more dramatic from moment to moment as "the things he has maltreated come to life," and they all attack him, until "the child falls back against the wall and shudders with fear and desolation."[25] The child escapes out of the home to a park,

---

under their treatment by the transference to a suitable mother-substitute" (Freud, *Complete Psychological Works*, 4592).
23 Freud, *Complete Psychological Works*, 3947–93.
24 David Bell, "Projective Identification," in *Kleinian Theory: A Contemporary Perspective*, ed. Bronstein Catalina (London: Whurr, 2001), 8n6.
25 "An arm-chair refuses to let him sit in it or have the cushions to sleep on. Table, chair, bench and sofa suddenly lift up their arms and cry: 'Away with the dirty little creature!' The clock has a dreadful stomach-ache and begins to strike the hours like mad. The teapot leans over the cup, and they begin to talk Chinese. Everything undergoes a terrifying change" (Klein, "Infantile Anxiety-Situations," 436).

where he is also attacked by all sorts of insects and animals. The turning point occurs when

> A squirrel which has been bitten falls to the ground, screaming beside him. He instinctively takes off his scarf and binds up the little creature's paw. There is great amazement amongst the animals, who gather together hesitatingly in the background. The child has whispered: "Mama!" He is restored to the human world of helping, "being good." "That's a good child, a very well-behaved child," sing the animals very seriously in a soft march—the finale of the piece—as they leave the stage.[26]

After relating the narrative, Klein begins to describe the child's pleasure at his acts of destruction from a broader perspective, which connects directly to her description in earlier works of a child's attack on what he perceives as the unity of mother and father. In the opera, this attack is depicted by sadistic weapons by means of which the child strikes at symbols of the father and mother, represented by the squirrel the child attacks and by the teapot he breaks. **In Klein's view, the opera's narrative enables us to locate the developmental stage in which infantile sadism emerges**: Klein argues that this stage is very early, manifesting even before the anal stage (the second stage of development according to Freud). The child's anxiety at the mother's threats expresses an even deeper anxiety, which is reflected in two revelations: The first is the initial appearance of the superego, and the second is the existence of internal objects, even at this early stage of development.

The design of the difference in size between the child and the props on the stage does not only represent an external difference between them, as the reviewer wrote about the opera. Rather, according to Klein, what happened was that the "child's anxiety makes things and people seem gigantic to him—far beyond the actual difference in size. Moreover, we see what we discover in the analysis of every child: that things represent human beings, and therefore are things of anxiety."[27]

Expounding on the language of the opera, Klein interpreted the differences in size as an expression of internal anxiety, and as an act of representation of internal objects. That is, in enabling deviation from reality, artistic language is able to represent the psyche's interior. The child's attack therefore expresses his anxiety at a counterattack by the external and internal objects (the mother and father). The sadism represents the anxiety of the child at the fact that the unity of the two parents is in doubt; at a later stage, castration anxiety evolves out of this primary anxiety. The child's battle with the animals symbolizes the attack of the mother as a function of

---

26 Klein, "Infantile Anxiety-Situations," 437.
27 Klein, "Infantile Anxiety-Situations," 439.

an Oedipus complex that appears already at an early stage of childhood. Klein's approach, according to which an early anxiety regarding the unity of the parents manifests between the first stage (the oral) and the second stage (the anal), represents a significant change from the view of Freud, who believed that the Oedipus complex appears at the third stage (the phallic).

The opera paved the way for Klein to oppose Freud on a deeper level: Early anxiety is not fear of castration, but rather fear of the attack of the mother, which also includes an attack on the penis. In effect, this represents anxiety at the unity of the parents, which is understood as an attack. Klein emphasized that the starting point of the essay was the opera, which illustrated for her the primacy of the sadistic attack. Another important finding is the dramatic change that occurs in the child, from the show of sadism toward the squirrel to a show of compassion. Using this plot point, Klein articulated an important innovation to Freud's position that the feeling of guilt and the conscience are social constructions.[28] The opera's narrative allowed Klein to demonstrate a case in which expressions of compassion and conscience can be individual and universal phenomena, as it is not clear from the narrative in what kind of society the child grew up and what kind of impact it had on him.

Klein argued that the child's compassion toward the squirrel expresses the early manifestation of the superego, even before the culmination of its development. According to Freud, the superego appears at a much later stage – following the struggle with the Oedipus complex, at the phallic stage. In the narrative, the child has compassion for the squirrel hurt by his outburst and covers it with his scarf. Two processes are portrayed simultaneously: The child calls for his mother, and the animals confirm that he is a good child. These two speech acts signal the internal expression of the child's guilt and conscience, which are represented by the mother and the animals. This is another revision by Klein to the theory of Freud, who ascribed the development of guilt and conscience to a later stage, in which the child understands and adopts social norms.

The first part of this essay may be conceived as an introduction and a basis for Klein's later and better-known essay from 1933: "The Early Development of Conscience in the Child."[29] In this essay, Klein argued that superego is already evident in young children of three or four.[30] Klein pointed to a crucial discovery that emerged from her observations of children. The emotional life of children is characterized by two primary types of anxiety: anxiety concerning their real parental figures (that they will leave

---

28 Freud, "Totem and Taboo," in Freud, *The Complete Psychological Works*, 2658.
29 Found in Melanie Klein, in *Contributions to Psycho-Analysis, 1921–1945* (London: Hogarth, 1965), 267–77.
30 Klein, *Contributions to Psycho-Analysis*, 267.

them, punish them, and so on), and anxiety that is the product of the imagination and has no connection to the real parental figures. According to Klein, these anxieties are the product of superego and the root of the formation of the conscience.

These anxieties lead to a "corresponding amount of repressed impulses of aggression"[31] and this aggression is directed – with the help of the narcissistic libido – externally, toward the object. Later, aggression is replaced with a positive relation to the object, just as the child in the opera changed his treatment of the squirrel. This is the point at which the conscience is formed. Klein summarized her many observations of children's play, which showed a close correspondence between the intensity of anxiety and the degree of violence. When the superego develops and anxiety recedes, it changes to a sense of guilt. That is, according to Klein, a sense of guilt is a product of the development of relations more suited to reality and a balanced relationship to the external object. This is in contrast to Freud, who saw guilt as regression to an earlier stage of development (of the superego) controlled by the Oedipus complex. Klein's discovery of the child's internalization of his relationship with his mother created a change in her view of art: As opposed to Freud, who saw it as a sublimation of instinct, Klein saw art as an expression of the desire to fix the relationship with the other, primarily with the mother. This can be seen in the first part of the essay.

Both in the concept of infantile anxiety and in the opera's narrative, the child's imagination generates anxiety. Alongside the real threat of suffering at the hand of his parents, there is also an imaginary element to the child's anxiety. Thus, it is not surprising that Klein drew inspiration from the opera's narrative in order to illustrate the workings of this imaginary aspect of anxiety. In the second part of the essay, Klein presented a further example of the aspect of imagination in an aesthetic work, as the result of which infantile anxiety is overcome.

This additional case study involved the creative development of a female painter. Klein analyzed an essay by Karin Michaelis, in which Michaelis describes how her friend Ruth Kjär changed from a woman with a "remarkable artistic feeling" for designing a home into a talented painter. Kjär is described by her friend as a woman who occasionally suffered from deep depression. An incident in which Kjär's brother-in-law aggressively took a painting of hers from her home led her first to depression, then to a burst of creativity, following which she became a painter. The empty space left after the brother-in-law took the painting at first embodied the empty space left by Kjär's mother, who had not been present in her life, in her childhood. Later, an interesting development occurred in Kjär's paintings, as she switched from painting an old woman, wrinkled and faded, to

---

31 Klein, *Contributions to Psycho-Analysis*, 268.

painting an impressive, domineering, and defiant woman. Thus, Klein revealed the maternal and reparative sides of creativity. Janet Sayers later read Klein's analysis as describing an attempt to fill the empty space that began to form with the absence of the mother and grew further when the painting was taken.

In the context of the present examination, the most interesting question is how Klein interpreted the creative act as clarifying the concept of anxiety, and reparation as a response to anxiety. Sayers's interpretation did not relate to the nature of creativity as enabling reparation.[32] Hanna Segal, on the other hand, argued that the problem of the empty space left by Kjär's absent mother was resolved by means of the painting, since it allowed her to re-symbolize her mother by means of painting.[33] However, both of these scholars ignored the contribution of the creative act to the conceptual investigation of anxiety, and in order to do so we must return to Klein's words in the essay.

Here, Klein examines the insights she gained from treating children and women: that the anxiety-situation precedes the dread of being alone, of the loss of love and of the love-object (according to Freud, the earliest anxieties). The question that concerns Klein is how the transition occurs from the anxiety at "an attacking mother to the dread that the real, loving mother may be lost." Since both in reality and for Ruth Kjär, the image of mother functions as an internal object, Klein asks how the image functions to generate creativity. The process of the development of the image of the mother in Kjär's paintings allowed her to "capture" the nature of creativity, which enables the transition from anxiety to reparation. Klein admits in the essay that she is "seeking the explanation of these ideas"[34] of anxiety and the transition to reparation, and that to do so

> it is instructive to consider what sort of pictures Ruth Kjär has painted since her first attempt. ... Drawing and painting are used as means to make people anew. The case of Ruth Kjär shows plainly that this anxiety of the little girl is of great importance in the ego-development of women, and is one of the incentives to achievement.[35]

With the analysis of the two works, the essay clarifies the ambiguity of the transition from infantile anxiety to reparation. The opera's narrative shows an apparently natural transition from the child's attack to compassion toward the squirrel. On the other hand, Kjär's painting series allows us to see

---

32 Sayers, *Mothering Psychoanalysis*, 311.
33 Hanna Segal, *Melanie Klein* (New York: Penguin, 1981), 139.
34 Klein, "Infantile Anxiety-Situations," 443.
35 Klein, "Infantile Anxiety-Situations."

the gradual change of the mother as an internal object, as expressed in the image of the mother as an external object in the painting. Creativity thus activates the process of reparation, which is not immediate or perfect, but rather develops. The change that occurs in the image of the mother in the paintings reflects the ego-development, and demonstrates that creativity enables a change in outlook, and in fact, self-formation.

The concept of creativity is explained in this essay as a motive for positive change. In the next essay, Klein showed that creativity as a factor that enables change can also create negative change, for instance, in a case where projective identification occurs.

The Second Article: *If I Were You* – Projective Identification and the Wish to Be Another Person

Klein's "On Identification" (1955) is one of her most important and central essays.[36] It is considered the chief essay in which she used a literary work to illustrate her model of the inner world, and especially the workings of the mechanism of projective identification. Here, Klein defined, expanded on, and developed the concept of "projective identification," which she first presented in her essay "Notes on Some Schizoid Mechanisms" (1946).[37] In "On Identification," Klein summarized the findings of the earlier essay, in which she showed that a three- to four-month-old infant has an unformed ego, and therefore addresses his anxieties by means of the defense mechanisms of splitting and identification.[38] In a later essay, Klein expanded on the concept of identification to also include a positive process.[39]

---

36 Melanie Klein, "On Identification," in *Envy and Gratitude and Other Works, 1946–1963*, ed. Masud R. Khan (London: Hogarth, 1975), 141–76.
37 "Much of the hatred against parts of the self is now directed towards the mother. This leads to a particular form of identification which establishes the prototype of an aggressive object-relation. I suggest for these processes the term 'projective identification'. When projection is mainly derived from the infant's impulse to harm or to control the mother, he feels her to be a persecutor" (Klein, "On Identification," 1–24, 8).
38 Klein, "On Identification," 143.
39 "Here I wish to go somewhat beyond my paper on 'Schizoid Mechanisms'. I would suggest that a securely established good object, implying a securely established love for it, gives the ego a feeling of riches and abundance which allows for an outpouring of libido and projection of good parts of the self into the external world without a sense of depletion arising. The ego can then also feel that it is able to re-introject the love it has given out, as well as take in goodness from other sources, and thus be enriched by the whole process. In other words, in such cases there is a balance between giving out and taking in, between projection and introjection. ... As I suggested, there are a variety of splitting processes (about which we have still a good deal to discover) and their nature is of great importance for the development of the ego" (Klein, "On Identification," 144).

The expansion suggested by Klein to the concept of projective identification is that in the process of development of the ego, many kinds of splitting can occur. In her 1936 essay, Klein only discussed splitting that results in the projection of negative aspects, while in the later essay Klein suggested that the infant may project positive aspects such as feelings of love. Likewise, Klein added that in a case of the projection of beneficent feelings, the ego may feel that it can introject those aspects as well. That is, this is a transformative process, not unidirectional.[40] To illustrate her findings, Klein turned to an analysis of Julian Green's novel *If I Were You*.[41]

Klein outlined the novel's narrative over six pages (!), an extended synopsis that speaks to her view on the importance of the creative work to understanding the concept of projective identification, far more than merely serving as an example. Indeed, further in the essay, Klein changed the goal of studying the novel from illustration to interpretation.[42] In a note to the Hebrew version of this essay, the translators remarked that Klein's use of the novel correlates with the interpretive tradition initiated by Freud, in which the purpose of using a literary work in a psychoanalytic study is to psycho-biographically analyze the author, or to analyze the characters as if they were patients.[43] I wish to argue, however, that this essay reflects a third method of literary interpretation, that is, a conceptual interpretation of the act of projective identification in the literary work. While Klein did not know Wittgenstein's work, she in fact implemented his methodological suggestion, according to which "concepts lead us to make investigations.[44] We are not analyzing a phenomenon ... but a concept."[45]

Klein explicitly stated the complicated motivation for her detailed discussion of the novel:

> The author of this story has deep insight into the unconscious mind; this is seen both in the way he depicts the events and characters and—what is of particular interest here—in his choice of the people into whom Fabian projects himself. My interest in Fabian's personality and

---

40 In the study of literature E. M. Forster defined the distinction between a flat versus a round character: "A 'flat' character, according to Forster, can be summed up in a single sentence and acts as a function of only a few fixed character traits. 'Round' characters are capable of surprise, contradiction, and change; they are representations of human beings in all of their complexity." E. M. Forster, *Aspects of the Novel* (1927; New York: RosettaBooks, 2002), 4–5.
41 Translated from the French by J. H. F. McEwen (London: Eyre & Spottiswoode, 1950). Klein, "On Identification," 144.
42 Klein, "On Identification," 152; emphasis in original.
43 Melanie Klein, *Selected Writings*, vol. 2, trans. Joshua Durban and Merav Roth (Tel Aviv: Bookworm, 2013), 227n15.
44 Wittgenstein, *Philosophical Investigations*, 569–70.
45 Wittgenstein, *Philosophical Investigations*, 383.

adventures, illustrating, as they do, some of the complex and still obscure problems of projective identification, led me to attempt an analysis of this rich material almost as if he were a patient.[46]

The reasons for Klein's use of the novel are far more substantial than its mere deployment as an example, and explain why she recapitulated the narrative at length. The first reason is the author's skill at describing unconscious processes. In contrast to the psychoanalytic therapist, whose approach to unconscious content is always indirect (such as translating a dream to everyday language, or the interpretation of transference relations), the author is endowed with "deep insight into the unconscious mind." This is reflected in the dominant theme that advances the narrative, in the choice of characters, and in the development of the main character, Fabian. The second reason is a conceptual investigation: Klein pointed out that the concept of projective identification is complex and ambiguous. The novel illustrates how this concept is realized in practice, and thus simplifies and clarifies its complexity and ambiguity. Klein fully recognizes that the character in the novel is not a patient at the clinic, but at the same time believes that his fictional literary formation can help in understanding real patients. Although scholars have noted the fact that Klein discussed the novel in the essay "On Identification," no scholar has delved into Klein's summary of the narrative of the novel, nor the novel's revelations regarding the process of projective identification.

Klein's Interpretation of the Work

The novel's narrative first and foremost exemplifies Klein's early definition of projective identification,[47] and later in the essay, Klein showed how Fabian's character expands the original definition of the concept. Klein pointed to Fabian's struggle with two central conflicts: The first is the conflict between his feeling of internal emptiness and the expanses of his imagination, which express grand ambitions. The second conflict is with his parents; it manifests in a strained relationship with the father, who is embodied in the image of Satan, and in his complicated relations of identification with his mother. This emotional structure, which contains two conflicts simultaneously, expands and deepens the meaning of projective identification, since two levels are involved: the level of relations with the parents, which is a starting point for diagnosis for the object-relations school

---

46 Wittgenstein, Philosophical Investigations.
47 "In my 'Notes on Some Schizoid Mechanisms' I described these fears as a consequence of the impulse to intrude into another person, *i.e.,* of projective identification" (Klein, "On Identification," 153).

(especially in the writings of Freud, Klein, and Winnicott), and the second level, less discussed in the rest of Klein's writing, which is the spiritual level of the relationship of the person with himself, or to the part of the superego that deviates from the values instilled by his parents.

In a unique and complicated way, these two levels combine, creating within Fabian aggression and a will to dominate other people. This internal struggle causes him to try to move from desire to action and realize his wish to become someone else by gaining physical control over the body of another person, who embodies a quality or characteristic that Fabian wishes to appropriate for himself.[48] In this context, the main innovation indicated by Klein in the concept of projective identification is "that the author has presented fundamental aspects of emotional life on two planes: the experiences of the infant and their influence on the life of the adult."[49] In Klein's view, the novel successfully shows how the emotional level functions simultaneously, so that Fabian's behavior and his words reveal both infantile emotions and their expressions in the emotional patterns of an adult. At this point, we can also see how poetic language is uniquely able to shape a rounded character, especially as there are significant differences between the greed, envy, and hatred that characterize an infant, and more complex expressions of these feelings in adulthood. Fabian's conduct shows his frustration at these emotions, as well as guilt and an urge to repair what he has destroyed. In the course of the narrative, the author shapes Fabian as a character who develops such feelings; thus, the narrative expresses an optimistic outlook, taken up by Klein, regarding the possibility of guilt and reparation.

It is important to note at this point that Klein's successors readily adopted the concept of "projective identification," but applied it only in the context of the treatment process, and not – as Klein did – as part of a complex understanding of the self. Thus, for instance, Elizabeth Spillius described three clinical "models" of projective identification, all of which relate to its use in the clinic, in the relationship between therapist and patient.[50] Herbert Rosenfeld demonstrated processes related to projective identification that play an important part in psychotic patients.[51] Betty Joseph presented several case studies

---

48 "Greed, envy and hatred, the prime movers of aggressive phantasies, are dominant features in Fabian's character, and the Author shows us that these emotions urge Fabian to get hold of other people's possessions, both material and spiritual; they drive him irresistibly towards what I described as projective identifications" (Klein, "On Identification," 154–55).
49 Klein, "On Identification," 155.
50 Elizabeth Spillius, "Clinical Experiences of Projective Identification," in *Clinical Lectures on Klein and Bion*, ed. Robin Anderson (London: Routledge, 1992), 57–70.
51 Herbert Rosenfeld, "Contribution to the Psychopathology of Psychotic States: The Importance of Projective Identification in the Ego Structure and the Object Relations of the Psychotic Patient," in *Melanie Klein Today: Developments in Theory and Practice*, vol. 1, *Mainly Theory*, ed. Elizabeth Spillius (1971; London: Routledge, 1988), 114–34.

in which the concrete quality of projective identification structuring countertransference was expressed,[52] and Michael Feldman highlighted an aspect important to the current discussion: Projective identification can also include the projection of good parts of the self such as love or an attempt to protect against attack. Furthermore, it is a sound process that is necessary for the growth of relationships and functions as a basis for empathy.[53] This emphasis enables us to understand how Klein interpreted the end of the novel, and thus, retrospectively, the complex character of Fabian from the outset.

At the stage of interpretation, Klein retells the narrative and underscores how the narrative breaks down the process of projective interpretation into stages. We should note that, in the first stage, Klein explicitly discussed the poetic techniques used by the author, with the basic technique being the instantiation of the metaphor of projective interpretation. After the meeting with Satan, in which he offers Fabian a spell by means of which he can become anyone he wishes, Fabian encounters all sorts of people with whom he wants to switch; at every meeting, he literally leaves his body and becomes another person. In addition, Satan allows Fabian to recall who he is throughout all his incarnations, by writing his name on a note and keeping it during all his incarnations. As Klein sees it, Fabian thus maintains his wish to maintain his connection to his original identity and to return to his home, whether out of feelings of guilt or a need to return to his original self.

This interpretation expands the psychoanalytic understanding of the process of splitting and projective identification, and depicts a pattern of behavior that is common and normative: Many people, in the process of the formation of their personalities, seek to resemble a person or a characteristic represented in a certain person. Alongside the wish to change, they also wish to remain loyal to their original selves. In the fictional narrative in which this fantasy is realized physically,[54] a literary mechanism allows the character of Fabian to embody a particular character in turn and to change according to the character's traits, while

---

52 Betty Joseph, "Projective Identification—Some Clinical Aspects," in Spillius, *Melanie Klein Today*, 135–48.
53 "Although it is not possible to go into all the ramifications of this process, I would like to mention that the projective identification may also involve good parts of the self—projected in love, or in an attempt to protect something valuable from internal attack. Up to a point, this process is a normal one, necessary for the satisfactory growth of our relationships, and is the basis, for example, for what we term 'empathy.'" Michael Feldman, "Splitting and Projective Identification," in Anderson, *Clinical Lectures on Klein and Bion*, 72–73.
54 "The processes underlying projective identification are depicted very concretely by the author. One part of Fabian literally leaves his self and enters into his victim, an event which in both parties is accompanied by strong physical sensations. We are told that the split-off part of Fabian submerges in varying degrees in his objects and loses the memories and characteristics appertaining to the original Fabian. We should conclude therefore (in keeping with the author's very concrete conception of the projective process), that Fabian's memories and other aspects of his personality are left behind in the discarded Fabian who must

at the same time maintaining his own core, which functions as a superego – evaluating and judging – and leads him to move on to another character. At the same time, the same core self that functions as a superego leads to the emotional apex of the story, which entails an "ethical leap," wherein Fabian understands that he has treated his mother poorly, regrets it, and expresses gratitude to her.

In the course of the narrative, Fabian changes into four characters. The first is Poujars, his wealthy employer, whose wealth Fabian associates with happiness: "'Ah! the sun. It often seemed to him that M. Poujars kept it hidden in his pocket.'"[55] The second character is the physically powerful Esménard, who is young and healthy, in contrast to the sickly Fabian. Esménard expresses feelings of hatred that lead to murder, which, according to Klein, allows Fabian to experience his hatred of his parents. On the other hand, the third character, Fruges, battles with Satan (as opposed to Fabian, who is tempted by Satan's offer), and represents an intellectual and religious aspect that Fabian desires, although he denies it. The fourth character is Camille, who has a beautiful wife, a married man with whom his wife's cousin, Elise, is enamored. According to Klein, Fabian does not have anything in common with Camille, but through him he identifies with Elise, and realizes a homosexual aspect of his psyche.

Although each of the characters has a trait that arouses envy in Fabian, dwelling within each of the characters becomes destructive for him. Fabian comes to understand that in becoming each of the characters, he becomes vulnerable to internalizing their "difficult" aspects. For instance, when he incarnates as Poujars and wishes to enjoy his great wealth, he experiences the kidney disease of his weak body and his unpleasant memories. In the end, he feels that he is losing parts of himself and longs to return home.

At the end of the journey, he succeeds in returning to himself and to his home. At the same time, the reader finds out that during the days the narrative took place, Fabian actually lay sick in his bed, unconscious. It may be, Klein suggests, that his experience may have been only an inner fantasy. However, it may be that this "death" represents the lack of vitality involved in such a massive projective identification, because it does not allow one to assume ownership over the elements projected. In Klein's terms, the splitting in the fantasy actually impacted the self, and Fabian became persecuted, depleted, and impoverished. It is as if parts of Fabian "got lost" in the characters in which he incarnated.

The most important section in which Klein presents the features of projective identification she derives from the novel is encapsulated here:

> The spatial and temporal terms in which the author describes these events are actually the ones in which our patients experience such

have retained a good deal of his ego when the split occurred" (Klein, "On Identification," 166).

55 Klein, "On Identification," 162.

processes. A patient's feeling that parts of his self are no longer available, are far away, or have altogether gone is of course a phantasy which underlies splitting processes. But such phantasies have far-reaching consequences and vitally influence the structure of the ego. They have the effect that those parts of his self from which he feels estranged, often including his emotions, are not at the time accessible either to the analyst or to the patient. The feeling that he does not know where the parts of himself which he has dispersed into the external world have gone to, is a source of great anxiety and insecurity.[56]

Klein notes the two basic terms by means of which a narrative is created: "the spatial and temporal terms." Although it is a fictional novel, Klein argues that the temporal and spatial terms function here identically to the way in which people experience these processes in reality. The invaluable contribution of the novel is that it makes these processes available to our consciousness, while in reality these processes are usually distant or concealed. In this way, the description of the feelings and other features of the processes of projective identification gain form and content and become real. Klein treats the novel as a realistic foundation and sums up the three aspects of projective identification, according to Fabian's story:

I shall next consider Fabian's projective identifications from three angles: (i) the relation of the split-off and projected parts of his personality to those he had left behind; (ii) the motives underlying the choice of objects into whom he projects himself; and, (iii) how far in these processes the projected part of his self becomes submerged in the object or gains control over it.[57]

The fiction acts as a magnifying glass for each stage of Fabian's projective identification, and allows the reader to understand its possibilities and complexities. As opposed to the process of projective identification in a patient in the clinic, which reveals in a concentrated fashion isolated features of the internalized objects that are projected onto the therapist, Klein outlines those aspects that emerge out of reading the novel. Following her, I will articulate these aspects as questions.

The first question is: What is the relationship between the features that are projected outward and those that remain internal? What is the relationship between Fabian's wish to be rich, healthy, ethical, and loving, and the memory of his name, which symbolizes his original personality – sick, not loving or loved, and not ethical in its ability to envy, to desire to murder, and so forth?

---

56 Klein, "On Identification," 166.
57 Klein, "On Identification," 167.

The second question is: What are his motives for Fabian's choice of characters? What tangential motives are revealed alongside the primary motives? For instance, does the choice of Camille represent a homosexual aspect of Fabian's character, as maintained by Klein? After all, there is no hint of this in the narrative.

The third question was already articulated by Klein: Did Fabian merge with the character to which he attached himself, or did he take over the character? Klein's questions reinforce the need to interpret the end of the novel, which could be said to be structured as an epiphany: Fabian wakes up and learns that he collapsed at the office where he worked three days earlier, and had actually been unconscious all that time.

The epiphany occurs in Fabian's consciousness and in the reader's consciousness simultaneously. Both understand that the mother took care of Fabian, thus showing her devotion and love for him. Fabian is filled with feelings of guilt toward her and agonizes over the negative emotions he experiences; he then dies young, as his father did. The striking conclusion of the novel is that sometimes it is too late to repent, or that it is impossible to escape the bitter fate of one's poor health. In any case, in this novel, guilt and reparation do not lead to a second chance at a satisfying life.

In conclusion, we can see that Klein interpreted the novel as a typical conceptual investigation. Her retelling of the stages of the narrative and her examination of the aspect represented by each character in Fabian's complex of desires, as well as his takeover of the character and its result, expands our understanding of the concept thus: There is a fundamental tension between a person's affinity to his selfhood and his feelings of envy, hatred, and aggression toward qualities and features that are not part of him. This tension may lead to various acts, but never negates the person's affinity toward himself. In a pathological emotional state, as Fabian experienced, there is no way to settle the affinity for selfhood with these feelings in a way that would enable integration and development. However, the existence of the epiphany in literature can also teach us about the potential for epiphany in the psyche of a person. In the novel *If I Were You*, the epiphany appears too late, but in the next essay, we will see the possible application of epiphany to life after it occurs.

The Third Article: Suffering, Depression, Guilt, and the Function of the Superego

The third essay in which Klein discussed a literary work examines Aeschylus's famous trilogy *The Oresteia*.[58] The essay consists of four parts:

---

58 Melanie Klein, "Some Reflections on 'The Oresteia,'" in *The Writings of Melanie Klein*, vol. 2, *Envy and Gratitude and Other Works, 1946–1963*, ed. Masud R. Khan (London: Virago, 1988), 275–99.

In the first part, Klein presents a synopsis of the three plays that compose the trilogy. In the second part, she summarizes her theoretical conclusions from her clinical work with children regarding the stages of emotional development, which start with anxiety and aggression and, at an advanced stage, end with guilt, compassion, and reparation. In the third part, Klein presents the Greek concept of "hubris," which captures the tension between the gods and the humans who attempt to resemble them in Greek mythology. In the final section, Klein uses the contents of the trilogy, and especially the concept of hubris, to flesh out an understanding of the concept of the depressive position.

Just as Freud leaned on the myth of Oedipus, so Klein borrows elements of Greek mythology, such as the relations between humans and gods, in order to understand a process of emotional development, and especially to clarify a certain complexity that is not available for clinical observation. Fiction therefore completes the discussion of reality. Klein starts with the seminal trilogy, as translated by Gilbert Murray,[59] stating that her goal is to examine "the variety of symbolic rôles in which the characters appear."[60]

Klein briefly presents the contents of the three parts of the trilogy. In the first, *Agamemnon*, Agamemnon returns from battle and his wife Clytemnestra murders him. The murder has a declared reason: "She justifies her murder as a revenge for the sacrifice of Iphigenia. For Iphigenia had been killed on Agamemnon's command in order to make the winds favorable for the voyage to Troy."[61] Alongside this declared reason, there are others: The first is that Clytemnestra witnessed the death of her daughter, and after that took a lover. The second is that the same lover, Aegisthus, is the son of Thyestes, who fell in love with the wife of his brother Atreus. In revenge, Atreus killed Thyestes's children, cooked them, and served them to Thyestes at a feast. Aegisthus was Thyestes's son, and therefore wanted to murder Agamemnon, Atreus's son. A third reason for revenge was that Agamemnon brought back Cassandra, the most beautiful of the hostages, with him from battle.

The second play, *Cheophoroe*, shows the continuation of the narrative. Clytemnestra has had two other children aside from Iphigenia, who was sacrificed by her father. These children are Orestes and Electra. Orestes wants to revenge the death of his father Agamemnon, but to do so he must kill his mother Clytemnestra. He hesitates, but his sister burns with anger at her mother, as Klein emphasizes, and convinces him to seek revenge on her. Likewise, he is commanded to do so "by the Delphic Oracle—a command

---

59 Aeschylus, *The Oresteia*, trans. Gilbert Murray, 2nd rev. ed. (London: George Allen and Unwin, 1946).
60 Klein, "Some Reflections," 275.
61 Klein, "Some Reflections."

which ultimately came from Apollo himself."[62] Orestes gives in to his sister and to the command of the god Apollo, and kills his mother and her lover. Before she is killed, Clytemnestra warns her son Orestes that if he kills her, he will be pursued forever by the Erinnyes; however, he does not take her advice, as Apollo has encouraged him to murder his mother. And indeed, immediately after he kills his mother, the Erinnyes appear.

The third play, the *Eumenides*, describes how Orestes is haunted by the Erinnyes and kept away from his home and his father's throne. Orestes wants to be pardoned, and the god Apollo advises him to consult the goddess of wisdom, Athena. Athena assembles the council of sages in order to decide whether to pardon Orestes, and the sages are divided. Athena then decides to support the pardon for Orestes. Athena later also addresses the claim of the Erinnyes that Orestes should continue to be punished, agreeing to share her power with them. Moreover, she commits to the maintenance of law and justice with regard to all sides and codifies a new law of compassion. In accordance with this law, the Erinnyes change from prosecutors to defenders of those who seek mercy. Although Klein did not note this, the end of the trilogy is surprising and unusual for a play that belongs to the genre of Greek tragedy, a genre in which it is rare to find forgiveness and reparation.

Why did Klein devote extensive attention to a detailed description of the trilogy? At this point in the essay, the reader cannot yet answer this question, and Klein still does not provide it.

At this point, she turns to a succinct description of child development, and summarizes the results of her research over the 20 years preceding this essay. The infant develops from a stage of anxiety and splitting, to the creation of symbols that allow integration and a transition to the depressive stage. In her description, Klein emphasizes that the child develops a superego in interaction with his attachment to his parents, and that this superego sometimes functions as a conscience. Seemingly, Klein explains here how the depressive position forms.[63] But she is not satisfied with this summary of her insights and observations.

At this stage, even before she reveals the reason she ascribes such importance to the narrative of the *Oresteia*, she adds a new concept to the discussion, a product of Greek thought: hubris. Klein quotes

---

62 Klein, "Some Reflections," 276.
63 "If the depressive position is being successfully worked through—not only during its climax in infancy but throughout childhood and in adulthood—the super-ego is mainly felt to be guiding and restraining the destructive impulses and some of its severity will have been mitigated. When the super-ego is not excessively harsh, the individual is supported and helped by its influence, for it strengthens the loving impulses and furthers the tendency towards reparation. A counterpart of this internal process is the encouragement by parents when the child shows more creative and constructive tendencies and his relation to his environment improves" (Klein, "Some Reflections," 279).

Murray's definition,[64] and establishes that the concept provides cover for the emotion a person feels when he presents a danger to himself and others. The concept of hubris includes, in Klein's opinion, all of the difficult emotions felt by the child: hatred, a will to destroy and humiliate, envy, sadism toward the parents, a sense of persecution, competitiveness, and ambition. At the root of all these feelings is a fear of punishment for hubris, since according to Hellenistic belief, hubris is forbidden and deserving of punishment. Another expression of hubris is a fear of success that stems from a fear of arousing others' envy. This fear can delay the realization of talent and potential. Klein gives examples from two case descriptions, one of a child and the other of an adult, of how hubris can deter people from succeeding, since one's success can be interpreted as hurting and humiliating others.

Klein returns to the *Oresteia* and describes Agamemnon as a character who operates out of hubris. Agamemnon is proud of the destruction he has caused; however, his hubris is not satisfied by his success, but rather hardens him further. His wife Clytemnestra also embodies hubris when she decides to murder her husband. The change, according to Klein, is hinted at in the *Oresteia* when Orestes consults with Apollo on whether to kill his mother. Orestes's deliberation and consultation with the god already reflects complexity of personality and not merely an aggressive and anxious act. After the murder, he does not submit to his fate but seeks pardon, and thus turns to Athena, who represents wisdom and justice. Klein interprets Orestes's murder of his mother as identification with his father and his suffering as a fear of persecution. But alongside this Klein points to the development of the depressive position, which includes a desire to atone for the sin, a perpetual hope, and a positive relation to the gods, especially to Athena. Klein ascribes this to the stage in which his relationship with his mother was positive and she taught him to be grateful. The mother functions as a beloved internal object, which, as Klein sees it, is a source of hope and pleasure.[65]

Klein interprets other aspects of the trilogy as emotional expressions; in this context, it is important to note that she argues that these convey the internalized images of the parents and thus express the superego at its early stages. Klein sees the whole trilogy as an articulation of the superego by means of various characters, who exhibit its various functions.[66] Likewise, a literary device like the transcription of characters' states of consciousness, as opposed to descriptions of their actions, works to portray decision as opposed to action in the depressive position, which enables the vicious cycle of

---

64 "The typical sin which all things, ... *Hubris*, a word generally translated 'insolence' or 'pride' ... Hubris grasps at more, bursts bounds and breaks the order; it is followed by *Dike*, Justice, which re-establishes them" (Klein, "Some Reflections," 280).
65 Klein, "Some Reflections," 289.
66 Klein, "Some Reflections," 291.

aggression and will for revenge to be dismantled.⁶⁷ The literary device of using main characters in contrast to secondary characters or opposing characters reflects connections between internal states of consciousness and actions taken in the world. Internal anger, as well as the possibility of reconciliation and acceptance, is manifested in external characters like Athena or the Erinnyes.

In conclusion, the trilogy's narrative reveals the potential of real change in a person. In contrast to existing patterns of envy, hatred, and revenge, the trilogy reveals the possibility of compassion and mercy, compromise and willingness to give up power, and, in the end, forgiveness and the return to family and society. It is notable that Klein wrote this essay after she had already articulated the features of the various positions, and backed them up with observations of the children she had treated. All the same, she clearly summarizes her choice to consider the key concepts of her thought anew in light of the trilogy, providing three main reasons. The first is the proof or the demonstration of the features of the transition between the paranoid-schizoid and the depressive position.⁶⁸ The second is that Aeschylus, in his vivid trilogy, succeeds in showing all the stages of emotional development, from the earliest to the most advanced.⁶⁹ The third reason, and the most important, is Aeschylus's artistic talent in using poetic language to create symbols by means of which he can express conflicts and complex emotional processes.⁷⁰

These three reasons clarify the nature of Klein's conceptual investigation in this complicated essay. Klein turned to a broad corpus of three tragedies, just as Freud did in his use of the Oedipus trilogy. However, in contrast to Freud, who used the trilogy in order to outline developmental patterns

---

67 Klein, "Some Reflections," 295.
68 "In my view he shows the mental state which I take to be characteristic of the transition between the paranoid-schizoid and the depressive position, a stage when guilt is essentially experienced as persecution. When the depressive position is reached and worked through—which is symbolized in the Trilogy by Orestes' changed demeanour at the Areopagus—guilt becomes predominant and persecution diminishes" (Klein, "Some Reflections," 286).
69 "Aeschylus presents to us a picture of human development from its roots to its most advanced levels. One of the ways in which his understanding of the depths of human nature is expressed are the various symbolic rôles which in particular the gods come to play. This variety corresponds to the diverse, often conflicting, impulses and phantasies which exist in the unconscious and which ultimately derive from the polarity of the life and death instincts in their changing states of fusion" (Klein, "Some Reflections," 298).
70 "The creative artist makes full use of symbols; and the more they serve to express the conflicts between love and hate, between destructiveness and reparation, between life and death instincts, the more they approach universal form. ... The dramatist's capacity to transfer some of these universal symbols into the creation of his characters, and at the same time to make them into real people, is one of the aspects of his greatness" (Klein, "Some Reflections," 299).

named after the characters (the Oedipus complex, the Electra complex, etc.), Klein turned to Aeschylus in order to undertake a conceptual investigation of the positions she had already established. Her conceptual investigation first included an exploration and an outline of the story of the trilogy, in order to map the entire course of the process of development in a comprehensive and complex way. In the second part, Klein then reflected on the technique of the symbolic shaping of the characters in order to understand the ways emotional states function dynamically, that is, in order to understand how certain feelings form, how conflicts work, and how conflicts may be resolved. The symbolic shaping allowed us to see Klein's concepts in a higher resolution than is available in clinical observation. In this way, Aeschylus's masterpiece enabled a more comprehensive conceptual investigation than did the literary works explored in Klein's other two essays.

Conclusion

Our discussion is the first to comprehensively examine three of Klein's essays in which she used literary and artistic works for a conceptual investigation. The first essay examined a relatively early stage of emotional development, in a nine-year-old child. Here, Klein showed how a transition from aggression to compassion occurs as a "leap," and not necessarily as a gradual process. In the second part of the essay, Klein portrayed such a leap in an adult, a female painter. In the second essay, Klein analyzed the complex process of projective identification in a relatively young person. In this case, too, reparation occurred as a "leap," although the narrative that preceded it prepared the ground for a gradual change. After all, Fabian died after the reparation, and did not manage to live in a "repaired" state. In the third essay, Klein used a trilogy in a much broader way: first, in order to show various stages of development in greater detail, from the infantile stage to a stage in which one can live after reparation and forgiveness. Second, she showed how emotional states are symbolically shaped by means of characters' actions, allowing her readers to understand her concepts in a fuller and richer way than is possible through descriptions of a clinical observation, which focuses on only one person. We may say that the conceptual investigation undertaken by Klein with the help of the literary works in these three essays allowed her to articulate her central concepts more deeply, no less than Freud did in his use of Greek mythology.

Chapter 3

Psychoanalysis and Obsessive-Compulsive Disorder

A Wittgensteinian-Existential Perspective

Nir Soffer-Dudek[1]

Chronology of an Impasse

In 1926 Freud described obsessional neurosis as "the most interesting and repaying subject of analytic research," admitting at the same time that "as a problem it has not yet been mastered."[2] During the near-century that has followed, several psychoanalytic and psychodynamic thinkers attempted to fill in this gap, most notably Anna Freud,[3] Ogden,[4] Bollas,[5] Brandchaft,[6] O'Connor,[7] and Amir.[8] Yet even with their insightful theoretical conceptualizations, currently psychodynamic therapies for obsessive-compulsive disorder (OCD) are considered ineffective or even harmful in mainstream clinical psychology.[9] This problem has also been pointed out by prominent

---

1 This work is partially based on the author's doctoral dissertation, submitted to Bar-Ilan University (accepted May 29th, 2018), under the supervision of Dr. Dorit Lemberger from the Program for Hermeneutics and Cultural Studies.
2 Sigmund Freud, "Inhibitions, Symptoms and Anxiety," in *The Standard Edition of the Complete Psychological Works of Sigmund Freud*, vol. 20, trans. James Strachey (London, Hogarth Press, [1926] 1959), 113.
3 Anna Freud, "Obsessional Neurosis: A Summary of Psycho-Analytic Views as Presented at the Congress," *International Journal of Psychoanalysis* 47 (1966): 116–22.
4 Thomas H. Ogden, *The Primitive Edge of Experience* (London: Jason Aronson, 1989), 47–81.
5 Christopher Bollas, *Cracking Up: The Work of Unconscious Experience* (London: Routledge, 1995), 71–102.
6 Bernard Brandchaft, "Obsessional Disorders: A Developmental Systems Perspective," *Psychoanalytic Inquiry* 21, no. 2 (2001): 253–88.
7 John O'Connor, "The Dynamics of Protection and Exposure in the Development of Obsessive-Compulsive Disorder," *Psychoanalytic Psychology* 24, no. 3 (2007): 464–74. John O'Connor, "A Flaw in the Fabric: Toward an Interpersonal Psychoanalytic Understanding of Obsessive-Compulsive Disorder," *Journal of Contemporary Psychotherapy* 38, no. 2 (2008): 87–96.
8 Dana Amir, "The Metaphorical, the Metonymical and the Psychotic Aspects of Obsessive Symptomatology," *International Journal of Psychoanalysis* 97 (2016): 259–80.
9 Dean McKay, Jonathan S. Abramowitz, and Erik A Storch, "Mechanisms of Harmful Treatments for Obsessive–Compulsive Disorder," *Clinical Psychology: Science and Practice* 28, no. 1 (2021): 55.

figures from within twenty-first-century psychoanalysis. Esman, for example, argues that since Anna Freud's 1966 review of obsessional neurosis, "virtually nothing has appeared in the psychoanalytic literature that has added to our understanding of the disorder or enhanced the very limited therapeutic influence of psychoanalysis in such cases."[10] Similarly, Gabbard acknowledges "the realization that psychoanalysis does not alter the obsessive-compulsive symptoms" and admits that "reports of symptomatic cures with psychoanalytic treatment are virtually nonexistent."[11] Rice remarks that "there is no published study that I am aware of that documents a complete cure for OCD through the psychoanalytic process."[12] And most recently, Csigó writes that "Since the introduction of [Freud's] obsessive neurosis, there has been no novel concept to further our understanding of OCD."[13] This deficiency in new theoretical ideas and techniques that can successfully accommodate therapy for OCD within the analytic framework brought about a steady decline in psychoanalytic writing on the subject in recent decades.[14] Furthermore, following the significant progress made by various cognitive-behavioral and biological approaches, psychoanalysis is no longer considered a recommended therapy for OCD by various national health agencies.[15]

As a practicing clinician, I do believe that psychoanalysis may be of value not just to the understanding of OCD but also to its treatment. However, if we wish to harness psychoanalytic insights into an effective therapeutic framework, it is first necessary to understand why the existing models have not been as effective as one would hope. I will try to address this question by using the ideas of Austrian-British philosopher Ludwig Wittgenstein (1889–1951), focusing on his key work, published in 1953,

---

10 Aaron H. Esman, "Obsessive-Compulsive Disorder: Current Views," *Psychoanalytic Inquiry* 21, no. 2 (2001): 145.
11 Glen O. Gabbard, "Psychoanalytically Informed Approaches to the Treatment of Obsessive-Compulsive Disorder," *Psychoanalytic Inquiry* 21, no. 2 (2001): 209.
12 Emanuel Rice, "Reflections on the Obsessive-Compulsive Disorders: A Psychodynamic and Therapeutic Perspective," *Psychoanalytic Review* 91, no. 1 (2004): 23.
13 Katalin Csigó, "Obsessive Position: The New Psychoanalytic Approach of Obsessive-Compulsive Disorder," *Current Psychology*, early online view (2021).
14 See: K. Mulhall, John O'Connor, and Katarina Timulakova, "Managing the Monster in the Mind: A Psychoanalytically Informed Qualitative Study Exploring the Experiences of People Diagnosed with Obsessive-Compulsive Disorder," *Psychoanalytic Psychotherapy* 33, no. 2 (2019): 118; O'Connor, "A Flaw in the Fabric," 87–89; Aya Zaidel, "Obsessive States: Aesthetics, Erotism, and Fantasy," *Psychoanalytic Review* 103, no. 4 (2016): 486.
15 See: American Psychiatric Association, "Practice Guideline for the Treatment of Patients with Obsessive-Compulsive Disorder," *American Journal of Psychiatry* 164 (2007): 9; Susan Chlebowski, and Robert J Gregory, "Is a Psychodynamic Perspective Relevant to the Clinical Management of Obsessive-Compulsive Disorder?" *American Journal of Psychotherapy* 63, no. 3 (2009): 245–56; "Obsessive-Compulsive Disorder and Body Dysmorphic Disorder: Treatment," National Institute for Health and Clinical Excellence, last Modified June 2020, https://www.nice.org.uk/guidance/cg31

Philosophical Investigations.[16] Wittgenstein himself never mentioned OCD, but his notions of selfhood, language, and meaning may serve as a framework for explaining psychoanalysis' shortcomings, and perhaps even for moving beyond them.

"A *Picture* Held Us Captive"

In *Philosophical Investigations* Wittgenstein maintains that we perceive the world through the lens of language. As grammar and vocabulary carry out their allegedly technical role, we learn to see some ideas as manifest truths and others as preposterous impossibilities, thereby creating "pictures" of reality.[17] Normally, we overlook the fact that these pictures are dependent on the vagaries of language and assume that we simply observe the world as it is. Nevertheless, there are certain instances when we do wish to verify the accuracy of our pictures, for example when we philosophize. And as we do so, we often encounter unexplained paradoxes and dead-ends (for reasons I shall elaborate upon later). However, since our pictures are so thoroughly interwoven into our thought and speech, we find it impossible to comprehend what went wrong in our investigations. Wittgenstein famously describes it in the following words:

> A *picture* held us captive. And we couldn't get outside it, for it lay in our language, and language seemed only to repeat it to us inexorably.[18]

I would like to suggest that obsessive rumination represents such a case of being held captive by a picture, specifically the picture of an inner world that exists inside our minds. In the following section I will describe how this picture is constructed through language, and then examine the catastrophic chain of events that may take place as we set out to grasp our inner world and investigate its contents.

The Augustinian Picture

People suffering from OCD try to suppress their doubts by looking *inwards*. Those who envisage violent images, for example, may spend days trying to clarify the true intention that had brought about the creation of such

---

16 Ludwig Wittgenstein, *Philosophical Investigations (4th Edition)*, trans. Gertrude E. M. Anscombe, Peter M. S. Hacker, and Joachim Schulte, ed. Peter M. S. Hacker, and Joachim Schulte (Oxford: Blackwell, 2009).
17 Wittgenstein, *Philosophical Investigations*, §§1, 115, 222. [**Note:** Due to the aphoristic character of *Philosophical Investigations* and the variability between its edited editions, references to this work feature the remark number rather than the page number, in the manner accepted among Wittgenstein's scholars].
18 Wittgenstein, *Philosophical Investigations*, §115.

images; Others, who obsess over their love for their partner, their faith in God, or their sexual orientation, try to scrutinize their thoughts and sensations to discover how they *really* feel; And many of those who perform compulsive rituals seek that ever-elusive sense of certainty, which will allow them to return to their daily lives. Paradoxically, the more all these individuals attempt to look into themselves and trace their true intentions, beliefs, emotions, and certainties, the further away those slip from their grasp.

Wittgenstein dedicates extensive parts of *Philosophical Investigations* to understanding why introspection often fails. He suggests that the problem lies not in our methods of looking inwards, but in our premises about the human mind. He opens his discussion of the subject by quoting a passage from Saint Augustine's fourth-century autobiographical magnum opus, *Confessions*. In this passage, Augustine describes how he acquired the use of language as a toddler: adults occasionally pointed to an object while pronouncing its name, until he gradually learned to associate the two.[19] According to Wittgenstein, this seemingly humdrum tale encapsulates our entire outlook on language. Like Augustine, we believe that language is there to name preexisting "things," whether they are physical objects, like an apple, or more abstract phenomena, like love. Consequently, when we encounter a given word, we assume it was created to describe something that was lying there, waiting to be pointed at and named. And since there are words describing inner states and processes (such as "understanding," "intention," "expectation," "love," or "certainty"), we suppose that there must be corresponding mental phenomena residing inside our minds. Thus, when we say that we intended to raise our arm, we believe that first we had had an experience of intention (as brief and fleeting as it may have been), and only then did we act upon it. Similarly, when we ask ourselves whether we love a person romantically, we suppose that there exists such a thing as a feeling of romantic love, and now we set out to find whether we feel it or not.

However, in *Philosophical Investigations* Wittgenstein leads us to realize that any attempt to grasp or verify inner states is doomed to fail. If we try to trace our intention upon saying or doing something, we may come up with various "thoughts, feelings, movements and also connections with earlier situations," but none of which is *intention itself*.[20] Gordon Bearn, one of Wittgenstein's most eloquent interpreters, elucidates this problem by providing another example from the field of young romantic relationships:

> How do you decide if you love the one or the other? As this should not be left to chance, you check. First you imagine the one, and look

---

19 Saint Augustine, *Confessions*, trans. Henry Chadwick (Oxford: Oxford University Press, 2008), 10–11.
20 Wittgenstein, *Philosophical Investigations*, §645. See also: §§621, 635.

inside yourself to see. Next you imagine the other, and look again. But this never helps. There is nothing to see. There are oil lights on the dashboards of cars; they are either on or off, and when they are on, you need oil. Sometimes I think I used to act as though there were a lovelight on the dashboard of my soul. I would look in to see if it was on or off, but I was never satisfied. I could never find the dashboard.[21]

But if inner states are so difficult to capture, why do we keep referring to them as if they are given facts? Wittgenstein proposes that this is the working of an unspoken (and mostly unconscious) social contract. We need to know that we are more than behaving machines: We wish to believe that when we raise our arm, it is because we *wanted to*, and that when people say that they love us, they *truly feel* something and not just use words. We need to know that our words are anchored to the solid ground of real phenomena, not just floating aimlessly in space. Hence, in our daily lives we speak of our inner world but at the same time mostly refrain from inspecting it too closely, let alone challenge its existence. We may gaze blankly into space in a peculiar practice called "introspection," or urge someone to "look into herself," yet rarely stop to think whether there is anything there to find in the first place.[22] Similarly, when people say that they *want* to do something, we hardly ever challenge them as to how they know that their will exists. Had we done so, interpersonal life would have turned into skeptical anarchy. We simply learn as children to talk about our inner world, and then, for the rest of our lives assume it is there because we talk about it. To use Wittgenstein's metaphor: "You think that after all you must be weaving a piece of cloth: because you are sitting at a loom – even if it is empty – and going through the motions of weaving."[23]

Having said that, it is important to clarify that Wittgenstein neither denies nor asserts the possibility of an inner world that exists prior to, and independent of, language. He merely argues that since our thinking is bound by language, we cannot transcend language and get a glimpse of what lies beyond. We must get by with the words we have, never knowing whether they refer to something which is there or not.[24]

As mentioned above, most people ignore this philosophical difficulty and casually report their non-verbal or pre-verbal experiences. However, certain

---

21 Gordon C. F. Bearn, *Waking to Wonder: Wittgenstein's Existential Investigations* (Albany: State University of New York Press, 1997), 105.
22 Wittgenstein, *Philosophical Investigations*, §§412–413.
23 Wittgenstein, *Philosophical Investigations*, §414.
24 Wittgenstein, *Philosophical Investigations*, §§304–08.

individuals feel an urgent need to verify the existence of these experiences or to explore their contents. This is mostly because they encounter a thought, image, sensation, or emotion which arouses a great deal of anxiety and needs to be clarified or ascertained. For example, as they envisage themselves brutally attacking their children, they seek to determine whether it attests to a hidden homicidal tendency or is merely a random thought. Yet, as they try to look inwards and find their actual intention, they discover, as Wittgenstein warns, that this cannot be accomplished. They cannot look into their mind and open a drawer with the label "intention" written on it. Only the alleged byproducts of their intention are available: various associated ideas, images, or sensations, but none of these embodies intention itself.

Notably, a prominent theory in the field of OCD suggests that individuals with obsessive-compulsive tendencies merely have attenuated access to their internal states.[25] This theory assumes that psychological states, such as love or intention, are as real as physical ones, and it posits that the problem of individuals who suffer from OCD is that they are worse than healthy people at accessing them. In contrast, following Wittgenstein, I suggest that psychological "internal states" are equally inaccessible to everyone, and that most people assign meaning to their actions only retrospectively, by using the *terminology* of intentions, emotions, etc. This is supported by current neuro-cognitive research, which demonstrates that the conscious experience of intention, for example, arises only after the neural activity for a given action had already started.[26] As Hommel comments, the notion of mental causality is not supported by empirical evidence; Our uniqueness as human beings does not lie in our capability to act out internal states of consciousness, but rather in our ability to give retrospective meaning to our actions and communicate this meaning to others.[27] Thus, I believe that what sets people with OCD apart is not their difficulty accessing their inner states, but their perpetual attempts at doing so. Whereas most individuals naturally accept the Augustinian picture of reality and effortlessly report their intentions, individuals suffering from OCD try to slow down the process and scrutinize their psyche. Yet each time they try to reach inside, they yield only more words and images which may be interpreted in various ways. One

---

25 Reuven Dar, Amit Lazarov, and Nira Liberman, "Seeking Proxies for Internal States (SPIS): Towards a Novel Model of Obsessive-Compulsive Disorder," *Behaviour Research and Therapy* 147 (2021): 1–3.
26 Atsushi Sato, "Both Motor Prediction and Conceptual Congruency between Preview and Action-Effect Contribute to Explicit Judgment of Agency," *Cognition* 110 (2009): 74; Chun Siong Soon, Marcel Brass, Hans-Jochen Heinze, and John-Dylan Haynes, "Unconscious Determinants of Free Decisions in the Human Brain," *Nature Neuroscience* 11, no. 5 (May 2008): 543–45.
27 Bernhard Hommel, "Dancing in the Dark: No Role for Consciousness in Action Control," *Frontiers in Psychology* 4 (June 2013): 2–3.

moment they may come up with the thought "I wanted to kill him" and an instant later tell themselves they would never hurt a fly. Which one of those thoughts expresses the true meaning of the intrusive image? Which interpretation is the correct one?

The Paradox of Rules

Here the plot thickens further, as Wittgenstein shows that philosophically speaking, competing interpretations are always equally justifiable. In fact, this is his main argument in what is known as the Paradox of Rules.[28] When one has a vivid murderous thought, for example, there is nothing in that thought that inherently dictates if it should be interpreted as a representation of one's true impulses or as a fleeting mental glitch. Similarly, the individual imagining that they had left the gas stove on will not find any marker in the image itself that may reveal whether it is a true memory or a fabrication. In Wittgenstein's words: "No state of affairs has, in itself, what I would like to call the coercive power of an absolute judge."[29] As in Jastrow's famous visual illusion of the duck-rabbit,[30] one can endlessly alternate between different ways of seeing a phenomenon, without ever reaching a resolution.

This instability of meanings is disturbing, and thus we try to keep it out of our collective mind. We convince ourselves and teach our children that everyday events and objects normally carry inherent meanings and that if we only ponder them long enough, we will discover the correct ones.[31] This again poses a challenge for those who suffer from OCD, as they realize to their horror that meanings are neither self-evident nor obligatory. They may come up with a series of compelling arguments, but then a host of similarly compelling counter-arguments appear. They may "feel" that they probably turned off the gas stove, only to have this feeling replaced by an equally tangible one of not doing so. This movement back and forth between equally valid yet fateful interpretations is an excruciating experience, especially since no one else seems to understand and share it. It is as if one discovers that the two seemingly integrated cogwheels of language and reality have been disengaged all along.

Curiously, this is also the experience that may consume anyone reading Wittgenstein's *Philosophical Investigations*. As we navigate the tangle of arguments and counterarguments, deliberations, and internal dialogues presented in the book, we feel that our grip on concepts is loosening. We may

---

28 Wittgenstein, *Philosophical Investigations*, §§139–40, 185–242.
29 Ludwig Wittgenstein, "A Lecture on Ethics," *Philosophical Review* 74, no. 1 (1965): 7.
30 Joseph Jastrow, *Fact and Fable in Psychology* (Boston: Houghton Mifflin, 1900), 294.
31 Wittgenstein, *Philosophical Investigations*, §§219–22.

have challenged all those pictures that hold our consciousness captive, but ultimately, we are left without a footing in the world. As Bearn describes it:

> Wittgenstein's destructive moments attempt just what Descartes refused to do: to shake our trust in our sense that THIS is relevant to THAT, our sense that THIS is a good reason for THAT, and so on.[32]

Wittgenstein readily acknowledges his bafflement as he discovers the cracks in the linguistic presuppositions that guide our lives. As he attests: "The more closely we examine actual language, the greater becomes the conflict between it and our requirement ... The conflict becomes intolerable."[33] Similarly, a few decades later, Psychoanalyst Thomas Ogden observed how patients who are also teachers and students of linguistics "often experience anxiety states bordering on panic in association with the feeling that they are dissolving as they dismantle the binding power of language." He adds that "this has in each case that I have encountered led to the patient's need to leave the field of linguistics at least temporarily."[34]

Yet individuals suffering from OCD do not have the privilege of "leaving the field of linguistics." For them, the dissolution of language's binding power is a daily, existential experience, from which they cannot escape. Captivated by the picture of an inner world, they try relentlessly to uncover it, only to find that it evades them. What was supposed to be the most intimate of realms suddenly becomes a shattered mirror, providing only fragments of impressions and ideas which must be interpreted like cryptic texts. The additional discovery that meanings can alternate indefinitely only intensifies this feeling of alienation, as their views of the world and of themselves ceaselessly change. This may explain the high levels of depersonalization and derealization empirically found among individuals with obsessive tendencies.[35] As the early psychiatrist and phenomenologist Viktor von Gebsattel describes it:

> What always fascinates us in encountering the compulsive person is the unpenetrated, perhaps impenetrable, quality of his being different ... the

---

32 Bearn, *Waking to Wonder*, 185.
33 Wittgenstein, *Philosophical Investigations*, §107.
34 Ogden, *The Primitive Edge of Experience*, 81.
35 See: Kieron O'Connor, and Frederick Aardema, "Living in a Bubble: Dissociation, Relational Consciousness, and Obsessive-Compulsive Disorder," *Journal of Consciousness Studies* 19, no. 7–8 (2012): 216–46; Nirit Soffer-Dudek, Dana Lassri, Nir Soffer-Dudek, and Golan Shahar, "Dissociative Absorption: An Empirically Unique, Clinically Relevant, Dissociative Factor," *Consciousness and Cognition* 36 (2015): 345–49.

strange remoteness of a mode of being completely different from our own ... for our world, in which he is found, does not seem to be his.[36]

At this point, many of those who suffer from OCD seek professional help to figure out why they cannot do what everyone else seems to be doing so effortlessly: to assign meaning to their inner states. Better understanding one's underlying motivations and desires sounds exactly like a job for psychodynamic therapy. Yet unfortunately, as reviewed above, it proves to seldom provide relief, and might even aggravate symptoms. If we wish to correct this, we must first understand why. Hence, in the next section, I will review psychoanalysis' outlook on the question of the inner world and observe how it interacts with the obsessive-compulsive situation.

In Search of the Unconscious

In private conversations, Wittgenstein described himself as "a disciple of Freud" and expressed admiration for the latter's originality and acuity of insight.[37] Yet, at the same time, he was passionately critical of what he perceived as the philosophical negligence of some of Freud's formulations, the most notable being Freud's core innovation: the very notion of the unconscious.

In its literal meaning, the adjective "unconscious" simply denotes what one is not aware of. Yet, as several critics point out, Freud was not fond of such "unscientific" negative definitions. Thus, he reestablished the unconscious as a noun, an entity, a distinct mental site, which could then be systematically explored.[38] This is evident, for example, in the following passage from his 1909 "Notes upon a Case of Obsessional Neurosis," wherein Freud depicts the unconscious as a subterranean hideout for forbidden impulses:

> The love has not succeeded in extinguishing the hatred but only in driving it down into the unconsciousness; and in the unconscious the

---

36 Viktor E. von Gebsattel, "The World of the Compulsive," trans. Sylvia Koppel, and Ernest Angel, in *Existence: A New Dimension in Psychiatry and Psychology*, eds. Rollo May, Ernest Angel, and Henri F. Ellenberger (New York: Basic Books, [1938] 1958), 170.
37 Ludwig Wittgenstein, *Lectures & Conversations on Aesthetics, Psychology and Religious Belief*, ed. Cyril Barrett (Berkeley: University of California Press, 1967), 41.
38 Michael Billig, *Freudian Repression: Conversation Creating the Unconscious* (Cambridge: Cambridge University Press, 1999), 14–17, 31–37, 42–46; Jacques Bouveresse, *Wittgenstein Reads Freud*, Trans. by Carol Cosman (Princeton: Princeton University Press, 1995), 19–20, 42–43, 50; Roy Schafer, *A New Language for Psychoanalysis* (New Haven: Yale University Press, 1976), 3–15, 102–05.

hatred, safe from the danger of being destroyed by the operations of consciousness, is able to persist and even to grow.[39]

Another example may be found in the 1917 "Resistance and Repression," wherein Freud compares the unconscious to "a large entrance hall," in which "mental impulses jostle one another like separate individuals," as they try to pass the watchman and push into the room of the preconscious.[40] Freud later apologizes for the crudeness of his metaphors, yet uses them nonetheless, adding that they are "very far-reaching approximations to the real facts."[41]

One might comment that the abovementioned examples are "just metaphors." Yet, as Wittgenstein teaches us, metaphors have the power to create reality. After we read Freud, we remember his vivid pictorial scenes, not his half-hearted reservations. We come to think of the unconscious as a space (an inner hallway, a prison cell, a hiding place), and of our impulses and desires as little entities, homunculi, dueling one another as they struggle to perform their prewritten roles. In other instances, Freudian imagery depicts the unconscious not just as a space but also as an entity in its own right, an inner *doppelgänger*, who, as Bouveresse describes it, "has its own desires, wishes, motives, intentions, purposes, ruses, and strategies, and is capable of achieving its ends with an intelligence, skill, and assurance often quite superior to those of the person himself."[42]

Such pictures of the human mind are not exclusive to Freud. Throughout the years they have been reincarnated, whether explicitly or implicitly, in other key psychoanalytic notions, such as Klein's idea of preverbal emotions,[43] Winnicott's "true self,"[44] or Bion's "O,"[45] to name a few. What they all share is the supposition that first there are one's inner, preverbal mental states, and only then can one become aware of them, articulate them, deny

---

39 Sigmund Freud, "Notes upon a Case of Obsessional Neurosis," in *The Standard Edition of the Complete Psychological Works of Sigmund Freud*, vol. 10, trans. James Strachey (London: Hogarth Press, 1955), 239.
40 Sigmund Freud, "Resistance and Repression," in *The Standard Edition of the Complete Psychological Works of Sigmund Freud*, vol. 16, trans. James Strachey (London: Hogarth Press, 1963), 295.
41 Freud, "Resistance and Repression," 296.
42 Bouveresse, *Wittgenstein Reads Freud*, 34.
43 Melanie Klein, "Envy and gratitude," in *Envy and Gratitude and Other Works* (London: Hogarth Press, 1975), 176–235; Melanie Klein, "The Psychological Principles of Infant Analysis," *International Journal of Psycho-Analysis* 8 (1927): 25–37.
44 Donald Woods Winnicott, "Ego Distortion in Terms of True and False Self," in *The Maturational Processes and the Facilitating Environment* (London: Hogarth Press, 1965), 140–52.
45 Wilfred R. Bion, *Attention and Interpretation* (London: Tavistock Publications, 1970), 26–91.

them, act them out, and so forth. And since these inner states purportedly lie in the dark recesses of one's unconscious, it is possible to rediscover them, provided we use the proper technique.

This outlook is susceptible to the same philosophical problems presented in the previous section. If we cannot take hold of our inner preverbal world by using simple introspection (whatever this practice may mean), why would we be able to do so by tracing our associations or discussing the intricacies of our relationships? Indeed, in private conversations, Wittgenstein argues that Freudian practices such as free-associating or dream analysis do not provide any bridges to the unconscious. Rather, they are culturally specific rituals, which merely grant an aura of authenticity to certain verbal ideas. And despite this aura, there is no indication that they express one's true nature any more accurately than other possible rituals.[46]

As I proposed above, those suffering from OCD had already encountered this problem before they entered the consulting room. They had already discovered that when they try to look "inwards," they come up with words and images, but never with those coveted pre-verbal inner states. Moreover, they had learned that whatever one may attain by using introspection is always subject to competing and equally justifiable interpretations. Yet, when they seek help, psychoanalysis guides them to keep doing exactly what they have been doing so far: to try and look inwards, this time using new techniques. Upon following this request, they generate additional ideas, images, and interpretable stories, but never attain that elusive sense of certainty that was supposed to be the result of getting in touch with their inner world.

Moreover, in the obsessive-compulsive context, the psychoanalytic technique of interpretation may bear harmful consequences. As I have argued, one of the main problems of those suffering from OCD is the over-fluidity of meaning. As Wittgenstein demonstrates in the Paradox of Rules, once we truly examine competing interpretations of any given phenomenon, we can see that none of them is self-evident nor logically superior to the others. Thus, when we offer an analytic interpretation, we present nothing but another contender to an already crowded and endless race of meanings. This may elucidate cases such as the one described by Meyer,[47] in which following psychoanalytic treatment, the patient's obsessions were not reduced but rather expanded to include additional objects and symbols. As

---

46 Wittgenstein, *Lectures & Conversations on Aesthetics, Psychology and Religious Belief*, 42–45.
47 Victor Meyer, "Modification of Expectations in Cases with Obsessional Rituals," *Behaviour Research and Therapy* 4 (1966): 276–77.

Wittgenstein complains: "Freud never shows how we know where to stop – where is the right solution."[48]

The ideas outlined above may account for psychoanalysis' limited achievements in treating OCD. Both the notion of the unconscious and the technique of interpretation are fundamental to psychoanalytically informed therapy, but at the same time, they drive the patient further into the ruminative turmoil. In the following sections, I shall propose a possible way to navigate this delicate situation, based on Wittgenstein's own theoretical and personal attempts at struggling with his daunting philosophical revelations.

"The Real Discovery"

Philosophical Investigations is a disheartening text for both its reader and its writer. Wittgenstein dissects commonplace notions, such as intention or understanding, by stripping away all their arbitrary and contingent characteristics, only to discover that nothing remains; that they are merely conversational conventions. We use terms such as "intending" or "knowing," but there is not necessarily something behind our usage.[49] Wittgenstein is constantly troubled by this discovery. He is neither a nihilist who wants to prove that everything can be refuted nor is he an early postmodernist making a case that discourse is everything. His skepticism belongs to the tragic kind, in which the world, as Cavell describes it, "vanishes exactly with the effort to make it present."[50] In a similar manner, Bearn poignantly comments upon Wittgenstein's investigations:

> We were looking for enlightenment. We wanted to know what the meaning of words and of our lives consisted in, and all we get is darkness ... Breaking the spell of our involvement with the world delivers us to nothing.[51]

The structure and style of *Philosophical Investigations* express exactly this struggle between Wittgenstein's desire to hold on to something certain and his coming to understand that he is unable to do so. This is why the book is constructed not as a series of consecutive arguments but as a disorderly assemblage of disputes with an imaginary interlocutor which never seems to

---

48 Wittgenstein, *Lectures & Conversations on Aesthetics, Psychology and Religious Belief*, 42.
49 Wittgenstein, *Philosophical Investigations*, §§304, 330–34, 645.
50 Stanley Cavell, "The Avoidance of Love: A Reading of King Lear," in *Must We Mean What We Say?* 267–353. (Cambridge: Cambridge University Press, 1976), 323. **See also:** Stanley Cavell, "The Uncanniness of the Ordinary," in *The Tanner Lectures on Human Values (Vol. VIII)*, ed. Sterling M. McMurrin (Cambridge: Cambridge University Press, 1988), 97–102, 111.
51 Bearn, *Waking to Wonder*, 187.

give up.[52] It is even possible to say that Wittgenstein's prose is similar in form and content to rumination – an inner dialogue that repeatedly breaks down its basic assumptions "without ever producing a clear, final statement on any of them."[53]

Like Wittgenstein's writing in *Philosophical Investigations*, obsessive rumination too presents an ongoing and incessant internal dialogue in which arguments and counterarguments are raised without reaching any conclusion. Patients suffering from OCD also feel they must answer an urgent, fateful question. But the more they try to distill something certain, the more certainty evades them, leaving only confusion and estrangement.

At this stage, we may ask if Wittgenstein is indeed the right candidate to provide us with an answer as to how to break this cycle. Upon reading *Philosophical Investigations*, we get the impression that he himself is desperately searching for a way to stop his rumination:

> The real discovery is the one that enables me to break off philosophizing when I want to. —The one that gives philosophy peace, so that it is no longer tormented by questions.[54]

As some commentators write, Wittgenstein never managed to stop, up to the point where philosophy indeed impeded on his daily life.[55] *Philosophical Investigations*, despite its enormous depth, offers the reader no key as to how to stop philosophizing. If anything, it manifests the opposite: how endlessly consuming the philosophical endeavor may be.

However, when one reads Wittgenstein's more private texts, specifically, his diaries and personal notes as well as recaps of his conversations with students, one sometimes encounters a seemingly different philosopher. These texts are less analytically rigorous, yet this is exactly their strength. They showcase Wittgenstein as an existential thinker, trying not to analyze the bewildering uncertainty presented by philosophy, but to figure out how to live in its midst. His thoughts on matters of faith, doubt, and personal salvation are consciously influenced by those of the existential Danish philosopher Søren

---

52 See: John Hughes, "Philosophy and Style: Wittgenstein and Russell," *Philosophy and Literature* 13, no. 2 (October 1989): 332–39; Alois Pichler, "The Interpretation of the Philosophical Investigations: Style, Therapy, Nachlass," in *Wittgenstein and His Interpreters*, eds. Guy Kahane, Edward Kanterian, and Oskari Kuusela (Oxford: Blackwell, 2007), 123–44.

53 Marie McGinn, *Wittgenstein and the Philosophical Investigations* (London: Routledge, 1997), 9.

54 Wittgenstein, *Philosophical Investigations,* §133.

55 Hughes, "Philosophy and Style", 335; Edward Marcotte, "Wittgenstein's Metaphysics of Contingency," *Metaphilosophy* 23, no. 1&2 (1992), 63; Ray Monk, *Ludwig Wittgenstein: The Duty of Genius* (London: Penguin Books, 1990), 3.

Kierkegaard (1813–1855), whom he admired. Thus, in the next section I shall take a small detour, reviewing Wittgenstein's private existential philosophy in light of Kierkegaard's work, and then come back to examine whether it may be of service for our efforts to understand and treat OCD.

Truth and Commitment

In his 1846 *Concluding Unscientific Postscript*, Kierkegaard introduces the idea of existential, rather than objective, certainty.[56] He maintains that we forge the truths that lead us through life not by observing objective evidence but rather with our actions. We do not decide to believe in God, for example, after being persuaded by evidence for His existence. Such a decision would be as trivial as believing in the existence of bacteria after looking into the microscope. Rather, we just believe, despite the possible lack of evidence. In Kierkegaard's words: "[existential] truth is precisely this venture of choosing an objective uncertainty with the passion of the infinite."[57] The leap of faith, the act of deciding to believe, is exactly what loads our core beliefs with meaning and turns them into existential truths.

Kierkegaard emphasizes that this undertaking is far from being easy or self-assuring. Since we create our personal truths through our own commitments and actions, each of us is alone as we face our doubts. No one can take the leap for us. Thus, our search involves both loneliness and shattering anxiety. It is a struggle that lasts throughout a lifetime, since "only eternity can give an eternal certainty, while existence has to be satisfied with the combative certainty, gained not as the conflict abates or becomes more illusory, but only by it becoming harder."[58] This theme is also prominent in *The Concept of Anxiety*, which Kierkegaard wrote around the same period.[59]

Wittgenstein's ideas about doubt and its imperfect resolution resonate with Kierkegaard's notions of faith and existential truth. Like Kierkegaard, Wittgenstein maintains that a person who declares, for instance, that they believe in God, is not making a claim about the nature of reality. Rather, they are committing themselves to an array of values and actions that give their life meaning.[60] "Hence," he writes, "although it's belief, it is really a

---

56 Søren Kierkegaard, *Concluding Unscientific Postscript*, trans. Alastair Hannay (Cambridge: Cambridge University Press, 2009), 159–251.
57 Kierkegaard, *Concluding Unscientific Postscript*, 171.
58 Kierkegaard, *Concluding Unscientific Postscript*, 190.
59 Søren Kierkegaard, *The Concept of Anxiety*, trans. Reidar Thomte, and Albert B. Anderson (Princeton: Princeton University Press, 1980), 42–44, 62, 155.
60 Ludwig Wittgenstein, *Culture and Value (Revised 2nd Edition)*, trans. Peter Winch, ed. Georg Henrik von Wright (Oxford: Blackwell, 1998), 58; Ludwig Wittgenstein, *Lectures & Conversations on Aesthetics, Psychology and Religious Belief*, 53–59. See also: William Child, *Wittgenstein* (New York: Routledge, 2011), 225.

way of living, or a way of judging life. Passionately taking up *this* interpretation."[61] The certainty Wittgenstein speaks of is not based on "truth" but rather on "taking-for-true."[62] Like Kierkegaard, he maintains that the value of such a venture lies precisely in the fact that it is done in the face of doubt. "If there were evidence, this would in fact destroy the whole business," he says in one of his lectures.[63]

According to this view, faith and certainty are not the *sources* of our actions (as we normally believe) but rather the *products* of our acts of faith. In his poetic words:

> First be redeemed & hold on tightly to your redemption ... then you will see that what you are holding on to is this belief. So this can only come about if you no longer support yourself on this earth but suspend yourself from heaven.[64]

Normally we believe that we should support ourselves on the earth of certainty, but then we arrive at those moments of doubt where we feel that the ground is slipping from under our feet. Wittgenstein offers a new, less intuitive way of supporting ourselves "from heaven," that is, from where we wish our love, our faith, our intentions, and our lives to be. We must contend with the terrifying act of walking in thin air, hoping that the ground will slowly materialize under our feet as we do so. Thus, Wittgenstein allows us to see our perpetual clashes with doubt as identity-forming events. Every time we act upon our wished-for truths despite the inherent uncertainty, we reaffirm or rather re-create them. Existentially speaking, we never receive our world ready-made, but must redeem it from the abyss of doubt through our actions.

"A Way of Living Life"

But what about therapy? Confronting doubt is an extremely lonely endeavor. The drama Kierkegaard and Wittgenstein portray calls for only one protagonist, who must take upon oneself a solitary leap over the void. Even God is depicted not as a provider of comfort and support, but as an abstract entity, whose existence depends solely upon one's resolutions. So where do we, as psychoanalytically informed therapists, fit in?

First, we should acknowledge what we *cannot* do: we cannot undertake the leap of faith for our patients. No one can. It is a life decision (or rather

---

61 Wittgenstein, *Culture and Value*, 73.
62 Wittgenstein, *Culture and Value*, 38.
63 Wittgenstein, *Lectures & Conversations on Aesthetics, Psychology and Religious Belief*, 56.
64 Wittgenstein, *Culture and Value*, 39.

a succession of decisions) that they must take upon themselves. It may be argued that what psychoanalysis unknowingly tried to do was to help patients evade that leap. It operated under the assumption that identifying and coming into terms with the forbidden impulses that fuel the compulsive behavior might spare patients the need to confront existential anxiety. It was hoped that realizing how one's compulsive cleaning is driven by their aggressive urges, for example, might eliminate their need to agonize over whether they're killing the household members by not sanitizing the toilet once again. However, as clinical experience shows, there is no way to outsmart the disease. Postulating the origins of one's obsessions and compulsions may be enlightening, sometimes even comforting, but it does not make existential terror go away. The only way to confront it is to eventually face it. This realization explains the effectiveness of behavioral therapy for OCD. Since what are exposure and response prevention if not a series of leaps of faith?

Thus, eliminating anxiety through exploring symbols, relationships, and associations is out of our reach as therapists. This has implications for what we should and should not do in psychodynamic therapy with the obsessive-compulsive patient. First, as I have argued above, we should limit our use of interpretations, since we can never win the paradox of rules. The person suffering from OCD is akin to a skeptical philosopher; they have already discovered the philosophical "secret" that the meaning of images, sensations, and emotions is never definitive. That things can always be interpreted one way and then the opposite, and both would be viable, despite the shattering consequences to one's well-being. Although as therapists we could use our prestige and the influence of transference to have our benign interpretation resonate with the patient as if it were the only correct answer, sooner or later this influence fades, and our patients realize that our interpretation is just one more way of seeing things. Each time this happens we lose credit, because our patients rightly feel that we must be somewhat naïve to have such confidence in a mere possibility.

Moreover, as I have argued above, everyone, including therapists of all schools but the strictest of behaviorists, uses deceptive language that persuades us that internal states are undoubtfully real, and it is therefore the person with OCD who is at fault for being so inept at accessing them. However, if we accept that mental states are created by language, we may conclude that none of us is better or worse than others in "accessing" them. Consequently, we should be very careful lest we suggest to our patients that they can acquire better insight into their problem by using whatever method of looking inwards in order to identify their internal mental states. I have yet to encounter a patient suffering from OCD who was able to reach a resolution for their anxiety by doing so.

So, what is it that we *should* do, as therapists? First, we need to realize the existential weight OCD inherently carries. The seemingly trifle ruminations about hand washing and doorknob checking actually present us with the big questions of life: questions of death and responsibility, love and fidelity, morality and meaning. It is never just germs, but the life one will not have the chance to live had they died of infection. It is not just the doorknob, but one's overwhelming responsibility for the safety and well-being of their loved ones. As the cultural anthropologist Ernest Becker observes, obsessive rumination serves to attenuate the terror of our frailness by limiting it to a single, concrete issue.[65] If we just check this button again, we shall not have to dread death anymore, at least temporarily. This is, of course, an illusion; The issues of our death, our morality, and our belief will always resurface one way or the other. It is our duty as therapists to help patients clarify the major life questions that lie under the barrage of obsessions and doubts. These questions cannot be solved intellectually, neither can they be solved by re-experiencing prior relationships in the consulting room. Eventually there is always the leap. Our task is therefore to help our patients regain enough ego-strength to accomplish it. This is where interpretation, transference, dream analysis, free association, reverie, and all the other tools of the psychoanalytic trade come in handy. They do not substitute the leap, but rather build up one's ability to commence it. They help patients find enough courage and compassion to encounter their love and their hate, their frailness and their hope, regardless of whether these are "internal" or created through discourse. It is through our attempts at empathy, through our efforts for holding and containing, that patients may, at last, muster enough faith and trust to jump. And when they finally attempt to stop grappling with the question of whether they had turned off the gas valve despite the fear that they are risking their family, or take it upon themselves to play the piano instead of ruminating about their love for their partner, we can help them realize the scope of this existential achievement.

In this sense, the obsessive patients who appear at our doorstep are given a rare opportunity to create their world anew. On every occasion in which they choose to continue daily life despite the torments of doubt, they constitute reality as they wish it would be. They buy back the world one choice at a time. As therapists, we are lucky enough to witness and accompany this terrifying process of certainty blooming amidst doubt. This certainty, which needs to be constantly earned and nurtured, is forever different than the one which has not been forged by pain. It is both fragile and at the same time extremely solid, as it is perpetually and repeatedly chosen, suspended from heaven.

---

65 Ernest Becker, *The Denial of Death* (New York: Free Press, 1973): 180–90.

Bibliography

American Psychiatric Association. "Practice Guideline for the Treatment of Patients with Obsessive-Compulsive Disorder." *American Journal of Psychiatry* 164 (2007): 1–56.

Amir, Dana. "The Metaphorical, the Metonymical and the Psychotic Aspects of Obsessive Symptomatology." *International Journal of* Psychoanalysis 97 (2016): 259–280.

Bearn, Gordon C. F. *Waking to Wonder: Wittgenstein's Existential Investigations*. Albany: State University of New York Press, 1997.

Becker, Ernest. *The Denial of Death*. New York: Free Press, 1973.

Billig, Michael. *Freudian Repression: Conversation Creating the Unconscious*. Cambridge: Cambridge University Press, 1999.

Bion, Wilfred R. *Attention and Interpretation*. London: Tavistock Publications, 1970.

Bollas, Christopher. *Cracking up: The Work of Unconscious Experience*. London: Routledge, 1995.

Bouveresse, Jacques. *Wittgenstein Reads Freud*. Translated by Carol Cosman, Princeton: Princeton University Press, 1995.

Brandchaft, Bernard. "Obsessional Disorders: A Developmental Systems Perspective." *Psychoanalytic Inquiry* 21, no. 2 (2001): 253–88.

Cavell, Stanley. "The Avoidance of Love: A Reading of King Lear." In *Must We Mean What We Say?*, 267–353. Cambridge: Cambridge University Press, 1976.

Cavell, Stanley. "The Uncanniness of the Ordinary." In *The Tanner Lectures on Human Values (Vol. VIII)*, edited by Sterling M. McMurrin, 81–117. Cambridge: Cambridge University Press, 1988.

Child, William. *Wittgenstein*. New York: Routledge, 2011.

Chlebowski, Susan, and Gregory, Robert J. "Is a Psychodynamic Perspective Relevant to the Clinical Management of Obsessive-Compulsive Disorder?" *American Journal of Psychotherapy* 63, no. 3 (2009): 245–56.

Csigó, Katalin. "Obsessive Position: The New Psychoanalytic Approach of Obsessive-Compulsive Disorder." *Current Psychology*, early online view (2021). 10.1007/s12144-021-01893-3

Dar, Reuven, Lazarov, Amit, and Liberman, Nira. "Seeking Proxies for Internal States (SPIS): Towards a Novel Model of Obsessive-Compulsive Disorder." *Behaviour Research and Therapy* 147 (2021): 1–13.

Esman, Aaron H. "Obsessive-Compulsive Disorder: Current Views." *Psychoanalytic Inquiry* 21, no. 2 (2001): 145–56.

Freud, Anna. "Obsessional Neurosis: A Summary of Psycho-Analytic Views as Presented at the Congress." *International Journal of Psychoanalysis* 47 (1966): 116–22.

Freud, Sigmund. "Inhibitions, Symptoms and Anxiety." In *The Standard Edition of the Complete Psychological Works of Sigmund Freud, Vol. 20*. Translated by James Strachey, 75–176. London: Hogarth Press, [1926] 1959.

Freud, Sigmund. "Notes upon a Case of Obsessional Neurosis." In *The Standard Edition of the Complete Psychological Works of Sigmund Freud, Vol. 10*. Translated by James Strachey, 153–318. London: Hogarth Press, [1909] 1955.

Freud, Sigmund. "Resistance and Repression." In *The Standard Edition of the Complete Psychological Works of Sigmund Freud, Vol. 16*. Translated by James Strachey, 286–302. London: Hogarth Press, [1917] 1963.

Gabbard, Glen O. "Psychoanalytically Informed Approaches to the Treatment of Obsessive-Compulsive Disorder." *Psychoanalytic Inquiry* 21, no. 2 (2001): 208–21.

Hommel, Bernhard. "Dancing in the Dark: No Role for Consciousness in Action Control." *Frontiers in Psychology* 4 (June 2013): 1–3.

Hughes, John. "Philosophy and Style: Wittgenstein and Russell." *Philosophy and Literature* 13, no. 2 (October 1989): 332–39.

Jastrow, Joseph. *Fact and Fable in Psychology*. Boston: Houghton Mifflin, 1900.

Kierkegaard, Søren. *Concluding Unscientific Postscript*. Translated by Alastair Hannay. Cambridge: Cambridge University Press, [1846] 2009.

Kierkegaard, Søren. *The Concept of Anxiety*. Translated by Reidar Thomte, and Albert B. Anderson. Princeton: Princeton University Press, [1844] 1980.

Klein, Melanie. "Envy and gratitude." In *Envy and Gratitude and Other Works*, 176–235. London: Hogarth Press, 1975.

Klein, Melanie. "The Psychological Principles of Infant Analysis." *International Journal of Psycho-Analysis* 8 (1927): 25–37.

Marcotte, Edward. "Wittgenstein's Metaphysics of Contingency." *Metaphilosophy* 23, no. 1&2 (1992): 57–67.

McGinn, Marie. *Wittgenstein and the Philosophical Investigations*. London: Routledge, 1997.

McKay, Dean, Abramowitz, Jonathan S., and Storch, Erik A. "Mechanisms of Harmful Treatments for Obsessive–Compulsive Disorder." *Clinical Psychology: Science and Practice* 28, no. 1 (2021): 52–59.

Meyer, Victor. "Modification of Expectations in Cases with Obsessional Rituals." *Behaviour Research and Therapy* 4 (1966): 273–80.

Monk, Ray. *Ludwig Wittgenstein: The Duty of Genius*. London: Penguin Books, 1990.

Mulhall, K., O'Connor, John, and Timulakova, Katarina. "Managing the Monster in the Mind: A Psychoanalytically Informed Qualitative Study Exploring the Experiences of People Diagnosed with Obsessive-Compulsive Disorder." *Psychoanalytic Psychotherapy* 33, no. 2 (2019): 117–32.

National Institute for Health and Clinical Excellence. "Obsessive-Compulsive Disorder and Body Dysmorphic Disorder: Treatment." Last Modified June 2020. https://www.nice.org.uk/guidance/cg31

O'Connor, John. "A Flaw in the Fabric: Toward an Interpersonal Psychoanalytic Understanding of Obsessive-Compulsive Disorder." *Journal of Contemporary Psychotherapy* 38, no. 2 (2008): 87–96.

O'Connor, John. "The Dynamics of Protection and Exposure in the Development of Obsessive-Compulsive Disorder." *Psychoanalytic Psychology* 24, no. 3 (2007): 464–74.

O'Connor, Kieron, and Aardema, Frederick. "Living in a Bubble: Dissociation, Relational Consciousness, and Obsessive-Compulsive Disorder." *Journal of Consciousness Studies* 19, no. 7–8 (2012): 216–46.

Ogden, Thomas H. *The Primitive Edge of Experience*. London: Jason Aronson, 1989.

Pichler, Alois. "The Interpretation of the Philosophical Investigations: Style, Therapy, Nachlass." In *Wittgenstein and His Interpreters*, edited by Guy Kahane, Edward Kanterian, and Oskari Kuusela, 123–44. Oxford: Blackwell, 2007.

Rice, Emanuel. "Reflections on the Obsessive-Compulsive Disorders: A Psychodynamic and Therapeutic Perspective." *Psychoanalytic Review* 91, no. 1 (2004): 23–44.
Saint Augustine. *Confessions*. Translated by Henry Chadwick. Oxford: Oxford University Press, 2008.
Sato, Atsushi. "Both Motor Prediction and Conceptual Congruency between Preview and Action-Effect Contribute to Explicit Judgment of Agency." *Cognition* 110 (2009): 74–83.
Schafer, Roy. *A New Language for Psychoanalysis*. New Haven: Yale University Press, 1976.
Soffer-Dudek, Nirit, Lassri, Dana, Soffer-Dudek, Nir, and Shahar, Golan. "Dissociative Absorption: An Empirically Unique, Clinically Relevant, Dissociative Factor." *Consciousness and Cognition* 36 (2015): 338–51.
Soon, Chun Siong, Brass, Marcel, Heinze, Hans-Jochen, and Haynes, John-Dylan. "Unconscious Determinants of Free Decisions in the Human Brain." *Nature Neuroscience* 11, no. 5 (May 2008): 543–45.
Von Gebsattel, Viktor E. "The World of the Compulsive." Translated by Sylvia Koppel, and Ernest Angel. In *Existence: A New Dimension in Psychiatry and Psychology*. Edited by Rollo May, Ernest Angel, and Henri F. Ellenberger, 170–87. New York: Basic Books, [1938] 1958.
Winnicott, Donald Woods. "Ego Distortion in Terms of True and False Self." In *The Maturational Processes and the Facilitating Environment*, 140–52. London: Hogarth Press, 1965.
Wittgenstein, Ludwig. "A Lecture on Ethics." *Philosophical Review* 74, no. 1 (1965): 3–12.
Wittgenstein, Ludwig. *Culture and Value (Revised 2nd Edition)*. Translated by Peter Winch. Edited by Georg Henrik von Wright. Oxford: Blackwell, 1998.
Wittgenstein, Ludwig. *Lectures & Conversations on Aesthetics, Psychology and Religious Belief*. Edited by Cyril Barrett. Berkeley: University of California Press, 1967.
Wittgenstein, Ludwig. *Philosophical Investigations (4th Edition)*. Translated by Gertrude E. M. Anscombe, Peter M. S. Hacker, and Joachim Schulte. Edited by Peter M. S. Hacker, and Joachim Schulte. Oxford: Blackwell, [1953] 2009.
Zaidel, Aya. "Obsessive States: Aesthetics, Erotism, and Fantasy." *Psychoanalytic Review* 103, no. 4 (2016): 483–513.

Chapter 4

"Look into the Depths within Yourself and Find the Outside World"

The Contribution of Rudolf Steiner's Monistic Philosophy to Psychoanalytic Conceptualization

Tali Sella

> "Look into the depths within yourself, and find the outside world;
> look into the outside world, and find yourself;
> Mark the pendulum-swing between the self and the universe,
> and unto you will reveal itself
> the human being as the universe;
> the universe as the human being."[1,2]

This chapter generates a dialogue between three psychoanalytic concepts and Rudolf Steiner's "monism of thought." To create and examine this interdisciplinary dialogue, it makes methodological use of tools and concepts from a number of fields: methodological tools proposed in Wittgenstein's later thought for the philosophy of language; interpretative-hermeneutic tools based on Gadamer's work; and the term "worldview" (*Weltanschauung*) as defined in Steiner's thought.

In Steinerian terms, this chapter proposes the unitive worldview established in Steiner's philosophy as a theoretical basis for the psychoanalytic conceptualization under study. In so doing, it also addresses the various functions of the term "worldview": In Steiner's doctrine, this term is defined as a conception at the foundation of a certain ideological system that pertains to the relationship between the human being and the world. Steiner uses this term to examine the changes that various systems undergo in terms of this relationship.[3]

---

1 This chapter is based on research carried out under the supervision of Dr. Dorit Lemberger in the Program for Hermeneutics and Cultural Studies at Bar-Ilan University. The author is grateful to the program for its support in producing this chapter.
2 Rudolf Steiner, *Wahrspruchworte* (Dornach: Rudolf Steiner Verlag, 1991), 237.
3 Rudolf Steiner, *The Riddles of Philosophy* (Great Barrington: SteinerBooks/Anthroposophic Press, 2009).

For Freud, it is an "intellectual construction which solves all the problems of our existence uniformly on the basis of one overriding hypothesis, which [...] leaves no question unanswered and in which everything [...] finds its fixed place" – the reverse of the scientific method in which he strives to anchor psychoanalysis.[4] Wittgenstein, for his part, notes the possibility for "surveyable representation," that is, "understanding which consists in 'seeing connections.'"[5]

In Wittgensteinian terms, the chapter relates to the language-games within which the psychoanalytic terms in question function, and positions them as "objects of comparison" with the language game instituted in Steiner's unitive-monistic philosophy.[6] This leads to the "aspect's lighting-up" – i.e., the ability to see aspects that had not been visible beforehand,[7] which is enabled by the comparison and dialogue between the language-games.

In terms of the Gadamerian method, the chapter creates a "fusion of horizons" between Steiner's philosophy and psychoanalytic concepts. This method defines the term "horizon" as a "range of vision [...] everything that can be seen from a particular vantage point,"[8] and argues that understanding is always contingent on a dialogic process and on the merging of horizons.[9] According to Gadamer, the dialogue between different fields enables the creation of a common language between them, along with an understanding, based on transformation into a communion, in which neither side remains as it was.[10] In this chapter, the horizon of Steiner's system of thought – what can be seen from the vantage point of this system – is cast upon three psychoanalytic terms, conducing the examination of the common language created in the dialogue between them.

---

4 Sigmund Freud, "Lecture XXXV: The Question of a 'Weltanschauung,'" in *New Introductory Lectures On Psycho-Analysis* (*The Standard Edition of the Complete Psychological Works of Sigmund Freud*, vol. 22, London: Hogarth Press, 1933), 1–182.
5 Ludwig Wittgenstein, *Philosophical Investigations* (4th rev. ed.), ed. P.M.S. Hacker and Joachim Schulte, trans. G.E.M Anscombe, P.M.S. Hacker and Joachim Schulte (Chichester: Wiley-Blackwell, 2010), § 122.
6 In accordance with Wittgenstein's argument that language-games "are not preliminary studies for a future regimentation of language [...]. Rather, the language-games stand there as *objects of comparison*" (*Philosophical Investigations*, § 130, italics in the original).
7 Ludwig Wittgenstein, "Philosophy of Psychology – A Fragment," in Ludwig Wittgenstein, *Philosophical Investigations* (4th rev. ed.), ed. P.M.S. Hacker and Joachim Schulte, trans. G.E.M Anscombe, P.M.S. Hacker and Joachim Schulte (Chichester: Wiley-Blackwell, 2009), §113.
8 Hans-Georg Gadamer, *Truth and Method (Second Revised Edition)*, translated by Joel Weinsheimer and Donald G. Marshall (New York: Continuum, 2004), 302.
9 Gadamer, *Truth and Method*, 367–74.
10 Gadamer, *Truth and Method*, 378–79.

Rudolf Steiner's Philosophy of Unity

Rudolf Steiner (1861–1925), an Austrian philosopher and thinker, is known mainly as the father of Anthroposophy, which is identified first and foremost with the educational approach for which it provides the foundation.[11] Nonetheless, the entirety of Steiner's thinking is significantly broader, and includes extensive philosophical thought besides the anthroposophic doctrine. This body of thought formulates a monistic ontology based upon an alternative epistemology to that constituted in Kantian thinking. The following are descriptions of the main contours of this philosophical approach.

Objective Idealism

The roots of Steiner's theory of knowledge are already present in his early writing, which addresses Goethe's scientific writings and the formulation of the epistemology upon which these writings may be based.[12] This epistemology views the laws of nature that reveal themselves in human knowledge as the objective laws of nature itself, and not as subjective laws of the human spirit, as maintained by Kant.[13] In his book *Truth and Knowledge* (1892), Steiner establishes objective idealism as his epistemological approach.[14] This approach contends that "everything necessary to explain and account for the world is within the reach of our thinking."[15] The function of knowledge is the convergence of the impression and the concept, which man receives from outside and inside respectively, and which both belong to the object known: "It is not due to the objects that they appear to us at first without corresponding concepts, but to our mental organization [...] from every real thing the relevant elements come to us from two sources, from perceiving and thinking."[16]

---

11 Anthroposophic education is a form of education that exists in many countries throughout the world and is based on Steiner's Anthroposophy. In 1919, in response to an invitation by the manager of the Waldorf-Astoria cigarette factory in Stuttgart, Germany, Steiner founded the first anthroposophic school for the children of factory workers. Anthroposophic education is based on the educational and developmental tenets of Steiner's philosophy, at the center of which is a detailed account of the child as a being of body, soul, and spirit. See Roy Wilkinson, *Rudolf Steiner on Education: A Compendium* (Stroud: Hawthorn Press, 2001).
12 Rudolf Steiner, *Goethe's Theory of Knowledge: An Outline of the Epistemology of His Worldview*, trans. Peter Clemm (Great Barrington: SteinerBooks, 2008); Rudolf Steiner, *Goethean Science*, trans. William Lindeman (New York: Mercury Press, 1988).
13 Shmuel Hugo Bergman, *Men and Ways; Philosophical Essays* (Hebrew) (Jerusalem: Bialik Institute, 1967), 242.
14 Rudolf Steiner, *Truth and Knowledge; Introduction to "Philosophy of Spiritual Activity,"* ed. Paul Allen, trans. Rita Stebbing (Great Barrington: SteinerBooks, 1981).
15 Steiner, *Truth and Knowledge,* 10.
16 Rudolf Steiner, *The Philosophy of Spiritual Activity [Freedom]*, 4th rev. ed., ed. R. F. Alfred Hoernlé and Hermann Poppelbaum (London & New-York: Anthroposophic Press; Rudolf Steiner Publishing, 1940).

Monism of Thought

Steiner's response to the question of knowledge is the basis for the formulation of the unitive ontological view that Steiner's approach constructs as "monism of thought." This view maintains that the perception of the distinctive existence of different elements in the world is illusory – "The tree which I perceive, taken in isolation by itself, has no existence; it exists only as a member in the immense mechanism of nature, and it is possible only in real connection with nature."[17] The same is true of the perception of man's separate existence: "A particular human individual is not actually cut off from the universe. He is a part of the universe, and his connection with the cosmic whole is broken, not in reality, but only for our perception."[18]

According to this approach, thinking is perceived as a spiritual force that exists both in man and in the world. It is the foundation shared by all beings and objects in the world, and therefore it constitutes the unity of the world, on the one hand, and is responsible for the human capacity to know the world, on the other. Unlike Kant, who defines concepts such as "functions of unity in judgments,"[19] for Steiner, concepts point to the ideal content that the unitive reality is imbued with. This content connects various objects that are subject to the impression of the perceiving subject, as well as between them and this subject: Thinking is the connecting apparatus that suffuses all impressions that appear separately in time and space. Beyond the impressions perceived through the senses, there is nothing other than the ideal connections between them, that is, beyond what we are able to discover by way of our thought.[20]

The attempt to establish universal unity upon a foundation other than the ideal content revealed through the act of thinking, is, according to Steiner, destined to fail.[21] As opposed to Schopenhauer, who contends that man is connected to the universe through his body and "whose affections [...] are the starting point for the understanding as it intuits the world,"[22] Steiner claims that our bodies' activities reach our consciousness solely through impressions of our selfhood, and as such, their status is no different than that of any other impression.[23] What man knows directly, not by way of impression, is, according to Steiner, thinking.[24] By observing thinking, man

---

17 Steiner, *Philosophy of Spiritual Activity [Freedom]*, 236.
18 Steiner, *Philosophy of Spiritual Activity [Freedom]*, 233–34.
19 Immanuel Kant, *Critique of Pure Reason*, ed. Paul Guyer and Allen W. Wood (Cambridge: Cambridge University Press, 1998), 206.
20 Steiner, *Philosophy of Spiritual Activity [Freedom]*, 82–83.
21 Steiner, *Philosophy of Spiritual Activity [Freedom]*, 78.
22 Arthur Schopenhauer, *The World as Will and Representation*, ed. Christopher Janaway, Judith Norman, and Alistair Welchman (Cambridge: Cambridge University Press, 2010), 124.
23 Steiner, *Philosophy of Spiritual Activity [Freedom]*, 76.
24 Steiner, *Philosophy of Spiritual Activity [Freedom]*, 30.

observes something he himself creates, and finds solid ground in the figure of an object, the reason of the existence of which he can gather from itself: "Such an object I am myself in so far as I think, for I qualify my existence by the determinate and self-contained content of the thinking activity."[25]

In a similar way, Steiner establishes a distinction between man's self-consciousness and his "I" Like consciousness of any other thing, consciousness of self, according to Steiner, is based upon man's impressions of himself. In contrast, the "I" is located within thinking,[26] which is not confined by the defined boundaries of impression.[27] Thus, the "I" does not overlap with the sphere that man perceives as the domain of his personality: man bears within himself the "activity which, from a higher sphere, determines [his] finite existence."[28]

The "I" in Steiner's Unitive Approach

The "I" to which Steiner's theory relates is anchored in thinking as a force with which the entire world is imbued. The content discovered by the "I" through thinking is derived from the world around him,[29] and is not like Kant's pure a priori consciousness – "independent of all experience and even of all impressions of the senses."[30] Unlike Fichte's "I,"[31] the "I" described in Steiner's paradigm is not an absolute being whose existence is based on the assumption of its existence and which creates the world from within itself: The "I" is a creative activity that establishes a worldview from the unification of the given and the concept.[32] Through human thinking, the thought-imbued essence of the world is mediated to the "I" Thus, like any other distinction, the distinction between the "I" and the external world is valid only within the framework of the given world as impression and without the activity of thinking.[33]

Steiner's philosophical approach institutes monism, which asserts the identification of the "ideal" dimension with the "actual" and the "real," and describes the world and man as imbued with thinking: "there is nothing unknown *behind* the sensory world, but [...] *within* the sensory world is the

---

25 Steiner, *Philosophy of Spiritual Activity [Freedom]*, 33.
26 Steiner, *Philosophy of Spiritual Activity [Freedom]*, 42.
27 Steiner, *Philosophy of Spiritual Activity [Freedom]*, 76.
28 Steiner, *Philosophy of Spiritual Activity [Freedom]*, 76.
29 Steiner, *Truth and Knowledge*, 66.
30 Kant, *Critique of Pure Reason*. 136.
31 Johann Gottlieb Fichte, *Science of Knowledge (Wissenschaftslehre), with the First and Second Introductions*, ed. Peter Heath and John Lachs (New York: Meredith Corporation, 1970).
32 Steiner, *Truth and Knowledge*, 81.
33 Steiner, *Truth and Knowledge*, 87.

spiritual world. [...] the realm of human ideas exists within the spiritual world."[34] According to Steiner, the creative power of thinking is manifested differently in the various kingdoms of nature and in man: in the plant kingdom, creative thinking appears in the form of the plant's living body, which carries the power to create its form from within itself and transmit it to members of its species; in the animal kingdom, it is expressed as sensations and impulses; whereas in man, thinking appears in its own form. Only in man does the spirit know itself as spirit, and only in man is there the possibility for development stemming from the conscious activity of the spirit: in man, the spirit has become his inner being.[35]

For Steiner, the spirit of man, his "I", constitutes part of the overall spirit with which the world is imbued.[36] At the same time, the "I" is also the human dimension that defines man's uniqueness, and through which every man is a species in his own right: "What a human being signifies begins, not where he is merely a member of a species, but only where he is an individual being. I have not in the least understood the nature of Mr. Smith of Podunk, if I have described his son or his father."[37] Thus, Steiner's approach is distinct from other monistic approaches in that it asserts the unity of man and the world alongside the essential uniqueness of every human being.

A Dialogue between Psychoanalytic Thinking and Steiner's Thinking

On the History of the Relationship between Psychoanalysis, Philosophy, and Spiritual Doctrines

In creating a dialogue between Steiner's monistic approach and psychoanalytic thinking, this chapter joins the considerable body of scholarship addressing the encounter of psychoanalysis with philosophy on the one hand and with spiritual doctrines on the other.

The initial attitude of psychoanalysis toward both of these domains is shaped by Freud's attempts to anchor psychoanalysis in science and distinguish it from the "philosophies." Unlike the philosophies, psychoanalysis,

---

34 Rudolf Steiner, *Autobiography: Chapters in the Course of My Life 1861–1907*, ed. Paul.M. Allen, trans. Rita Stebbing (Great Barrington: Steiner Books, 2006), 126 (italics in the original).
35 Rudolf Steiner, *Theosophy; An Introduction to the Supersensible Knowledge of the World and the Destination of Man*, ed. Henry B. Monges (New York and London: Anthroposophic Press; Rudolf Steiner Publishing, 1946), 185–91.
36 Rudolf Steiner, *An Outline of Esoteric Science*, trans. Catherine E. Creeger (Great Barrington: Anthroposophic Press, 1997), 46.
37 Rudolf Steiner, *Theosophy; An Introduction to the Supersensible Knowledge of the World and the Destination of Man*, 71.

according to Freud, "is not a system starting out from a few sharply defined basic concepts, seeking to grasp the whole universe with the help of these"; psychoanalysis "keeps close to the facts in its field of study, [...] gropes its way forward by the help of experience, is always incomplete and always ready to correct or modify its theories."[38]

In his chapter "The Question of a 'Weltanschauung'" (1933), Freud sets psychoanalysis, which "has a special right to speak for the scientific Weltanschauung," against the worldviews of philosophy and religion, which are based, in his view, on the human need for a sense of security.[39] Philosophy behaves, according to Freud, as a science, but is unlike science in its adherence to the illusion that it is capable of creating a complete and coherent worldview. In terms of its method, according to Freud's approach, philosophy is misguided in its tendency to over-estimate the epistemological value of logical operations, and in its acceptance of other sources of knowledge such as intuition.[40] As for religion, Freud presumes it to be an enemy: the attempt it represents to rule the world of the senses by way of the world of wishes, developed by man as a result of his biological and psychological needs, is "a counterpart to the neurosis which individual civilized men have to go through in their passage from childhood to maturity."[41]

In his essay "Civilization and its Discontents" (1930) – following Romain Rolland's response to his chapter "The Future of an Illusion"[42] – Freud addresses man's experience of unity with the world as the source of religious sentiment and the objective of spiritual practice.[43] The origin of this experience, which Rolland refers to as "'Oceanic' feeling," is linked, according to Freud, to the preservation of the early developmental state of the infant who "does not yet distinguish his ego from the external world as the source of the sensations flowing in upon him."[44] Religious needs are derived, in his view, "from the infant's helplessness and the longing for the father aroused by it [...] The origin of the religious attitude can be traced back in clear outlines as far as the feeling of infantile helplessness."[45]

---

38 Sigmund Freud, "Two Encyclopaedia Articles," *The Standard Edition of the Complete Psychological Works of Sigmund Freud*, vol. 18, London: Hogarth Press, 1923, 233–60, 253–54.
39 Freud, "Lecture XXXV: The Question of a 'Weltanschauung,'" 158–59.
40 Freud, "Lecture XXXV: The Question of a 'Weltanschauung,'" 160–61.
41 Freud, "Lecture XXXV: The Question of a 'Weltanschauung,'" 168.
42 Sigmund Freud, "The Future of an Illusion," *The Standard Edition of the Complete Psychological Works of Sigmund Freud*, vol. 21, London: Hogarth Press, 1927, 1–56.
43 Sigmund Freud, "Civilization and Its Discontents," *The Standard Edition of the Complete Psychological Works of Sigmund Freud*, vol. 21, London: Hogarth Press, 1930, 57–146, 64–73.
44 Freud, "Civilization and Its Discontents," 66–67.
45 Freud, "Civilization and Its Discontents," 72.

The relationship of psychoanalysis to philosophy has changed significantly since Freud. Many writers set psychoanalytic thinking in dialogue with various philosophical methods and create a relationship between them – a relationship different from the one instituted by Freud. Tauber argues that in the express rejection of formal philosophy, Freud "eschewed significant self-reflection on his own intellectual commitments."[46] Thus, he opines that scrutiny of the Freudian project using philosophical tools may lead to important insights regarding psychoanalysis, and suggests its placement within its broadest intellectual and cultural contexts;[47] Mills argues that "psychology is the child of philosophy; although psychology has grown up and has flown from the nest, philosophy will always remain its Gracious Mother ('alma mater')";[48] while Orange contends that "psychoanalysts [...] are practicing philosophers. Doing philosophy every day, [...] [the] dialogue with great philosophers can help us to keep thinking and questioning."[49]

The attitude of psychoanalysis toward religious, spiritual, and mystical doctrines is also undergoing significant changes. In his study "Psychoanalytic Approaches to Faith," Gideon Lev describes the opening-up of psychoanalytic thinking to engagement and dialogue with a wide range of spiritual, religious, and mystical doctrines. Buddhism, Hinduism, Judaism, and Kabbalah are just a few examples of the doctrines and practices with which this type of dialogue has been maintained in recent decades.[50] After nearly a century in which the psychoanalytic establishment took a critical and reductive stance toward – or completely ignored – religion, spirituality, and faith, from the end of the twentieth century, psychoanalysis has been going through a process that renders it, in Lev's view, "spiritually sensitive."[51]

The Unique Encounter between Psychoanalytic Thinking and Steiner's Thinking

Steiner's philosophy is absent from the conventional repertoire of philosophical and spiritual theories with which psychoanalytic thinking conducts a dialogue. This is the case despite the common chronological, geographical, and cultural

---

46 Alfred I. Tauber, *Freud, The Reluctant Philosopher* (New Jersey: Princeton University Press, 2010), xiv.
47 Tauber, *Freud, The Reluctant Philosopher*, 1.
48 Jon Mills, *The Unconscious Abyss: Hegel's Anticipation of Psychoanalysis* (New York: State University of New York Press, 2002), 189.
49 Donna M. Orange, *Thinking for Clinicians; Philosophical Resources for Contemporary Psychoanalysis and the Humanist Psychotherapies* (New York and London: Routledge, 2010), 2.
50 Gideon Lev, "Denigration, Indifference, Fascination: Psychoanalytic Approaches to Faith" (Hebrew), Ma'arg: *The Israel Annual of Psychoanalysis* 3 (2012): 53–90.
51 Lev, "Denigration, Indifference, Fascination," 74.

contexts in which the two theories emerged. Freud and Steiner frequented the same circles in late nineteenth-century Vienna and shared a similar cultural environment, as well as a special veneration for the philosopher Franz Brentano, with whom both studied,[52] and a connection to a renowned acquaintance, Joseph Breuer.[53] Nonetheless, the only intersection between their doctrines appears in Steiner's sharp criticism of the conceptual and practical aspects of psychoanalysis, which he expressed in several of his lectures.[54]

This chapter argues that a dialogue between psychoanalytic thinking and Steiner's comprehensive theory bears potential for the fertilization of both disciplines.[55] It proposes the monism of Steiner's thinking as a unique solution to the psychoanalytic quest for a philosophical foundation that does not denote a contradiction or fissure between the subject and the world.[56] This paradigm's uniqueness is related, on the one hand, to the alternative it proposes to the dualism that entails a separation and a rift between "I" and "world," "spirit" and "matter," and "subject" and "object,"[57] as well as a juxtaposition of the "ideal" and "real" dimensions.[58] On the other hand, its

---

52 Patricia Herzog, "The Myth of Freud as Anti-Philosopher," in *Freud – Appraisals and Reappraisals: Contributions to Freud Studies,* vol. 2, ed. Paul E. Stepansky (New York and London: Routledge, 1988), 163–90, 181.
53 Steiner, *Autobiography; Chapters in the Course of My Life 1861–1907,* 28.
54 In various lectures on the subject, Steiner attacks Freud's view of the sexual impulse as the cause of an explanation for different mental states. The connection Freud makes between hysterical symptoms and unconscious sexual drive is, according to Steiner, rooted in examination and knowledge of the soul using unsuitable means of knowing. According to Steiner's claim, the attempt to explain and know the soul through unsuitable means of knowing is also found in Adlerian thinking and Jungian depth psychology. See Rudolf Steiner, *Freud, Jung & Spiritual Psychology,* trans. May Laird-Brown, ed. Sabine H. Seiler, and Richard Smoley (Great Barrington: Anthroposophic Press, 2001). Steiner maintains that the human soul must be examined through a perspective that relates to the spiritual dimension of human existence. See Rudolf Steiner, "The Mission of Anger," in *Metamorphoses of the Soul; Paths of Experience,* vol. 1, trans. C. Davy and C. von Arnim (Forest Row: Rudolf Steiner Press, 1983), 17–31.
55 The current chapter relates to the contribution of the dialogue between psychoanalytic thinking and Steiner's philosophical approach. A dialogue with different aspects of his anthroposophic method will be explored in other contexts.
56 Stolorow, Orange, and Atwood, who are identified with this quest, argue that at the basis of all schools of analytical thought is the doctrine of the Cartesian "isolated mind" (Robert D. Stolorow, Donna M. Orange and George E. Atwood, "Psychoanalysis without Descartes," *The International Journal of Psychoanalysis* 82, no. 6 (2001): 1263–66; Stolorow et al. "Cartesian and Post-Cartesian Trends in Relational Psychoanalysis," *Psychoanalytic Psychology* 18, no. 3 (2001a): 468–84. This doctrine divides the subjective world into "inside" and "outside" spheres, renders this division concrete, and describes the mind as an objective entity among the other objects of the world: as a "thinking thing," with an interiority full of content, the mind looks from within upon the world outside itself, from which it is estranged (Stolorow et al., 2001a, 469).
57 Steiner, *Philosophy of Spiritual Activity [Freedom],* 15.
58 Steiner, *Philosophy of Spiritual Activity [Freedom],* 80.

uniqueness is related to the fact that it offers an alternative to unitive theories such as Buddhism, with which psychoanalytic thinking has been engaged in a developing dialogue over the past decades.[59] In contradistinction to Buddhism, which proposes that reality constitutes a unity and the "I" is an illusory concept, Steiner's paradigm maintains the uniqueness of the "I" and a unified view of reality at one and the same time.

The Steinerian doctrine can also benefit from a dialogue with psychoanalytic thinking: as exemplified in his criticism of psychoanalysis, Steiner's doctrine underscores the importance of referring to the spiritual dimensions of man, but it ignores the importance of acknowledgment of various dimensions of the emotional experience and dynamic. This chapter argues that Steiner's framework lacks both attention to emotional processes and the creation of a basis for understanding and working with them. A dialogue with psychoanalytic thinking is essential, therefore, for filling this gap, and for creating a practice of psychological therapy based on this framework.

In what follows, the dialogue between psychoanalytic thinking and Steiner's "monism of thought" is accomplished by examining the implications of the latter philosophical approach for three psychoanalytic concepts – "projective identification," "transitional space," and "self-object"/"selfobject." In a number of ways, these concepts formulate the connection between the psyche and selfhood of an individual and that of another individual or external object. In Steiner's terms, they constitute a distinctive, though suffuse, expression of a philosophical view regarding the relationship between "man" and "world." In practice, each of these concepts subverts conceptions describing this relationship in terms of separation and difference. Steiner's unique unitive perspective is proposed in the following as a philosophical foundation in which it is possible to anchor different dimensions of these concepts.

Steiner's Monism of Thought as a Foundation for Psychoanalytic Conceptualization

Monism of Thought and Projective Identification

In his essay "On Projective Identification," Ogden holds it to the detriment of psychoanalytic thinking that a concept as important as projective identification remains one of the most loosely defined and incompletely understood

---

59 Erich Fromm, "Psychoanalysis and Zen Buddhism," in *Zen Buddhism & Psychoanalysis*, ed. D.T. Suzuki, Erich Fromm, and Richard De Martino (London: Souvenir Press [Educational and Academic], 1974), 77–141; D. T. Suzuki, "Lectures on Zen Buddhism," in *Zen Buddhism & Psychoanalysis*, ed. Erich Fromm, D. T. Suzuki, and Richard De Martino (London: Souvenir Press [Educational and Academic], 1974), 1–76; Anthony Molino, *The Couch and the Tree: Dialogues in Psychoanalysis and Buddhism* (New York: North Point Press, 1998).

psychoanalytic conceptualizations.[60] The current study argues that basing the concept of projective identification on Steiner's philosophy may enable a clearer definition, as well as a better understanding of the processes and mechanisms it indicates.

As a mechanism with a communicative function and a real impact on the consciousness of the other[61] – as it is described by Klein's successors,[62] as well as in her own "On Identification" (1955)[63] – projective identification requires a philosophical foundation that notes the influences of one individual's processes of consciousness on the other. The unified worldview constituted in Steiner's philosophy is proposed as such a framework.

Steiner's philosophy describes "thinking" not only as a basis for man's faculty of consciousness, but also as the spiritual dimension on which the existence of man and the world are founded and that constitutes their unity. As "monism of thought," this viewpoint describes the lack of distinction between human beings and creates a framework for understanding the actual connection between the various contents of their consciousnesses.

The choice to base the term "projective identification" on Steiner's philosophy establishes the link created in Bion's writing between projective identification and thinking and its development.[64] The anchoring of the possibility of transferring elements of consciousness between human beings within the unity of the world of consciousness creates a basis for understanding the process wherein thoughts which are intolerable for the infant are transferred to the mother. This possibility facilitates, in Bion's terms, the infant's capacity for thinking, that is, the infant's ability to make use of sense data as alpha-elements after having been converted by the mother's alpha-function.[65] In combining Bion's and Steiner's approaches, one can say

---

60 Thomas H. Ogden, "On Projective Identification," *International Journal of Psychoanalysis* 60 (1979): 357–73, 357.
61 In other words, not only as a concept that points to an intrapsychic process related to unconscious fantasy, as first defined by Klein in 1946 (Melanie Klein, "Notes on Some Schizoid Mechanisms," *International Journal of Psychoanalysis* 27 [1946]: 99–110), but "as one that has an actual impact on the mental reactions [...] of the other" (Durban and Roth in Melanie Klein, *Selected Writings*, vol. 2 [Hebrew], eds. Joshua Durban and Merav Roth, trans. Orah Zilberstein [Tel Aviv: Bookworm, 2013], 213).
62 Durban and Roth in Melanie Klein, *Selected Writings*, 212.
63 In which she writes: "One part of Fabian literally leaves his self and enters into his victim, an event which in both parties is accompanied by strong physical sensations" (Melanie Klein, "On Identification," in *The Writings of Melanie Klein, Vol. III: Envy and Gratitude and Other Works 1946–1963* (New York: The Free Press, 1975), 141–47, 166.
64 "The activity we know as 'thinking' was in origin a procedure for unburdening the psyche of accretions of stimuli and the mechanism is that which has been described by Melanie Klein as projective identification" (Wilfred R. Bion, *Learning from Experience* [London and New York: Routledge Taylor and Francis Group, 1962, 31]).
65 Wilfred R. Bion, "The Psycho-Analytic Study of Thinking," *International Journal of Psychoanalysis* 43 (1962): 306–10, 308.

that the mother's ability to think thoughts that cannot be thought by her child – and which are transferred to her by way of the unity of thinking – enables the development of the child's capacity to think.

Monism of Thought and the Transitional Space

Winnicott's well-known terms "transitional object" and "transitional phenomena" – which point to an intermediate area "to which inner reality and external life both contribute"[66]– were received generously in the psychoanalytic community, as Winnicott himself testifies.[67] However, according to Kolka, their conceptual background and widespread implications barely registered in the psychoanalytic consciousness.[68] Erel claims that the broad use of the idea of the existence of "transitional space" – of which these terms are specific iterations – does not necessarily attest to the idea's clarity: "it can even be said that in this case the opposite is true […] the potential space is one of the more puzzling and complex ideas in Winnicott's theory."[69]

This chapter argues that Steiner's monism of thought constitutes a philosophical foundation for the concept "transitional space." The existence of a common and unified world of ideas asserted by Steiner's philosophical approach creates a basis for understanding the Winnicottian term: this "world" is, according to Steiner, the origin – or, paraphrasing Winnicott, "the place"[70] – of all ideas, concepts, notions, and thoughts.[71] This space is also the origin from which stems the uniqueness of every individual – defined, according to Steiner, by way of the various intuitions that the individual receives from this unified spiritual world.[72]

The anchoring of the concept "transitional space" in Steiner's "unified world of ideas" serves as a basis for the potential and necessary existence of a "space" that is both common and private – a space that is the basis for both the creation of a connection with the world[73] and the experience of the self.[74] This type of anchoring establishes this space as the origin and place of

---

66 Donald W. Winnicott, "Transitional Objects and Transitional Phenomena – A Study of the First Not-Me Possession," *International Journal of Psychoanalysis* 34 (1953): 89–97, 90.
67 Donald W. Winnicott, *Playing and Reality* (London and New York: Routledge, 1999), 40.
68 Ra'anan Kulka, "Foreword: Revolutionary Continuity in Psychoanalysis (Hebrew)," in Donald W. Winnicott, *Playing and Reality*, ed. Ra'anan Kulka (Tel Aviv: Am Oved, 1995), 9–30, 22.
69 Osnat Erel, "The Secret of His Charm" (Hebrew), in *True Self, False Self*, ed. Emanuel Berman (Tel Aviv: Am Oved Publishers, 2009), 9–21, 14.
70 Winnicott, *Playing and Reality*, 41, 100.
71 Steiner, *Philosophy of Spiritual Activity [Freedom]*, 148–59.
72 Steiner, *Philosophy of Spiritual Activity [Freedom]*, 152.
73 Winnicott, *Playing and Reality*, 13.
74 Winnicott, *Playing and Reality*, 54.

play, art, philosophy, science, religion, and culture;[75] the placement of the transitional space as an intermediate area between the external reality and the inner world;[76] the universality of the phenomena related to the transitional space;[77] and the description of the developmental process of the experience of selfhood and the ability for objective knowledge springing from the unified being and experience.[78]

From the dialogue with Steiner's philosophy, one can understand the developmental process described by Winnicott as a transition between a state of being in the unity of thinking and a state in which thinking also functions in individual consciousness. At the beginning of life, just as later in life, the individual is part of the all-encompassing unity of thought. At the stage where a thinking consciousness does not yet exist in the infant, the infant is in an experience of unity with its mother and with the world, and therefore, in Winnicottian terms, is incapable of object-relating and the use of an object.[79] These only become possible when, during the child's development, "the thinking activity of the soul" – as Steiner calls it – appears; knowledge of this activity allows one to "understand what is meant by knowledge of something."[80]

The encounter between the terms "transitional space" and Steiner's "monism of thought" allows for an inspection of these two thinkers' attitudes toward the dimensions of subjectivity and objectivity. Winnicott's theory identifies the experience of unity that characterizes early life with subjectivity, and assigns objectivity to the stage at which the infant's merger with the object ends.[81] Steiner's philosophy, in contrast, delineates the connection between unity and separateness on the one hand, and subjectivity and objectivity on the other hand, differently: in a manner that strengthens Winnicott's logic, the knowledge of and objective attitude toward things are described in terms of the activity of thinking in man's consciousness – that is, as a situation in which they are aware of the separateness between them and the world. However, this separateness is a subjective state for Steiner: "The subject does not think because it is a subject, rather it conceives itself to be a subject because it can think."[82] Arriving at objective knowledge is possible, according to Steiner, through the unifying

---

75 Winnicott, *Playing and Reality*, 14.
76 Winnicott, *Playing and Reality*, 2.
77 Winnicott, *Playing and Reality*, 41.
78 Winnicott, *Playing and Reality*, 107, 151.
79 Winnicott, *Playing and Reality*, 86–94.
80 Steiner, *Philosophy of Spiritual Activity [Freedom]*, 10.
81 Winnicott, *Playing and Reality*, 107.
82 Steiner, *Philosophy of Spiritual Activity [Freedom]*, 46.

activity of thinking – by way of which man "embraces himself and the rest of the world."[83]

The primary state is described by Winnicott as subjective, and is contingent on conceptualization: objectivity, which in his view is connected to perception,[84] develops from within this state,[85] when the infant progresses to the stage of "separating out the mother from the self."[86] In contrast, Steiner asserts subjectivity of perception and objectivity of conceptualization: While for Winnicott, the infant separates the object from itself, for Steiner, the infant separates itself from the object. Subjectivity, according to Steiner, is related to the experience of separateness produced by thinking, while objective knowing is linked to the development of thinking toward an essential knowledge of the unity between the individual's unique selfhood and the world.

The dialogue with Steiner's monism of thought enables the grounding of the Winnicottian term in an ontology that establishes the existence of the transitional space as a reality within which the world, every human being's unique selfhood, and the activity of consciousness originates. The external and internal realities are anchored in this actual space in a way that shows objective and subjective experience to be different aspects of its realness.

Between Monism of Thought and "Self-Object" and "Selfobject"

The terms "self-object" and "selfobject" are at the foundation of and express the Kohutian theory regarding the relationship between the self as a subject and another individual, who is perceived as an object into which narcissistic energy is invested.[87] The dialogue with Steiner's monism of thought embeds these concepts in a philosophical framework that describes the experiential and ontological dimensions of the relationship between the self and the object, as well as the connection between these dimensions. In addition, this philosophical paradigm provides a justification for the transition from the concept "self-object" – which refers to the relationship between both its parts in terms of the experience of the object as part of the self[88] – to the concept "selfobject," which describes the relationship between them as necessary for the formation of the self.[89]

---

83 Steiner, *Philosophy of Spiritual Activity [Freedom]*, 47.
84 Winnicott, *Playing and Reality*, 151.
85 Winnicott, *Playing and Reality*, 13–14.
86 Winnicott, *Playing and Reality*, 107.
87 Heinz Kohut, *The Analysis of the Self: A Systematic Approach to the Psychoanalytic Treatment of Narcissistic Personality Disorders* (Chicago and London: The University of Chicago Press, 2009), 326.
88 Kohut, *Analysis of the Self*, xiv.
89 Heinz Kohut, *How Does Analysis Cure?* ed. Arnold Goldberg and Paul Stepansky (Chicago and London: The University of Chicago Press, 2013), 51–52.

The relationship between the self, the subject, and the object is derived, according to Steiner's theory of knowledge, from the reciprocal acts of thinking and observation in human knowing. When man receives an impression of something, he regards the thing as given and as separate from him; when thinking is directed upon the observation, he has consciousness of objects. As a thinker, he experiences himself as active; when he directs his thinking toward this activity, he defines himself as subject. The conception of the self comes into being as self-consciousness when man contemplates his nature as a thinking subject. Thinking is located, according to this theory, beyond the subject and object: It is that which creates these two concepts.[90]

This account of the relationship between impressions and concepts allows us to examine man's perception of himself as self and as subject – as well as his perception of the other individual as object – through a perspective that aims to identify the realness of these impressions. Steiner's monism of thought suggests that while the impression of the self delineates man within defined boundaries,[91] the reality of this impression belongs to the entirety of the "universal world process."[92] The reality of the rest of the impressions – which man defines by way of his thinking of them as objects – belongs to the entirety of the same process, so that self and object, or self and other, constitute real unity.

Steiner's philosophy differentiates between the real unity of the subject and object and their definition as separate concepts: This definition is created through the capacity for thinking, on the basis of the separateness inherent in the impression. This distinction enables us to relate to the transition in the Kohutian conceptualization – from "self-object" to "self-object" – as a transition from a concept that denotes the experiential dimensions of the relationship between the self and the other, to a concept that denotes the unified dimensions of the ontological connection between them.

The initial definition of the concept "self-object" refers to the experiential dimension of the relationship to the object in which narcissistic libido is invested. Such an object is experienced as part of the self, the implication being that in reality it is indeed separate from the self, and therefore it is an "object," but is not experienced as such. This definition – coined by Kohut in his monograph *The Analysis of the Self* (1971) – is related to the view that relates to self-objects as archaic objects, positions their formation and function in early childhood, and defines healthy development in terms of their internalization and assimilation into the mature personality.[93] In Kohut's next book – *The Restoration of the Self* (1977) – a footnote expresses a change in this perception: "The psychologically healthy adult

---

90 Steiner, *Philosophy of Spiritual Activity [Freedom]*, 46.
91 Steiner, *Philosophy of Spiritual Activity [Freedom]*, 76.
92 Steiner, *Philosophy of Spiritual Activity [Freedom]*, 92.
93 Kohut, *Analysis of the Self*, 26–28.

continues to need the mirroring of the self by self-objects [...] No implication of immaturity or psychopathology must, therefore, be derived from the fact that another person is used as a self-object."[94]

The implications of this view, according to which man continues to need the self-object throughout his entire life, lead to the conceptual shift from "self-object" to "selfobject," in which the hyphen connecting the self to and separating it from the object is omitted. This shift – which takes place in Kohut's *Self Psychology and the Humanities* (1978) – establishes the term "selfobject" to mark the need for the permanent existence of "a matrix of emphatic selfobjects that is held to be as much a prerequisite of psychological existence as oxygen for biological life."[95]

In its first incarnation, the Kohutian framework maintains the distinction between the self and the object or an-other. From a dialogue with Steiner's philosophical approach, it can be anchored in a view according to which the conceptualization of separateness is established on the level of the experience and the impression, with its inherent limitations. Kohut's later concept, by contrast, can be anchored in the ontological dimension of Steiner's approach and his description of the real unity of human beings with each other and with the world.

By relinquishing the hyphen between "self" and "object," the Kohutian paradigm transitions from a concept that relates to the unity of the self and the object within the experiential dimension alone, to a concept that denotes their real unity. This process receives a philosophical justification from Steiner's monism of thought, which establishes the distinction between the dimensions of the experience and the dimensions of the reality as a reversal of the distinction upon which Kohut bases the first concept, in which the hyphen separates the self from the object. While Kohut begins with the assumption that in the real dimension, the self and the object are separate from one another, and that their unity exists in the experiential dimension, Steiner's approach enables the argument that their unity – which is manifested in the hyphen-less concept – is real, and that their separateness exists only on the experiential level.

Summary

This chapter compared the language-games within which the concepts "projective identification," "transitional space," and "self-object"/"selfobject"

---

94 Heinz Kohut, *The Restoration of the Self* (Chicago and London: The University of Chicago Press, 2009), 188.
95 Heinz Kohut, *Self Psychology and the Humanities: Reflections on a New Psychoanalytic Approach*, ed. Charles B. Strozier (New York and London: W. W. Norton and Company, 1985), 74.

function to the language-game established by Steiner's philosophical approach. The fundamental worldview of this approach describes the unity of man and world and anchors this unity in the same dimension that distinguishes every human as "I" Steiner terms this dimension, which suffuses reality in its totality, "thought" or "spirit." Steiner's monism of thought was proposed as a philosophical foundation for three psychoanalytic concepts that cannot be based on a conception of absolute distinction between one human being and another.

The dialogue between the psychoanalytic terms and this view enables an ontological approach to the phenomenon indicated by each term: The foundation of "projective identification" in the conception of unity of consciousness explained the ability of one individual's consciousness to influence another; the placement of the "unified world of ideas" described in Steiner's ontology at the basis of the Winnicottian concept "transitional space" enabled us to relate to it as a unified space that at once connects between human beings and constitutes the origin of their uniqueness; the Kohutian concepts, which link the self and the object, were based on the dialectic between the real unity of human beings with one another and the experience of separateness and self-consciousness.

In terms of Gadamer's hermeneutics, the dialogue between psychoanalytic thinking and Steiner's unitive framework enables a fusion of horizons between the two, as well as the creation of a language based on the encounter. I claim that the uniqueness of this language is related to the possibility it establishes of relating to the real dimensions of interpersonal processes and events, as well as to the relationship between the reality of these processes and the ways in which they are experienced. This language allows for the description of interpersonal and intrapsychic processes in terms of the "thinking" that creates the real spiritual unity of human beings with one another, as well as the uniqueness of every human as an "I"; the experience of human beings' separateness and consciousness of self; and their potential for essential knowledge of themselves and of the world.

Chapter 5

Malfunctions in the Symbolic Space
A Psychoanalytic-Semiotic View[1]

Sharon Strasburg

Symbolization is one of the most influential mechanisms of human existence. It is linked to psychological processes related to development, pathology, and psychic structuring, as well as to philosophical questions associated with the production of meaning. It constitutes a key component in both the capacity for complex comprehension of the world and the formation of the individual's subjectivity, as well as in the individual's awareness of the subjectivity of the other. The capacity for symbolization is necessary for interpersonal communication and for the ability to cope with absence and separation.

This chapter aims to explore situations in which the symbolic space is disrupted, thereby giving rise to a malfunction. This malfunction, in turn, undermines the potential for a full and rich life given that the attempt to represent reality has failed. Perception of reality is experienced as concrete fact, not as a construction or as one of multiple options. The impairment of this ability means the impairment of basic mental functioning, which may cause significant human suffering.

The chapter proposes that the psychoanalytic literature tends to relate to the symbol, and subsequently to symbolic malfunction, in two contrasting ways – perception of the malfunction in symbolization as a difficulty in producing defense, as opposed to a view of the malfunction as the destruction of the symbolic link. Still, the question arises as to whether these approaches indeed negate one another. Semiotics, as propagated by philosopher C. S. Peirce,[2] sheds a different light on this dichotomy, and enables the proposition of a spectrum of a wide range of potential avenues for examining symbolic malfunctions. Thus, this chapter offers an integrative psychoanalytic-semiotic

---

1 This chapter is part of a Ph.D. thesis carried out under the supervision of Dr. Dorit Lemberger in the Program for Hermeneutics and Culture Studies at Bar-Ilan University. I wish to thank Dr. Lemberger and the program for their professional and financial support.
2 Charles Sanders Peirce, *The Collected Papers of Charles Sanders Peirce*, reproducing vols. I-VI, Charles Hartshorne & Paul Weiss (eds.), Cambridge, MA: Harvard University Press, 1931–1935; vols. VII-VIII, Arthur W. Burks (ed.) (same publisher, 1958).

model for conceptualizing malfunctions in symbolization. Moreover, its application in therapy will be demonstrated by way of possible clinical interventions based on different types of malfunctions.

Symbolic Malfunctions in Psychoanalysis

From the psychoanalytic literature dealing with symbolization, it is possible to identify two essentially different ways of relating to symbol formation. Although both approaches view the growth of the symbolic capacity as a developmental achievement, their origins and aims differ, and from each a different understanding of malfunctions in symbolization is derived.

Malfunction as Difficulty in Creating Defense

The first vantage point stems from Freud's perception of the symbol as a means of distancing from anxiety-arousing content. His research on symbolism focused on the dream, and he argued that the censorship of the dream employs symbolism to render the dream incomprehensible.[3] Hysteria, as well, constitutes a symbolic product that distances the core traumatic or conflictual events from consciousness. The symbolic system is, of course, unconscious to the individual, and therapy focuses on translating the symbol back to consciousness. Jones's notion that all that is symbolic is repressed is a development of this view.[4]

Melanie Klein, and in her wake, Hanna Segal, continued this line of thought when describing the symbolization that takes place in the first months of life as a healthy action of the ego whose purpose is to cope with anxieties in relation to the object.[5,6] When during the symbolization process, something turns into something else that symbolizes it, its initial threatening status is neutralized. Klein and Segal described the "symbolic equation" – a situation that characterizes the paranoid-schizoid position in which there is no clear distinction between the symbol and symbolized, that is, symbolic objects are experienced as identical to the object. With the development of the depressive position, a mature symbolic capacity develops in which the distinction between symbol and object becomes possible, and the symbol

---

[3] Sigmund Freud, "Introductory Lectures on Psycho-Analysis," *The Standard Edition of the Complete Psychological Works of Sigmund Freud*, Volume XV (1915–1916): Introductory Lectures on Psycho-Analysis (Parts I and II), 1–240.

[4] Erenst Jones, "The theory of symbolism" in *Papers on Psychoanalysis*. London: Bailliere, 1916.

[5] Melanie Klein, "The importance of symbol-formation in the development of the ego," *International Journal of Psychoanalysis* 11 (1930): 24–39.

[6] Hanna Segal, "Notes on symbol formation," *International Journal of Psychoanalysis* 38 (1957): 391–97.

becomes a representation of the object. Thus, the defense becomes more sophisticated when the distance between the symbol and the symbolized is greater.

This approach views the development of the symbolic capacity as an achievement whose significance is the development of a defense against the encounter with elements that the psyche struggles to contain. Malfunction in symbolization indicates an inability to carry out the necessary distancing from the symbol, thereby sustaining perception of the symbol and symbolized as identical. This type of malfunction leads to a surge of anxiety, and the subject is forced to utilize mental mechanisms, such as projective identification, in order to eliminate and cast these elements from their psyche. Undoubtedly, this stance proves extremely valuable for the psychoanalyst as it constitutes a basis for formulating therapeutic interventions. While working in analysis on dreams, free associations, and images, as well as in play therapy with children, it is extremely important to relate to the symbol as defense and try to reveal unconscious content. Nevertheless, focusing on the repressed symbol alone entails a limiting of both the range of possibilities in which the symbol can be used, and the various possible malfunctions.

Malfunction as Destruction of the Connection

Beginning in the 1950s, there arose an essentially different approach to symbolization, which viewed it not only as the production of a substitute for impulse gratification, but also as a basic characteristic of the mind. This approach pointed to the connection the symbol produces between detached parts and perceived it as a bridge between the interpreting subject and the object.[7] From this point of view, symbolic malfunction expresses the need to reject the connection. The individual senses that the connection threatens their mental wholeness, and that they must turn to concrete forms of thinking as an escape. This is a fundamentally different approach than that proposed by Freud, according to which the use of symbolization itself constitutes defense and from Klein's position which views the symbol as a means for creating distance from the anxiety-provoking object.

Several psychoanalytic theorists have pointed to the symbolic malfunction as an absence of connection. Winnicott described how the psychic structure produces this detachment.[8] When the infant's spontaneous gestures are not sympathetically accepted by the mother, the false self is forced to split from

---

7 Bonomi, Carlo. & Borgogno, Franco, "The broken symbol: The fear of the mind of the other in the symbolic history of the individual," *International Forum of Psychoanalysis*, 15 (2006): 169–77.
8 Donald, W. Winnicott, *Playing and Reality.* London and New York: Routledge, 1971.

the true self and defend it in order to protect it. The infant lives, but in a compliant fashion, lacking spontaneity. The absence of the connection to the true self is also the origin of the symbolic malfunction.

> Where there is a high degree of split between the true self and the false self which hides the true self, there is found a poor capacity for using symbols, and a poverty of cultural living. Instead of cultural pursuits one observes in such persons extreme restlessness, an inability to concentrate, and a need to collect impingements from external reality so that the living-time of the individual can be filled by reactions to these impingements.[9]

Following Winnicott, Ogden positioned the development of the symbol in the potential space, which exists as a transitional space between concrete adherence to the object and its symbolization.[10] According to Ogden, if at first the symbol and the symbolized are not differentiated from one another, later the ability to differentiate between the thought and the object of thought develops, which requires an interpreting subject. He described a triangular model of the symbol, the symbolized, and the thinker, which shares points of similarity with Peirce's model as described later in this chapter. Derived from this triangular view is Ogden's conception of symbolic malfunctions: "Potential space ceases to exist as any two of these three elements become differentiated: the thinker and the symbol, the symbol and the symbolized, or the thinker and the object of thought (the symbolized)."[11] The malfunction is defined, therefore, as the product of detachment in the symbolic connection.

Bion proposed an additional perspective on disruption in the production of the symbol in his paper "Attacks on Linking,"[12] in which he referred to the attack on the actual function of the link, in other words, an attack on verbal thought itself. In his opinion, the origin of this disorder is double: there is a congenital tendency for destructiveness and envy, supplemented by the environment which does not enable the use of projective identification. As a result of the attack on the link, the capacity for curiosity is destroyed and the possibility for learning is blocked.

Hans Loewald challenged Jones's claim that everything symbolic is repressed and argued that what is repressed is not the impulse but rather the

---

9 Donald, W. Winnicott, "Ego distortion in terms of true and false self," in *The Maturational Processes and the Facilitating Environment*, 140–52. London: Hogarth Press, 1965, 150.
10 Thomas. H. Ogden, *The Matrix of the Mind*. New Jersey, London: Jason Aronson Inc, 1986.
11 Ibid., 225.
12 Wilfred. R. Bion, "Attacks on linking," *International Journal of Psychoanalysis,* 40 (1959): 308–15.

link between the symbol and the symbolized.[13] Mental health, in his view, is contingent on an open channel between "primary process," in which language is manifested in the bodily experience, and "secondary process," which is constituted in a language prone to generalization. When proper conditions in development are lacking, there is a detachment between the sensory and the abstract, or alternatively, there appears a difficulty in differentiating between the entities, which leads to psychotic or regressive speech.

Other theorists also focused on the symbolic malfunction as the destruction of the link. Freidman and Russell suggested that in contrast to symbolization characterized by linkage, "de-symbolization" is characterized by equivalence, which facilitates a reduction of possible choices.[14] In a similar vein, Target and Fonagy proposed that when the mother reacts to her infant by way of a precise reflection of reality, not in a symbolized fashion (a situation they call "psychic equivalence"), the infant learns that the inner reality is identical to the external reality, and as a result, there develops a rigidity and difficulty in tolerating a different way of thinking than that of the subject.[15]

These theoretical conceptions point, then, to a malfunction that stems from the existence of a disconnect in the symbolic link. The emphasis is on the individual's need to create a detachment as a way to defend vulnerable parts of the self. The role of psychoanalytic therapy is, therefore, to create the conditions to produce the link between the detached parts.

Thus, one can see that each of the two contrasting psychoanalytic approaches to malfunctions in symbolization outlined above tends to focus upon a single aspect of symbolization and to present its conception as exclusive. As a result, it appears that they both retain a certain lack. The classic approach ignores situations in which the individual avoids the connection that the symbol creates, while the second approach ignores situations in which the symbol indeed serves to disguise anxiety-evoking contents. This points to the need for a broader classification of symbolic malfunctions that takes both approaches into account. We suggest viewing them not as contradictory but as different points on a wider spectrum.

Moreover, the review of the psychoanalytic literature reveals a considerable deficiency in psychoanalytic approaches dealing with symbolization. Despite the fact that psychoanalysis is a "talking cure" it largely lacks

---

13 Hans. W. Loewald, *Sublimation: Inquiries into Theoretical Psychoanalysis*. New Haven: Yale University Press, 1988.
14 Freedman, Norbert & Russell, Jared, "Symbolization of the analytic discourse," *Psychoanalysis and Contemporary Thought*, 26 no. 1 (2003): 39–87.
15 Mary Target & Peter Fonagy, "Playing with reality: II. The development of psychic reality from a theoretical perspective," *International Journal of Psychoanalysis*, 77 (1996): 459–79.

acknowledgment of the symbolization process as inherently related to issues of language. The emphasis here is not on the ways in which language is used, but on examination of the semiotic nature of the mechanisms at the basis of symbolization. Thus, the need arises for a comprehensive discussion on symbolization which also takes into account its linguistic nature, that is to say presents a detailed account of the symbol's components and means to distinguish between them.[16] This new way of thinking will enable a broader classification of symbol types, and subsequently, of types of symbolic malfunctions. Beyond its theoretical contribution, this type of interdisciplinary model also unlocks for the therapist a variety of possibilities for understanding the patient struggling with symbolization.

The Contribution of Semiotics for Understanding Symbolization

Theories from the field of the philosophy of language are the obvious choice for studying processes of symbolization. C. S. Peirce, a pioneer of philosophical pragmatism, established the field of semiotics, which endeavored to explore the ways in which symbols are produced and differentiated from other signs. Today, semiotics constitutes a field of research that serves as a major hermeneutic apparatus in social studies and the humanities.

For Peirce, at the basis of understanding the concept of the symbol is the sign: "all thought is in signs."[17] To understand symbols, he delves into the manner in which the individual perceives the world and creates meaning. He defined a symbol as "something which stands to somebody for something,"[18] and thus referred to the symbol in its broadest sense – from diagrams, metaphors, and symptoms to symbols, texts, and even ideas. In contrast to de-Saussure,[19] who proposed a dyadic theory of signs, Peirce created a *triadic theory*; in other words, he argued that the symbolic process requires three components. This position is similar to Segal's,[20] and later Ogden's,[21] according to which the triad is at the basis of symbolization. Winnicott's term "transitional space" also echoes Peirce's triadic conception, because it exists in the third space created between the mother and the

---

16 Dorit Lemberger, "'Love is a curious mixture of opposites': The Symbolic Function of Language in Psychoanalysis and Its Use in a Study of Amos Oz's A Tale of Love and Darkness," *The Soul Beetle: Interdisciplinary Perspectives in Psychoanalysis*. Tel-Aviv: Resling, 2020, 17–52.
17 Peirce, *Collected papers*, § 5.253.
18 Peirce, *Collected papers*, § 2.228.
19 Ferdinand Saussure, *Course in General Linguistics*, trans: Wade Baskin. New York: Philosophical Library, 1959.
20 Segal, 1957.
21 Ogden, 1986.

infant, between reality and imagination, and between inside and outside. Peirce divided the levels of consciousness in three: firstness – the physical, sensory experience through which we perceive the world; secondness – the encounter with reality itself which produces reaction; and thirdness, which is the abstract, symbolic level.

In his comprehensive and unprecedented study on the theory of signs, Peirce created several divisions in order to explore in-depth the ways symbols function in the world. These divisions constitute an enormous contribution to scholarship from two important perspectives: first, they present a thorough investigation of the characteristics of symbols, including their different types, components, and the related states of consciousness. Second, for researchers from various disciplines, the various categories constitute fertile terrain for research and provide accessible tools for examining the performance of symbols and signs in additional content worlds. The first division is between symbol types:

Icon – a sign linked to its object in terms of similarity or imitation (for instance, a map and the terrain signified in it). The comparison that Freud presented in the interpretation of symbols in dreams based on similarity ("the essence of this symbolic relation is that it is a comparison")[22] is based on this type of relationship. It constitutes a two-dimensional sign which presents a neutral, not interpretive, relationship. However, this relationship is only one of many proposed by Peirce.

Index – a sign connected to the object by way of a causal physical connection, either real or imagined (for example, smoke signifies fire). The indexical sign is based on contiguity. In Peirce's words, "Psychologically, the action of indices depends upon association by contiguity, and not upon association by resemblance or upon intellectual operation."[23] The index calls attention to the object, however, not by way of verbal communication. We can only follow the index, not control it, and it does not enable us to imagine that reality is as we would want it to be. In Muller's words, the index "insults infantile grandiosity."[24] In being irreversible, the index underscores that we must suffer loss, in a manner that calls to mind the achievements of the depressive position described by Klein.

Symbol – the most developed relationship between the object and the sign. This is a sign whose meaning constitutes a matter of social convention, and which is based upon a relationship of convention or repetition (for instance, the scales of justice). The prime example for the sign is, obviously, a word. While its phonetic manifestation is arbitrary, it takes on its meaning by way of its being agreed upon by a social group.

---

22 Freud, Introductory lectures, 152.
23 Peirce, *Collected papers*, § 2.306.
24 Muller, 1996, 60.

An additional division proposed by Peirce is related to the components of the sign: **sign** is the representation of a concept (verbal, graphic, etc.); **object** is the subject of the sign; and **interpretant**, which is Peirce's important addition, is the concept created in the mind as a result of its encounter with the sign, its meaning. The importance of the interpretant's role stems from its being a mediator between the other two, in such a way that the three parts are linked to each other.

These distinctions can be extremely valuable for psychoanalysis when exploring processes in the symbolic development, for instance, in the context of Winnicott's aforementioned theory on the development of the false self. In semiotic terms, the infant's spontaneous gestures can be construed as signs to which the mother responds. When it is possible for the infant to express their self in a live and spontaneous fashion, the sign will constitute an index, one that points to the infant's intentions and feelings. However, when the mother replaces these gestures with a gesture of her own, and the infant responds with a "compliant response," the gesture becomes an icon, an imitation of the mother. The intact developmental process from icon to index is reversed and its fate for the infant is destructive. In fact, instead of receiving the infant's signs as potentials for a range of interpretants, and assisting the infant in broadening the creative boundaries of the true self, the mother forces upon the infant an interpretant of her own for the sign.

In the last few years, several psychoanalytic writers have acknowledged the value of semiotic thinking for comprehending the development of symbolization in all its aspects. However, they tend to focus on intact symbolization or on a general understanding of the symbolic malfunction as an expression of a malfunction within the normal developmental process. Thus, Muller formulated what he called "developmental semiotics" and proposed a Peircean reading of the developmental process in semiotic terms.[25] According to him, the mother-child relationship is sustained by a cultural system of signs. In the course of development, the infant gradually acquires a greater ability to point at objects and develop a growing semiotic capacity to move from iconicity to a wider usage of the index, and finally to the use of symbolic language. Thus, for example, in Oliver Sacks's famous interview with autistic scientist Temple Grandin, he responds with amazement to her advanced ability to understand icons and indices in communication with animals. However, he also called attention to a deficiency in her ability to communicate with human beings as a result of a difficulty in perceiving culturally determined symbols or social conventions.[26] This discernment of malfunctions in "developmental

---

25 John. P. Muller, *Beyond the Psychoanalytic Dyad: Developmental Semiotics in Freud, Peirce, and Lacan*. New York: Routledge, 1996.
26 Ibid., 62.

semiotics" demonstrates how Peirce's distinctions can help determine the type of the symbolic malfunction.

Keinanen proposed the term "psychosemiosis," which assumes that the human psyche grows by way of sign coding in reciprocal interaction with significant others.[27] His emphasis is on the capacity for self-regulation which is formed in the primary relationship and internalized through symbolization. Utilizing Peirce's terms, Keinanen proposed different modalities of experience which generate meaning for information channeled to the infant from both within and outside their body. If the psychosemiotic process is delayed, mental disorders will appear. In working with borderline personality disorder, upon which Keinanen focuses, the therapist conceptualizes experiences for the patient in words, and thus gradually, the patient unravels their self from the constraints of the immediate experience. Thus, the patient's capacity for self-regulation grows, thereby internalizing the image of the therapist in a symbolic fashion which is not contingent on the therapist's physical presence.

Philips presented another application of Peirce's triadic terms for understanding the development of symbolic discourse, arguing that at the beginning of life every component of the triad is embodied in a *real human being*.[28] In the developing discourse in the mother-father-child triad three types of pathological situations may arise. First, when the mother does not enable the presence of the father as third, so that he is absent both as semiotic object and interpreter, the language will remain subjective (in the relationship between the mother and the infant), and it will be impossible to speak of something truly external to the speakers. Second, when the parents fail to render the infant an object of *their* discourse, the infant will not be able to experience their self as interpreter. The third pathological situation is that in which the interaction between the infant and the father in which they relate to the mother as object is not feasible, and subsequently, the infant will not have an experience of the mother as an object separate from them, or as a subject in and of herself.

It appears then, that Peirce's classifications have been used in several important ways for the examination of symbolic development. However, the differentiation between different types of malfunction remains unsolved. This paper proposes to utilize Peirce's distinctions to create a comprehensive model of malfunctions and suggest an alternative paradigm for relating to the dichotomy so far described in psychoanalysis – not as two exclusive

---

27 Matti Keinanen, "The psychosemiotic model for understanding the body–mind continuum: Implications for epistemic and psychotherapeutic applications," in *Making Our Ideas Clear: Pragmatism in Psychoanalysis,* edited by Philip Rosenbaum, 15–242. Information Age Publishing Inc, 2015.
28 James Philips, "Peircean reflections on psychotic discourses," in *Peirce, Semiotics and Psychoanalysis,* edited by John Muller & Joseph. Brent, 16–36. Baltimore: The Johns Hopkins University Press, 2000.

depictions of malfunction, which contradict one another, but as possibilities located on a broader spectrum. This expansion leans on Peirce's notion that there are multiple possibilities for describing the relationship between sign and signified, as mentioned above.

Moreover, Peirce's semiotics describes the interpretive process of the sign as infinite. Every sign can produce an additional sign in the interpreter's mind thereby instigating the formation of an infinite chain of signs: "We here see thoughts determining and causing other thoughts, and a chain of reasoning or of association is produced. But the beginning and the end of this chain, are not distinctly perceived."[29] Put differently, each time a sign appears, and the individual links it to an object, an interpretant is produced. However, this meaning can become itself a sign for the next interpretant, and it is in this manner that the individual's interpretive capability can be broadened. Hence, the symbolic malfunction is also part of the infinite chain of signs. An individual fails to signify something, and this failure leads to a certain interpretant, that is, to the construction of the meaning of the situation. This meaning can, in turn, produce a new sign, which will lead to a new malfunction, or alternatively, to a departure from the malfunction cycle.

For example, a patient's friend did not want to share with her the details of a traumatic event she had experienced. The patient did not perceive this as a sign of protecting privacy, but rather interpreted the situation as rejection. The interpretant of rejection now became in its turn a sign for the friend no longer being interested in maintaining contact with the patient, which led to their cutting off ties. Whereas the psychoanalytic view of the situation would suggest seeing it as a repetition of experiences of rejection familiar to the patient, and her response as a defense against the pain it generates, the semiotic viewpoint clarifies the understanding that what occurred here was a chain of malfunctions in interpreting signs. Examination of the chain of malfunctions in symbolization enables the therapist to call the patient's attention in a more precise way to how the malfunction is produced, and help them examine their interpretations of it.

From the understanding that there is a broad range of relationships between the sign and object, and that the process of interpreting the sign includes an infinite chain of interpretations, there arises the need to examine, in a similar manner, the possible malfunctions in symbolization as well.

Symbolic Malfunctions: A Psychoanalytic-Semiotic Integrative Model

The distinction between different types of malfunctions is valuable both on the theoretical level, which facilitates expansion of the range of possible

---

29 Peirce, *Collected papers*, § 7.337.

malfunctions, and on the clinical level, for understanding the distinctive forms of intervention in the different malfunctions. In the psychoanalytic literature there are few and partial depictions of work with symbolic malfunctions. Melanie Klein's account of treating a boy named Dick is probably the most well-known.[30] Klein helped the boy progress from symbolic equation toward verbal symbolic capacity. Yet, as Lemberger noted, Klein acted intuitively, and her account lacks the theoretical component to explain this process.[31] This criticism is valid as well for Winnicott's two partial accounts of two cases he treated. First, of a child concerned, symbolically, with connecting objects with strings as an expression of his separation anxiety from his mother,[32] and second of a woman preoccupied with futile fantasizing instead of with the creative thinking of the fantasy.[33] These are expressions of symbolic malfunctions, however, they lack explanation of how therapy enables their correction.

The employment of Peirce's semiotics and the classifications he proposed constitute powerful tools that help examine the processes of change at a "higher resolution." For instance, a patient is late for a session, saying that he is late because he had to stay at work. The therapist proposes a different interpretation for the delay and associates it with the previous difficult session. At first, the patient rejects this connection, then tells the therapist that he had experienced unrest all week, which he related to stress at work; however, now he associates it with content raised in the previous session. From a psychoanalytic point of view, this is a malfunction that includes rejection of the connection, followed by the interpretation which facilitated a renewed connection to the anxiety-inducing content (the previous session). The contribution of semiotics expands the understanding of the malfunction by positioning it on the continuum of the sign's production – after the therapist proposed an interpretant for the delay and linked it to the previous meeting, the interpretant itself became the object that provided new meaning to an additional sign (the unrest). The therapist's awareness of the semiotic process would have enabled them to show the patient not only how the previous session unconsciously affected them, but also how semiotic malfunctions prevent them from understanding the meaning of other occurrences, and would consequently focus the therapy on broadening the patient's symbolic capacity. The understanding that the delay could have additional meanings also helps the patient soften the rigid stance according to which every sign has one signifier, to broaden his point of view, and in this way experience the

---

30 Klein, 1930.
31 Lemberger, 2020.
32 Winnicott, 1971, 15–20.
33 Winnicott, 1971, 26–37.

variety of possibilities for interpretation in life situations. When their experiences acquire new meaning, the patient can create a new narrative for themselves.[34] In other words, the therapist helps the patient explore different interpretants in their communication with others or with the therapist, as manifested in the transference relationship. Andre Green suggested that hope in therapy is constituted in creating potential meaning – not a situation that points to "it has no meaning" but also one that does not point to "this is the meaning of this" – but rather in a space of potentialities, of absence in which representation occurs.[35] It is important to remain in the potential area and not hurry to fill the void in such a way that prevents the unconscious derivatives to arise, like in the case of a therapist who immediately provides the sign or bridge to overcome the malfunction, while not enabling the patient the necessary process. There is no doubt that overcoming the malfunction can occur only in the encounter between therapist and patient. Only in the presence of an "other," who also creates distance from the sign, can the transformation occur and make development possible. In Green's words, "symbolic structures are probably innate. However, today we know [...] that they require the intervention of the object in order to move from potential to realization at a certain point in time."[36]

One can see, therefore, that it is important to examine the range of possible malfunctions which can arise in the process of the production of the sign, and which can likewise be expressed in the therapeutic encounter. In order to arrive at an integrative psychoanalytic-semiotic model, we propose the following model which comprises six archetypes of symbolic malfunctions. The first two malfunctions are parallel to the two possible malfunctions proposed by psychoanalytic theorists, while the next four represent examples of additional possible malfunctions. All the malfunctions will be described by way of leaning on Peirce's proposed divisions, and through an examination of their significance in the clinical domain. It is important to note that this model does not define levels of the malfunctions' severity, for indeed, different malfunctions can have different levels of severity. Moreover, every individual can demonstrate a range of malfunctions in different states of stress in their life. The intensity of the mental pathology will be examined according to the extent

---

34 Roy Schafer, "Narration in the psychoanalytic dialogue," in *Essential Papers on Literature and Psychoanalysis*, edited by Emanuel Berman. & William. E. Butler, 341–65. New York University Press, 1993.
35 Andre Green, "The analyst, symbolization, and absence in the analytic setting (On changes in analytic practice and analytic experience) – In memory of D. W. Winnicott,"*International Journal of Psychoanalysis,* 56 (1975): 1–22.
36 Ibid., 13.

to which the malfunction occupies a central place in the individual's characteristic manner of symbolization.

Iconic Malfunction – Symbolic Equation

This malfunction is the most basic and prevalent of the different types of malfunctions.[37] Peirce's description of the icon as based on a relationship of imitation or similarity between the sign and the signified is compatible with this phenomenon, and it also characterizes the first psychoanalytic approach described earlier which perceives the sign as a defense meant to avoid anxiety. As mentioned, Freud related to the equation relation in dreams and viewed the symbol as a displacement of the anxiety-inducing object. Klein and Segal described the symbolic equation as a lack of distinction between symbol and symbolized, as demonstrated by Britton's example of a patient who was afraid that if she did not see her mother, she would become blind (not seeing the beloved object literally means not seeing).[38] Ogden effectively described this type of malfunction:

> The dialectic of reality and fantasy collapses in the direction of fantasy (i.e., reality is subsumed by fantasy) so that fantasy becomes a thing in itself as tangible, as powerful, as dangerous and as gratifying as the external reality from which it cannot be differentiated [...] the hallucination does not sound like a voice, it *is* a voice [...] One does not feel like one's father, one's father *is* in one's blood and must be bled out in order for one to be free of him.[39]

Put differently, one thing cannot represent another thing, but rather becomes the thing itself. In this situation, the ambiguity necessary for "metaphorical thinking" is absent.[40] The therapeutic work in this case must first focus on examining the connection between the sign and the object, stressing that they are not identical and gradually exploring the points of difference.

---

37 Alvarez added two levels of pre-symbolization which describe the void and the addictive tendency that appear prior to the symbolic equation, that is, before the appearance of the sign. Accordingly, their descriptions exceed the boundaries of this discussion on malfunctions in the sign and signified relations. Alvarez, Anne. *The Thinking Heart: Three Levels of Psychoanalytic Therapy with Disturbed Children*. Routledge, 2012.
38 Ronald Britton, *Belief and Imagination: Explorations in Psychoanalysis*. Routledge, 1988, 18.
39 Ogden, 1996, 215–16.
40 Antal. F. Borbely, "Metaphor and psychoanalysis," in *The Cambridge Handbook of Metaphor and Thought*, edited by Raymond. W. Gibbs, 412–24. Cambridge University Press, 2008.

This will gradually enable the patient to create an indexical relation, and later to develop a symbolic connection as well.

Rejecting the Connection between Sign and Object

This malfunction is characterized by the detachment that the individual generates between the symbolized object and the sign that represents it. As a result, a symbol is not produced but rather its two parts remain detached from one another. This state is parallel to the second psychoanalytic conception described earlier, which presents the connection produced by the symbol as threatening, and as a result, generates the individual's need to reject it. The refusal to know the *meaning of the connection* indicates the destruction of the interpretant.

Ogden referred to this type of malfunction as collapse of the fantasy pole in the direction of reality, which serves mainly as a defense against the fantasy. In these situations "imagination is foreclosed" and the individual finds it difficult to play, imagine, and even feel fully alive. To exemplify, Ogden described a child whose exposure to reality was traumatic (saw his parents engaging in sexual intercourse and was present at his sister's birth). The child had difficulty enjoying puppet shows, because, as he claimed, the puppets were just wooden figures hanging from strings.[41] Patients presenting this type of malfunction either hardly ever describe dreams or repudiate them as stupid and meaningless. Such patients are highly cognizant of details in the therapy room and in life in general, and concretely adhere to them. They can be described as suffering from a tendency toward metonymy and a malfunction in metaphoric production.[42] The complex therapeutic objective therefore focuses on exploring the origins of the fear of fantasy, paralleled by expanding the space for playing and creativity.

An extreme situation of the disruption of the connection produced by the symbol can occur during an experience of mental trauma. The traumatized patient is incapable of giving the trauma symbolic representation and it remains "frozen," without the possibility for change.[43] Bonomi called this phenomenon "broken symbols": "What is broken when a person is struck by trauma is a symbol."[44] He stressed that the symbol connects between feelings and representations, and between the body and the world. While in Freud's conception the construction of post-traumatic

---

41 Ogden, 1996, 219–22.
42 Roman Jackobson, "Two Aspects of Language and Two Types of Aphasic Disturbances," in *Volume II Word and Language*, 239–59. Berlin, New York: De Gruyter Mouton, 2010.
43 Borbely, 2008.
44 Carlo Bonomi, "Trauma and the symbolic function of the mind," *International Forum of Psychoanalysis*, 13 (2004): 45–50, 47.

symptoms is mediated through the mind, in Bonomi's view, it is mediated through the body. Thus, in a traumatic situation, the emotional world retreats to physical sensations; in Peirce's terms, the thirdness that provides meaning collapses, and a regression to firstness occurs.

Indexical Malfunction

The formation of an index necessitates, as described by Peirce, a slightly more complex conception of the sign than that of the icon. Both reality testing and the acknowledgment of causal relationships are required to create an index. However, retaining the indexical state indicates a malfunction in the transition to the tertiary and the production of a symbol. What characterizes this malfunction is that, despite that it is perceived by the senses (the level Peirce referred to as firstness) and is connected to reality (secondness), it still lacks the third level of meaning. This malfunction may be deceiving, given that the individual distinguishes between the sign and signified, but at the same time has difficulty in giving the sign its meaning. For instance, an individual enters a room and notices a social event. They detect what is happening with their senses and are also aware of the feeling it arouses in them, but cannot interpret its meaning.

In another example, Winnicott writes about a mother who assumes she recognizes her infant's needs (based on experience with her other children), and in her response, prevents the child from spontaneously expressing their needs.[45] In effect, she responds to signs as if automatically without understanding their meaning. There is a profound difference between this type of response and that of a mother who responds to her child symbolically, that is, enables their gestures, and manages to construe their meaning and how they symbolize the child's distress.[46]

In therapy, the therapist will attempt to mediate for the patient between the object and the interpretant, i.e., the meaning. In their refusal to submit to the secondary, they will repeatedly attempt to instill the tertiary meaning, and thereby move toward the symbolic. The use of metaphor as a therapeutic tool can facilitate the transition from indexical malfunction to the development of the symbolic capacity, since the metaphor produces the distance between both its parts necessary for the insertion of the meaning.[47]

---

45 Donald, W. Winnicott, "The theory of the parent-infant relationship," in *The Maturational Processes and the Facilitating Environment*, 37–55. London: Hogarth Press, 1965.
46 Corradi Fiurama, Jemma, "The symbolic function, transference and psychic reality," *International Review of Psychoanalysis*, 4 (1977): 171–80.
47 Floyd Merrell, "Charles Sanders Peirce's Concept of the Sign," in *The Routledge Companion to Semiotics and Linguistics*, edited by Paul Colbey, 28–39. London: Routledge, 2001.

Confusing Levels of Symbolization

This is a malfunction of confusion between the types of connections between object and sign, for instance, between index and symbol. Philips described this type of confusion in a patient who sensed sexual arousal toward a woman at work.[48] In contrast to the normal situation in which the woman is the object of the desire, the arousal is an index that points to the desire, and the thought (I want her) is the interpretant, this patient experiences that the woman was ordered from outside to cause his arousal. In other words, *the sense of arousal turned from index to symbol*, and a psychotic thought was produced.

Very often, therapists encounter a less severe manifestation of this malfunction. For example, a patient who was going through a period of many changes in his life sent his therapist a message precisely at their session's designated hour asking if they were meeting. The surprised therapist responded that she was waiting for him. When he arrived a moment later, the patient said that he was not sure of the hour and was afraid that he would interrupt another patient's session. The therapist interpreted this as the patient not being certain of having a secure place with her, to which the patient responded: "I'm drowning and you're describing the water." According to the patient, the confusion regarding the hour of the meeting reflected the general sense of disorientation he had been experiencing during that period of time. The therapist construed the event as an expression of symbolic malfunction and sensed that while she understood it as a symbol of a personality trait, for the patient, it was an index – an event that points to a similar mode of confused and forgetful conduct in recent days. Even if the therapist's interpretation was correct, it failed to identify the manner in which the patient used the sign. As a consequence of this insight, she said to the patient: "You are focused on survival, and I asked you to pause and look at the symbolism in the event." The patient now felt better understood and calmed down. Thus, it appears that the way to cope with this type of malfunction is to return to the original sign and examine how the confusion between index and sign came about.

Empty Sign or Pseudo-Sign

This type of malfunction is sometimes more difficult to identify, because the production of the symbol seems to have been completed, when in fact, what has been produced is a symbol that can be defined as an empty symbol or pseudo-symbol. Many times, this situation emerges as a consequence of a split between different components of the psychic order. Winnicott's description of

---

48 Philips, 2000.

the split between the true and false self calls attention to this type of malfunction. Following the split, a deficient symbol is produced – born from the need to match expectations – which does not originate in the vitality and creativity that characterizes the production of a symbol from within a true experience of self. Wright proposed that if an impingement occurs that leads to trauma to the pre-verbal self, there will be a split between the pleasing verbal self (false), which speaks the words of others, and the pre-verbal self (true), which remains hidden and lacking means of expression.[49] Target and Fonagy referred to "pretend play" as a split between mental and emotional representation, with the symbol remaining empty.[50] The individual feels disconnected, even dissociative, and displays a discourse that seems communicative, but lacks meanings to the words.

The purpose of the therapy will be to produce a bridge that will fuse the split, whether it be by creating a connection to the true self (Winnicott) or by creating a connection between the emotional and mental dimensions (Target and Fonagy). When the interpretation succeeds in creating this kind of connection, the two dimensions are linked through a symbolic bridge created by the therapist's words, and there is hope for producing a symbol that is connected, more authentically, to the patient's inner world.

Symbol Externalization Malfunction

There are severe situations in which the sign does not serve to refer to an object, but rather becomes an entity in and of itself in the world. For Peirce, man himself is a sign:

> The word or sign which man uses *is* the man himself. For, as the fact that every thought is a sign, taken in conjunction with the fact that life is a train of thought, proves that man is a sign [...] Thus my language is the sum total of myself, for the man is the thought.[51]

Philips notes that here Peirce is calling attention to the point that, in contrast to the notion that we are in direct contact with objects in the world, the process mediates through our consciousness, which is itself a sign, however, we are unaware of this when we are speaking.[52] The language blurs itself and becomes unnoticed, so that the signs are rendered transparent. We see the world *through them*, and we do not linger on them while speaking. On the

---

49 Kenneth Wright, *Mirroring and Attunement. Self-realization in Psychoanalysis and Art.* London: Routledge, 2009, 100.
50 Target & Fonagy, 1996.
51 Peirce, *Collected papers*, § 5.314.
52 Philips, 2000.

other hand, in psychotic thinking, the thoughts and the words do not transmit the individual beyond them to the object and they remain stuck in them. Thus, a patient may not understand the meaning of the word "chair" momentarily when asked to sit in the chair. The basic semiotic structure of the experience is broken, and the fear that arises is unbearable. While psychoanalysis bases its understanding of psychosis on the blurring of the boundary between inside and out, self and object, the significant contribution of semiotics in this context is the comprehension of the sign's exteriority. Deciphering the psychotic mechanism is rooted in awareness that it fully externalizes the sign. While an individual observing from the outside is aware of the signs' externalization and the psychotic's bizarre use of them, the psychotic individual is unaware of the process, and this is an expression of his own malfunction. The therapeutic objective in such a case will be to gradually create a connection between the sign and the object, and in doing so, decrease the sign's externalization and detached existence.

Applying the Model to Clinical Work

Awareness of these six types of malfunctions serves to refine the therapist's ability to identify the state of malfunction that the patient is in. This implies that the therapist must ask their self in every session, and sometimes even at different moments in the session, how is the symbol functioning now? What level of malfunction is the patient presenting? The absence of this kind of discernment can make it difficult to create an appropriate therapeutic intervention.

For example, Steiner wrote about a patient who entered the clinic looking suspicious and uncalm, and who refused to lie down on the sofa.[53] The therapist noticed that he was holding something under his pullover. After a few minutes, the patient began whispering: "I must protect … I must protect the baby." When Steiner told the patient he felt that he was threatening the baby-patient himself, the patient took out from under the pullover a little doll and a pair of scissors and told him not to say anything more, because his words would physically hurt the "baby." The patient was prepared to use the scissors to cut the therapist's words and throat. Steiner presented this vignette as an example of symbolic equation; however, he ignored the gap between the patient's malfunction and the therapist's response. The patient used the doll as an iconic representation, but it appears that the therapist's symbolic interpretation did not take into account the depth of the infringement on the symbolization, and as a result, intensified the anxiety.

---

53 Riccardo Steiner, "Does the Pierce's semiotic model based on index, icon, symbol have anything to do with psychoanalysis?" in *Language, Symbolization and Psychosis,* edited by Giovanna Ambrosio, Simona Argentieri & Jorge Canestri, 219–72. London: Karnac, 2007.

Following diagnosis of the type of malfunction, the therapist will be able to choose from the proposed model a range of therapeutic interventions to help their patient in the process of symbolization development. It is notable here that despite the theoretical division of malfunctions, in the clinical reality, there may appear a variety of presentations, including numerous integrated malfunctions or partial expressions of malfunction. Moreover, the production of the sign, as well as disentangling the malfunction, is not singular, closed events, but part of a chain of signs that constitutes another tool the therapist can use while helping the patient progress from one level of symbolization to the next.

It is important to note that the investigation of malfunctions in symbolization, and all their complexities, includes not only expressions amongst patients, but also malfunction amongst therapists.[54,55] The therapist is in fact both an object that needs to be symbolized and one that promotes symbolization, and thus the symbolic malfunction deeply influences them. Occasionally, they are trapped in a situation in which their ability to produce symbols is limited. There can be over identification with the patient's sense of helplessness and passivity, which will lead to concreteness and the therapist's forgoing the possibility of thinking and inducing associations. The therapist's increasing awareness to possibilities of malfunction will enable them to see themselves as also prone to malfunctions and to take these possibilities in account.

Summary

Despite the important place of symbolization in psychoanalytic thinking, the research lacks a methodical discussion of types of symbols and the relations between them, and consequently, of the ways in which symbolization might be disrupted. This chapter presented two ways in which psychoanalytic writers related to symbolic malfunction, and proposed to expand this perspective and examine additional potential malfunctions. Peirce's theory of signs was found suitable for this objective given that it places at the center of its investigation the classification of the distinct types of signs. The linguistic aspects, which hitherto did not receive enough attention in psychoanalytic literature, provide an opportunity to examine in-depth symbolic processes and malfunctions from a new vantage point, and the current study demonstrates how symbolization is grounded in linguistic mechanisms. Few researchers have begun to acknowledge the contribution of Peirce's semiotics for exploring clinical situations, and this study continues this line of

---

54 Steiner, 2007.
55 Louise Gyler, "'The violence of the real' in unrepresented experience," *The 22nd Annual Frances Tustin Memorial Prize and Lectures.* Tel Aviv University, November 2019.

research for examining the potential malfunctions in symbolization. It presented an integrative psychoanalytic-semiotic model consisting of six prototypes of malfunction and distinguished their characteristics while exploring options for the model's clinical application.

The semiotic attention to malfunctions, as well as to symbolization processes in general, contributes to increasing the awareness to language in the therapeutic discourse and to enhancing the therapist's linguistic sensitivity. Identification of the symbolic level in which the patient is located, and where the malfunction occurs, can help the therapist in conducting symbolic transformation. In addition, the presentation of the connection between semiotics and psychoanalysis demonstrates the manner in which psychoanalysis can benefit from its connection with other disciplines, as well as contributing to them, and thus constitutes a step in the direction of expanding interdisciplinary thought. It appears that the opening of psychoanalysis to additional disciplines, such as semiotics, can add to its strength as a vital and creative discipline which continues to evolve. Therefore, it is extremely important that future research should continue to explore the significant link between psychoanalysis and semiotics and examine additional aspects of language as it is expressed in therapy.

Chapter 6

"Bring Words back from their Metaphysical to their Everyday Use" – Meaning in Life through Ordinary Language Use[1]

Yael Mishani-Uval

Introduction

A sense of meaning in life has been found to be essential for living a full life, for a sense of well-being, and for strengthening a person's resilience in the face of adversity and crisis.[2] Psychologists, psychiatrists, and other therapists testify that more people seek treatment out of a sense of emptiness and meaninglessness,[3] or, as the psychoanalyst Michael Eigen puts it, out of "a sense of psychic deadness."[4] On the surface, many people's lives may appear healthy, successful, and even meaningful; however, this may be accompanied by a sense of "inner deadness," stagnation, or a lack of spiritual animation. This can stem from various sources and is manifested in different guises, from a complete lack of passion for life, apathy, and inability to make decisions, to people whose psychic deadness takes over all aspects of life and transforms it into an experience of ongoing suffering. The most recent Diagnostic and Statistical Manual of Mental Disorders (DSM 5), which was published in 2013, even includes a separate chapter titled "Depressive Disorders," which lists symptoms such as negative mood, hopelessness, lack of interest in everyday activities, exhaustion, changes in appetite, feelings of worthlessness, indecision, and others.[5]

As part of the field of existential psychotherapy, which aims to address universal existential concerns, a new method of therapy has emerged in the

---

1 This research was supported by The Program for Hermeneutics and Cultural Studies at Bar-Ilan University and is part of a doctoral thesis written within the Program under the supervision of Dr. Dorit Lemberger.
2 For a review and meta-analysis, see Katarzyna Czekierda, Anna Banik, Crystal L. Park, and Aleksandra Luszczynska, "Meaning in life and physical health: Systematic review and meta-analysis," *Health Psychology Review*, 11(4) (2017): 387–418, https://doi.org/10.1080/17437199.2017.1327325.
3 Irvin David Yalom, *Existential Psychotherapy* (New York: Basic Books, 1980).
4 Michael Eigen, *Psychic Deadness* (London: Routledge, 2004).
5 American Psychiatric Association. 2013. *Diagnostic and Statistical Manual of Mental Disorders: DSM-5.* (Arlington, TX: American Psychiatric Association Publishing).

DOI: 10.4324/9781003326588-6

last three decades called "Meaning Therapy." This is a positive integrative approach to counseling and psychotherapy with roots in the Logotherapy of Viktor Frankl, a student of Freud and the founder of the Third Viennese School of Psychotherapy. The starting point of Meaning Therapy is that the main motivation in human life is the will to meaning.[6] This kind of therapy (or counseling) aims to help clients[7] discover or infuse meaning into their lives and as such equip them with tools to deal with life's challenges, unavoidable suffering, changing life circumstances, and uncertainty. This therapeutic approach urges the subject to take responsibility for their decisions, choices, and actions.[8]

Such therapeutic approaches, whose popularity in the Western world has skyrocketed in the last few decades, have filled the void left by classical psychotherapy. In the post-modern era, which is characterized by doubt in the concept of "Truth," challenging of values, and constant change and uncertainty about the future (including, due to the climate crisis, the question of whether life on Earth will continue), psychological analysis that limits itself to the patient's perspective have abandoned questions in the realm of value, such as the question of the meaning of life.

Psychoanalysis focuses on a causal study of the subject's mental (and partially also physical) phenomena, and as such sheds light on the deterministic-biological aspect of the human psyche. Since Freud's time, symptoms have been seen as meaningful and connected to the patient's past experiences.[9] Through analysis – interpretation or translation of symptoms, dreams, and mistakes, such as slips of the tongue, slips of the pen, forgetfulness, and more – it is possible to trace the source of problems observed on the surface – to the depths of the unconscious. The assumption is that exposing the causal relation between the symptom and its source leads to healing. The analysis thus serves as an *interpretation* and *translation* of symptoms in that it raises their unconscious roots to the surface. However, psychoanalysis' focus on instincts, impulses, or the causes of mental states, has left unanswered many questions within the ethical realm, which focus, among other things, on a subject's need for a meaningful life.

---

6 Viktor Frankl contrasted the will to meaning with Freud's pleasure principle (will to pleasure) and Adler's striving to superiority (will to power). Viktor Frankl, *Man's Search for Meaning* (Boston: Beacon Press, 2006 [1946]).
7 As part of this approach the terms "patient" is usually avoided, and "client" is used instead.
8 Louis Hoffman, Mark Yang, Francis J. Kaklauskas, and Albert Chan, *Existential Psychology East-West*, Colorado Springs, CO: University of the Rockies Press; Paul T. P. Wong, "Meaning therapy: An integrative and positive existential psychotherapy," *Journal of Contemporary Psychotherapy*, 40 (2) (2010): 85–93; Emmy Van Deurzen, *Existential counselling & psychotherapy in practice* (2nd ed.). (London: Sage, 2012).
9 Sigmund Freud, "The meaning of the symptoms," in *A General Introduction to Psychoanalysis*, trans. G. Stanley Hall (New York: Horace Liveright, 1920), 221–235.

There is a great deal of subjective choice when it comes to the way one grasps the meaning of one's own life, or the attitude one adopts towards life; the answer to these questions need not be causal. In Viktor Frankl's *Man's Search for Meaning* he provides a first-person description of the shocking experiences he endured in both body and soul in concentration camps such as Auschwitz and Dachau.[10] In this description, he says that even among the SS guards some took pity on the prisoners. He describes, for example, how it became clear after the war that a commander of the camp from which Frankl was released, had paid significant sums of money from his own pocket to purchase medicine for prisoners. In contrast, Frankl describes a senior camp warden who was a prisoner himself and behaved more cruelly than any SS officer. In other words, nothing can be concluded from the fact that a person belongs to a particular group; human kindness can be found anywhere, even in the cruelest places imaginable.

Observing Holocaust survivors, they also serve as an example of the possibility of subjective choice and our inability to predict the future based on events of the past. Among the survivors, there were many who, like Viktor Frankl, managed to establish a sense of meaning in their lives after the war and even to live full and meaningful lives, whereas others, like Paul Celan and Primo Levi, decided to end their lives years after being released from the concentration camps. The fact that people experienced something in their past does not necessarily attest to their present and future actions, choices, or attitudes. This lacuna within Freud's psychoanalysis was also demonstrated by the pioneer of the early twentieth-century linguistic-philosophical turn, the philosopher Ludwig Wittgenstein (1889–1951).

The present chapter aims to offer a method of conceptual investigation that is inspired, or more precisely guided, by early and late Wittgenstein;[11] a method that can then be utilized to help clarify the concept of "meaning in life" and the processes involved in its realization. "Meaning in life" is, of course, an abstract and elusive concept that is involved in abstract and complex processes, the sources and causes of which are difficult to pinpoint and track. This raises the question of how such a concept can be investigated and studied. This chapter will discuss the two revolutions that Wittgenstein sparked in the study of language, as they are reflected in his *Tractatus Logico-Philosophicus* (the *Tractatus*), published in 1921, and his *Philosophical Investigations*, published posthumously in 1953. Discussing these two revolutions will supply the foundations for the proposed qualitative-empirical

---

10 Frankl, *Man's Search for Meaning*.
11 It is customary to distinguish between Wittgenstein's early thought as it is expressed in his *Tractatus Logico-Philosophicus*, which was published in 1921, according to which meaning was understood in terms of "truth" and "correspondence," and his later work, which is reflected most clearly in his *Philosophical Investigations*, which was published in 1953, according to which meaning was understood in terms of use.

method of inquiry that can be applied in the clarification of ethical (and aesthetic) philosophical concepts, such as the one at the heart of this chapter. In so doing, it will also draw a straight methodological line between Wittgenstein's early work and his later work.

Meaning through Language – the Limits of the Inquiry

Wittgenstein's groundbreaking treatise *Tractatus Logico-Philosophicus* belongs to and has a central place in a tradition within analytic philosophy that developed in the late nineteenth and early twentieth centuries, which used logical tools and analytic examination of language to critique and expose the nonsensicality of earlier metaphysical traditions. The purpose of analytic philosophy was to "clean" philosophical discourse from confusion and to conduct controlled and rigorous inquiries by which concepts could be clarified and sensible claims could be distinguished from claims that are the outcome of misuses of language and are therefore senseless or nonsense. Analytic philosophers aspired to utilize an ideal (logical) language to reach objectivity and universality.

That the *Tractatus Logico-Philosophicus* is included within this tradition can already be concluded from its introduction. In the introduction, Wittgenstein declares that the book deals with a range of different philosophical challenges, among them "the problem of life,"[12] and argues that the source of many of these challenges is "that the logic of our language is misunderstood."[13] As Wittgenstein explains, the essence of the book is "to draw a limit to thinking, or rather – not to thinking, but to the expression of thoughts; for in order to draw a limit to thinking, we should have to be able to think both sides of this limit (we should therefore have to be able to think what cannot be thought). The limit can, therefore, only be drawn in language and what lies on the other side of the limit will simply be nonsense."[14]

Wittgenstein was the first philosopher to draw a direct line between the question of the meaning of life and that of meaning in language. The three sections of the *Tractatus* that address this relation explicitly are the following:

> The sense of the world must lie outside the world. In the world everything is as it is and happens as it does happen. *In* it there is no value—and if there were, it would be of no value. If there is a value

---

12 Ludwig Wittgenstein, *Tractatus Logico-Philosophicus*, trans. C. K. Ogden. (New York: Dover, 1998 [1921]), §6.521.
13 Wittgenstein, *Tractatus Logico-Philosophicus*, 3.
14 Ibid.

which is of value, it must lie outside all happening and being-so. For all happening and being-so is accidental. What makes it non-accidental cannot lie *in* the world, for otherwise this would again be accidental. It must lie outside the world.[15]

Hence also there can be no ethical propositions. Propositions cannot express anything higher.[16]

It is clear that ethics cannot be expressed. Ethics is transcendental. (Ethics and aesthetics are one.)[17]

Toward the end of the *Tractatus*,[18] Wittgenstein makes good on his promise from its introduction. He shows us how a philosophical question such as the question of the meaning of life is meaningless – whether it is a semantic question that attempts to clarify the meaning of the world or an ethical question that attempts to clarify the value and purpose of life.[19] This is so because talking about the meaning of life is meaningless. Ethics must essentially be transcendental, and because it is transcendental, it can have no expression in language. Why? Because ethics speaks of absolute, unconditional, values that dictate how one should or how it is appropriate for one to live. Yet, if life has absolute and unconditional value, this cannot be demonstrated by the contingent facts of life. To understand the meaning of the world one must be outside it, and that, of course, is impossible.[20]

To see why Wittgenstein thinks that ethics and aesthetics, which he takes to be identical, cannot be expressed in language, we must first understand the distinction he draws between logical propositions, empirical propositions that describe the world, and ethical and aesthetical propositions. Of logic, Wittgenstein says:

The propositions of logic are tautologies.[21]

The propositions of logic therefore say nothing. (They are the analytical propositions.)[22]

---

15 Ibid, §6.41.
16 Ibid, §6.42.
17 Ibid, §6.421.
18 The *Tractatus* ends with a single sentence, no. 7, that has no sub-sections.
19 Yuval Lurie, *Tracking the Meaning of Life: a Philosophical Journey* (Columbia Missouri: University of Missouri Press, 2006), 126.
20 Both Freud and Frankl thought that it was useless to speak of the ultimate meaning of life. (Sigmund Freud, *Civilization and Its Discontents,* trans. J. Strachey (New York: W. W. Norton, 1961 [1929]), 20; Frankl, *Man's Search for Meaning*, 114.)
21 Wittgenstein, *Tractatus Logico-Philosophicus*, §6.1.
22 Ibid, §6.11.

> Logical research means the investigation of all regularity. And outside logic all is accident.[23]

The study of logic concerns necessary laws. In the propositions of logic there is no chance, they are derived a priori and therefore say nothing about the world. In contrast, everything outside of logic is accidental. In this sense, a "genuine" law involves necessity, and, as such, only logical necessity exists. Everything that lacks logical necessity must therefore be accidental. In this way, Wittgenstein undercuts the possibility of natural necessity. According to Wittgenstein, the propositions of logic mark the limits of the world, that is, all that can be expressed in language. In contrast, natural propositions, such as the propositions of the natural sciences that describe the world, are not logical and therefore are not necessary. They describe worldly states of affairs, or facts, and their truth value is contingent upon empirical proof.

By contrasting what Wittgenstein says about logic with what he says about the world, his significant claim about the world emerges: that it is contingent. With this claim, Wittgenstein rejects the law of causality that Freud placed at the foundation of his psychoanalytic theory and with which our discussion began.

> The law of causality is not a law but the form of a law.[24]
>
> There is no compulsion making one thing happen because another has happened. The only necessity that exists is logical necessity.[25]
>
> States of affairs are independent of one another.[26]
>
> From the existence or non-existence of one state of affairs it is impossible to infer the existence or non-existence of another.[27]

Wittgenstein shows that the law of causality does not express necessity, and therefore, as he emphasizes, is not a law but a form of a law. There is no necessity in the world that would compel us to think that one thing will lead to another or that from one state of affairs we could infer another. Necessity exists only in logic. That is, from the events of the past it is impossible to infer or predict the events of the future or the present:

---

23 Ibid, §6.3.
24 Ibid, §6.32.
25 Ibid, §6.37.
26 Ibid, §2.061.
27 Ibid, §2.062.

> There is no possible way of making an inference from the existence of one situation to the existence of another, entirely different situation.[28]
>
> We *cannot* infer the events of the future from those of the present.
>
> Superstition is nothing but belief in the causal nexus.[29]

Immediately after rejecting the law of causality and our ability to infer one event from another, Wittgenstein turns to discuss freedom of the will. He emphasizes that it is embodied in our inability to predict future actions.

> The freedom of the will consists in the impossibility of knowing actions that still lie in the future. We could know them only if causality were an *inner* necessity like that of logical inference [...][30]

We can now return to ethical and aesthetical propositions and clarify what Wittgenstein means when claiming that ethics is transcendental, by appealing to another of his early texts. In "A Lecture on Ethics," which Wittgenstein delivered in Cambridge in 1929, he looks at different synonyms of "ethics" and shows that what is common to them all is that each is used in two senses – relative and absolute and that a fact cannot be transformed into an absolute judgment. Beyond the fact that properties such as "good" or "bad" do not "belong" to objects but are attributed to them by people,[31] Wittgenstein emphasizes that a fact that is describable in language cannot be good or bad. In other words, ethical and aesthetical propositions involve absolute, non-accidental, values, and therefore cannot describe states of affairs in a world where everything is accidental.

> Our words used as we use them in science, are vessels capable only of containing and conveying meaning and sense, *natural* meaning and sense. Ethics, if it is anything, is supernatural and our words will only express facts; as a teacup will only hold a teacup full of water and if I were to pour out a gallon over it.[32]

---

28 Ibid, §5.135
29 Ibid, §5.1361
30 Ibid, §5.1362
31 "The interpretant" in Peirce's terms (Charles Sanders Peirce, *The Collected Papers of Charles Sanders Peirce*, reproducing vol. I-VI, Charles Hartshorne and Paul Weiss (eds.), Cambridge, MA: Harvard University Press, 1931–1935; vols. VII-VIII, Arthur W. Burks (ed.) (same publisher, 1958), § 2.228).
32 Ludwig Wittgenstein, (1965). "A lecture on ethics," *The philosophical review*, 74 (1), (1965 [1933]), 3–12: 6.

Accordingly, an answer to an ethical question can be personal, particular, and contextual, but cannot be expressed in scientific-objective language. In this, Wittgenstein is expressing a position similar to that of the nineteenth-century Danish philosopher, Søren Kierkegaard (1813–1855),[33] who believed that ethics, which is intertwined with subjective truth, goes beyond scientific-objective language.[34] For Wittgenstein, ethics is described as "supernatural" or transcendental. That is, for both Kierkegaard and Wittgenstein ethics is bound up with subjective experience. It therefore goes beyond the limits of the world and of language and cannot be communicated directly or expressed scientifically.[35] In this respect, as Wittgenstein emphasizes, "The *limits of my language* mean the limits of my world,"[36] that is, the subject is the limit of the world.

I am my world. (The microcosm.)[37]

The subject does not belong to the world but it is a limit of the world.[38]

At each step, the *Tractatus* directs us toward an understanding that we must abandon the possibility of solving the general, universal, question of the meaning *of* life. According to Wittgenstein, this question has no answer, and even if it does – we have no way of knowing it. As such, the question is nonsensical. Instead, Wittgenstein directs us toward what we should *do*.[39] The purpose of philosophy, according to Wittgenstein, is "the logical clarification

---

33 Kierkegaard framed the question of the meaning of life as the key to human existence and rejected the thought that theoretical, objective, universal, and abstract rationality, which makes no contact with the concrete life of the individual, might guide the subject on how to act in life. (Søren Aabye Kierkegaard, *Fear and Trembling and the Sickness unto Death* (Princeton University Press), 2013 [1843]; Søren Aabye Kierkegaard, *Concluding Unscientific Postscript to Philosophical Fragments,* Vol. 1, trans. H. V. Hong and E. H. Hong (New Jersey: Princeton University Press, 1992 [1846])).
34 At various point, Wittgenstein testifies to his fondness of Kierkegaard. (Jens Glebe-Møller, "Wittgenstein and Kierkegaard," *Kierkegaardiana* 15 (1991), 55–68; Norman Malcolm, *Ludwig Wittgenstein. A Memoir* (London: Oxford University Press, 2001 [1958])).
35 This may be the reason that Kierkegaard chose to use irony, which is an indirect method of communication. (Shlomi Mualem, "Running up against the Limits of Language: Wittgenstein and Kierkegaard," *Iyyun: The Jerusalem Philosophical Quarterly* 54 (2005), 131–148 [Hebrew]).
36 Wittgenstein, *Tractatus Logico-Philosophicus*, §5.6.
37 Ibid, §5.63.
38 Ibid, §5.632.
39 Yuval Lurie, "Wittgenstein on the meaning of life," *Iyyun: The Jerusalem Philosophical Quarterly* 49 (2000), 115–136 [Hebrew], 115.

of thoughts."⁴⁰ And, he adds: "philosophy is not a body of doctrine but an activity."⁴¹ Philosophical *activity* is contrasted with the silence with which Wittgenstein seals the *Tractatus* in his most quoted sentence:

What we cannot speak about we must pass over in silence.⁴²

It must now inquire whether the silence that Wittgenstein advocates at the end of the *Tractatus* entails that we cannot speak, and a fortiori investigate, the concept of "meaning *in* life." An answer to this question is critical for the possibility of understanding the concept, which is at the center of this chapter. In light of *Philosophical Investigations*, which I will discuss in the next section, I wish to adopt an interpretation according to which the silence Wittgenstein suggests does not mean that it is useless to speak about meaning *in* life; rather, it is a demand for scientific humility – silence as expressing the recognition that some claims can neither be proven nor refuted.⁴³ The two branches that attempt to provide answers to the question of the meaning of life – science and religion – fail to do so.⁴⁴

Wittgenstein, himself, does not remove from the discussion such familiar feelings as the feeling of wonder at the very existence of the world, the feeling of absolute security, of delight, and of guilt; rather, he shows that even though there is some absolute value in such feelings, they are no more than experiences that have occurred at a specific place and time, that had a beginning and have come to an end. Therefore, it is meaningless to say that they have some inherent, absolute, supernatural, value.⁴⁵ To those who object that such experiences have absolute value and that this is a fact like all others, though one for which a logical description has yet to be found, Wittgenstein responds that not only is there no way to describe these expressions but their senselessness is their essence. Everyone who deals with these matters tends to push against the limits of the world, against the limits of language, and that, of course, is hopeless.

---

40 Wittgenstein, *Tractatus Logico-Philosophicus*, §4.112.
41 Ibid.
42 Ibid, §7.
43 Ulman-Margalit writes that "we can ask what constitutes a meaningful life even without searching for an answer to the explicit question of what is the meaning of life." She then notes that, in a different way, members of the Viennese Circle of the 1920s and 1930s redirected the focus of the philosophical-semantic debate from the question of the meaning of a sentence to the question of the difference between a meaningful sentence and a meaningless one. (Edna Ullman-Margalit, "The meaning of life and meaningful life," in Yeshayahu Tadmor, and Amir Freimann eds., *Education – Core and Essence* (Tel-Aviv: Mofet Institute, 2012), 123–132 [Hebrew].))
44 Wittgenstein, *Tractatus Logico-Philosophicus*, §6.341, §6.342, §6.371.
45 Wittgenstein, "A Lecture on Ethics," 8.

> For all I wanted to do with them was just to go beyond the world and that is to say beyond significant language [...] This running against the walls of our cage is perfectly, absolutely hopeless. Ethics so far as it springs from the desire to say something about the ultimate meaning of life, the absolute good, the absolute valuable, can be no science.[46]

How might one, nonetheless, experience life as meaningful? Wittgenstein's solution is grounded in an attitude shift: "one must want life by experiencing it as something wonderous."[47] In this respect, ethics and aesthetics are one and the same, not only because their propositions are meaningless, but because both give expression to a certain attitude toward life, that is, to the subject's individual choices.[48] In this respect, ethics and aesthetics are identical because both emphasize the "how" and not the "what," that is, the form of the expression rather than its essence.

Summarizing our discussion of Wittgenstein's first revolution in the study of language and its relevance to the conceptual clarification of the concept of "meaning in life," the *Tractatus* seemingly leaves us at a dead end. Wittgenstein marks a clear boundary between what can be empirically investigated and is within the limits of language, and what is beyond the limits of language, and therefore cannot be empirically investigated. As a metaphysical question that aims to articulate the universal meaning of life, the question is nonsensical and so there is no point in addressing it. Yet, from the fact that we have no way of approaching the general meaning *of* life, it cannot be concluded that it is impossible to speak of how a subject establishes a subjective meaning *in* life. People can provide linguistic expression to how they grasp the meaning of their lives. As a result, people's linguistic expressions of their attitudes toward life can serve as the subject matter of an investigation that focuses on everyday linguistic expressions. As part of Wittgenstein's conception of philosophy as an activity that purports to clarify ideas and thoughts, it is thus possible to clarify the concept within the limits of language. That is, it is possible to take the subject to be the limit of the investigation and his choices and attitudes to serve as instruments in the clarification. Wittgenstein's second revolution in the study of language will further ground this research method.

Meaning in Ordinary Language Use

In his posthumously published *Philosophical Investigations*, Wittgenstein brings about a revolution in his understanding of language that has

---

46 Ibid, 12.
47 Lurie, "Wittgenstein on the Meaning of Life," 128
48 Ibid, 133.

significant implications for the study of language. In its very first section, he rejects the Augustinian picture, which is representative of the referential theory of meaning, according to which "every word has a meaning. This meaning is correlated with the word. It is the object for which the word stands."[49] In his later thought, Wittgenstein attacks the notion, which he too shared, that logic is "sublime" and that its study provides a glimpse into the structure of thought and the deep structure of language. While in the *Tractatus* meaning is understood along the axis between language and the world, in *Philosophical Investigations* meaning is determined by the use of language within a particular form of life.[50]

By appealing to everyday language, Wittgenstein illustrates, much as Frege did,[51] that these assumptions, along with the assumptions of logic, are mistaken. He suggests that we treat words and sentences as pieces in a game and emphasizes that "[...] the meaning of a word is its use in language."[52] In this respect, meaning is no more than a role within a specific game. Thus, Wittgenstein moves away from the logical picture of language and turns the spotlight to other characteristics of language that depend on how people *use* it.

Philosophical Investigations includes criticism of semantic and scientific truths and reflects a shift in thought concerning the study of language. Wittgenstein replaces the logical vocabulary that includes such concepts as "reference," "correspondence," "rules," "categories," etc., with a dynamic vocabulary that includes such concepts as "use," "family resemblance," and "language games." The study of language is no longer treated as an activity whose goal is to uncover logical structures that underlie the foundations of language. Rather it is taken to be a practice that traces different ways of using language, which is now perceived as a living and changing mechanism with many varied functions that serve not only to convey thoughts but other human purposes.[53]

At the same time, transitioning to meaning in use does not entail abandoning the search for the abstract essence or common denominator among the varied uses of language. In the *Investigations*, Wittgenstein still adheres to his Tractarian notion that "essence is expressed in grammar"[54] and that "grammar tells us what kind of object anything is (Theology as grammar)."[55] According to (later) Wittgenstein's methodological directive, even if concepts

---

49 Wittgenstein, *Philosophical investigations*, §1.
50 Dorit Lemberger, "Between theology as grammar and religious point of view in Wittgenstein philosophy of religion," *Iyyun: The Jerusalem Philosophical Quarterly* 52, 2003: 399–424 [Hebrew], 416.
51 Gottlob Frege, "Sense and reference," *The Philosophical Review* 57(3) (1948 [1892]), 209–230.
52 Wittgenstein, *Philosophical Investigations*, §43.
53 Ibid, §304.
54 Ibid, §371.
55 Ibid, §373.

do not have clear boundaries, they can still be studied based on their usage. Thus, for example, Wittgenstein emphasizes that there is no hierarchy between words or concepts in language:

> [...] If the words "language," "experience," "world" have a use, it must be as humble a one as that of the words "table," "lamp," "door."[56]

According to Wittgenstein, there are no higher-order (metaphysical) words or super-concepts, just as there is no meta-language.[57] Accordingly, Wittgenstein urges us to ground all metaphysical concepts, which are the objects of our philosophical investigations, and to investigate them in their real usage in everyday language:

> When philosophers use a word – "knowledge," "being," "object," "I," "proposition/sentence," "name" – and try to grasp the essence of the thing, one must always ask oneself: is the word ever actually used in this way in the language in which it is at home? – What we do is to bring words back from their metaphysical to their everyday use.[58]

If we adopt Wittgenstein's methodological directive, we can describe and clarify a philosophical-psychological concept such as "meaning in life," its contents, aspects, and modes of constitution by tracing how it is used in language. The notion of "meaning in use" means that what gives words meaning is their concrete use. In other words, to clarify the meaning of some concept, we need nothing more than to trace its actual usage in everyday language. Such an investigation will not strive to uncover an abstract meaning that dictates how a word is or will be used because in everyday language there is no necessity. Language is constantly changing, it operates in different ways, people use it for different purposes, old and new, and in so doing they expand and redefine its boundaries. This conception of languages is captured nicely in Wittgenstein's metaphor of "language as a city."[59]

My proposal is, thus, to follow Wittgenstein and reevaluate the meaning of the concept "meaning in life" according to its concrete usage in everyday language. Given that the question of meaning in life is a subjective question that largely involves the subject's choice, the best way to investigate it is through a relational investigation that reflects the intentions of the speaker at a particular point in time and within a particular context.

---

56 Ibid, §97.
57 Wittgenstein, *Tractatus Logico-Philosophicus*, §5.5563.
58 Wittgenstein, *Philosophical Investigations*, §116.
59 Ibid, §18.

This mode of investigation can be incorporated into a qualitative research program, based on in-depth interviews, which is first and foremost characterized by being conducted in "the language of words."[60] Thus, I suggest that we acknowledge the possibility of carrying out a conceptual investigation by means of the qualitative research method that has gained popularity in the last few decades across many disciplines. In the course of such interviews, participants are asked to respond to questions concerning their conception of the meaning of their life from a subjective perspective.

"A Lecture on Ethics," which has been discussed in the previous section, provides suggestions for questions concerning the way a person conceives the meaning of his life. To clarify the subject matter of ethics to his audience, Wittgenstein presents a range of phrases that are synonymous with "ethics," and in so doing attempts to paint a picture, as he says, of their common characteristics.

> Now instead of saying "Ethics is the enquiry into what is good" I could have said Ethics is the enquiry into what is valuable, or, into what is really important, or I could have said Ethics is the enquiry into the meaning of life, or into what makes life worth living, or into the right way of living.[61]

This quotation has two important implications for our purposes: First, it provides an example of the application of a research methodology that aims to clarify a philosophical concept such as "ethics" by attending to its synonymous expressions in language. Second, it provides examples of concrete questions that we can ask when we turn to investigate, directly or indirectly, how people grasp the meaning of their lives, for example: What is important for you in life? What do you take to be valuable? What makes your life meaningful and worth living? What do you think is the correct way to live life? Such qualitative inquiry can provide a perspective on different ways that certain subjects at a certain time constitute meaning in their lives, and, in this respect, provides a linguistic corpus of everyday expressions that are synonymous with the concept "meaning in life" and exposes its relevance in the lives of the research participants.

Additionally, a qualitative investigation for the purposes of conceptual clarification can utilize other methodological tools that Wittgenstein makes available in the *Investigations*. Exploring the different uses can be carried out within the framework of language games. In the Socratic form, Wittgenstein shows us that nothing in common can be found among everything that we call "game," such as board games, games of imagination, ball games, etc. The only things common among them are "similarities, affinities," which he calls

---

60 Asher Shkedi, *The Meaning Behind the Words: Methodologies of Qualitative Research: Theory and Practice* (Tel-Aviv University, Ramot Press, 2014), 13 [Hebrew].
61 Wittgenstein, "A Lecture on Ethics," 5.

"family resemblances" – the resemblance, which cannot be characterized clearly, that holds among family members.[62] In *Philosophical Investigations*, Wittgenstein proposes that we treat language as a collection of language games, that is, as an entire set of behaviors that serve different purposes among groups of people.[63] The centrality of the concept of "language game" in Wittgenstein's later thought emphasizes the fact that speaking a language is "part of an activity, or of a form of life."[64] In other words, speaking a language is part of a wider context and is a changing, emergent, thing. It is, therefore, also unpredictable and ungrounded. This conception of language as a collection of "language games" reflects a sharp departure from traditional logical categorization and turns the spotlight onto language use.[65] In light of this conception, which examines meaning in use, we can inquire as to which language games speakers play when speaking of the meaning of their lives and identify some "family resemblance" between them. The conception of meaning in use also sets in advance the limits of the investigation. A description of the concrete uses of a concept will never purport to encompass and exhaust all the uses of some specific concept in language. Conceptual clarification in terms of concrete usage offers a limited perspective, but one that can nonetheless provide clarifications and insights.

Finally, Wittgenstein's demand to replace the search for abstract meanings in favor of concrete meanings is also methodological-ethical; it urges us, as researchers, to attend and be alert to the different and varied roles that people give their words at a given time. It demands us to withhold our often-hasty judgments concerning the meanings of words and sentences and abandon our preconceptions and be open to new and creative meanings.[66]

In sum, qualitative research that examines the concrete usage of some concept or other in everyday language does not bring us from the everyday concrete level to an abstract metaphysical level. Thus, we remain within the limits of language that Wittgenstein already charts in the *Tractatus*. We do not attempt to go beyond this limit and articulate a scientific theory concerning the meaning of life. Such an inquiry helps us clarify the concept within its circumstances of usage by a given speaker.[67] Nonetheless, this does not amount to giving up on an important and relevant conceptual clarification. On the contrary, it is of great significance that even though the concept "meaning in life" is abstract, complex, and elusive, it has expression

---

62 Wittgenstein, *Philosophical Investigations*, §66-7.
63 Tamar Sovran, *Language and Meaning: The Birth and Growth of Cognitive Semantics* (Haifa University Press, 2006) [Hebrew], 76.
64 Wittgenstein, *Philosophical Investigations*, §23.
65 Sovran, *Language and Meaning*, 77.
66 Eliezer Malkiel, An *Analytic Commentary on the Philosophical Investigations §1-§315 by Ludwig Wittgenstein* (Jerusalem: Carmel, 2017) [Hebrew], 24.
67 Adi Ofir, "Definition," *Mafte'akh* 11 (2017), 71–99: 84. [Hebrew]

in language. Therefore, even if it cannot be subject to scientific investigation, it can be subject to qualitative research that traces the subject's choices as these are reflected in his linguistic decisions. As Wittgenstein says:

> Philosophers very often talk about investigating, analyzing, the meaning of words. But let's not forget that a word hasn't got a meaning given to it, as it were, by a power independent of us, so that there could be a kind of scientific investigation into what the word *really* means. A word has the meaning someone has given to it.[68]

Meaning as Choice – Methodological Application in Ordinary Language

In the above, I proposed a methodological interpretation of Wittgenstein's early and late comments on the question of the meaning of life, which we can apply in our investigation of the concept of "meaning in life" and its relevance to (post)modern life. In this section, I will exemplify this methodological tool by analyzing three semi-structured deep interviews with Hebrew-speaking octogenarian Israelis.[69] The interviews were conducted as part of a study that aims to understand how different speakers understand and construct the meaning of their lives.[70] The questions that comprise the interviews are similar; they concern the ways that the interviewees grasp the meaning of their lives as well as their attitudes toward events, people, and other aspects of life they take to be meaningful in their life stories.

The assumption is that when a speaker uses language, he makes certain (conscious or unconscious) selections from his linguistic repertoire; the investigation of these choices may expose his modes of understanding and conceptualization.[71] As I cannot here detail the great variety of themes that

---

68 Ludwig Wittgenstein, *The Blue and Brown Books*. (Oxford and Cambridge: Blackwell, 1958), 27–28.
69 The choice to interview speakers over the age of 80 stems from the assumption that this stage in life calls forth growing preoccupation with questions regarding meaning in life that is characterized by retrospective observation, a summary of achievements and failures, and an attempt to establish a "unified self." (Erik H. Erikson, *Childhood and Society* (W.W. Norton And Company, 1950)).
70 The interviews were conducted as part of a study in The Program for Hermeneutics and Cultural Studies that received the approval of the ethics committee of Bar-Ilan University (confirmation no.: ISU202010001).
71 Michael A. K. Halliday, "A brief sketch of systemic grammar," in Gunther Kress ed., *Halliday: System and Function in Language: Selected Papers* (Oxford University Press, 1976 [1969]), 3–6; Michael A. K. Halliday, "Meaning as choice," in Lise Fontaine, Tom Bartlett, and Gerard O'Grady eds., *Systemic Functional Linguistics: Exploring Choice* (Cambridge: Cambridge University Press, 2013), 15–36.

came up during the interviews, I will present, as an example, one major theme that emerged from the three interviews. This theme captures a common aspect in how the different interviewees grasp the meaning of their lives, which can be generalized through the motto: "Meaning in life as choice."

The first interviewee (83) lost her son in an IDF operational activity (when he was 28). Her interview began with the question "what is meaningful for you in life?". The first thing the interviewee said in response is: "What is meaningful for me in life is that it wasn't simple." After a few long seconds of silence, she continued: "My starting point is the terrible disaster that befell me." Though, as an interviewer, I had no prior knowledge of her life story, the interviewee chose to begin with the most significant fact of her life – the loss of her son. This was the starting point of our conversation, but also the starting point of her thoughts about the meaning of her life and about a life worth living.

> The decision was to live with dignity, and to be a grandmother as a grandmother ought to be. To continue to host them every Friday, to participate in raising the kids. That was the decision I made, I think, courageously, because it was not easy, and to this day I thank myself for this good choice that I made, because when you stand between life and death and you choose life it is the correct choice [...] I felt that in life, the choice between life and death is unequivocal. It isn't a little bit of life and a little bit of death. If you chose life, then live and respect your life.

The meaning of her life was reflected in her active decision, a decision she can pinpoint in space and time – an existential decision to choose life and to live it fully, that is, to transform it into a meaningful life, despite and in the shadow of the disaster. She describes the trauma of losing her son using the metaphor of an "atom bomb," one that destroys every part of life and barely leaves the possibility for renewed healthy growth. As she tells it, the mourning and bereavement eliminated any possibility of establishing mental and linguistic meaning. Nonetheless, as she describes the situation, the years have made it possible for her to bring about new growth, as she put it, growth alongside mourning, activity, and productivity alongside pain and bereavement.

> This is something that I had no knowledge of. What real mourning, from the gut, amounts to. I wasn't even able to read the news headlines. I wasn't able to do anything. I wasn't able to cook [...] I wasn't able to do any regular daily activity. Everything would go wrong [...] It's as though some kind of scarf envelopes your brain. You can't speak the right words [...]
>
> The upheavals in my life, especially that of the loss of my son, is so dramatic and so overwhelming [...] it is not something soft, tender,

dreamy. It's an atom bomb. And yet there is still growth later on. I once said that my heart was cleaved in two. I constantly feel that there are parts within me that are active; they do, they create, they write, and there is a part that is always crying. And this combination of this divided heart, this soul split in two, is me.

The second interviewee (85) spoke of the meaning of his life as a conscious choice to be an observant person of faith, who spends most of his day studying the Bible and the Talmud, in prayer and teaching. This interview also began with major trauma – namely, his experiences as a young child during the Holocaust and the many family members, including his father, that were lost during that time. Yet the vast majority of the interview revolved around his life today, which, he claimed, is full of the joy of learning and of curiosity, which lends his life deep spiritual content, enriches it with meaning, and transforms it into a life "with not one wasted day."

[...] to feel that life is passing through you, not beside you, I think is a great thing. Many people feel that life passes them by, and I feel that life is passing through me, thanks to the studies [...] The Talmud gives me deep inner content.

This interviewee emphasized his conscious decision to live as an observant person. He too can identify a point in his life when he actively chose his attitude toward life after the Holocaust. He describes the way he decides to look at life every day as a miracle – an attitude to which he largely attributes his choosing a life of faith. Additionally, he sees himself as part of something grander – as a part of the Jewish people who survived the Holocaust and who now has the task of attending to the continuity of the Jewish people.

In my opinion, we, as Jews, have a role to play. We have the role of attending to the continuity of the Jewish people [...] The meaning of life for me is the continuity of the Jewish people, and I do all that I can so that it carries on [...] In my mind, the resurrection of the people of Israel, the resurrection of the State of Israel, is a great miracle [...] I cannot imagine my life not in Israel.

The third interviewee (85) spoke of the last five years as the most meaningful in her life. Unlike the previous two interviewees, who spent most of the interview speaking about how they imbued their lives with meaning, the third interviewee actually spoke at length of her difficult life, described in "oppressive" terms. At a very young age, her mother died, and she lived under the shadow of a "domineering" father, as she put it, who expected her to bear the burden of raising the other children. In adulthood, she married a husband who she also described as "domineering." In so doing, she drew a straight line between her childhood under the shadow of her father and her adulthood under the shadow of her husband. She often repeated the sentence "I was missing something" in reference to her life and told of many dreams she had (to enlist in the army, to become a nurse, and more), which she claimed dissolved because of external circumstances or fate. When asked in the interview "what is meaningful to you in life?" she responded:

> Bless him, my husband is now in an institution. The significant thing that happened to me is that he got out of the house. Suddenly I felt freer, I did things I have never done, to walk out without asking anyone, to go to the [seniors'] club every day, which he also didn't allow me [...] This is what's meaningful – what made me an independent woman.

The fact that her husband left the house, upon falling ill with Alzheimer's and needing to receive treatment at an institution, is described as the key to her freedom to choose. Only in the last few years, when she is no longer bound by the will of others and no longer "dominated," as she put it, does she feel that her life is full of meaning – in the very fact of her being free to choose as she pleases.

From the three interviews, it thus follows that what makes their lives meaningful is their choice to navigate their lives in their own way and according to their own decisions. Although for the third interviewee freedom of choice was born of necessity, it is what she highlights as the most meaningful in her life. Additionally, in all three interviews it is a salient fact that the linguistic expression of how the speakers grasp the meaning of their lives is formally shaped by drawing a contrast with their past experiences: for the first interviewee it was the choice of life in the face of her son's death; for the second interviewee it was the choice to take responsibility for the continuity of the Jewish people in the face of the Holocaust, and for the third interviewee it was the very possibility of choice in contrast to the years in which she was "dominated." In other words, it seems that meaning emerges out of contrast, both in form-structure, that is, in terms of linguistic expression, and mentally. The purpose of the contrast established by the interviewees in their narratives is, on the one hand, to emphasize and reinforce the significance of the events they chose to speak about in their interviews, and, at the same time, to sharpen and highlight the role these stories play within their experiences and how significant aspects of their lives were constituted.

To summarize, this chapter proposes an interpretation of Wittgenstein's comments on the question of the meaning of life that can be transformed into a methodological tool that emphasizes inquiry in action, within the limits of the world and language, at a concrete everyday level. The chapter shows how using this methodology can expand our knowledge of abstract, vague, and complex concepts, which need not be involved in causal processes. In this case, we examined the different uses of the concept "meaning in life" in everyday language among three octogenarian Hebrew speakers. Of course, the presented conclusion provides only a partial perspective on the concept's usage. To expand our knowledge concerning the concept of "meaning in life" we must apply the methodological tool with other speakers, of different ages, and in different contexts. Yet I believe that this is the conceptual investigation that is most loyal to Wittgenstein's thought. Returning to his metaphor of the city, this has been but a short stroll through its streets. To learn more, we must continue walking.

Bibliography

American Psychiatric Association. *Diagnostic and Statistical Manual of Mental Disorders: DSM-5*. Arlington, TX: American Psychiatric Association Publishing, 2013.

Czekierda, Katarzyna, Banik, Anna, Park, Crystal L., and Luszczynska, Aleksandra. "Meaning in Life and Physical Health: Systematic Review and Meta-analysis." *Health Psychology Review* 11, no. 4 (2017): 387–418, 10.1080/17437199.2017.132 7325

Eigen, Michael. *Psychic Deadness*. London: Routledge, 2004.

Erikson, Erik H.. *Childhood and Society*. W.W. Norton And Company, 1950.

Frankl, Victor. *Man's Search for Meaning*. Boston: Beacon Press, 2006 [1946].

Frege, Gottlob. "Sense and reference." *The Philosophical Review* 57, no. 3 (1948) [1892]: 209–230.

Freud, Sigmund. "The Meaning of the Symptoms," Seventeenth Lecture in *A General Introduction to Psychoanalysis*, trans. G. Stanley Hall. New York: Horace Liveright, 1920.

Freud, Sigmund. *Civilization and Its Discontents*, trans. J. Strachey. New York: W. W. Norton, 1961 [1929].

Glebe-Møller, Jens. "Wittgenstein and Kierkegaard," *Kierkegaardiana* 15 (1991): 55–68.

Halliday, Michael A. K. "A Brief Sketch of Systemic Grammar" In *Halliday: System and Function in Language: Selected Papers*, edited by Gunther Kress, Oxford University Press, 1976 [1969].

Halliday, Michael A. K. "Meaning as Choice," In *Systemic Functional Linguistics: Exploring Choice*, edited by Lise Fontaine, Tom Bartlett, and Gerard O'Grady, 15–36. Cambridge: Cambridge University Press, 2013.

Hoffman, Louis, Yang Mark, Kaklauskas Francis J., and Chan Albert. *Existential Psychology East-West*. Colorado Springs, CO: University of the Rockies Press, 2009.

Kierkegaard, Søren Aabye. *Fear and Trembling and the Sickness unto Death*. Princeton University Press, 2013 [1843].

Kierkegaard, Søren Aabye. *Concluding Unscientific Postscript to Philosophical Fragments*, Vol. 1, trans. H. V. Hong and E. H. Hong. New Jersey: Princeton University Press, 1992 [1846].

Lemberger, Dorit. "Between Theology as Grammar and Religious Point of View in Wittgenstein Philosophy of Religion," *Iyyun: The Jerusalem Philosophical Quarterly* 52 (2003): 399–424 [Hebrew].

Lurie, Yuval. "Wittgenstein on the Meaning of Life," *Iyyun: The Jerusalem Philosophical Quarterly* 49 (2000): 115–136 [Hebrew].

Lurie, Yuval. *Tracking the Meaning of Life: a Philosophical Journey*. Columbia Missouri: University of Missouri Press, 2006.

Malcolm, Norman. *Ludwig Wittgenstein. A Memoir*. London: Oxford University Press, 2001 [1958].

Malkiel, Eliezer. An *Analytic Commentary on the Philosophical Investigations §1-§315 by Ludwig Wittgenstein*. Jerusalem: Carmel, 2017 [Hebrew].

Mualem, Shlomi. "Running up Against the Limits of Language: Wittgenstein and Kierkegaard." *Iyyun: The Jerusalem Philosophical Quarterly* 54 (2005): 131–148 [Hebrew].

Ofir, Adi. "Definition." *Mafte'akh* 11 (2017): 71–99 [Hebrew].

Peirce, Charles Sanders. *The Collected Papers of Charles Sanders Peirce*, reproducing vol. I-VI, edited by Charles Hartshorne and Paul Weiss, 1931–1935. Cambridge, MA: Harvard University Press; vols. VII-VIII, Arthur W. Burks (ed.) (same publisher), 1958.

Shkedi, Asher. *The Meaning Behind the Words: Methodologies of Qualitative Research: Theory and Practice*. Tel-Aviv University, Ramot Press, 2014 [Hebrew].

Sovran, Tamar. *Language and Meaning: The Birth and Growth of Cognitive Semantics*. Haifa University Press, 2006 [Hebrew].

Ullman-Margalit, Edna. "The Meaning of Life and Meaningful Life." In *Education – Core and Essence*, edited by Yeshayahu Tadmor, and Amir Freimann, 123–132. Tel-Aviv: Mofet Institute, 2012 [Hebrew].

Van Deurzen, Emmy. *Existential Counselling & Psychotherapy in Practice* (2nd ed.) London: Sage, 2012.

Wittgenstein, Ludwig. *Tractatus Logico-Philosophicus*, trans. C. K. Ogden. New York: Dover, 1998 [1921].

Wittgenstein, Ludwig. "A lecture on ethics," *The Philosophical Review* 74, no. 1 (1965) [1933]: 3–12.

Wittgenstein, Ludwig. *The Blue and Brown Books*. Oxford and Cambridge: Blackwell, 1958.

Wong, Paul T. P. "Meaning Therapy: An Integrative and Positive Existential Psychotherapy," *Journal of Contemporary Psychotherapy* 40, no. 2 (2010): 85–93.

Yalom, Irvin David. *Existential Psychotherapy*. New York: Basic Books, 1980.

Chapter 7

Language Game and Separations
A Psychoanalytic-Philosophical View about the Infinity of the Separation Experience

Ophira Schorr Levy[1]

> "*Certain events would put me into a position in which I could not go on with the old language-game any further.*"[2]

During the cycle of life all human beings experience separations. No man can escape the pain of separation, from feelings and the thoughts it evokes. Separation and being apart are necessities and need that frequently clash with other human needs such as belonging, support, and security. Separation is defined in the Oxford Dictionary as follows: "The act of separating people or things; the state of being separate from someone or something, a period that people spend separately from each other."[3] Some separations will be experienced positively but many will experience it painfully, sometimes, even to the point of dysfunction. Separations have the power to shape relationships, both in structuring the past and in influencing the future. Separations within close relationships can cause a potential risk for the development of emotional problems and at the same time may lead to growth and development.[4]

This chapter presents two main arguments: First, the impact of separations on self-development and the experience of being apart is continued and is created throughout life and is not fixed in infancy. A second argument claims that this impact is constructed and established through processes that occur by language use.

---

1 This chapter is based on a Ph.D. thesis carried out under the supervision of Dr. Dorit Lemberger in the Program for Hermeneutics and Culture Studies at Bar-Ilan University. I wish to thank Dr. Lemberger and the program for their professional and financial support.
2 Ludwig Wittgenstein, *On Certainty* (Oxford: Basil Blackwell, 1969), §617.
3 Oxford Advanced American Dictionary, Oxford University Press, 2021.
4 George A Bonanno, Loss, trauma, and human resilience. Have we underestimated the human capacity to thrive after extremely aversive events? *American Psychologist*, 59(2004): 20–28.

DOI: 10.4324/9781003326588-7

This chapter will present the reference of main psychoanalytic theories regarding separations, Wittgenstein's contribution to the examination of separation and separateness through the use of language and will propose a connection between psychoanalysis and the philosophy of language through a study case of Shira, a six-year-old girl and through discussion of the novel "The Lying Life of Adults."[5] The choice of analyzing a literary work expresses Bakhatin's conception of literature as conveying to us something of the diversity of human existence, the constant movement between the variety of possibilities of man in front of other humans, who constitute speakers at any given moment. There are endless dialogical possibilities and psychoanalysis finds it hard to deal with this richness, due to the lack of sufficient discourse theory.[6] Literature, then, can fill this gap, it allows for the presentation of separation processes and self-establishment from the individual point of view, which are reflected in the literary writing. The use of a literary work, such as the novel "The Lying Life of Adults," allows analysis of poetically worded ideas about separation. These ideas appear in the literary work concerning a concrete situation but are formulated as a generalization concerning reality outside the work. Literature thus becomes a philosophy – universal wisdom about the nature of the world.[7] It will be demonstrated how separation experiences are shaped in both cases and how interpretive change of parting events is possible through language mechanisms.

Change and Permanency – the River of Life

Separation and being apart experience are cross-cultures and periods of human phenomena and they are a formative factor in everyone's lives, from the moment of birth to death. The question of change and permanency in the world has preoccupied humans since the dawn of history, as can be understood from the fifth-century BCE Greek philosopher Heraclitus's words: "Upon those who step into the same rivers different and again different: waters flow."[8]

Heraclitus provides us with various images of how functioned the river of life and argues for the uniformity of contrasts. The river is the same river, which always flows through the same channels, even though those who enter it are washed in different water. The person inside the river is watching the same river and at the same time, he is also watching the constant change of

---

5 Elena Farrante, *The Lying Life of Adults*, Ann Goldstein (Translator) (Europa Editions, 2020).
6 Mikhail Bakhtin, *Speech Genres and Other Late Essays*. Trans. Vern W. McGee (Austin, Tx: University of Texas Press, 1986).
7 According to Wimsatt the literary text is both universal and individual in that the concrete and private statements in literature paradoxically become universal. See: Wimsatt, W. K. Jr. *The verbal icon: Studies in the meaning of poetry* (Kentucky: University of Kentucky Press, 1954).
8 Heraclitus, *Fragments of Heraclitus*, translated by John Burnet, 1920, fr. 12.

the water surrounding him. In the same way, man sees the world in rational uniformity even though it contains patterns of diversity and variability.

Wittgenstein also used the river as an image for the relationship between change and uniformity, though not in the same way as Herculithus' conception. Wittgenstein wrote: "The mythology may change back into a state of flux, the river-bed of thoughts may shift. But I distinguish between the movement of the waters on the riverbed and the shift of the bed itself, though there is not a sharp division of the one from the other."[9]

Wittgenstein made a distinction between the water flowing in the river and the riverbed. According to Wittgenstein, the river channel is not entirely composed of hard rocks, moreover at any time they can undergo a gradual erosion, meaning a change.[10]

In his book "On Certainty" Wittgenstein examined the nature of our basic assumptions and revealed the distinction between these assumptions and knowledge.[11] Wittgenstein proposed what is known as the "hinge propositions" according to it we use doubt-exempt claims as we use door hinges. These provide a well-established foundation on which, metaphorically, "the door can turn," and from which we can seek answers to our questions and doubts.[12] These claims are, in fact, the basic foundations of our logic. Wittgenstein showed that certainty differed from knowledge (in the sense of justified true beliefs), "I know" does not indicate knowledge but subjective certainty. Many hinges on which our certainty hangs on are common to all people, but some hinges differ from one to another and are culture and background dependent.[13] Moyal-Sharrock calls this type of certainty "non-epistemic" which is not the result of logic, nor is it empirical in a scientific sense. This is the certainty of our worldview, it "is the inherited background against which I distinguish between true and false."[14]

When this background is shaken and changed, certainty falls beneath our feet, and we cannot play the familiar language games through which we operate in the world. The question of change is directly related to the constant separation experiences that human beings experience and the challenges they pose in the self and relation to the world. Whenever reality changes we part from the previous conditions in which our being used to exist, we part from parts we knew within ourselves and from a sense of

---

9 Ludwig Wittgenstein, *On Certainty* (Oxford: Basil Blackwell, 1969) §97.
10 Roger A. Shiner, Wittgenstein and Heraclitus: Two river-images, *Philosophy, 49* (1974): 191–97.
11 Daniele Moyal-Sharrock, William H. Brenner, (Eds.), *Readings of Wittgenstein's On Certainty* (Palgrave Macmillan, 2005).
12 "But it isn't that the situation is like this: We just can't investigate everything, and for that reason we are forced to rest content with assumption. If I want the door to turn, the hinges must stay put." Ludwig Wittgenstein, *On Certainty*, 1969, §343.
13 Danièle Moyal-Sharrock, Logic in Action: Wittgenstein's Logical Pragmatism and the Impotence of Scepticism, *Philosophical Investigations*, 26:2 (2003): 125–48.
14 Ludwig Wittgenstein, *On Certainty*, 1969, §94.

security we feel. Separation experiences can be seen as events that change the human mythology, the riverbed of our life. Human beings experience a sudden interruption of the familiar reality, the continuity of their mental experience, their identity changes at once, and the recognition that what was in the past will never return, floods and shapes them.

The Use of Language and the Connection to Separations

How closeness and distance are created through different linguistic mechanisms is relevant to understanding the processes of separation and separateness. The article proposes to examine these processes from a linguistic point of view because according to Wittgenstein the experience of human beings in the world is always influenced by their language, its context, and manner of use. However, there is equally no stable meaning, because meaning is determined by our diverse uses of words in concrete contexts.[15]

Freud, Klein, and Winnicott contributed greatly to the understanding of the development of the ability to symbolize, from the early stages of development.[16] At the same time, it is hard to find in these approaches a satisfactory description of the cognitive process that characterizes the ability to symbolize. The philosophical concepts regarding language and the relationship between the subject and the world can constitute a significant contribution to understanding this practice. Describing the complexity and the various possible relationships in the symbolization process can also allow psychoanalysis to understand more complex situations and to define a relationship of merging and separation in a richer way.[17]

---

15 According to Wittgenstein the ability to use words is not at all conditioned by the ability to define them. We will usually know how to use the word even though it has unclear boundaries and blurred margins – "One might say that the concept 'game' is a concept with blurred edges. – "But is a blurred concept a concept at all? – Is an indistinct photograph a picture of a person at all? Is it even always an advantage to replace an indistinct picture by a sharp one? Isn't the indistinct one often exactly what we need?" Ludwig Wittgenstein, *Philosophical Investigations*: The German Text, with a Revised English Translation (Blackwell, 1953), §71.

16 See for example: Melanie Klein, The Importance of Symbol-Formation in the Development of the Ego. *International Journal of Psychoanalysis* 11 (1930): 24–39. Donald W. Winnicott, Transitional Objects and Transitional Phenomena – A Study of the First Not-Me Possession1, *International Journal of Psycho-Analysis*, 34 (1953): 89–97.

17 Lemberger phrased: "This requirement stems from the fact that at the heart of psychoanalytic thought are discussions about the importance and necessity of symbolization in separation processes and subjective founding processes, but none of them defines what a sign or symbol is, how they are created and how they function in these processes." In: Dorit Lemberger, "'Love is a curious mixture of opposites': The Symbolic Function of Language in Psychoanalysis and Its Use in a Study of Amos Oz's A Tale of Love and Darkness," *The Soul Beetle: Interdisciplinary Perspectives in Psychoanalysis* (Tel-Aviv: Resling, 2020): 17–52, 26.

Separations and Separateness in the Psychoanalytic Theories of Freud, Klein, and Winnicott

It can be said that the genesis of psychoanalysis is in separation. In his constitutive book, "The Interpretation of the Dreams," Freud wrote that his father's death is what made him go in search of the meaning of his dreams.[18] Thus, the experiences of separation and loss formed the basis of Freud's work from its early stages and influenced him throughout his writing.

In his well-known work "Mourning and Melancholia," Freud described the process of mourning as a conflict between the demand of the ego, which recognizes the reality, the detachment of the libido from the missing object, and the resistance of the id who refuses to accept the rough reality.[19] This resistance can lead a grieving person into losing interest in the outside world, in loving and self-perception – then the grief becomes pathological grief. In a state of normal grief, reality takes its place until the ego is released from the grasp of the object. This statement of Freud raises the question: Can we truly be completely free from the significant objects from which we were separated? Later, Freud changed his conception and claimed that the primary objects continue to exist in the mind throughout life.[20] Many times in the clinic, we see how separations during early life continue to resonate throughout the rest of our lives, even after years of therapy.

Freud described a process in which man chooses to love the object for a narcissistic motive, in fact, through the object he loves himself. In situations in which the object harms him, hatred is created, however since the libido is invested in the same object in a narcissistic way, a conflict of love-hate is formed. Underlying the melancholic patient's suffering there is a pathological, ambivalent, and aggressive connection between the subject and the object. There is a relationship in which there is insufficient separateness, and the sick self identifies with the aggressive, introverted narcissistic object. This is how Freud connected between losing an object, narcissism, and identification. "In this way, an object-loss: was transformed into an ego-loss and the conflict between the ego and the loved person into a cleavage between the critical activity of the ego and the ego as altered by identification."[21]

---

18 Sigmund Freud, *The Interpretation of Dreams*. Third Edition. Trans. by A. A. Brill. New York: The Macmillan Company, 1913 (Bartleby.com, 2010).
19 Sigmund Freud, Mourning and Melancholia, *The Standard Edition of the Complete Psychological Works of Sigmund Freud*, Volume XIV (1914–1916): On the History of the Psycho-Analytic Movement, Papers on Metapsychology and Other Works (1917): 243–58.
20 Sigmund Freud, Analysis Terminable and Interminable. *Int. J. Psycho-Anal.*, 18 (1937): 373–405.
21 Sigmund Freud, Mourning and Melancholia (1917), 249.

One of Freud's main theories concerns shaping the subject's identity through the solution of the Oedipal complex.[22] Freud assumes the claim that the subject is created within the family, social and cultural system, and that at the base of this formation lies the desire for the murder of the father.[23] Although Freud focused the drama on sexuality, it is notable that this drama emphasizes the fact that separation from the mother's body during birth does not take on psychological significance but at a much later stage. The growing child recognizes his sexuality and the father's sexuality as a factor that has an increasing influence both on his identity and as a barrier in his relationship with his mother.[24]

Freud initially assumed that the origin of childhood neurosis was in the repression of childhood trauma of sexual seduction by an adult. Later, he abandoned this theory and concluded that the neurotic symptoms were not directly related to events that happened (in reality) but to hallucinations and sexual expectations.[25] This change led to Freud's psychoanalysis becoming a journey into the patient's inner world, especially as it manifested itself in the early childhood years. Consequently, Freud's theory downplayed the importance of actual events affecting human life. When it comes to separation and separateness process, the importance of events that took place cannot be underestimated. One cannot ignore the fact that separation often includes the involvement of other actual persons.

Compared to Freud, Klein focused on investigating the infant's mental life from birth. Klein described an infant with a primary and emerging self-nucleus that is in contact with the object from the moment of birth, but his perception of himself and the object is influenced by physiological maturity, from the intensity of his impulses and needs, and his unconscious fantasies. The infant moves between a sense of merging between self and the other, and between an evolving perception of separation and a distinct sense of self. There is a movement between a rigid split to protect from anxiety and give meaning and a longing to unite with the mother's body and its contents. This can be seen in the initial position that Klein called the paranoid-schizoid position characterized by the movement between the splitting mechanism representing complete separation and the projective identification mechanism representing mixing and merging.[26]

---

22 Sigmund Freud, A Special Type of Choice of Object made by Men (Contributions to the Psychology of Love I). *The Standard Edition of the Complete Psychological Works of Sigmund Freud*, Volume XI (1910): 163–76.
23 This argument also appears in the context of culture in the book: Sigmund Freud, *Totem and Taboo: Resemblances between the Psychic Lives of Savages and Neurotics*. Harmondsworth, Middlesex (Penguin Books, 1938).
24 Nick Mansfield, Freud and the Split Subject in: *Subjectivity theories of the self from Freud to Haraway*, Australia: Allen & Unwin (2000): 25–38.
25 Anthony Storr, *Freud: A Very Short Introduction* (Oxford University Press, 2001).
26 Melanie Klein, Notes on Some Schizoid Mechanisms. *The International journal of psychoanalysis*, 27 (1946): 99–110.

In the more advanced position, the depressive position, the capacity for integration increased and there is a separate entity. There is a willingness to accept the separate existence of the object, which increases the feeling of depression and loneliness but also allows one to process them. According to Klein, the human condition is characterized by partiality, finality, separateness, and otherness, therefore the recognition of separateness is an achievement and from it, the recognition of responsibility toward the other is built. The depressive position contains a recognition of all parts of the self, for better or worse. There is a sense of responsibility that moderates loneliness through reparation and creativity in the inner world and connections in the outer world.[27] In the paranoid-schizoid position, there is no gap between the symbol and the symbolized and both are emotionally equivalent while in the depressive position the symbol stands instead of the object and represents it. The constructed capacity for symbolism creates a space between the self and the object and allows the separation.[28] The symbol is created in the transition between the two positions and its formation allows the development of the depressive position. According to Klein, in different life situations, we relate to reality and perceive it in different symbolic ways that match the characteristics of the different positions.

Unlike Klein, the starting point of the development process according to Winnicott is not the infant itself but a unit of infant-environment or infant-mother, a unit from which the infant cannot be distinguished as an independent entity. The dependence of the baby is so absolute at this point that it means that the environment is a part of it.[29]

One of the essential roles of the mother at this stage is to allow the baby to experience an existence in which his needs are met and invasive interventions by the environment are avoided. Beyond a certain amount, the baby will experience the invasion of the world as an existential threat and as a cause of anxiety. On the other hand, in the ideal situation, in which the baby turns to the world and discovers it spontaneously, without losing the sense of self, the necessary illusion in which the baby feels that he has an omnipotent control over his environment is preserved. Continuing the baby's progress toward separation and reality involves developing the ability to use the object and not just in terms of object-relating. The use of the object is possible only when the object is perceived as a thing for itself, when the subject accepts his independent existence and being part of reality and not just as the result of projections.[30]

---

27 Melanie Klein, A Contribution to the Psychogenesis of Manic-depressive States. *International Journal of Psychoanalysis*, 16(1) (1935): 145–74.
28 Melanie Klein, The Importance of Symbol-Formation in the Development of the Ego. *International Journal of Psychoanalysis* 11 (1930): 24–39.
29 Donald W. Winnicott, The Theory of the Parent-Infant Relationship1. *Int. J. Psycho-Anal.*, 41 (1960): 585–95.
30 Donald W. Winnicott, *Playing and Reality* (London: Penguin, 1971).

The discovery of the externality of the object has enormous importance, because the baby enters with its help into a world of external and autonomous objects, with their uniqueness and features, which enrich his experience remarkably. Winnicott assumed that this task never ends, and the constant struggle involved in it creates great stress, and each of us needs to rest from it from time to time. The stage of transition between subjective and objective perception and the moments of rest (in which the claim to sharply distinguish between external and internal reality is not required) is called by Winnicott "a transitional phenomenon," "transitional object," "transitional space," and "potential space."[31] This is where the use of symbols develops, representing at the same time the phenomenon of the outside world and the phenomena of the individual human being.

The psychoanalytic theories presented so far have given a central place to separation from the object which also involves the development of the capacity for separateness and symbolization. This chapter seeks to broaden the psychoanalytic point of view through Wittgenstein's philosophical concepts of language and how it is expressed in the actions of life. In this sense, every action of language is, on the one hand, an act of connection and on the other hand action of separations.[32] Therefore, there is a place to explore the processes of separation and separateness from a linguistic point of view and to discuss questions of formation, content, and context.

Wittgenstein's Contribution to Understanding Separation and Separateness Processes

Wittgenstein clarified that "To understand a sentence means to understand a language. To understand a language means to be master of a technique."[33] For example, if we look at the way a mother separates from her daughter who goes study at a distant university compared to a woman who separates from her husband, we will allegedly think that the difference between them is minor since in both situations there are separation processes. However, according to Wittgenstein, we can observe two different language games. The first is related to social rules that occur when a boy or girl reaches young adulthood. On the other hand, the language game of separation between a woman and her husband is a complex game related to the tradition of the family social system, legal and economic discussions. This is how Wittgenstein opened a new era in the study of meaning – he turned to the use

---

31 Donald W. Winnicott, Transitional Objects and Transitional Phenomena – A Study of the First Not-Me Possession1, *International Journal of Psycho-Analysis*, 34 (1953): 89–97.
32 Julia Kristeva, Soleil Noir. Dépression et mélancolie, Gallimard, Paris, 1987 (trans. *The Black Sun: Depression and Melancholia*, (New York: Columbia University Press, 1989).
33 Ludwig Wittgenstein, (1953). *Philosophical Investigations*: The German Text, with a Revised English Translation (Blackwell, 1953), §199.

of language as the behavioral and linguistic agreements that are an expression of human needs and systems of behavior and thinking.[34]

Language Games and the "Dawning" of an Aspect

For Wittgenstein, philosophy is meant to extract us from the grip of deceptive world – pictures, and therefore philosophy is therapy. Humans are subject to deceptive vision schemes that lead them to existential crises. Getting out of this alienated image is an important ethical project since in the end, one can see the self and the other as they are.[35] Reading Wittgenstein's thought allows one to see how the things he perceives as natural and necessary visions are nothing but partial perspective on life and thought. Doing so Wittgenstein allows the reader liberation through language, a new dawning of an aspect, through which one can experience reality as it is.[36] According to Wittgenstein, "the meaning of a word is its use in the language,"[37] that is philosophers must try to clarify the rules of language use, meaning, the various "language games" humans share. Since language games do not take place in an empty space, but in human communities, they should not be explained by a logical explanation but rather a psychological one.

Wittgenstein was a central figure in the historical development of analytic philosophy, the most important philosophical branch in the second half of the twentieth century. Analytic philosophy is characterized by an emphasis on language according to which, philosophical problems should be understood and analyzed as problems of linguistic expression because the way people experience the world is always influenced by their language. According to this approach, there are no pure sensory experiences that are not embodied by thought expressed in language. However, equally, there is no clear meaning because language is always meaningful.[38] Following Wittgenstein's thought we are forced to recognize that the tools by which man seeks to establish order, meaning thinking and language, do not regulate reality "per se," but are models whose purpose is to explain the world according to the scale of personal rules of the game.[39] The boundaries of language are the boundaries of our world since the choice of words of our thinking rises from the limited capabilities of the human race. It can,

---

34 Tamar Sovran, *Language and Meaning – The birth and Growth of Cognitive Semantic* (Jerusalem: Hemed Press, 2006).
35 Richard David Precht, *Who Am I and If So, How Many? A Journey Through Your Mind* (New York: Random House Publishing Group, 2011).
36 Ludwig Wittgenstein, *The blue and brown books* (Oxford: Basil Blackwell, (1958[1933–35]).
37 Ludwig Wittgenstein, *Philosophical Investigations*, §43.
38 Richard David Precht, *Who Am I*, 2011.
39 Peter Michael Stephan Hacker, *Wittgenstein: connections and controversies* (Oxford: University Press, 2001).

therefore, be argued that the mission of language is to "mislead us" in relation to the realistic nature of our statements. It was created to shape reality and the world according to the needs of humanity.[40]

The language is a system of activities, each of which serves a different purpose. For each of these distinct ways in which language can be used Wittgenstein called "language-game."[41] Utterance requires rules and without it, it is meaningless, when meaning is created within a particular context and time. Every language game has rules; however, these rules are modifiable. Through the variety of language games, we can perform a very wide range of actions including formulating actions of separation and experiences of being apart.

Sometimes, however, when we try to condense many language games into a single pattern, we do not properly understand the ways in which the language works. Wittgenstein saw this as one of the sources of philosophical embarrassment. Wittgenstein found another important source of philosophical embarrassment by searching for generalization, the feature common to all things called by the same name. He assumed that such a feature did not have to be present. In that case, Wittgenstein spoke of "family resemblance." There is no need to seek, as has traditionally been done, for one necessary core of the meaning of a word common to all its uses. Instead, "we see a complicated network of similarities overlapping and criss-crossing."[42] Family resemblance reveals the lack of boundaries that characterize different uses of the same concept.

Wittgenstein argued that the meaning of words is determined within the context of language games, based on mutual agreements between speakers. This means that to understand a language and use it in a way that will be understood by others, a common basis and interactions are needed. The ability to recognize a sense of longing and loss after separation, to attribute meaning to it, is rooted in exposure to people's response to loss and in the shared conceptualization of the experience. According to him, even a person's reference to himself does not exist in isolation but is woven in a broader language game. How, if so, should we understand a mental state? The idea is to examine the use of concepts in a particular context and not the concepts themselves. When the usage seems confusing and the definitions are inaccurate, Wittgenstein recommended returning to the context in which the meaning of the word was first learned "What we do is to bring words back from their metaphysical to their everyday use."[43]

---

40 Baker Gordon, and Peter Michael Stephan Hacker, *Wittgenstein: Meaning and Understanding: Essays on the Philosophical Investigations*, vol. 1 (Oxford: Blackwell, 1983).
41 Ludwig Wittgenstein, *Philosophical Investigations*, §7.
42 Ibid., §66.
43 Ludwig Wittgenstein, Philosophical Investigations, §116.

Wittgenstein's contribution to philosophy, therapy, and other aspects of life is revolutionary and very important, mainly because of the emphasis he puts on the problematic uses of human beings in language.[44] Most of us, in an attempt to make experiences understandable, turn to language not only for what it can represent but also as a social activity. Wittgenstein described how human beings impose their own meaning and theories on an experience and then forget that they do so, in order to remain meaningful or logical with each other. All of this is done using the rules of grammar. Eventually, it is our interactions with each other that establish the truth or meaning of any language game based on grammar or "rules" that stem from social relationships rather than some abstract logic or laws beyond us.[45]

Heaton has translated this principle into psychological understandings. To clarify the changing patterns of the ways in which symbols symbolize one must turn to the concrete use of language. Heaton argued that psychoanalytic theorists have based their understanding of language on mental theory in which "thinking is conceived as rule-bound information processing and manipulation of symbols, mirroring an autonomous, pre-existing reality."[46] This way of thinking opposes how we talk to each other. Clarifying our linguistic confusions leads to a recognition of the autonomy of language and the comprehension that language as a system has no basic structure beyond use.[47]

It can be said that we find it difficult to separate and deal with parting because language produces different illusions and bewitches us, in Wittgenstein's words.[48] We are addicted to the erroneous comparison that results from a grammatical similarity that exists between sentences. We can say "my heart broke" because of a breakup and give it a similar meaning as the phrase "my cup broke." Yet while the cup can be re-attached, we have no ability to do so with the emotions that arise because of a breakup pain. Language allows us to produce the illusion that emotions are definite objects. Exploration in the spirit of Wittgenstein can help in understanding the language games that characterize diverse situations of separation and hence to see how language, through language games, serves opposing needs of dependence versus being apart, desire to be loved, and safe versus the need for independence, etc. Mixing these language games causes embarrassment and mental difficulty. In a certain way, psychoanalysis has failed to give

---

44 John M. Heaton, *Wittgenstein and Psychotherapy: From paradox to wonder* (New York: Palgrave Macmillan, 2014).
45 Ludwig Wittgenstein, *Philosophical Investigations*, §23.
46 John M. Heaton, *The Talking Cure: Wittgenstein's Therapeutic Method for Psychotherapy* (New York: Palgrave Macmillan, 2010): 96.
47 John M. Heaton, The Talking Cure, 109.
48 Ludwig Wittgenstein, *Philosophical Investigations,* §109.

proper place to the basic practices of discourse and the many language games we hold, and it can benefit from Wittgenstein's philosophical ideas.

Lifetime Changes Compared to Object Relations

Freud, Klein, and Winnicott did not pay much intention to the question of the influence of the present and the future on dealing with separations. Freud argued that the past, meaning early development, is what influences our conduct throughout life.[49] According to Klein's approach, the initial object relationship pattern is preserved and restored in adult relationships.[50] Winnicott's assumption was also that personal growth and the ability to change origin in the early relationship between the baby and the maternal care he receives.[51] Is that so? What is the role of meaningful life experiences that occur throughout life? How does all this affect the initial object relations? What is the role of the language, society, and culture in which we live in this context?

Several theorists have dealt with the subject of evolution throughout the life cycle. Their main contribution was in the understanding that development lasts throughout life, and that personality does not form in a definitive way in infancy, as Klein and Winnicott argued, or until the age of latency, as Freud claimed.

These theories describe stages of development from birth to death, with each stage including developmental tasks, which, if completed in a proper manner, will bring a positive change.[52] Each stage includes one's inner world, the socio-cultural context in which he operates, and the nature of the relationship that exists between the self and the world.[53]

---

[49] Freud wrote: "But, whatever the character's later capacity for resisting the influences of abandoned object-cathexes may turn out to be, the effects of the first identifications made in earliest childhood will be general and lasting." In: Sigmund Freud, The Ego and the Id. The Standard Edition of the Complete Psychological Works of Sigmund Freud, Volume XIX (1923–1925): *The Ego and the Id and Other Works*, 1–66, 2003, 31. In his late work he also wrote about the Id: "This oldest portion of the mental apparatus remains the most important throughout life, and it was the first subject of the investigations of Psycho-Analysis." In: Sigmund Freud, An Outline of Psycho-Analysis. *Int. J. Psycho-Anal.*, 21, 27–84 (1940): 28.

[50] Elizabeth Spillius, Pricilla Roth & Richard Rusbridger, (Eds.). *Encounters with Melanie Klein, Selected papers of Elizabeth Spillius* (London: Routledge, 2007).

[51] "If there is a good-enough environmental provision, these things take place in that child. But if the facilitating environment is not good enough, then the line of life is broken and the very powerful inherited tendencies cannot carry the child on to personal fulfillment." In: Donald W. Winnicott, Clare Winnicott, Ray Shepherd, and Madeleine Davis. *Home is where we start from: essays by a psychoanalyst* (New York: Norton, 1968): 119.

[52] Erik H. Erikson, *Identity, youth and crisis* (New York: W. W. Norton Company, 1968).

[53] Daniel J. Levinson, A Conception of adult Development. *American Psychologist, 41* (1986): 3–13.

The world and human beings are dynamic and change all the time. Humans may experience self-awakening, self-criticism, or other significant experiences that can lead to internal and external changes. These external events and internal changes cause us to incorporate new insights and perspectives into our lives. Issues of separation, anxiety, and loss resonate within us and can also affect our continued development and the way we act throughout life. This article seeks to argue that separation events that take place throughout life undermine the certain, change the riverbed, and force the self to re-evolve through language.

Case Studies from Literature and Clinic

To demonstrate the effect of object-relations and life events of a separation and how they function in language, a case from the clinic and from the novel "The Lying Life of Adults" will be presented.[54] Each case presents a unique and different kind of separation and separateness experiences. Linguistic and psychoanalytic investigation of the examples allows exploring the interpsychic mental processes, the connections to the parental figures, and the effect of the separation states on self-development.

"The Lying Life of Adults"

The book opens with the sentence: "Two years before leaving home my father said to my mother that I was very ugly."[55] While many of the critics have mainly referred to the last part of the sentence, attention should be paid to the first one. The book's protagonist, Giovanna, notes the events that will lead to a fundamental change in her life: her father will leave home and thus split apart the family and at the same time also affect the way she perceives herself.

The book is a "coming of age" novel in which Giovanna describes the adolescent processes she goes through that also involve questions of separateness and are expressed in acts of separation from the parental characters. These acts of separateness and separation are woven throughout the book. The protagonist of the story is a girl who feels owning her mother. When it turns out that the father has betrayed the mother for 15 years with her best friend the mother becomes a shadow of herself. Giovanna finds it difficult to bear the change and she describes how she perceived her mother as belonging only to her: "I discovered then that I could become incurably jealous. Until that moment I had been sure that my mother belonged to me and

---

54 Elena Farrante, *The Lying Life of Adults*, Ann Goldstein (Translator) (Europa Editions, 2020).
55 Ibid., 7.

that my right to have her always available was indisputable. In the puppet theater of my mind my father was mine and legitimately also her ... . But incongruously, I felt that outside of that relationship my mother was indivisible and inviolable, she belonged to me alone."[56]

Italian and Dialect – Different Language Apparel

Following the father's statement that she is getting ugly and thus becomes like his hated sister, Giovanna goes on a journey of self-discovery and otherness. This journey takes place in the different regions of Naples and is clearly expressed through various language games in which Giovanna takes part. To determine if she is indeed like her aunt Vitoria, Giovanna develops an intense relationship with her hunt that brings her to a roller coaster of emotions. These in turn lead to states of closeness and a sense of identification and on the other hand to periods of separation and distance.

Giovanna, a 12-year-old girl, is the daughter of two parents who are involved in teaching, literature, and words. So, books and language play an important role in this novel. The protagonist refers to the use of language in the context of status, geographical location in the city of Naples, and mainly to the way it is perceived by the speaker. While her intellectual parents speak Italian and give importance to reading books and philosophical discussions, her aunt Vitoria speaks in a dialect embedded in vulgarity. The aunt's language game represents the language game of the poor neighborhoods but mostly produces for Giovanna intimacy and authenticity: "She said words like that but more vulgar, with a familiarity that disoriented me ... ."[57] Vittoria's rude and direct words create in Giovanna the feeling that she is perceived as an adult and should not be protected and hidden from reality, especially the reality of the adult world – "While my father and mother didn't blink in the face of my questions, but evaded them when they were embarrassed and sometimes consulted with each other before answering, Vittoria got irritated, cursed, displayed her impatience openly, but answered, explicitly, as no adult had ever done with me."[58]

Through the aunt's language game, Giovanna encounters for the first time in her life the adult world loaded with lies and concealments. She is busy understanding the meaning of the words "truth" and "lies" and finds that the concepts, which she has understood and recognized so far as having clear boundaries, are in fact fluid and given to the various language games that take place around her. She uses both to the point of confusion and flexes them in accordance with her understanding of the laws of use and according

---

56 Ibid., 85.
57 Ibid., 46.
58 Ibid., 61.

to her needs. She shares how the lie functions differently in each language game – "I discovered that lying to my parents made me anxious, while lying to Angela and Ida was fun."[59]

The "Dawning" of an Aspect – Loss of Innocent

Language games of separations appear as part of the triad's relationships in the novel – Giovanna follows her mother's secret phone calls, she begins to understand the body language of an intimate relationship between a man and a woman when she discovers that her parents' best friend's ankles touch her mother's ankles hidden beneath the dinner table. She becomes aware of her father's different voices which he adjusts according to the circumstances, a voice full of affection, as opposed to a cold voice, the use of formal Italian versus dialect. Giovanna moves in a world of words and symbols and experiences a "dawning" of an aspect – a change in her point of view reveals to her what was hidden, and she is forced to part with the previous way she perceived her parents. All the new language games create confusion related to a lack of understanding of language actions – what does the meaning of the argument between her father and his good friend Mariano that took place intentionally using the dialect? Why did Costanza, her mother's best friend and Mariano's wife leave the house with a slam of a door and Giovanna's father ran after her and not her husband?

All of these are part of a painful process of separateness and forming a self-identity. In trying to understand who she is she gives a central place to words and thoughts. These even affect her appearance, similarly to her aunt Vitoria "We two are made like that, when we have good thoughts we're pretty, but we turn ugly with mean ones … ."[60]

Giovanna is having a hard time experiencing her parents' two-year separation process. She tries to rebel, to go out against the father and cut herself off from him. These emotional efforts impair her ability to function at school. Even the relationship with the mother begins in a union, lasts in a painful separation, and ends in the acceptance of the reality of separation. Giovanna is developing following her separation from her mother, her journey into the world of adult sexuality and language games.

The transition between childhood and adulthood is marked in the novel by an act of speech – Giovanna shares with her aunt the act of betrayal of her mother and notes that in doing so childhood is over. Giovanna (like Shira, whose treatment will be brought next) holds within herself a desire to go back in time, to early childhood, to erase all the words and events that threaten the unity of the family.

---

59 Ibid., 51.
60 Ibid., 98.

The novel introduces us to separation events in adolescence. The protagonist of the novel moves between the desire to cling to the familiar (her parents, culture, language) and the desire to create a unique identity and a place of her own in the world. The separation between the parents and the departure of the father lead to harsh consequences, the "normal" language is dismantled, a process of defamiliarization occurs and new perspectives on the language are needed to overcome the destruction.

A Case Study – Shira

This case description presents the effect of separation at the age of latency. The separation event created a regression to infancy and affected the relationship with the parental figures. Shira was referred for treatment by her parents when she was seven, the eldest daughter with a young brother about one year old. The parents said that since the baby was born Shira has been behaving like a baby: refusing to eat if she is not fed, talking like a baby, returning to wetting occasionally at night. The mother said that the relationship with Shira was characterized by many conflicts. She also shared that she stopped contact with her father about two years ago because she was no longer willing to accept his violent behavior toward her mother and toward her.

In the first meeting with Shira, she said that two bad things happened to her. The first is that all her balloons flew away and the second that her grandfather was angry and cursed so they had to say goodbye to him. Since then, they didn't speak with Grandpa. In another meeting, while playing with dolls she spoke about lost babies and that she herself wants to be a baby. I referred to the fact that she felt that nothing is unstable and even things that were born disappear, even relationships end. She looked at me and said she had secrets she could not tell me. The separation was meaningless, so it threatened her and led to an examination of the concept of relations.

In subsequent sessions, she stressed again that she has secrets and I mentioned that if she would reveal it to me, it could be dangerous. Shira repeatedly mentioned the violent encounter with the grandfather and the detachment from him. She felt the mother was scared of him, but it was not clear to her why. I thought it must be hard for her to share her feeling since the mother herself was burdened with hard feelings regarding her father. According to Aharoni, the secret is not material that the person does not want to reveal to another, but a mental content that the significant other was not able to hear.[61] The secret, by its very nature, seeks to be heard, and the

---

61 Ahorioni Hagit, Hidden Secrets Between an attentive ear and containing Mind, *Sihot* 19(2) (2005): 159–67.

moment it is told to another person is a moment of trust and hope. Aharoni argued that at the base of the secret is a failure in containing. Such a situation, in which there is no attentive ear that is willing to absorb any content, is experienced as a gap and as a difficult separation.

Hide and Seek: A Game of Parting and Connection

During one of the sessions, Shira entered the space behind the clinic's couch, stayed there until the end of the session, and occasionally called my name. I mentioned that she was hiding from me but at the same time wanted to be in touch. She sent her hands from behind the couch and pulled it back. She laughed as I reached out to her. Then she reached out her foot and so she played with me until the end of the hour. I said with a smile that she was showing me parts of her but still not sure she wanted to show me herself.

The hiding game behind the couch lasted many sessions. In one of the sessions, there was a change in the game. Shira tied my hand with string, got in behind the couch, and tied her hand too. She was asking me to pull the string and so she would try to get out. We played like that, tied to each other until the end of the session. I said that a relationship is a complicated thing, both connect and threaten. Shira in response came out, stood in front of me, pulled the string in all sorts of directions, directed me to move with her so that the string would not tear, and then before the end of the session forcibly untied the knots she had tied.

This game reflected an experience of traumatic loss and attempts to control it. The context in which the game arrives, the form of play, and the transfer patterns that are expressed through it are significant signs of identifying the child's defenses and the threat to which he responds.[62] Shira made me simultaneously helpless and herself in control of the parting situation, contrary to what she felt within her. Alongside, she also experienced a temporary separation which always ended in a reunion.

Shira created similar but different hiding games and changed the rules as she did so. According to Wittgenstein, it is not enough to formulate one common factor for all Shira's games but to examine the differences and similarities in the rules.[63] Thus, Shira seemed to use the Hide and seek games in two ways. Shira wanted to be found and not to be found according to her will and control. At first, she allowed me to find parts of her body, parts of the self, and with the connection formed (literally), the words (interpretations) suggested in the therapy, she allowed me to find her whole and even rejoice in my presence.

---

62 Rita V. Frankiel, Hide-and-Seek in the playroom: On object loss and transference in child treatment. *Psychoanal. Rev.*, *80*(3) (1993): 341–59.
63 Ludwig Wittgenstein, *Philosophical Investigations*, §66.

The Fear of Growing up – an Encounter with Reality

One of the sessions marked the beginning of a series of sessions in which a new kind of language game took place – Shira asked to be a baby and that I would be the mother. The language became infantile as it was accompanied by daily acts of maternal care – I made her porridge, she rolled on the rug and spoke to me in a demanding infantile voice, and more. The event of the separation from the grandfather represented within her an unbearable reality of too early separations and separateness. At one of the meetings, she suddenly said that she better stay a baby because that way she might be able to go back in time and prevent what happened between her mother and her grandfather.

Shira's therapy allowed an encounter with the desire to remain a baby and the fear of growing and developing a true self. Throughout the treatment, I met Shira's defenses against the anxieties of death and loss as she tried to keep the good apart from the bad, thus not losing things and not allowing them to end. She struggled to contain the duality of relationships with the other, the love and security that such a relationship can provide, and on the other hand the danger inherent in the most significant relationships. By containing her wish to become a baby, get dirty, and attack me in the protected room, and by giving words to her feelings it became easier for Shira to deal with her anxieties. In the last part of the therapy, Shira was happy to share with me her growth. She was able to enjoy growing and developing. The need for the infant attachment to her mother diminished and the understanding of the significance of losing contact with the grandfather increased.

Conclusion

The chapter presented the importance of lifelong separation experiences and how those experiences shape the self through language. The reality of humans often forces them to deal with separations at different ages. The case descriptions presented in the chapter illustrated how dynamic and unpredictable life is. Following the events of separation, there is usually a change in one's mental world. In case that the possible movement between merging and separating expands, better integration of the self can be formed. The ability to bear oneness and separation at the same time enables the formation of beneficial relationships, as well as to bear separations during life.

According to Wittgenstein when we think of ourselves in states of separation and wonder who we are and what is our relationship with the other, we are within a particular context and therefore the meaning of our words is not within us but in the way they are used at the same time. The images we have in mind about relationships, about what is fixed and what changes, what must be, and what is impossible without it, often distort the relevant contingent meaning.[64] Human beings can make claims about themselves and perceive them as facts, as well as regarding the other in separation, but these are not facts about the world but concepts that have a fluid meaning and are therefore changeable.

The way we act with words to give meaning or fail in this task is a central theme in Wittgenstein's philosophy and one can see how this idea functions in the case studies presented in the chapter. For example, when we are tempted to think that our parents are a part of us and that we will never separate from them, or how the meaning of the concepts of "truth" and "lie" has been reconstructed in Ferrante's novel. It is therefore important to understand the way we use words in practice instead of giving a theoretical account of a psychological phenomenon.

Understanding how we give meaning allows us to examine how concepts function, how their original meaning was constructed, and in what context. It is possible to examine whether the context is appropriate for the familiar language game, whether it is necessary to build a new language game, to redefine the mental concepts of the abandoned/leaving self, of relationship, change, etc. All of these are dictated to us through the language and meaning we have given them. Through such an inquiry it is possible to resolve the paradoxes and alleviate the despair that characterizes many of the separation experiences.[65]

Unlike Freud who focused his attention mainly on the content of what was being said, Wittgenstein suggests focusing on how things are said, how language functions in different mental states, and how meaning is given, and in what context.[66] This model places language as a significant factor in shaping reality, the self, and social constructionism. Attention is given to how language sustains and organizes for us a sense of separate self, shapes our experiences of separation, and our subjectivity. In this way, one can better understand the inner world, give it meaning and make an alternative to the fixed thought patterns that only increase anxiety, sorrow, and dysfunction.

---

64 Ludwig Wittgenstein, *Tractatus Logico-Philosophicus* (London: Kegan, Paul, Trench, Trubner & Co, 1922).
65 For details on the role of the therapist and the therapy, see Dorit Lemberger, "Wittgenstein's 'Lighting Up of an Aspect' and the Possibility of Change in Psychoanalytic Therapy," *British Journal of Psychotherapy* 33(2) (2017): 192–210, 202. "The therapist acts as a sort of translator in two stages. In the first stage, he is supposed to understand the patient's world-picture and help him see the grammar he used to construct it. After the patient understands the grammar of seeing and can disassemble the causal perspective it contains, the therapist can propose an alternative way of seeing ... ."
66 John Heaton, The Talking Cure, 2010.

Chapter 8

Unhappy-Certainty*

Alice Maya Keinan

Freud: Repetition Compulsion

Vanity of vanities, says the Teacher, vanity of vanities! All is vanity. What do people gain from all the toil at which they toil under the sun? A generation goes, and a generation comes, but the earth remains forever. The sun rises and the sun goes down, and hurries to the place where it rises. The wind blows to the south, and goes around to the north; round and round goes the wind, and on its circuits the wind returns. All streams run to the sea, but the sea is not full; to the place where the streams flow, there they continue to flow. [...] What has been is what will be, and what has been done is what will be done; there is nothing new under the sun. Is there a thing of which it is said, "See, this is new?" It has already been, in the ages before us.[1]

From the melancholy words of Ecclesiastes, it appears that even in ancient times, repetition was recognized as a fundamental movement of nature and human life. As such, from the beginning of psychoanalysis, which is concerned with the subject and with healing their ailments, it needed to be in discussion with mental processes involving the inner grammar of repetition. Routine key concepts such as symptom, impulse, wish, unconscious, transference, fixation, regression all express variations of this movement.[2]

---

* This article is part of a study to obtain a doctorate in the Psychoanalysis and Hermeneutics Track of the Program for Hermeneutics and Cultural Studies at Bar-Ilan University, under the guidance of Dr. Dorit Lemberger, to whom I am deeply grateful. The work was written with the support of the Continental Foundation of the Program for Hermeneutics and Cultural Studies.
1 New Revised Standard Version (NRSV) Ecclesiastes 1: 1–11.
2 Jean Laplanche and Jean-Bertrand Pontalis, *The Language of Psycho-Analysis*, trans. Donald Nicholson-Smith (London: The Hogarth Press and the Institute of Psycho-Analysis, 1973 [1967]), 78–79; Lazar and Erlich, *Repetition Compulsion: A Reexamination*, 30.

DOI: 10.4324/9781003326588-8

Freud first proposed the term **repetition compulsion** (*wiederholungszwang*) in his paper *Remembering, Repeating and Working-Through* (1914.) He used this term in regard to the discussion on transference relationships. He claimed that past experiences that left a great impression on the subject and were not understood, tended to be expressed in the present in the form of acting out. That is, the patient does not remember anything of what had been forgotten and repressed, but instead unknowingly acts it out and repeats it.[3] Freud believed that the greater the patient's resistance, the more extensively acting out (repetition) would replace remembering. Therefore, he argued, attempts to get close to the repressed may be followed by the patient yielding to the kind of repetition compulsion that may deviate from the realms of analysis into other activities and relationships.[4]

According to Freud, the subject's repetition of their own pathological characteristics serves as a means for the repressed to turn into manifested essence. This is the psyche's way of making the unconscious present and reachable. As such, repetition compulsion expresses resistance to change but simultaneously constitutes an opening for reconciling with the repressed. In this context, Freud says that if one directs the spreading fire of repetition compulsion to the thorn field of analytical relations, it can be curbed and even rendered useful. When given the right to exist in a defined sphere (transference), it becomes a playground in which the patient can display almost freely all the pathogenic instincts hiding in their psychic life. Thus, repetition compulsion is converted into a motive for remembering with the potential to create a bridge between illness and life.[5] In my view, in this formulation Freud places repetition compulsion in a paradoxical sphere replete with contradictions and negations, thus undermining the psychoanalytic understanding as well as the subject trapped in repetition: between the danger of stagnation and the hope for change.

In *Beyond the Pleasure Principle* (1920) Freud attaches paramount importance to repetition compulsion in a discussion aimed at reexamining the foundations of psychoanalytic theory. He defines the phenomenon as an unconscious mechanism that compels the subject to experience perpetual recurrence of situations that inevitably bring them sorrow.

These passive experiences, which the person seemingly has no influence over, create the impression that they are predestined. For instance, a woman

---

3 Sigmund Freud, "Remembering, Repeating and Working-through (Further Recommendations on the Technique of Psycho-Analysis II)" (1914), in *The Standard Edition of the Complete Psychological Works of Sigmund Freud, Volume XII (1911–1913):The Case of Schreber, Papers on Technique and Other Works*, ed. James Strachey (London: The Hogarth Press and the Institute of Psycho-Analysis, 1958), 149–150.
4 Ibid., 150–151.
5 Ibid., 153–154.

who repeatedly married men who fell ill soon afterward, whom she had to care for until they died.[6] Freud attributes this phenomenon to the person's "demonic" nature. He suggests that repetition compulsion is related to the actions of a conservative primary instinct that aims to return the person to an inorganic (zero) state he calls: the *death instinct*.[7]

Freud argues that only in rare instances can we observe repetition compulsion in its pure form, driven by the death instinct alone without the involvement of other motives. He refers to children's play, to the recurring nightmares in war neurosis, and to repetition in the transference relationship. In all these, he says, there is some convergence between the death instinct and the life instinct.[8] Despite attempts to conceptualize repetition compulsion as an expression of the death instinct, in my view, the arguments here draw it back to the paradoxical intermediate field in which it was originally placed: a field in which past and present, suffering and hope – and now life and death – are tied together with a knot that is difficult to disentangle.

From Freud's formulations on repetition compulsion, it appears that most of his clinical and theoretical attention was aimed at understanding the intrapsychic processes underlying it. This trend was also reflected in a later work, *Inhibitions, Symptoms and Anxiety* (1926), in which he presented the phenomenon as the power of resistance of the repressed.[9] It also appears that the connection he proposed between repetition compulsion and the transference relationship served later as a conceptual substrate for developing the concept in interpersonal directions as well.

Repetition Compulsion from the Standpoint of Contemporary Theories

In contemporary psychoanalytic discourse, repetition compulsion is perceived as a pattern that manifests in the relationship between the person and others. The associated assumption is that its roots are oftentimes in the

---

6 Sigmund Freud, "Beyond The Pleasure Principle" (1920), in *The Standard Edition of the Complete Psychological Works of Sigmund Freud, Volume XVIII (1920–1922): Beyond the Pleasure Principle, Group Psychology and Other Works*, ed. James Strachey (London: The Hogarth Press and the Institute of Psycho-Analysis, 1955), 18–22.
7 Ibid., 35–36.
8 Ibid., 23, 32.
9 Sigmund Freud, "Inhibitions, Symptoms and Anxiety" (1926), in *The Standard Edition of the Complete Psychological Works of Sigmund Freud, Volume XX (1925–1926): An Autobiographical Study, Inhibitions, Symptoms and Anxiety, The Question of Lay Analysis and Other Works*, ed. James Strachey (London: The Hogarth Press and the Institute of Psycho-Analysis, 1959), 159–160.

arena of interpersonal events.[10] This line of thinking, as I will demonstrate below, developed in the writing of psychoanalysts from the object relations approach.

Fairbairn argues that in early childhood, when there is ongoing interaction with non-beneficial parental figures, the child has a basic tendency to identify with them.[11] The child is compelled to internalize these objects in an effort to control them, but mainly because they need them.[12] Fairbairn reasons that the child uses repression to defend themselves against the (inner and outer) bad objects. This defense, combined with the feeling that the evil (or blame) is inside them, enables them to remove these objects' stings and to experience them as good.[13]

When the repression cracks, for whatever reason, the person faces the significant challenge posed by the evil objects, which break out of the basements of the unconscious. These incessantly haunt the self and threaten its integrity.[14] According to Fairbairn, that is the demonic expression that Freud identified in repetition compulsion. He maintains that the source of the recurring same thing, of the same cruel fate, is not in the death instinct but in the presence of evil internal objects that have returned from the repressed.[15] In analysis, he says, it is important to bring about the release of those evil spirits through transference relations. To this purpose, the analyst is first required to base themselves as a good object in the patient's world.[16]

Like Fairbairn, Winnicott attaches paramount importance to aspects of connection and dependence.[17] He argues that it is only natural for the individual to be able to protect the self against environmental failure by freezing the experience in their inner world. Behind this move is the hope that one day what has been frozen will thaw, and a more beneficial environment will make correction possible. According to Winnicott, repetition compulsion – which is part of regressive situations in treatment – entails such an opportunity.[18]

---

10 E.g: Pine, "The Four Psychologies of Psychoanalysis and Their Place in Clinical Work," 573.
11 Fairbairn, "The Repression and the Return of Bad Objects (with special reference to the war neuroses)," 62.
12 Ibid., 67.
13 Ibid., 64–65.
14 Ibid., 65.
15 Ibid., 78–79.
16 Ibid., 70.
17 Donald W. Winnicott, "Metapsychological and Clinical Aspects of Regression within the Psycho-Analytical Set-Up" (1954), in *Through Paediatrics to Psycho-Analysis* (New York: Basic Book, Inc., 1975 [1958]), 278–294.
18 Ibid., 280–283.

Joseph, who belongs to the Kleinian tradition, focuses on the blind and passive aspects of the phenomenon.[19] She suggests that the vicious circle of repetition compulsion is connected to dealing with unconscious anxieties stimulated by dependence on a primary object.[20] Joseph contends that attempts to control these anxieties help to create a balance between destructiveness and love, but also prevent the individual from developing and really taking part in intimate, close relationships. Thus, the inner object as well as the self that is in a relationship with it are preserved in a state of paralysis, as if they had been frozen alive.[21] Like Winnicott's formulations, Joseph's formulations regarding repetition compulsion are tied in a motive of freezing. But while he sees the phenomenon as a possibility for renewing movement in what has been paralyzed, she sees it as a balancing psychic compromise that reduces the person's range and quality of relationships.

Loewald, who integrated Freudian terminology with that of ego psychology, addresses the phenomenon through aspects of activity and passivity.[22] He proposes seeing it as a mechanism that is activated and managed not only by destructive instincts but as also by expressing the person's creativity.[23] Loewald explains that these aspects of repetition do not contradict each other, but rather, can be merged into a given action. Passive repetition, he says, which stems from unconscious repressed experiences, inevitably entails the possibility of transforming into creativity. Realizing this possibility depends on the extent to which these psychic materials are taken over by the ego's organizing activity. He adds that in analysis, the patient should be helped to feel an active agent of their agonizing experiences. Through the analyst's interpretations, repetitive and passive patterns of transference can acquire a quality of constructive active repetition – activity in which the person turns the old into a new creation.[24]

In their paper, Lazar and Erlich offer an important discussion of the phenomenon and its origins.[25] Based on how Lacan interpreted Freud's understandings regarding this matter, their observation illuminates the interpretive aspects of repetition compulsion.[26] According to them, the sense of fate that characterizes the phenomenon is created by the subject's interpretive action. That is, a repetition compulsion is not an observable actual factual occurrence but one that occurs in the **representation** of the

---

19 Joseph, "An Aspect of the Repetition Compulsion," 213–222.
20 Ibid., 213.
21 Ibid., 220–222.
22 Loewald, "Some Considerations on Repetition and Repetition Compulsion," 59–66.
23 Ibid., 59.
24 Ibid., 60–62.
25 Lazar and Erlich, "Repetition Compulsion: A Reexamination of the Concept and the Phenomenon," 29–55.
26 Ibid., 29–30.

experience. The subject themselves – through these and those signs – attributes the compulsive repetitive meaning to the collection of experiences/events.[27] Thus, Lazar and Ehrlich stress the relevance of language to understanding the phenomenon – an aspect that this work seeks to expand and enrich.

Kitron, from the standpoint of self-psychology,[28] examines repetition compulsion, arguing that it is a twofold expression of the dread of traumatic repeated disappointment and of the wish for a new benign relationship. He explains that any deviation from one's familiar script is perceived as dangerous, and as such, causes anxiety. Sometimes the person subconsciously prefers to "take the blow" by activating the inevitable pessimistic event. One of Kitron's arguments that I find interesting is based on Sandler's formulations.[29] He claims that by repeating the familiar script, the other is forced into their assigned disappointing role.[30] At the same time, says Kitron, the repeated appeal to the other through the action also contains hope for a new experience.[31] Furthermore, he believes that processing the disappointing experiences in a safe therapeutic environment may create the kind of strengthening impact that enables them to become non-traumatic disruptions.[32]

These claims indicate that over time, the conceptualization of repetition compulsion has received a wide range of references. Some of these focus on instinct dynamics while others place most of the weight on what occurs in relationships. They take the subject through changing fields of meaning of death and life, fear and hope, stagnation and creativity, and repetition of the same thing and the possibility of change. Perhaps this resembles the intricate phenomenon that repetition compulsion seeks to describe. Its broad meaning, its contradictions, and the ambiguity surrounding its origins, all repeatedly return it to the paradoxical, ambiguous sphere in which Freud placed it. After all, as he claimed: "… a thing which has not been understood inevitably reappears; like an unlaid ghost, it cannot rest until the mystery has been solved and the spell broken."[33] This inability to rest around the conceptualization and the phenomenon indicates that further investigation is necessary.

---

27 Ibid., 47.
28 Kitron, "Repetition Compulsion and Self-psychology," 427–441.
29 Ibid., 427–428.
30 Joseph Sandler, "Countertransference and role-responsiveness," *Int. R. Psycho-Anal.* 3 (1976): 43–47.
31 Kitron, "Repetition Compulsion and Self-psychology," 429.
32 Ibid., 435–439.
33 Sigmund Freud, " Analysis of a Phobia in a Five-Year-Old Boy" (1909), in *The Standard Edition of the Complete Psychological Works of Sigmund Freud, Volume X (1909): Two Case Histories ('Little Hans' and The 'Rat Man')*, ed. James Strachey (London: The Hogarth Press and the Institute of Psycho-Analysis, 1955), 122.

The current move connects to some ideas presented by contemporary writers who emphasized the relationship dimension, such as Kitron,[34] as well as to Lazar and Erlich,[35] who positioned language as an important component in experiencing the compulsion to repeat. By bringing together concepts from Hegel's philosophy and Wittgenstein's perception of language, I seek to further develop existing understandings: to thoroughly explore the dynamics of repetition compulsion from an intersubjective angle while addressing the ways in which language functions in reconstructing the familiar relationships scenario, and in the possibility of deviating from it.

Hegel: The Subject's Unhappiness

In describing the dialectic in which the subject constitutes their self, Hegel uses the image of a plant. He describes how the bud develops into a blossom, which develops into a fruit. These forms are seemingly incompatible, yet at the same time, he says, they are part of an organic unity.[36] Taking this image further, we know that in nature this process of wilting and re-growth will perpetually repeat itself. This cyclical pattern expresses the movement of the person: from a given existent reality toward a more unified, ideal reality, which negates it; from a given self-state to another that transcends it; and so forth. This is the essence of being a subject – to be that which is not identical to the self; to move from being at rest in a state of self-overlap, of identity, to a state of unrest, difference, separation – and to overcome this, time and again.[37]

Hegel argues that with each completion of a cycle in which the actual merges with the ideal, a circle is closed "that presupposes its end as its goal, having its end also as its beginning."[38] In this work, he gives dialectic movement the shape of a spiral. With every turn, the subject goes through a process of alienating a part of their self, externalizing it in another, and returning again to the realms of their consciousness. According to Hegel, movement in a spiral without returning to the initial point is enabled because the subject's self becomes different. That is, they develop a more integrative self-concept that "sublates" (*aufhebung*) their previous positions. For this purpose, the person must come out of the reality of a subject–object relationship and recognize the other as a subject like themselves.[39] They

---

34 Kitron, "Repetition Compulsion and Self-psychology," 427–441.
35 Lazar and Erlich, "Repetition Compulsion: A Reexamination of the Concept and the Phenomenon," 29–55.
36 Georg W. F. Hegel, Preface to the *Phenomenology of Spirit*, trans. Arnold V. Miller (New York: Oxford, 1977 [1807]), 2.
37 Ibid., 10, 12.
38 Ibid., 10.
39 Hegel, *Phenomenology of Spirit*, §184.

must open themselves up to allow otherness to enter, direct their gaze at it in reality, and allow it to permeate them.

In the canonical chapter of phenomenology: "Independence and Dependence of Self-Consciousness: Lordship and Bondage," Hegel seeks to illustrate this process through the plot of the lord and slave. The chapter begins with an internal split within the one consciousness, which is externalized to the interpersonal reality in the characters of the lord and slave. In this reality, they each see in the other the part that they have lost in themselves.[40] Although Hegel holds the position that self-consciousness is meant to transcend the lord-slave (subject–object) split and understand therefore that the other is part of it, the plot comes to a tragic conclusion: In a frozen picture of the relationship, the lord and slave remain trapped within their consciousness and fail to fulfill their subjectivity.[41]

The lord, who believed he was the subject, is eventually revealed as having forgotten his inner essence by becoming addicted to pleasure.[42] He stops taking an active part in the world, and his needs are mediated by another, who serves as an object (slave) for him. The lord sinks into a state of self-overlap in which he tries to transcend himself, so to speak, by appropriating increasingly more material elements for himself. We can recognize the existential state that the lord represents in people who seek to fill themselves through consumption: purchasing another garment, car, flight … . As experience shows, attaining these goals offers fleeting happiness but leaves the person hollow inside.

The slave's story is slightly different, but nonetheless tragic. Through the work he does for the lord, he learns to change his nature in relation to an idea. He thereby manages to outwardly express something of the potential inherent in his subjectivity but remains trapped within the slave consciousness. The formative negation (deviation), becomes an external skill that controls and changes certain things but does not become an internal principle by which the slave feels the vitality beating within, deviating from the concept of his self.[43] In this context, Butler argues that the master and slave experience their death while still alive:[44] "Domination and enslavement are projects of despair … . Life or determinate existence requires the sustained interrelationship of physical existence and the cultivation of identity."[45]

---

40 Ibid., §179–§184.
41 Ibid., §196.
42 Ibid., §192.
43 Ibid., §195–§196.
44 Judith p. Butler, *Subjects of Desire: Hegelian Reflections in Twentieth-Century France* (New York: Columbia University Press, 1987).
45 Ibid., 54.

Both the lord and slave are unaware of their otherness. They live in the consciousness of "the same thing," which also dictates a relationship reality in which only more of the same happens.

The Lord and Slave in the Shadow of the Unhappy Consciousness

The next chapter in the phenomenology tells us the future awaiting the lord and slave. Here, Hegel deals with a particular position of consciousness that constitutes part of the subject's dialectical development. He calls this *unhappy consciousness*,[46] where unhappiness is a state of existence that appears before the consciousness returns to itself. This is restlessness incarnate. Unhappy consciousness, says Hegel, is a consciousness of duplication based entirely on contradictions and duality. In this state, the duplication that was previously divided into two people – the lord and the slave, returns to one, such that the consciousness **feels** the split within it. It feels its loss, but does not know what it lacks. Because it does not have the reflective ability to think or conceive what it feels, the split is experienced as an internal rupture and not as a unity of opposites (as in the third stage of dialectic) in which consciousness reconciles with itself and others.[47]

The parts of the self alienated by the consciousness continue to exist outside it, experienced as foreign and as not belonging to it. That is, the unhappy consciousness is blind to itself. It does not understand that the split it experiences is with itself. This condition, according to Hegel, brings the subject terrible suffering:[48] Looking at such a consciousness, "we have here only a personality confined to its own self and its own petty actions, a personality brooding over itself, as wretched as it is impoverished."[49]

Jean Wahl is a pioneer in interpreting Hegelian phenomenology in language close to the human experience.[50] For Wahl, the concept of unhappy consciousness forms the basis for interpreting the whole phenomenology.[51] He perceives dialectics as a process in which the subject adopts other aspects of themselves.[52] According to him, in every transition between one self-state and another that deviates from it, we will find an unhappy consciousness.

---

46 Hegel, *Phenomenology of Spirit*, §206–§230.
47 Ibid., §206.
48 Ibid., §207, §217, §225.
49 Ibid., §225.
50 Jean Wahl, "'Mediation, Negativity, and Separation':from Le Malheur de la Conscience dans la Philosophie de Hegel" (1929), in *Hegel and Contemporary Continental Philosophy*, ed. D. K Keenan (State University of New York Press, 2004).
51 Gary Gutting, *Thinking the impossible: French Philosophy Since 1960* (Oxford University Press, 2011), 26.
52 Wahl, "Mediation, Negativity, and Separation," 3.

Unhappiness, then, is a condition for happiness,[53] and happiness, in the existential drama of the subject longing to be different passes and is soon replaced by a feeling of unhappiness.

From the conceptualization of the unhappy consciousness, it follows that the lord and slave will experience many torments until they regain the aspects of themselves that they have lost in otherness. Here we may ask: Why do the lord and slave remain imprisoned in their miserable consciousness even though the interpersonal reality reveals to them their other essence?

This question does not only concern the lord and the slave, but deals with the individual in general's ability to break through the boundaries of their consciousness and see additional possibilities of being their selves; the kind that intertwines their private subjectivity with generality and expands it. It is likely that, while movement and flow frequently occur in both outer and psychic reality, our ability to change our concepts, our perceptions of ourselves and of the world, is limited. We see in therapy that such a change in consciousness is not common and requires much time and effort.

In the following section, I will examine the matter under discussion from a Wittgensteinian approach that explores in-depth aspects of language.

Wittgenstein – the Limits of My Unhappiness Means the Limits of My Language

In his famous saying, "The limits of my language means the limits of my world,"[54] Wittgenstein marked the inseparable connection between the individual and their experience of the world. Thus, he argued that "the world of the happy man is a different one from that of the unhappy man."[55] These worlds are dictated by different *language-games* that create a distinct array of meanings.[56]

Language is multifaceted, Wittgenstein says. It is playful – the edges of its boundaries are blurred, so the speaker is invited to use it creatively, thus allowing a movement of meaning.[57] On the other hand, language is like a witch. When it encounters one's aspiration for finite definitions, it may become unequivocal, concrete, and closed.[58] Then one can mistakenly think that the game is reality; that what is being described really exists.[59]

---

53 Ibid., 14.
54 Ludwig Wittgenstein, *Tractatus Logico-Philosophicus*, trans. D. F. Pears and B. F. McGuinness (London and New York: Routledge & Kegan Paul, 1961), §5.6.
55 Ibid., §6.43.
56 Wittgenstein, *Philosophical Investigations*, §23.
57 Ibid., §71, §203.
58 Ludwig Wittgenstein, *The Blue and the Brown Books: Preliminary Studies for the 'Philosophical Investigations'* (Blackwell Publishing Ltd, 1958), 45, 59.
59 Wittgenstein, *Philosophical Investigations*, §371, §373.

Wittgenstein maintains that this state of being closed is related to the person's need for certainty. Certainty, he claims, is a state of self-conviction[60] that allows one to feel safe and navigate the world without providing justifications.[61] At the same time, he says, for a person to be able to make changes in their own life, they must also make room for doubting what seems obvious.[62]

Wittgenstein believes that the source of certainty lies in our world-picture.[63] This **picture** is not a choice based on proofs. It is created in language and instilled in us by using language.[64] That is, our certainty is projected into us through the language-games that we inherited and take part in. Moreover, he says, this certainty derives its strength and stability from the common agreements in language in opinions, but also in the form of life.[65] In this sense, our certainty is not entirely private. Our meaning is also the meaning of otherness.

Under the person's basic need for certainty, the world-pictures that penetrate the consciousness through language (and reflect a particular way of attributing meaning to life) solidify and take on the position of mythology; of truth.[66] They are not experienced as ways of looking at reality but as reality itself: "This would give us a picture of knowing as the perception of an outer event through visual rays which project it as it is into the eye and the consciousness."[67] When the slave looks at the lord, he has no doubt that he **sees** a lord there. This, without being aware that he (in the relationship between them and in the speech that he developed with him) created the possibility **of seeing** him **as** a **lord.** Wittgenstein calls this phenomenon, which involves thinking but is perceived as direct seeing: "**seeing as**" or "continuous seeing of an aspect."[68] According to him, without the ability to see reality under aspects or to see reality in pictures, the person has no possibility of attributing lasting meaning to things.[69]

According to Wittgenstein, it is certainty – the lord and slave's consciousness that becomes bewitched by language – that does not allow them to deviate from themselves and establish another meaning. As he implies,

---

60 Wittgenstein, *On Certainty*, §8, §12, §42.
61 Ibid., §7, §344, §355, §358.
62 Ibid., §115, §160.
63 Ibid., §162.
64 Ibid., §94: But I did not get my picture of the world by satisfying myself of its correctness: nor do I have it because I am satisfied of its correctness. No: it is the inherited background against which I distinguish between true and false.
65 Ibid., §358; Wittgenstein, *Philosophical Investigations*, §241.
66 Wittgenstein, *On Certainty*, §95.
67 Ibid., §90.
68 Wittgenstein, *Philosophical Investigations*, part II, §11.
69 Yoav Ashkenazy, *Fractured Mirror: On Creation of the Self in Wittgenstein and Murdoch* (Ramat Gan: Bar-Ilan University Press, 2012), 24.

different language-games are learned and internalized through a person's relationships with other people. Furthermore, in the framework of the relationship between the lord and slave, an entire system of ways of speaking between them is constituted: The lord gives orders, the slave fulfills them and translates demands into products; the lord accuses, complains, the slave admits, apologizes … .

Along with the development of language-games, the lord and slave develop a certain form of life. They pour their experiences into meaning patterns that together create a kind of world-picture. Each in their own way, they form a perception of others and of their self around this image. Beneath the human need for certainty, the patterns of meaning solidify into a stable ground of consciousness. Metaphorically, as we understand from Wittgenstein, this ground activates a kind of **gravitational field of meaning** that attracts new experiences and trials that could have been awarded other interpretations.[70] Thus, the work in which the slave expresses being an element of formative negation falls into the certainty of slave consciousness. Under the slave aspect, the consciousness may see its creation as the creation of the lord; as one that functions like a well-oiled machine performing actions determined by someone else.

The "gravitational force" of the existing patterns of meaning, of certainty, does not allow the lord and slave to see additional possibilities of being themselves. With time, the patterns of relationships between the lord and slave become further established. This form of life, of relationships and language, appears to lead them to the painful continuation: a situation in which the lord and slave seemingly become trapped in a rigid position of self, relationships, and language; trapped by what I propose to call **unhappy-certainty:** an unhappy-certainty that they failed to break free from "… for it lay in our language, and language seemed to repeat it to us inexorably."[71]

Unhappy-Certainty and the Paradox of Repetition Compulsion

Unhappy-certainty is a hybrid concept that combines Hegelian ideas with Wittgenstein's approach to language. In this context, I propose that unhappy-certainty describes an excruciating conflicting existential state in which a foreign element penetrates the person's certainty and undermines the safe ground they stand on. This state, according to Hegel's conception, is an inherent part of the subject's dialectical development; a stage containing the possibility of leading a person toward a different, richer order of self, relationships, and language. As I will demonstrate later, with the entry of

---

70 Wittgenstein, *On Certainty*, §96.
71 Wittgenstein, *Philosophical Investigations*, §115.

foreignness into the familiar, the individual's certainty seemingly tries to resist what is happening and grasps them more tightly. Thus, the subject finds themselves unintentionally drawn with increasing intensity to their existing patterns of meaning. This repeatedly throws them **back** into the suffocating bosom of their disrupted certainty, which becomes more compulsive, and they are miserable within it.

Unhappy-certainty may have manifestations in a person's life. It may be an island within a fuller, richer existence, but under certain circumstances, it may spread across the entire mental and linguistic space. When it is widespread and persistent, unhappy-certainty becomes a real chronic disease that inflicts much suffering on the subject. This existential distress in its various manifestations often leads different people to knock at the doors of psychoanalysis.

There, in the inner chambers of psychoanalysis, this distress was identified in the phenomenon that Freud awarded the conceptual category of repetition compulsion, in which the person incessantly and ostensibly without control repeats distressing experiences or relationship patterns.

Furthermore, I propose to see repetition compulsion as a symptom of the existential distress I have termed unhappy-certainty. I will discuss various aspects of repetition compulsion that arise from this proposed interpretation, presenting references that provide justification for the current move and for developing this concept. Special emphasis will be given to examining the paradox of the phenomenon and the experience of unhappiness that arises from it.

To understand what occurs in repetition compulsion, I will rewind the dialectical script slightly back. By combining Hegel and Wittgenstein's ideas, we see that the pre-unhappiness phase is characterized by the fact that the person perceives every foreignness that they detect around them – and even more so, within them – as threatening. In order to produce some sense of stability and security, their inner and outer worlds are arranged together into a picture with very clear lines – with sharp distinctions (splits) between the inner and outer, between me and the other, between a lord and a slave ... .

This picture is our certainty, as Wittgenstein claimed – a world-picture rooted in the relationships, language-games, and forms of life we share with other people.[72] Certainty defines the boundaries of the person's world, i.e., the way in which they perceive and see reality. It gives them a feeling of walking in a familiar and known place.

Unhappy-certainty describes an existential state that is one step ahead from there in the process. The dialectic tells us that in this state, an alienated aspect of a person's self returns to the one consciousness: not as a reflective

---

72 Ibid., §241; Wittgenstein, *On Certainty*, §358.

thought with a unifying effect, but as a foreign, other element that seemingly infiltrates a person's home. Taking a wider perspective, we see that the rigid separations previously determining the boundaries of the subject's world become askew. The sharp lines are breached, and the otherness that was outside permeates into the certain, familiar, and long-known order. It is important to note that as Hegel argued,[73] this otherness can be an alienated (or repressed) self-aspect, but can also be a completely foreign, invading component. For example, a self-aspect of another that has been projected into the subject, or even an event experienced as traumatic.

It appears that the further this otherness spreads into the certainty and instills unfamiliar elements in it, the more the subject clings to the existing formations. It is as if their certainty is repeatedly forcing them into familiar patterns of meaning, acting as a moment that opposes the potential change that seeks to turn the wheel back. In this situation, the routine aspect of certainty that offers the person security – repeating the familiar relationship patterns, walking along known paths, seeing things in a particular way – may take on the character of Sisyphean and compulsive repetition.

In *The Uncanny Essay*, Freud describes dynamics regarding the experience of helplessness he attributed to repetition compulsion:

> As I was walking, one hot summer afternoon, through the deserted streets of a provincial town in Italy which was unknown to me, I found myself in a quarter of whose character I could not long remain in doubt. Nothing but painted women were to be seen at the windows of the small houses, and I hastened to leave the narrow street at the next turning. But after having wandered about for a time without enquiring my way, I suddenly found myself back in the same street, where my presence was now beginning to excite attention. I hurried away once more, only to arrive by another detour at the same place yet a third time. Now, however, a feeling overcame me which I can only describe as uncanny.[74]

Repetition compulsion is like a maze in which the person tries to escape from a certain place (of self, relationship, and language), but finds themselves repeatedly returning to the same point or "street" of certainty that has become terrifying. Therefore, instead of moving in a spiral, they are trapped in an unchanging circular motion. In a broad view of dialectics, this maze, being a derivative of unhappy-certainty, is a necessary stage in the process of

---

73 Hegel, *Phenomenology of Spirit*, §178–§179.
74 Sigmund Freud, "The Uncanny" (1919), in *The Standard Edition of the Complete Psychological Works of Sigmund Freud, Volume XVII (1917–1919): An Infantile Neurosis and Other Works,* ed. James Strachey (London: The Hogarth Press and the Institute of Psycho-Analysis, 1955), 236–237.

subject constitution that holds within it a living and kicking conflict between the need to cling to the known, and the desire to transcend the given limits of certainty, to be what is not identical to oneself – to be a subject. This is consistent with Kitron's perception, who saw in repetition compulsion a restrictive and limiting relationship pattern that also contains hope for a new experience.[75]

One important understanding regarding repetition compulsion emerging from this discussion is that the accompanying suffering is not caused only by the repetition of an unpleasant past experience. It most likely stems from the very paradox, among other things, in which the person feels torn between two positions; between moments pulling them simultaneously in opposite directions. Inspired by Hegel's metaphor for dialectics, we can say that this is like the tension exerted on the plant when the blossom retreats into itself, closing and hardening. Then fruit begins to emerge. A person caught in repetition experiences a **contradictory** consciousness of this kind; an experience of terrible misery stripped of words in which they deeply **feel** the split but do not know its meaning. As such, Hegel says, "Its thinking as such is no more than the chaotic jingling of bells, or a mist of warm incense, a musical thinking that does not get as far as the notion, which would be the sole, immanent objective mode of thought."[76]

In light of these claims, one can better understand the sense of the uncanny that Freud attributed to repetition compulsion.[77] This feeling describes the panic that grips one when conflicting elements come together, creating a foreign, unfamiliar imprint in the canny, in the certainty, in what the person was fully convinced of. Consistent with the Hegelian conception, Freud says that what leads to this is the return of the repressed; that is, the return of an alienated self-aspect to one's frame of reference. As Hegel argued, the person in this situation does not understand that the contradiction lies within, but perceives it as standing between them and the other; between them and the world. Therefore, the person often finds it difficult to see themselves as an active agent in the recurrence of the same thing. Instead, they tend to attribute what is happening to them to the other person, or alternatively, to a general, abstract and outer otherness that adopts the character of a cruel fate.[78]

This contradiction is also reflected in the behavioral manifestation of repetition compulsion. The foreign, split aspect appears to speak itself through the "language of action," as Freud identified in the analyzes he performed. For instance, the patient does not say that he remembers being a

---

75 Kitron, "Repetition Compulsion and Self-psychology," 427–441.
76 Hegel, *Phenomenology of Spirit*, §217.
77 Freud, "The Uncanny," 236–237.
78 Freud, "Beyond The Pleasure Principle," 22.

defiant and critical child toward his parents. Instead, he behaves similarly toward the analyst.[79] This kind of conscious memory would surely contradict how the patient perceived himself until that point. Furthermore, the patient's rebellious behavior would most likely have attracted some counter-reaction from the analyst and eventually led the patient to believe the analyst was being critical of him. That is, that the foreignness was not his but that of the other, whom he would now also see as the source of his unhappiness.

Under the conceptualization of unhappy-certainty, repetition compulsion is no longer perceived as a manifestation of individual pathology but as a human phenomenon with existential significance. According to Hegel, the experience of unhappiness that is its essence serves as a critical and **necessary** element that brings us closer to the foreign. It opens up in our being a kind of corridor of (possible) movement between a given reality of life and another reality of self-relationship-language. It is similar to a birth canal in which repetitive and compulsive contractions push the fetus toward an encounter with the foreign world that in the known cycle of life, soon becomes their familiar **world**; a certain world that gives incense clouds clear contours, lyrics to music, and to otherness – a place within us that is an integral part of our selves.

But how does this process occur? How does repetition compulsion allow a person to get close to the foreign and emerge toward the otherness within and without?

Repetition Compulsion and the Transparent Prison of Language

Through the plot of the lord and slave, I showed earlier how a foreign, alienated part of a person's self receives a renewed life in the relationship in the form of a real other. Within the lord and slave's life routine, and in the language-games between them, otherness is seemingly abandoned and forgotten in the orderly separateness of their certainty. Meanwhile, the discussion between the two also becomes static and predictable: Language functions as a tin can that preserves their current consciousness; a discussion in which various events and other possibilities of experience that reality presents them with (for example, the slave's creative work) fall into a gravitational field of a given, familiar meaning.

In this context, Wittgenstein would certainly have argued that part of the person's difficulty in crossing the boundaries of their certainty and dictate their form of life, lies in the fact that they don't see them. After all, how can

---

79 Freud, "Remembering, Repeating and Working-through," 150.

you deviate from something you are blind to, that you do not know exists at all as a boundary line?

> The aspects of things that are most important for us are hidden because of their simplicity and familiarity. (One is unable to notice something—because it is always before one's eyes.) The real foundations of his enquiry do not strike a man at all. ... we fail to be struck by what, once seen, is most striking and most powerful.[80]

This indicates that the subject may easily be swallowed up in a world in which the patterns by which they see/interpret reality have become so self-evident that their existence can no longer be detected; a world limited in possibilities, where things appear a certain way such that the otherness and difference of the living actuality have been engulfed and covered in shades of the same.

Here the phenomenon we are interested in enters the picture. I suggest that repetition compulsion functions as a kind of futile move, the very **paradoxicality** in it serves as a key for exposing the lines of language, for illuminating forgotten aspects of existence that have become transparent due to their simplicity and regularity. With this move, the person seems to be captured more tightly by their own certainty. Despite their attempts to evade, to take new, roundabout paths, they find themselves repeatedly returning to the same point. The compulsive returning to the same dead-end place (in the self, relationships, and language) makes it **striking**. Therefore, something that was hidden for us becomes **felt, present,** and suddenly arouses our attention.

This experience is reflected in the following experience that Freud describes:

> ... we naturally attach no importance to the event when we hand in an overcoat and get a cloakroom ticket with the number, let us say, 62 ... But the impression is altered if two such events, each in itself indifferent, happen close together—if we come across the number 62 several times in a single day, or if we begin to notice that everything which has a number—addresses, hotel rooms, compartments in railway trains—invariably has the same one ... We do feel this to be uncanny. And unless a man is utterly hardened and proof against the lure of superstition, he will be tempted to ascribe a secret meaning to this obstinate recurrence of a number; he will take it, perhaps, as an indication of the span of life allotted to him.[81]

---

80 Wittgenstein, *Philosophical Investigations*, §129.
81 Freud, "The Uncanny," 237–238.

Consistent with Lazar and Ehrlich's argument,[82] Freud explains how repetition compulsion is constructed in language. In this process, reminiscent of the **"condensation"** of objects in a dream, a "normal" sign (such as the number 62, or alternatively, an aspect of criticism in a relationship) attracts more events and occurrences that resemble them. Thus, it fills up with and is condensed into the cumulative repetitive meaning of itself. It becomes an impressive sign that the subject can no longer fail to notice. This sign simultaneously holds the familiar and foreign within it, as if calling the subject to pause and really listen to what is happening. Therefore, if we don't rush to lay the gravestone on these impressive events by attaching one or another explanation – if we only allow ourselves to dwell on the paradox that repetition compulsion faces us with – it opens up a space for the person to **think;** to **doubt** what exists; to **question** what is; to not accept things as they are.

In addition, I suggest that the unhappiness that comes with repetition compulsion embodies the pain caused by the person's collision with the transparent prison of their certainty, their relationships, and their language. With Wittgenstein's help, this (existential) state can be likened to a fly trapped in a jar.[83] The fly repeatedly bumps into the glass sides – and it is only this that substantiates their existence. Wittgenstein says that in language, as in a jar, there is always an exit, some kind of open back door.[84] Escaping the maze (or paradox) is possible "only if we make a radical break with the idea that language always functions in **one** way, always serves the same purpose."[85] If we apply this to the category of repetition compulsion, then we can say that the possibility of extricating oneself from it lies precisely in our ability to be swept into it, despite the panic; to see it as more than a repetition of the same thing: to give space for the relations of similarity between things – but also for the distinctions and difference; for what reveals itself to be other from what we know.

Psychoanalysis: To Extricate Oneself from the Entanglement of Unhappiness

Wittgenstein argues that although the way out from the transparent prison of our certainty – from a particular attribution of meaning to the world – is not at all simple, it is possible. What seems like mythology to us can return

---

82 Lazar and Erlich, "Repetition Compulsion: A Reexamination of the Concept and the Phenomenon," 29–55.
83 Wittgenstein, *Philosophical Investigations*, §309.
84 Ibid., §99.
85 Ibid., §304.

to a state of flux, or as he puts it, the "river-bed of thoughts may shift."[86] This shift, he says, is related to the changing of language-games, concepts, and the meanings of words.[87]

In the second part of *Philosophical Investigations*, he describes the process by which a compulsive mode of vision is seemingly replaced by another. He illustrates this by using Jastrow's "duckrabbit," which at any given moment can be seen in only one way: as a rabbit's head, or as a duck's.[88]

This illustration is a metaphor for the interpreting subject's attitude to a reality of multiple aspects that one's ability to perceive is limited and narrow. Wittgenstein "plays" with the duckrabbit illustration and says: "I have been shown this picture before, but I have not seen anything in it other than a rabbit."[89] He thereby demonstrates a state of "seeing as." (Seeing the duckrabbit as a rabbit.) At the same time, Wittgenstein notes, we may suddenly notice a duck in the illustration. With this distinction, a fundamental perceptual shift occurs, and the picture may appear to change before our eyes, even though we know that it has not. Wittgenstein calls the phenomenon "**a dawning of an aspect.**"[90] Through this experience, which contains a paradoxical and thought-provoking quality, the person realizes that what they perceived as factual reality is but only one possible way of seeing – it is an **interpretation.**[91]

In a criticism of Freud's dream interpretation method, Wittgenstein refers directly to a change of an aspect in the analytical situation context. He advises not to rush to explain dream images by wish-fulfillment; to a way of seeing that replaces one explanation or certainty with another. Instead, he suggests inviting the patient to observe various aspects of the dream. Thus, he says, the person can produce a new meaning each time, thereby opening up a different way of seeing themselves.[92]

Wittgenstein's understandings are highly relevant to treating repetitive compulsion – a phenomenon in which the person's self and relationship with another appear to be captured in existing, unchanging language-games, imprisoned in a subjective interpretation that does not allow the subject to see something else (a duck's head) where the rabbit's head is. Developing Wittgenstein's view further, I suggest that the analytical discourse should enter the gap that is full of the contradictions and pain that repetition

---

86 Wittgenstein, *On Certainty*, §97.
87 Ibid., §65.
88 Joseph Jastrow, *Fact and fable in psychology* (New York: Houghton Mifflin, 1900).
89 Wittgenstein, *Philosophical Investigations*, part II, §11.
90 Ibid.
91 Stephen Mulhall, *On Being in the World: Wittgenstein and Heidegger on Seeing Aspects* (London and New York: Routledge, 1990).
92 Ludwig Wittgenstein, *Lectures and conversations on aesthetics, psychology and religious belief*, ed. Cyril Barrett (Berkeley: University of California Press, 1967), 45–47.

compulsion causes. It should wander the uncanny, anxiety-evoking street that the patient repeatedly returned to on their way. It should visit the homes and dark alleyways, listen to the old and new stories that arise; allow the living speech, the evolving dialog between analyst and patient to wash over every inch with new meaning and changing aspects that illuminate differently the same lines of reality. In so doing, repetition is turned into **repetition with a difference.**

In those paradoxical moments of the dawning of an aspect that take place in the analytical conversation, the subject's thinking and seeing seem to awaken to renewed action. This allows them to become acquainted with the unbridgeable gap where one stands as an interpreting subject between language and world. Becoming acquainted with it is similar, perhaps, to the fly noticing the opening in the jar and making its way out of the maze it had landed in. For the person, this state expresses their release from the transparent prison of language, from the enchanted circle of repetition compulsion, and movement toward other language-games.

The change of language-games, as in a system of cogwheels, results in movement in the relationship and in the self. When the subject sees the revealed world in another way, they allow the other to appear differently than in the familiar painful script. In this situation, the patient will be able to see the analyst beyond an object who restores to them the alienated aspects of their self. As Hegelian phenomenology teaches, with this shift, the subject frees the other from themselves and recognizes them as a subject – similar but different from themselves. With this recognition, they return differently to the bosom of their consciousness and certainty. The otherness, which was previously external, and later felt inside like a foreign element lacking words and form, becomes part of them: a moment that has merged into the fabric of its selfhood through the action of reflection,[93] in which the person's broken, ripped certainty also heals. This allows them to extricate themselves (at least temporarily) from the entanglement of their unhappiness. In this painful process, in which a person brings the foreign closer to them, allows it into their home, language, and relationship, certain possibilities of self lose their importance while the importance of others increases.

Summary

Through the meeting between Hegel and Wittgenstein's ideas and psychoanalysis, I observed repetition compulsion as part of a broader phenomenon – existential unrest – that I called *unhappy-certainty*. In this conceptualization, repetition compulsion was positioned as a paradoxical, painful but necessary step in the process of self-constitution. I showed that

---

93 Hegel, *Phenomenology of Spirit*, §178–§184.

unhappiness, which contains the rending of the person between certainty (security) and the unfamiliar, is a critical element that brings the person closer to the foreign – to their inner otherness and to that of others. Repetition compulsion that repeatedly creates collisions with one's language boundaries reveals as it were the most basic structures of depth (that have become invisible to us due to their ordinariness). Through these we attribute meaning to the world. In the process described, the subject becomes aware that what they perceived as reality is only a mode of vision, an interpretation. Herein also lies the importance of psychoanalytic conversation, which offers the person the possibility of seeing something under changing aspects; of seeing repetition compulsion as repetition with a difference and as something that brings the subject into contact with other possibilities of being themselves. It allows them to move from the order of certainty, in which they are imprisoned, to a different, other order of self, relationships, and language.

Bibliography

Ashkenazy, Yoav. *Fractured Mirror: On Creation of the Self in Wittgenstein and Murdoch*. Ramat Gan: Bar-Ilan University Press, 2012.

Butler, Judith p. *Subjects of Desire: Hegelian Reflections in Twentieth-Century France*. New York: Columbia University Press, 1987.

Fairbairn, Ronald W. D. "The Repression and the Return of Bad Objects (with special reference to the war neuroses)." In *Psychoanalytic Studies of the Personality*, 59–81. London: Routledge & Kegan Paul, 1952.

Freud, Sigmund. "Analysis of a Phobia in a Five-Year-Old Boy" (1909). In *The Standard Edition of the Complete Psychological Works of Sigmund Freud, Volume X (1909): Two Case Histories ('Little Hans' and The 'Rat Man')*, edited by James Strachey, 3–148. London: The Hogarth Press and the Institute of Psycho-Analysis, 1955.

Freud, Sigmund. "The Uncanny" (1919). In *The Standard Edition of the Complete Psychological Works of Sigmund Freud, Volume XVII (1917–1919): An Infantile Neurosis and Other Works*, edited by James Strachey, 217–256. London: The Hogarth Press and the Institute of Psycho-Analysis, 1955.

Freud, Sigmund. "Remembering, Repeating and Working-through (Further Recommendations on the Technique of Psycho-Analysis II)" (1914). In *The Standard Edition of the Complete Psychological Works of Sigmund Freud, Volume XII (1911–1913): The Case of Schreber, Papers on Technique and Other Works*, edited by James Strachey, 18–22. London: The Hogarth Press and the Institute of Psycho-Analysis, 1958.

Freud, Sigmund. "Inhibitions, Symptoms and Anxiety" (1926). In *The Standard Edition of the Complete Psychological Works of Sigmund Freud, Volume XX (1925–1926): An Autobiographical Study, Inhibitions, Symptoms and Anxiety, The Question of Lay Analysis and Other Works*, edited by James Strachey, 77–175. London: The Hogarth Press and the Institute of Psycho-Analysis, 1959.

Gutting, Gary. *Thinking the Impossible: French Philosophy Since 1960*. Oxford University Press, 2011.

Hegel, Georg W. F. *Phenomenology of Spirit*, translated by Arnold V. Miller. New York: Oxford, 1977 [1807].
Jastrow, Joseph. *Fact and Fable in Psychology*. New York: Houghton Mifflin, 1900.
Joseph, Betty. "An Aspect of the Repetition Compulsion." *The International Journal of Psychoanalysis* 40 (1959): 213–222.
Kitron, David. "Repetition Compulsion and Self-psychology." *The International Journal of Psychoanalysis* 84, no. 2 (2003): 427–441.
Laplanche, Jean, and Jean-Bertrand Pontalis. *The Language of Psycho-Analysis*, translated by Donald Nicholson-Smith. London: The Hogarth Press and the Institute of Psycho-Analysis, 1973 [1967].
Lazar, Rina, and Shmuel Erlich. "Repetition Compulsion: A Reexamination of the Concept and the Phenomenon." *Psychoanal. Contemp. Thought* 19, no. 2 (1999): 29–55.
Loewald, Hans W. "Some Considerations on Repetition and Repetition Compulsion." *Internat. J. Psycho-Anal.* 52 (1971): 59–66.
Mulhall, Stephen. *On Being in the World: Wittgenstein and Heidegger on Seeing Aspects*. London and New York: Routledge, 1990.
Pine, Fred. "The Four Psychologies of Psychoanalysis and Their Place in Clinical Work." *J. Amer. Psychoanal. Assn.* 36 (1988): 574–596.
Sandler, Joseph. "Countertransference and Role-responsiveness." *Int. R. Psycho-Anal.* 3 (1976): 43–47.
Wahl, Jean. "'Mediation, Negativity, and Separation':from Le Malheur de la Conscience dans la Philosophie de Hegel" (1929). In *Hegel and Contemporary Continental Philosophy*, edited by D. K Keenan, 1–17. State University of New York Press, 2004.
Winnicott, Donald W. "Metapsychological and Clinical Aspects of Regression within the Psycho-Analytical Set-Up" (1954). In *Through Paediatrics to Psycho-Analysis*, 278–294. New York: Basic Book, Inc., 1975 [1958].
Wittgenstein, Ludwig. *Philosophical Investigations*, translated by G. E. M. Anscombe. Basil Blackwell: Oxford, 1953.
Wittgenstein, Ludwig. *Tractatus Logico-Philosophicus*, translated by D. F. Pears and B. F. McGuinness. London and New York: Routledge & Kegan Paul, 1961.
Wittgenstein, Ludwig. *The Blue and the Brown Books: Preliminary Studies for the 'Philosophical Investigations'*. Blackwell Publishing Ltd, 1958.
Wittgenstein, Ludwig. *On Certainty*, translated by Denis Paul and G. E. M. Anscombe. Basil Blackwell: Oxford, 1969.
Wittgenstein, Ludwig. *Lectures and Conversasions on Aesthetics, Psychology and Religious Belief*, edited by Cyril Barrett. Berkeley: University of California Press, 1967.

Chapter 9

"Tragic Knots" Following Acquired Chronic Medical Conditions

A Relational Perspective in Psychotherapy in Medical Settings[1]

Orin Segal

Introduction

Overview

Psychological literature describes severe and disabling acquired chronic medical conditions, as causing traumatic loss of control over one's own body and world, as well as fundamental changes in interpersonal relations.[2] These changes can shatter previously established self and self-other concepts. As theoretical literature regarding these interpersonal changes and their corresponding intrapersonal changes in medical settings is scarce, this chapter attempts to integrate contemporary psychoanalytic ideas to theoretically explore these experiences.

Specifically, this chapter explores and utilizes Roy Schafer's psychoanalytic concept of "tragic knots" and Jessica Benjamin's relational concept of complementarity, applying them in medical contexts.[3] Following this, two common relational complementarities, in which individuals experiencing acquired medical conditions place themselves and the other in mirroring roles, are described: (a) victimhood vs. agency (b) maintaining privacy and autonomy vs. belonging and dependence. These interpersonal interactions

---

1 This chapter is based on a chapter in my PhD dissertation, under the supervision of Prof. Dorit Lemberger in the Culture and Hermeneutics Program at Bar-Ilan University.
2 Orin Segal, "'I Am Not Myself, but I Am Not an Other': Self-Dissolution Narrative in Medical Rehabilitation Psychotherapy," in *Memories and Monsters: Psychology, Trauma, and Narrative*, ed. Severson Eric R. and Goodman David M. (New York: Routledge, 2018).
3 Roy Schafer, "The Reality Principle, Tragic Knots, and the Analytic Process," *Journal of the American Psychoanalytic Association* 55, no. 4 (2007): 1151–68; Jessica Benjamin, *Beyond Doer and Done To. Recognition Theory, Intersubjectivity and the Third*, Angewandte Chemie International Edition, 6(11), 951–952, vol. 13 (London and New York: Routledge, 2018).

DOI: 10.4324/9781003326588-9

are described and illustrated through clinical illustrations from medical and rehabilitation situations throughout the chapter.

Self-Dissolution Following Acquired Medical Conditions

Miriam,[4] a young woman in her early 20s, is trying to cope with a neurological-muscular degenerative illness, which she acquired during late childhood. The main effect of her illness has been a gradual decline in control over muscle tone and motor abilities. Accordingly, over the years Miriam has lost the ability to walk or stand. It is also difficult for her to use her hands when needed for fine motor activities, such as writing, using a touch screen on a cell phone, using a knife when eating, or even dressing. Presently, Miriam uses a wheelchair and needs help from others to perform many of the basic daily routines. As a result, her main relationships today are with her caregivers, and those that could not help her functionally, have been gradually rejected by her.

For a couple of years, Miriam has been in psychotherapy. She initially sought a rehabilitation psychologist in order to help her find the motivation to work harder in physiotherapy, so her physical condition could improve and she could accomplish her dreams to travel around the world. When therapy started, she rejected all negative aspects of her condition and repeatedly stressed that the fact that she is alive is a miracle. Nevertheless, she did not feel happiness or satisfaction; in fact, she hardly expressed emotions at all. She also described how she felt alone and isolated. Although Miriam wanted to be cured, she did not think she could ever feel a part of human society again, as she did when she was younger and healthy.

In this brief example, we can see how Miriam's medical condition has affected her sense of self and sense of others and how these are interconnected. Her physical impairments have made her more dependent on others, on the one hand, yet feeling more socially isolated, on the other. Miriam is one of many individuals coping with acquired chronic medical conditions[5] (henceforth ACMC). As Miriam and others experience ACMC, they are confronted by a threefold psychological toll. First, they have to cope with a body that is often painful, weak, and vulnerable. Second, as physical and emotional needs and abilities change, one has to face

---

4 There has been a thorough disguising of the identity and pertinent identifying information of the client presented in the vignette in this paper.
5 I will refer to acquired chronic medical conditions as a general term describing a multitude of acquired physical conditions, such as chronic illness, acquired physical injuries or other acquired medical conditions that result in physical impairments. Using ICF (International Classification of Functioning) language, the term ACMC solely refers to the physical impact of an acquired condition.

fundamental changes in interpersonal relations as well. Third, there is a need to adjust to the disruption of the foundations of self-knowledge, causing a sense of self-dissolution. I define self-dissolution as the feeling of a shattered or split self, between a previously known and seemingly stable self, and a present unknown and unpredictable self. This sense of self-dissolution is frequently caused by sudden onsets of disabling and distressful lasting physical conditions.[6] It is a feeling of a split and disintegration If persistent over time, self-dissolution can cause profound distress.

Therefore, living with ACMC involves coping with many debilitating outcomes: physical, emotional, and socio-economical. Research focusing on long-term and short-term psychological impact of acquired chronic medical conditions, describe devastating emotional and interpersonal outcomes, especially high rates of prolonged clinical depression, anxiety, and PTSD for individuals coping with ACMC and their caregivers.[7]

Despite the ample literature describing the emotional and interpersonal toll of ACMC, up to date there have been relatively few attempts to explore and develop this from a theoretical perspective.[8] Accordingly, the goal of this paper is to further explore the psychological experience of ACMC, focusing on the changes to the sense of self and sense of other, and on the

---

6 Segal, "'I Am Not Myself, but I Am Not an Other': Self-Dissolution Narrative in Medical Rehabilitation Psychotherapy."
7 Jane M. Gunn et al., "The Association between Chronic Illness, Multimorbidity and Depressive Symptoms in an Australian Primary Care Cohort," *Social Psychiatry and Psychiatric Epidemiology* 47, no. 2 (2012): 175–84; Israel Ministry of Health: The department for research and development for mental health, "Anxiety and Depression Disorders in Israel (Hebrew)," 2012, http://www.health.gov.il/publicationsfiles/depression_anxiety_israel.pdf; Mary L. Burke, Georgne G. Eakes, and Margaret A. Hainsworth, "Milestones of Chronic Sorrow: Perspectives of Chronically Ill and Bereaved Persons and Family Caregivers," *Journal of Family Nursing* 5, no. 4 (1999): 374–87; Cassandra J. Crangle and Tae L. Hart, "Adult Attachment, Hostile Conflict, and Relationship Adjustment among Couples Facing Multiple Sclerosis," *British Journal of Health Psychology* 22, no. 4 (2017): 836–53; Donna R Falvo, *Medical and Psychosocial Aspects of Chronic Illness and Disability* (Burlington: Jones & Bartlett Learning, 2014); Pamela Naidoo et al., "The Association between Biopsychosocial Factors and Disability in a National Health Survey in South Africa," *Psychology, Health and Medicine* 23, no. 6 (2017): 653–60; Scott C. Bezeau, Nicholas M. Bogod, and Catherine a Mateer, "Sexually Intrusive Behaviour Following Brain Injury: Approaches to Assessment and Rehabilitation," *Brain Injury: [BI]* 18, no. 3 (2004): 299–313; Samantha DeDios-Stern and Eun Jeong Lee, "Blame, Coping, and Psychosocial Outcomes in Caregivers of Individuals with Brain Injury," *Rehabilitation Psychology* 62, no. 3 (2017): 353–62.
8 Erin Martz and Hanoch Livneh, *Coping with Chronic Illness and Disability Theoretical, Empirical, and Clinical Aspects* (Springer, 2007); Rona Moss-Morris, "Adjusting to Chronic Illness: Time for a Unified Theory," *British Journal of Health Psychology* 18, no. 4 (2013): 681–86; Segal, "'I Am Not Myself, but I Am Not an Other': Self-Dissolution Narrative in Medical Rehabilitation Psychotherapy"; Dana S. Dunn and Timothy R. Elliott, "The Place and Promise of Theory in Rehabilitation Psychology Research," *Rehabilitation Psychology* 53, no. 3 (2008): 254–67.

changes in interpersonal interactions. Through the exploration of different relational aspects of this experience, namely *complementarity* in interactions with others and common *tragic-knots* shaping senses of self and other, I suggest a theoretical and practical self-illness narrative framework to further understand this experience.[9]

Self-Illness Narrative Model

Following the notion that self-dissolution is one of the major psychological sequelae following ACMC, I would like to refer to post-modern psychoanalytic concepts of self. Post-modern approaches view the self not as an entity to be found in our minds, but more as a mental construct. One way of conceptualizing the self, according to this view, is as an active mental construct through which the individual achieves a sense of continuity over time, and through which he perceives the world, organizes, and selects information about it and grants it meaning and sense.[10]

Narrativists and constructivists add to this idea that humans make meaning and organize their life experiences through narratives.[11] The self, or self-narrative, is viewed as a "… 'macro-narrative' that consolidates our self-understanding, establishes our characteristic range of emotions and goals, and guides our performance on the stage of the social world.[12] Based on this view, the self is conceptualized as a contingent mental narrative construct, serving a twofold purpose: to gain a sense of continuity in a non-continuous experience and to organize and make sense of the world, in a chaotic and non-organized world. This mental function is done effortlessly and in most cases without conscious deliberation.

---

9 Jessica Benjamin, "Beyond Doer and Done to: An Intersubjective View of Thirdness," *The Psychoanalytic Quarterly* 73, no. 1 (2004): 5–46; Schafer, "The Reality Principle, Tragic Knots, and the Analytic Process"; Tammar Zilber, Rivka Tuval-Mashiach, and Amia Lieblich, "The Embedded Narrative. Navigating Through Multiple Contexts," *Qualitative Inquiry* 14, no. 6 (2008): 1047–69.

10 Stephen A. Mitchell, "Contemporary Perspectives on Self: Toward an Integration," *Psychoanalytic Dialogues* 1 (1991): 121–47; Daniel N. Stern, *The Interpersonal World Of The Infant: A View From Psychoanalysis And Developmental Psychology* (New York: Basic Books, 2000).

11 Susan Roos and Robert A. Neimeyer, "Reauthoring the Self: Chronic Sorrow and Posttraumatic Stress Following the Onset of CID," in *Coping with Chronic Illness and Disability: Theoretical, Empirical, and Clinical Aspects*, 2007, 89–106; Roy Schafer, "Narration in the Psychoanalytic Dialogue," *Critical Inquiry* 7, no. 1 (1980): 29–53, https://doi.org/10.1086/448087.

12 Robert A. Neimeyer, Olga Herrero, and Luis Botella, "Chaos To Coherence: Psychotherapeutic Integration Of Traumatic Loss," *Journal of Constructivist Psychology* 19, no. 2 (2006): 129, https://doi.org/10.1080/10720530500508738.

Using this conceptualization, if self or self-narrative serves as a function of meaning-making, then experiencing ACMC can alter this meaning in a fundamental way.[13] The disruption of a self-narrative by a sudden or ongoing medical condition can leave the individual with a dissolution of meaning when meaning is needed the most. The self-dissolution narrative is a rigid narrative in which there is a former self, recognized as a previously organized construct, and a new sense of self, not totally meaningful. The two are split by an illness, a physical injury, or an ongoing acquired impairment. The relationship between the two selves is an ambiguous one, causing a weird sense of familiarity and estrangement simultaneously.

As I will soon discuss more comprehensively, the focus of this paper will be to discuss self-dissolution as it presents itself in a wider self-illness narrative. Specifically, I would like to explore how self-dissolution affects and is affected by one's connections to others, specifically in the form of what I will describe as *tragic knot complementarities.*

It is important to note that by emphasizing the contextual, interpersonal characteristics of the self-illness narrative, I do not mean to imply that the intrinsic "intra-psychological" characteristics of self-dissolution are of less importance to understanding the individual experience of ACMC. Rather, the two fields are mutually interdependent, constantly shaping and influencing each other. many thinkers believe that human experiences, ACMC among them, are rooted in intersubjective and social contexts, thus affecting the construction of self accordingly.[14] At the same time, as individual subjects we constantly shape and construct our lives, world views, and self-narratives, thus affecting the social interactions we are part of. As the scope of this paper is limited, we will not further discuss directly the effect of the structural field on self-dissolution or other self-illness aspects.

---

13 Kaethe Weingarten, "Making Sense of Illness Narratives: Braiding Theory, Practice and the Embodied Life (2001)," *International Journal of Narrative Therapy Community Work*, 2006, 1–11, http://www.dulwichcentre.com.au/illness-narratives.html; Arthur W Frank, "Just Listening: Narrative and Deep Illness," *Families, Systems, & Health* 16, no. 3 (1998): 197–212.

14 Judith Butler, *Precarious Life* (London and New York: Verso, 2004); David A. Jopling, "Cognitive Science, Other Minds, and the Philosophy of Dialogue," in *The Perceived Self. Ecological and Interpersonal Sources of Self-Knowledge (1993)*, ed. Ulric Neisser (Cambridge, UK: Cambridge University Press, 2006), 290–310; Ulric Neisser, "The Self Perceived," in *The Perceived Self. Ecological and Interpersonal Sources of Self-Knowledge (1993)*, ed. Ulric Neisser (Cambridge, UK: Cambridge University Press, 2006); Veronica Nanton et al., "The Threatened Self: Considerations of Time, Place, and Uncertainty in Advanced Illness," *British Journal of Health Psychology* 21, no. 2 (2016): 351–73; Michael White and David Epston, *Narrative Means to Therapeutic Ends* (New York and London: W.W. Norton and Company, 1990).

Complementarity and Tragic Knots following Acquired Chronic Medical Conditions

Acquired Chronic Medical Conditions and Relational Complementarities

As mentioned earlier, the self is a way in which humans organize their past experiences, understand their relationships and roles, and direct their present and future actions.[15] Relational and interpersonal postmodern thought in philosophy and psychology tells us that the self, whether viewed as a narrative, or as an organizing construct, is always formed in the context of a real or imagined other.[16] Through the self constituting act, the individual positions herself in different interpersonal roles. However, through this act, not only is the self-subject positioned in a role but the other's role is shaped as well. In the context of ACMC, self-other narratives should be viewed in light of the real effect a medical condition has on interpersonal experiences.[17] For example, in many cases of ACMC, such as Miriam's example, there is a growing dependency upon others to assist in medical treatment or in everyday life activities that were previously accomplished independently. Obviously, this change in dependency alters the relationships and interactions one has with others and forces one to re-form views of self and others accordingly.

When the act of self-construct becomes rigid and restrictive, there is a risk that both partners in a dyad will be forced into a complementary relation: For example, a helpless man suffering from diabetes submissively relies on his strong and benevolent sister to take care of his every need; the girl that is fighting cancer angrily rejects any offer of help and support from her close friends, so on. Jessica Benjamin (2004) describes these complementary relations as: "... those push me/pull-you, doer/done to dynamics that we find in most impasses, which generally appear to be one-way—that is, each person feels *done to, and not like an agent helping to shape a*

---

15 Stephen A. Mitchell, "Contemporary Perspectives on Self: Toward an Integration"; Robert A. Neimeyer, "Re-Storying Loss: Fostering Growth in the Posttraumatic Narrative," in *Handbook of Posttraumatic Growth: Research and Practice*, ed. Lawrence G. Calhoun and Richard G. Tedeschi (Mahwah, NJ: Lawrence Erlbaum, 2006).
16 Lewis Aron, "Self-Reflexivity and the Therapeutic Action of Psychoanalysis," *Psychoanalytic Psychology* 17, no. 4 (2000): 667–89; Lewis Aron, "Analytic Impasse and the Third: Clinical Implications of Intersubjectivity Theory," *International Journal of Psychoanalysis* 87 (2006): 349–68; David A. Jopling, *Self-Knowledge and The Self* (New York and London: Routledge, 2000); Weingarten, "Making Sense of Illness Narratives: Braiding Theory, Practice and the Embodied Life (2001)."
17 Weingarten, "Making Sense of Illness Narratives: Braiding Theory, Practice and the Embodied Life (2001)."

co-created reality."[18] Lewis Aron (2006) adds to this: "Dyads, couples, and systems tend to get stuck in complementary relations. This complementarity is characterized by a variety of splitting, in which one side takes a position complementary to—the polar opposite of—the other side."[19]

Thus, complementarities are a process in which self-other relationships and self-narratives are formed or maintained. One of the most important aspects of Benjamin's concept of complementarity is that it precludes perceiving the other as a subject and the relationship as a mutual one.[20] Rather, being in a complementary relationship means perceiving the other in a restrictive and anticipated role, thus perceiving him as an object.[21] Benjamin describes that this could happen when one does not develop a perception of intersubjectivity, or when "more traumatized, abandoned or hated parts of the self, arise."[22] In this sense, experiencing self-dissolution following medical conditions frequently gives rise to rejected and unwanted parts of oneself in the past and present.[23] Furthermore, many times this experience not only alters the ability to perceive the other as a subject but to perceive the self as a subject as well, thus establishing a restricted and minimized self-narrative.[24] Accordingly, I suggest that relations formed in the medical setting are especially vulnerable to complementarities.

Complementarities and Tragic Knots

While there are many possible complementarities shaping the self-other narratives, I would like to focus on self-narratives that emerge when confronted with "tragic knots" following illness experiences. This concept, shaped by Roy Schafer (2007), is defined by him in the following passage: "Consciously or unconsciously, a person must confront a recognizably fateful situation that is insufficiently under his or her control. [...] However

---

18 "Beyond Doer and Done to: An Intersubjective View of Thirdness," 9.
19 "Analytic Impasse and the Third: Clinical Implications of Intersubjectivity Theory," 353.
20 Jessica Benjamin, *Beyond Doer and Done To. Recognition Theory, Intersubjectivity and the Third.*
21 Jessica Benjamin, "Recognition and Destruction: An Outline of Intersubjectivity (1990)," in *Relational Psychoanalysis. The Emergence of a Tradition*, ed. Stephen A. Mitchell, and Lewis Aron (New York: Routledge, 1999), 181–99.
22 Jessica Benjamin, "Beyond Doer and Done to: An Intersubjective View of Thirdness," 20.
23 Nanton et al., "The Threatened Self: Considerations of Time, Place, and Uncertainty in Advanced Illness"; Segal, "'I Am Not Myself, but I Am Not an Other': Self-Dissolution Narrative in Medical Rehabilitation Psychotherapy."
24 Robert A. Neimeyer, James W. Pennebaker, and Jessica G. van Dyke, "Narrative Medicine: Writing through Bereavement," in *Handbook of Psychiatry in Palliative Medicine*, ed. Harvey M. Chochinov and William Breitbart, 2nd ed. (New York: Oxford University Press, 2009); Robert A. Neimeyer, "Narrative Disruptions in the Construction of the Self," in *Constructions of Disorder. Meaning-Making Frameworks for Psychotherapy*, ed. Robert A. Neimeyer and Jonathan D. Raskin (Washington, DC: American Psychological Association, 2000), 207–42.

great its potential advantages, achievements, and gratifications, each course of action will involve suffering, impairment, or loss for the self, of the self, or in the lives of loved others."[25]

In short, tragic knots describe a situation characterized by a need to take action that will inevitably have a psychological cost. Schafer describes these situations as rooted in the external reality which underlies one's actions (internal and external). As such, they can be described as contexts upon which one acts. However, all tragic knot contexts described by Schafer, and adopted here, are of an interpersonal nature. Therefore, being in a tragic knot forces one to choose to act in an interpersonal context, and by doing so, to compose and shape a self through action.

Taking action in a tragic knot, according to Schafer, involves making a choice, to take one course of action over another.[26] It is important to note that these psychic choices can, and in most cases are, unconscious resolutions of internal conflicts or negotiations. In line with Schafer's conceptualization, I will use the term "choice" throughout this paper when referring to the positioning of oneself in a complementary relation pole in a tragic knot context.

Viewed through a relational prism, tragic knots can be seen as specific situations triggering complementarities. In these tragic situations, one shapes a self-narrative in opposition to the other, thus giving rise to complementary relations. As one chooses a position in a tragic knot, one dissociates from aspects of self that may threaten this polar choice. This process of dissociation "pushes" the other in the tragic knot relationship, forcing the other to enact the opposing role or to adopt the dissociated parts through the mechanism of projection identification.[27]

It is important to note that in this paper, tragic knots, as well as complementary relationships, are perceived as a relational mechanism that happens in various kinds of dyadic relationships, and are not limited to the psycho-therapeutic ones. Specifically, the focus in this paper is on relationships formed in medical contexts, serving as a platform for tragic knot complementarities, which will be described.

---

25 "The Reality Principle, Tragic Knots, and the Analytic Process," 1151.
26 Roy Schafer, "Conflict: Conceptualization, Practice, Problems," *The Psychoanalytic Quarterly* 74 (2005): 47–63; see Roy Schafer, "Action Language and the Psychology of the Self," *Annu. Psychoanal.* 8 (1980): 83–92.
27 Melanie Klein, "The Origins of Transference," *The International Journal of Psycho-Analysis* 33, no. 4 (1952): 433–38; H. Racker, "The Meanings and Uses of Countertransference," *Psychoanalytic Quarterly* 76, no. 3 (2007): 725–77; Michael Parsons, *The Dove That Returns, The Dove That Vanishes. Paradox and Creativity in Psychoanalysis* (London: Routledge, 2000).

As presented earlier, ACMC can alter one's life fundamentally, causing a sense of self-dissolution which undermines the ability to understand the situation of infirmity. Re-establishing sense in a situation of ACMC and reconstructing a self in this context confront the individual with many "tragic" choices. Two seemingly common tragic knots in the medical situation are introduced here. These two tragic knots include (1) *being victimized – gaining agency*, and (2) *maintaining privacy – negotiating autonomy and feeling of belonging*. The two "knots" are a loose adaptation of Schafer's concepts theoretically implemented in medical situations.[28]

Tragic Knot I: Being Victimized vs. Gaining a Sense of Agency

Schafer describes this knot as a consequence of being a victim of human violence, sudden loss of someone dear, or suffering an injury. These real-life experiences "disrupt the capacity for personal growth and attachment to others."[29] In the face of becoming a victim due to illness or physical trauma, one can find oneself in a tragic knot dichotomy between feeling responsible but possibly guilty for the medical affliction as opposed to feeling an innocent victim but stripped off a sense of agency.[30] To this dichotomy, I should add other conflicts such as viewing oneself as passive or active, full of rage, and wanting revenge as opposed to surrendering helplessly in the face of the medical experience.

For example, when confronted by a life-changing illness or injury, such as Miriam's neurological-muscular degenerative illness, she can feel she is a victim of an unfair world and construct a self-illness narrative of victimhood. This narrative includes a shattering of her belief in existential justice and safety in her own physical strength and self-control. At the same time, by feeling this sense of loss and helplessness, she is also able to grieve over her emotional and physical losses. This could hopefully help her move on and explore other aspects of her life and self.

On the other hand, by perceiving oneself as responsible for an illness or injury, one can acknowledge guilt and posit blame for the onset or consequences of the physical condition, accompanied by possible feelings of shame and misery. At the same time, the choice of viewing oneself as

---

28 Roy Schafer describes a third tragic knot, he defines as "approaching intimacy with others" Schafer, "The Reality Principle, Tragic Knots, and the Analytic Process," 1159. Although this is an important tragic knot, relevant to the therapeutic interaction, I believe that at this point, there is little for me to further elaborate on, beyond Schafer's general description and my previous focus on maintain privacy – negotiating autonomy and feeling of belonging
29 1155.
30 e.g., J. Scott Richards et al., "Attribution of Responsibility for Onset of Spinal Cord Injury and Psychosocial Outcomes in the First Year Post-Injury," *Rehabilitation Psychology* 42, no. 2 (1997): 115–24.

responsible for a medical condition can also be viewed as a way of establishing control, mental or physical, over the experience. This can lead to a possible sense of empowerment and even paradoxically be emotionally appeasing. Self-control makes these experiences, difficult and painful as they might be, intelligible. As well as enabling a person to find the meaning and reason for the medical condition, a story of self-responsibility can also be translated into real self-care actions, facilitating autonomy, adjustment to one's situation and personal growth.

In short, the tragic knot of victimhood-vs.-agency presents the following conflict: one feels one needs to choose between responsibility or guilt on the one hand, possibly accompanied by a conceivable sense of control; or feeling a victim of the circumstances, losing a sense of control and a sense of ability to predict future outcomes, while expressing anger and grief toward one's losses. Obviously, what makes a tragic knot choice tragic is that there is no one "good" decision. Each pole consists of psychological advantages intertwined with personal prices.

As noted earlier, choosing a side in a tragic knot, not only constructs the narrative one tells about the self and the illness but also shapes others in the relevant interpersonal contexts. It is difficult to formulate a simple relationship between the choices one makes in the victimhood knot, and the way the other is shaped accordingly in the interaction. The other is not only a passively reacting object, but is an interacting subject. She can surrender to the complementarity but can defy it too.[31] To add to this, not only does the other choose how to react to the choices imposed on her, but she also brings into the interaction her own tragic knots choices and her own self-other narrative.

For example, a man coping with a spinal cord injury can experience a sense of being a helpless victim of the situation. This subconscious choice could lead to an idealized view of his doctors and the rest of the medical and rehabilitation staff. As he views himself as passive in the face of his injury, the medical staff is viewed as omnipotent saviors, thus projecting onto them full responsibility for his condition. Viewing them this way, he might be compliant in different therapies, participating and fulfilling demands and tasks made by his therapists. On the other hand, if they do not manage to help him recover the way he hopes, he might feel enraged by them, similar to his rage toward the injury.

The medical staff – the relevant others, in return, can surrender to the complementary role into which they are cast, thus identifying with the beneficial and maybe grandiose health-care professional depicted in this illustration. It is highly possible that the therapist/caregiver will not perceive her self-perceptions as reactions to a limited choice she was confronted with

---

31 Jessica Benjamin, "Beyond Doer and Done to: An Intersubjective View of Thirdness."

but rather as expressing her own self-identity. That is, the tragic knot complementarity is an unconscious dynamic and the caregiver would probably identify with the dichotomous complementary role inflicted on her.

Following Aron's "seesaw" metaphor, the other could try to reverse the roles, while remaining in the complementarity.[32] For example, the other can resist the role of an omnipotent health-care professional, perceiving herself as unworthy and feeling "performance" anxiety. She might then perceive the patient as demanding and offensive, constantly "pushing" her to her limits.

Although it can be a difficult task, the other can try to reject or change the complementarity altogether, by helping to create an intersubjective understanding between the sides in the interaction. This will be discussed later.

It is important to stress that this interpersonal process is not one-directional. Not only does the person coping with ACMC influence the other-narrative, but this can and is a mutual interpersonal construction. The tragic knot choice is affected not solely by the reaction of the individual to his injury, but also by the reactions and perceptions others have regarding the individual and themselves in the tragic knot interaction. That is, the other enters the interaction not only as a respondent to the tragic choice, but as an initiator as well. Thus, tragic knot complementarity narratives are co-authored in a complex matrix.

Tragic Knot II: Maintaining Privacy vs. Belonging and Dependency

Schafer describes that "Privacy is intimately involved in developing and stabilizing a sense of self, autonomy, social competence, integration, and freedom of imagination. At the same time, maintaining an optimal degree of privacy is a steady source of tension, for others often interpret visibly maintaining privacy as a sign of aloofness, mistrust, indifference, or rebellion."[33] He adds that "Being careless about one's privacy can lead to indiscretions, charges of exhibitionism, and exposure to humiliation and exploitation" (ibid). In light of this, ACMC forces changes in a previous balance between privacy and sociability, as one faces growing physical dependency and self-exposure to caregivers, physicians, medical staff, etc. These changes can include depending on others to help with medical treatment, to help with ADL (activities of daily living) previously accomplished independently, or to give emotional support previously unneeded.

In all of these situations, choosing sociability stresses social dependency and support at the risk of a loss of privacy and a sense of autonomy. On the other hand, in rehabilitation and other medical surroundings, choosing

---

32 Lewis Aron, "Analytic Impasse and the Third: Clinical Implications of Intersubjectivity Theory," 354.
33 Schafer, "The Reality Principle, Tragic Knots, and the Analytic Process," 1161.

privacy cannot only be perceived by others as rejection of others and of social bonds, but it can also be perceived as a refusal to participate in one's treatment plan.

Elaborating on Schafer's inclusion of the sense of autonomy as part of the privacy dimension, I would like to stress the importance of this in ACMC experiences. As described earlier, one of the main consequences of ACMC is the increasing physical dependency on others. Because independence is highly valued in western, individualistic-focused cultures, a perceived lack or loss of independence is commonly followed by a certain degree of self-devaluation.[34] In line with this, while accepting help from others might prove physically or functionally useful, it comes with a potential price: the dissolution of the sense of self as an autonomous agent and possible social exclusion thereafter. This was a price Miriam had felt too. Although dependency per se was not the main reason she had felt non-human, but rather the social scrutiny and rejection she felt, certainly was a contributing factor.

Focusing on the idea of physical dependence, Judith Butler (2004) emphasizes two roles our body has in this self-other tragic knot. She suggests that the body has a social role: potentially vulnerable, exposed, and scrutinized by others, while simultaneously being a source of contact and social connectedness. "The body has its invariably public dimension. Constituted as a social phenomenon in the public sphere, my body is and is not mine."[35]

In light of Butler's ideas, ACMC can abruptly undermine the social balance one has previously achieved. The ill or injured body is a more vulnerable one, succumbing to heightened public scrutiny, exposure, and dependency. Simultaneously, this same experience is felt by many as uniquely private and subjective, not intelligible to others.[36] This is the reason why the sense of belonging is another important aspect of the tragic knot of privacy. Abundant clinical literature stresses the impact that chronic illness, injury, and disability have on the sense of loneliness and social isolation.[37]

It is worth mentioning briefly that the perception of belonging has social-political and social-subjective aspects. Regarding the social-subjective

---

34 Lennard J Davis, "Constructing Normalcy: The Bell Curve, the Novel, and the Invention of the Disabled Body in the Nineteenth Century," in *The Disability Studies Reader*, ed. Lennard J Davis, 2nd ed. (New York, 2006), 3–16; Dominique Van de Velde et al., "The Illusion and the Paradox of Being Autonomous, Experiences from Persons with Spinal Cord Injury in Their Transition Period from Hospital to Home," *Disability and Rehabilitation* 34, no. 6 (March 6, 2012): 491–502; Mitchell G. Weiss, Jayashree Ramakrishna, and Daryl Somma, "Health-Related Stigma: Rethinking Concepts and Interventions," *Psychology, Health and Medicine* 11, no. 3 (2006): 277–87; Katie Wang and John F. Dovidio, "Disability and Autonomy: Priming Alternative Identities," *Rehabilitation Psychology* 56, no. 2 (2011): 123–27.
35 *Precarious Life*, 26.
36 Frank, "Just Listening: Narrative and Deep Illness."
37 e.g., Falvo, *Medical and Psychosocial Aspects of Chronic Illness and Disability*.

aspect, Atwood et al. (2002) argue that "... the experience of personal annihilation reflects an intersubjective catastrophe in which psychologically sustaining relations to others have broken down at their most fundamental level."[38] Although this paragraph was written in the context of psychotic and dissociative states, I suggest it also reflects the social-subjective sense of belonging (or lack of it) following ACMC. There are many causes for the distancing of emotionally sustaining relationships following ACMC. These include the fears others have of the physical condition the individual is experiencing or the fear the individual has of being scrutinized and feared by others; feeling one cannot help the person experiencing ACMC emotionally or physically; feeling the relationship alliance has been compromised because of the personal changes that are due to the physical condition.

On the social-political side, when a person acquires a medical condition, such as diabetes, cancer, HIV, head injury, limb amputation, etc., he involuntarily acquires a social identity as well.[39] Thus, in many aspects of one's perception of social identity, there is no longer a sense of belonging to pre-ACMC "healthy" social groups. At the same time, new but not necessarily desired "ill" groups offer shared experiences and shared narratives. Apart from the fact that members of the new group could be perceived by the individual as reflecting his traumatic experience, in many cases belonging to such a group means belonging to a minority that is stigmatized, underestimated, and under-privileged.[40]

Moreover, in a world where great importance is attached to health, youthfulness, and strength, no longer having these attributes means being valued less.[41] Hence, the fear of being associated with a "disability" minority group may exist whether or not individuals coping with ACMC have encountered harsh discriminatory acts toward them or have been directly devalued.

In summary, in the face of ACMC, one frequently has to choose between two extremes; one representing privacy, individuality, autonomy, and

---

38 George E Atwood, Donna M. Orange, and Robert D Stolorow, "Shattered Worlds/Psychotic States: A Post-Cartesian View of the Experience of Personal Annihilation," *Psychoanalytic Psychology* 19, no. 2 (2002): 288.
39 Michael Davidson, "Universal Design: The Work of Disability in an Age of Globalization," in *The Disability Studies Reader. Second Edition*, ed. Lennard J. Davis (New York: Routledge, 2006).
40 Davis, "Constructing Normalcy: The Bell Curve, the Novel, and the Invention of the Disabled Body in the Nineteenth Century"; Ruth Hubbard, "Abortion and Disability: Who Should and Who Should Not Inhabit the World?," in *The Disability Studies Reader. Second Edition*, ed. Lennard J Davis (New York: Routledge, 2006); Weiss, Ramakrishna, and Somma, "Health-Related Stigma: Rethinking Concepts and Interventions."
41 Davis, "Constructing Normalcy: The Bell Curve, the Novel, and the Invention of the Disabled Body in the Nineteenth Century."

singularity of life experiences; and the other, representing sociability, a feeling of belonging, dependence, self-exposure, and possible exploitation.

Returning to the self-illness complementarity, the perception of the relevant other, as part of an in or out-group, healthy or ill, affects the expectations the individual has toward the interaction: whether it will be one of empathy and belonging, or of scrutiny, intimidation or rejection.

What does it mean for the relevant other to react to a privacy complementarity? Similar to the tragic knot of victimhood, the relevant other can surrender to the complementary role that is imposed upon her. If confronted by dependence and helplessness, the other might identify with the helpful, care-giving, and nurturing role, or may become domineering and authoritarian. She, the relevant other, could also give in to a position of indifference, scrutiny, or dismissal, if confronted by the need for privacy and the fear of not being socially accepted.

The relevant other can and does actively project her perceptions, prejudices, and predispositions toward people with disabilities and physical impairments, thus affecting the privacy tragic knot. Moreover, because the tragic knot of privacy has many different aspects, as we have seen here, the other can comply with some of the choices on a complementarity interaction, and avoid others. For example, the wife of a man coping with lymphoma could take a complementarity role in the choice of dependence, providing for her husband's every need; at the same time, she could disagree with playing a complementary role in his choice of self-exposure, criticizing him for sharing his illness experience with others or not feeling embarrassed to expose his body to medical staff, and encouraging him to be more private in these situations.

Interpreting Tragic Knots Interaction in Therapy – Case Example

I will now turn to a clinical vignette taken from a therapy session with Miriam, who was presented in the beginning of this paper. For a few months prior to the session presented here, a major issue in therapy was the nursing care Miriam was receiving from her family. She felt there was a demand and expectation, which I, the therapist, was a part of as well, for her to gradually let go of her family's caretaking and accept external nursing help at home. This demand was perceived by Miriam as part of the general expectation for her to "grow up" and be more independent. Initially, Miriam was reluctant to agree to this demand. Her main concern was that having a stranger take care of her would fundamentally change and damage the relationship with her parents and increase her sense of loneliness. As she felt the pressure from her parents and me increasing to engage in independent activities, she became more and more frustrated with us. It had also caused her to emotionally and physically withdraw, "proving" to us that she needed help.

The following vignette is taken from a therapy session that occurred shortly after Miriam had started getting daily help at home by a nursing caretaker. I did not know this had happened, but realized this when Miriam entered the clinic escorted by a foreign woman. Nevertheless, throughout the first 20 minutes of therapy, Miriam did not mention the existence of the caretaker in her life, and spoke about other, seemingly banal daily experiences, such as university papers she had to hand in. The more she did not speak about it, or show any sign this was important to her, the more I felt upset she had not told me this was about to happen. Eventually, after a short silence in the conversation, I felt I had to directly ask.

Therapist: I noticed that an unfamiliar woman brought you here. Who is she?
Miriam: Oh ... That is Julia ... She is my new caretaker. She started about a week ago ... She is very nice.
Therapist: (surprised by Miriam's nonchalant reaction): How do you feel about this?
Miriam: It's fine. Ordinary ... She helps me with what I need, and my parents have the time to do their things now. So it's all good. For them too. You know, they are aging and it's not easy to pick me up and move me from place to place.
Therapist (slightly puzzled and starting to feel a little annoyed with Miriam's indifference, after this had been such a matter of fear and resistance on her part; at the same time starting to feel guilty for feeling annoyed with Miriam): I was thinking about how your reaction today is surprisingly different to what I had expected from you. For so long you rejected the idea and now you feel it is ordinary to you.
Miriam (shrugs her shoulders): I adapt quickly ... If there is something this life has taught me, it is that I have to adapt, whether I want to or not... People don't understand this because they don't have to cope with what I am dealing with. I have to put all my trust in the people that take care of me, otherwise I might die... I can't withhold this trust (Miriam gazes directly towards me).
Therapist (feeling blamed for goading Miriam and not understanding her): You told me in the past that this was the main thing that made you hold tighter to your parents; the fear of not having someone take care of you. For you this is the way to survive. I think the magnitude of this is difficult for others to understand, including your parents and me ... I guess you feel I did not understand this ...
Miriam: Right. It's the same thing ... If things don't work in relationships, people my age can just get up and leave. I can't ... I am totally physically dependent on the people around me ... I can't just leave, and I can't have them just leave. I need them for everything I do: for getting into the bath; for taking my medication; for going from place to place;

for making food ... Maybe I can do more than I actually do, but it doesn't change the fact that I need them constantly in my life.

Therapist (empathically): That's very intense emotionally. You feel so dependent on others that you think you literally couldn't exist without them. It must be frightening?

Miriam: I don't mind it ... I really don't mind being dependent. My body is nothing to me ... I mind it if people don't understand this dependency. I'm afraid if I do things alone, they will think I don't need them as much and leave me alone.

I would like to briefly interpret this vignette from a tragic knot complementarity narrative point of view. To me the most prominent tragic knot apparent in this vignette is the tragic knot of maintaining privacy vs. belonging and dependency. First and foremost, Miriam feels that her physical illness has made her dependent on others in a real existential level. She needs others to take care of her daily physical needs in such a way that not receiving this help is perceived by her as a matter of life or death. It is important to note that this existential sense of urgency Miriam feels and its connection to the thought of her own possible death, is a fairly common issue following ACMC.[42] When confronted by ACMC, one also has to face one's own vulnerability and limitations and is, therefore, faced with a feeling of mortality too. Hence, it is not surprising that in light of Miriam's severe medical condition, death plays a real and crucial role in her self-illness narrative.

For Miriam, her close family relationships sustain her existence. Therefore, it is a matter of life or death to hold onto these relationships. This connection, together with the fear of death, makes every possible change in her close relationship's dynamics feel like a threat, which has to be resisted. That is why she has feared getting help from a caretaker for so long. Independence comes at the price of separation, and separation brings mortality with it.

Another aspect of privacy expressed in this text is the issue of self-exposure and trust. In order for Miriam to receive care, she has to fully expose her body to others, even strangers, such as physicians, nurses, and the new caretaker. She has to trust others to do so without harming her, as others have the power to take care of or take advantage of Miriam. In Miriam's mind, once a person becomes a caretaker, she feels she cannot withhold her trust, as this would be counter-productive to her many needs. Whatever fears she might have regarding trust in the relationship she is in, Miriam cannot express them consciously, once the choice has been made. It seems to me that is why her response seemed indifferent and detached

---

42 Mary Ann McColl et al., "Changes in Spiritual Beliefs after Traumatic Disability," *Archives of Physical Medicine and Rehabilitation* 81, no. 6 (2000): 817–23; Ernest Becker, *The Denial of Death* (New York: The Free Press, 1973).

regarding the new and very intimate relationship with the caretaker. The fact that Miriam felt she had to develop a connection with the caretaker in a very short time meant that she had to reject possible feelings of conflict that usually appear in new relationships. This dissociative emotional process leaves her seemingly fearless, but also apathetic and indifferent.

A third aspect of the privacy dimension is the issue of belonging. Miriam feels that the same people she is dependent on, her family and the therapist, are also the people that cannot actually understand her. She is dependent on them because of their good health and physical abilities, but at the same time feels distant from them for being healthy. In that sense, the people closest to her are also perceived by her as an out-group, not able to truly grasp her self-illness experience. To this she reacted in anger and frustration when she felt the demands for independence where not congruent with her own sense of self. In comparison to the privacy-autonomy dimension, in which Miriam places herself on the public pole, perceiving herself as dependent and choosing to be exposed to others; on the privacy-belonging dimension she places herself on the opposite pole, emphasizing privacy and loneliness.

How do Miriam's tragic knot of unconscious choices affect the complementary roles in the interpersonal interaction? The first complementarity was apparent long before the particular session described above. It started when I, like Miriam's family, impelled Miriam to gain independence. The more we encouraged this, the more Miriam resisted and was anxious about the outcomes of this possible form of separation from her parents. The more we pushed for separation, i.e., privacy, the more Miriam pulled for dependency. This dynamic made Miriam perceive her parents and me as insensitive, even aggressors, forcing her to do what she did not what to do. She battled to make us understand how dependent she was, but the more she did this, the more she was perceived as taking advantage of her situation and the demand for her to be independent was exacerbated. We were all stuck in this "doer-done-to" dynamic.

Although this aspect of the privacy complementarity is in the background of the session presented, it seems that the most salient issue enacted in the therapy room is the issue of understanding and belonging. While Miriam felt misunderstood and withdrew, I felt that I didn't understand her and felt I had to address it. While Miriam felt she could not trust me, because I didn't understand her existential fear, I felt she was intentionally not telling me about the caretaker. Miriam felt that her experience was so unique and subjective, that others who do not experience a similar physical dependency could not understand or identify with her. We were both experiencing this unspoken disconcerting gap between us.

Furthermore, the gap on the privacy-belonging dimension placed each of us as isolated subjects, while viewing the other as a foreign and unknown object. I, the therapist, was identified by Miriam as part of the "healthy" out-group. As such, my role in Miriam's self-illness narrative was a stereotypical one of a "healthy" person that could not and did not want to understand Miriam's world; that cannot open to another form of experience; that does not share any similar experiences with her. At the same time, in my self-narrative, Miriam was perceived as an "ill" individual in need for an authoritarian figure to tell her what she should do. I disregarded her fears, maybe silencing them in previous therapy sessions, and kept on pushing her to do more, to take responsibility for her life, and to mature and become independent. While all might be appropriate therapeutic goals, I lost a sense of Miriam's subjectivity, and I lost awareness of my impact on the distance that was growing between us.

Freeing the Dyad from a Tragic Knot Complementarity

What can be done when a dyad is "stuck" in a complementarity, forcing each side to construct a rigid self-other narrative, as is the case in the vignette that has been described and in so many medical situations?

An exhaustive solution for this is beyond the scope of this paper, but I will offer a general suggestion, based on Aron and Benjamin's ideas.[43] Both suggest that the solution begins with at least one of the partners in the dyad recognizing a mutual effect in the specific interaction and taking responsibility over his part. Once this occurs, the path to being freed from the I-subject/You-object complementarity and moving toward an intersubjective relationship lies in addressing each of the partners' dispositions as well as the mutual influence they have on each other.

In the vignette, a beginning of leaving the complementarity began with understanding the position I was enacting in the room, being both the person Miriam depends on, in the privacy-autonomy dimension, and at the same time being part of the apparent ignorant healthy out-group: the insensitive and aggressive "pusher." By understanding this, I could understand my feeling of estrangement and my impulse to "push" Miriam to my idea of independence, prior to the presented session.

Acknowledging my role as part of a healthy out-group, I could start to understand the resentment and need for withdrawal Miriam felt toward me. I also began to be aware of my feelings of frustration, estrangement, and lack of empathy toward Miriam, as a result of this tragic knot. By frankly communicating my limited perception and its possible effects on our relationship, I could allow her to re-choose her wish to communicate or not to communicate her experience with me and re-negotiate her sense of belonging and dependence. The more we do so, the more we both can expand our self-other narratives. Obviously, this process is an ongoing one, its roots only planted in this vignette.

---

43 Aron, "Analytic Impasse and the Third: Clinical Implications of Intersubjectivity Theory"; Jessica Benjamin, "An Outline of Intersubjectivity: The Development of Recognition," *Psychoanalytic Psychology* 7 (1990): 33–46; Benjamin, "Beyond Doer and Done to: An Intersubjective View of Thirdness"; Benjamin, *Beyond Doer and Done To. Recognition Theory, Intersubjectivity and the Third*.

Discussion

The Role of the other in Self-Illness Narratives

In this paper I have focused on one of the ways interpersonal interactions shape the narrative one tells about the self and the other in the context of chronic medical conditions through a complementarity construct.[44] I have further suggested two common dimensions, or tragic knots, that shape the relational complementarities following ACMC: (1) Being victimized – gaining agency; (2) Maintaining privacy – vs. dependency and belonging.

As was stressed throughout this paper, it is impossible to directly correlate the tragic-self choice and the other's choice. The other can comply with the role forced upon him in the tragic-knot complementarity, or try to reverse the roles, i.e., swinging the complementarity seesaw. Furthermore, the other can also force his-own tragic-knot choice, thus making the interplay of interaction even more complicated. However, both partners can also free the couple from the complementarity knots. As suggested by many relational thinkers, a start is when at least one partner in the dyad can perceive the relationship in its intersubjectivity, i.e., two subjects mutually affecting each other.[45] Directly addressing and relating to the tragic knot and the complementary roles, reactions, and emotions afflicted by it can help open a new co-authored interpersonal narrative which is not ruled by complementarity.

I would like to briefly emphasize the role of self-dissolution following ACMC in the process of self-illness complementarity. As mentioned in the introduction, the sense of self-dissolution is followed by tremendous anguish, suffering, and distress. It denies the individual a sense of meaning that his life once had, thus leaving him in a void and chaos. As long as the sense of dissolution of the self is dominant, the self-construct tends to be rigid and limited.[46] One is constantly trapped in dissociation between the person I used to be, and the ill person I am now.

Although this needs further research I suggest that this general self-illness narrative reduction and dissociation also has an effect on tragic-knot

---

44 Aron, "Analytic Impasse and the Third: Clinical Implications of Intersubjectivity Theory," 354.
45 Lewis Aron, "Analytic Impasse and the Third: Clinical Implications of Intersubjectivity Theory"; Philip M. Bromberg, "Truth, Human Relatedness, and the Analytic Process: An Interpersonal/ Relational Perspective," *International Journal of Psychoanalysis* 90, no. 2 (2009): 347–61; T H Ogden, "The Analytic Third: Working with Intersubjective Clinical Facts," *The International Journal of Psycho-Analysis* 75 (Pt 1), no. September 1993 (1994): 3–19; Benjamin, *Beyond Doer and Done To. Recognition Theory, Intersubjectivity and the Third*.
46 Robert A Neimeyer, "Reconstructing the Self in the Wake of Loss: A Dialogical Contribution," 2011, 374–89; Segal, "'I Am Not Myself, but I Am Not an Other': Self-Dissolution Narrative in Medical Rehabilitation Psychotherapy."

choices. That is, self-dissolution not only reduces the general self-illness narrative, but it causes rigidity in self-other interactions, thus triggering tragic-knot complementarities. Furthermore, as described earlier, as one dissociates oneself from unwanted aspects of the self that represent one's unwanted "ill" self, they are projected onto the other.

Another possible factor contributing to the link between ACMC and complementarities comes from disability studies. Different disability theorists suggest that as a society we tend to perceive persons with disabilities and physical illnesses as "ill" or "handicapped" objects, thus dehumanizing them.[47] These social constructs are internalized by both individuals experiencing ACMC and their partners in the dyad. That is, the perception of an individual solely as "ill," "handicapped" or as "healthy" and "normal" on the other hand, reduces self-other narratives and shapes rigid roles and interactions.

Both these processes, the process of self-dissolution and the process of objectifying individuals with ACMC, while different from each other, contribute to the perception of the individual coping with ACMC as an object, thus giving way to the complementarity in the dyad. This should be further explored, theoretically and empirically.

Future Directions

One possible and important direction that should be further explored is the intrinsic, intrapsychic field affecting self-dissolution and changing self-narratives following acquired chronic medical conditions. It is important to remember that the self is not only a public construct but a subjective and private mental phenomenon. Integrating between intra- and intersubjective processes will give us a better and more thorough understanding of the individual experience following acquired chronic medical conditions.

Another important issue that should be further addressed is the cultural and politico-social affect over self-illness construction.[48] The individual self

---

47 Davis, "Constructing Normalcy: The Bell Curve, the Novel, and the Invention of the Disabled Body in the Nineteenth Century"; Hubbard, "Abortion and Disability: Who Should and Who Should Not Inhabit the World?"; Shelley Tremain, "Foucault and the Government of Disability" (Ann Arbor: The University of Michigan Press, 2008).
48 Judith Butler, *Precarious Life*; Michel Foucault, *The History of Sexuality I (1976)*, Hebrew ver (Israel: Hakibbutz Hameuchad Publishing House, 1996); Michel Foucault, *Power/ Knowledge: Selected Interviews and Other Writings 1972–1977, New York*, vol. 23, 1980; Shelley Tremain, "Foucault and the Government of Disability"; Michael White, "Working with People Who Are Suffering the Consequences of Multiple Trauma: A Narrative Perspective," *International Journal of Narrative Therapy & Community Work*, no. 1 (2004): 44–75; Tammar Zilber, Rivka Tuval-Mashiach, and Amia Lieblich, "The Embedded Narrative. Navigating Through Multiple Contexts."

is embedded in a manifold of social and cultural circles that continuously affect how the individual and the social environment define and react to each other. I have briefly touched upon this topic when discussing the issue of belongingness, but this should be further explored and elaborated upon.

Further research should also continue to explore the topic of relational tragic-knots in ACMC contexts in depth, both theoretically and empirically. Further research could shed light on conditions that trigger specific tragic-knots dimensions or common choices in a dimension. For example, one direction could be to address the question of how particular medical conditions, such as coping with a head injury as compared to a muscular-skeletal illness, facilitate specific common tragic-knot narratives; or how specific interactions related to ACMC, such as interactions with medical personal as compared to family members, contribute to specific tragic-knot choices. Another possible direction is to gain a better understanding of the influence that others' tragic-knots choices have on the individual dealing with acquired chronic medical conditions.

Finally, as self-dissolution following ACMC causes so much intrapersonal and interpersonal distress, it is of utmost importance to establish specific therapeutic approaches focusing on these psychological outcomes for individuals coping with acquired chronic medical conditions, their families, caretakers, and medical staff working with them. The ideas described in this paper can serve as an interpretive basis for interventions dealing with the interpersonal aspects of acquired chronic medical conditions.

Bibliography

Aron, Lewis. "Analytic Impasse and the Third: Clinical Implications of Intersubjectivity Theory." *International Journal of Psychoanalysis* 87 (2006): 349–368.

Aron, Lewis. "Self-Reflexivity and the Therapeutic Action of Psychoanalysis." *Psychoanalytic Psychology* 17, no. 4 (2000): 667–689.

Atwood, George E, Donna M. Orange, and Robert D Stolorow. "Shattered Worlds/Psychotic States: A Post-Cartesian View of the Experience of Personal Annihilation." *Psychoanalytic Psychology* 19, no. 2 (2002): 281–306.

Becker, Ernest. *The Denial of Death*. New York: The Free Press, 1973.

Benjamin, Jessica. "An Outline of Intersubjectivity: The Development of Recognition." *Psychoanalytic Psychology* 7 (1990): 33–46.

Benjamin, Jessica. "Beyond Doer and Done to: An Intersubjective View of Thirdness." *The Psychoanalytic Quarterly* 73, no. 1 (2004): 5–46.

Benjamin, Jessica. *Beyond Doer and Done To. Recognition Theory, Intersubjectivity and the Third. Angewandte Chemie International Edition, 6(11), 951–952*. Vol. 13. London and New York: Routledge, 2018.

Benjamin, Jessica. "Recognition and Destruction: An Outline of Intersubjectivity (1990)." In *Relational Psychoanalysis. The Emergence of a Tradition*, edited by A. Mitchell Stephen and Lewis Aron, 181–199. New York: Routledge, 1999.

Bezeau, Scott C, Nicholas M Bogod, and Catherine a Mateer. "Sexually Intrusive Behaviour Following Brain Injury: Approaches to Assessment and Rehabilitation." *Brain Injury: [BI]* 18, no. 3 (2004): 299–313.

Bromberg, Philip M. "Truth, Human Relatedness, and the Analytic Process: An Interpersonal/ Relational Perspective." *International Journal of Psychoanalysis* 90, no. 2 (2009): 347–361.

Burke, Mary L., Georgne G. Eakes, and Margaret A. Hainsworth. "Milestones of Chronic Sorrow: Perspectives of Chronically Ill and Bereaved Persons and Family Caregivers." *Journal of Family Nursing* 5, no. 4 (1999): 374–387.

Butler, Judith. *Precarious Life*. London and New York: Verso, 2004.

Crangle, Cassandra J., and Tae L. Hart. "Adult Attachment, Hostile Conflict, and Relationship Adjustment among Couples Facing Multiple Sclerosis." *British Journal of Health Psychology* 22, no. 4 (2017): 836–853.

Davidson, Michael. "Universal Design: The Work of Disability in an Age of Globalization." In *The Disability Studies Reader. Second Edition*, edited by Lennard J. Davis. New York: Routledge, 2006.

Davis, Lennard J. "Constructing Normalcy: The Bell Curve, the Novel, and the Invention of the Disabled Body in the Nineteenth Century." In *The Disability Studies Reader*, edited by Lennard J. Davis, 2nd ed., 3–16. New York: Routledge, 2006.

DeDios-Stern, Samantha, and Eun Jeong Lee. "Blame, Coping, and Psychosocial Outcomes in Caregivers of Individuals with Brain Injury." *Rehabilitation Psychology* 62, no. 3 (2017): 353–362.

Dunn, Dana S., and Timothy R. Elliott. "The Place and Promise of Theory in Rehabilitation Psychology Research." *Rehabilitation Psychology* 53, no. 3 (2008): 254–267.

Falvo, Donna R. *Medical and Psychosocial Aspects of Chronic Illness and Disability*. Burlington: Jones & Bartlett Learning, 2014.

Foucault, Michel. *Power/Knowledge: Selected Interviews and Other Writings 1972–1977*. New York: Random House, Vol. 23, 1980.

Foucault, Michel. *The History of Sexuality I (1976)*. Hebrew ver. Israel: Hakibbutz Hameuchad Publishing House, 1996.

Frank, Arthur W. "Just Listening: Narrative and Deep Illness." *Families, Systems, & Health* 16, no. 3 (1998): 197–212.

Gunn, Jane M., Darshini R. Ayton, Konstancja Densley, Julie F. Pallant, Patty Chondros, Helen E. Herrman, and Christopher F. Dowrick. "The Association between Chronic Illness, Multimorbidity and Depressive Symptoms in an Australian Primary Care Cohort." *Social Psychiatry and Psychiatric Epidemiology* 47, no. 2 (2012): 175–184.

Hubbard, Ruth. "Abortion and Disability: Who Should and Who Should Not Inhabit the World?" In *The Disability Studies Reader. Second Edition*, edited by Lennard J. Davis. New York: Routledge, 2006.

Israel Ministry of Health: The department for research and development for mental health. "Anxiety and Depression Disorders in Israel (Hebrew)," 2012. http://www.health.gov.il/publicationsfiles/depression_anxiety_israel.pdf

Jopling, David A. "Cognitive Science, Other Minds, and the Philosophy of Dialogue." In *The Perceived Self. Ecological and Interpersonal Sources of Self-Knowledge (1993)*, edited by Ulric Neisser, 290–310. Cambridge, UK: Cambridge University Press, 2006.

Jopling, David A. *Self-Knowledge and The Self*. New York and London: Routledge, 2000.
Klein, Melanie. "The Origins of Transference." *The International Journal of Psycho-Analysis* 33, no. 4 (1952): 433–438.
Martz, Erin, and Hanoch Livneh. *Coping with Chronic Illness and Disability Theoretical, Empirical, and Clinical Aspects*. Springer, 2007.
McColl, Mary Ann, Jerome Bickenbach, Jane Johnston, Sharon Nishihama, Millard Schumaker, Karen Smith, Marsha Smith, and Brian Yealland. "Changes in Spiritual Beliefs after Traumatic Disability." *Archives of Physical Medicine and Rehabilitation* 81, no. 6 (2000): 817–823.
Mitchell, Stephen A. "Contemporary Perspectives on Self: Toward an Integration." *Psychoanalytic Dialogues* 1 (1991): 121–147.
Moss-Morris, Rona. "Adjusting to Chronic Illness: Time for a Unified Theory." *British Journal of Health Psychology* 18, no. 4 (2013): 681–686.
Naidoo, Pamela, R. Sewpaul, A. Nyembezi, P. Reddy, K. Louw, R. Desai, and D. J. Stein. "The Association between Biopsychosocial Factors and Disability in a National Health Survey in South Africa." *Psychology, Health and Medicine* 23, no. 6 (2017): 653–660.
Nanton, Veronica, Dan Munday, Jeremy Dale, Bruce Mason, Marilyn Kendall, and Scott Murray. "The Threatened Self: Considerations of Time, Place, and Uncertainty in Advanced Illness." *British Journal of Health Psychology* 21, no. 2 (2016): 351–373.
Neimeyer, Robert A. "Narrative Disruptions in the Construction of the Self." In *Constructions of Disorder. Meaning-Making Frameworks for Psychotherapy*, edited by Robert A. Neimeyer and Jonathan D. Raskin, 207–242. Washington, DC: American Psychological Association, 2000.
Neimeyer, Robert A. "Re-Storying Loss: Fostering Growth in the Posttraumatic Narrative." In *Handbook of Posttraumatic Growth: Research and Practice*, edited by Lawrence G. Calhoun and Richard G. Tedeschi. Mahwah, NJ: Lawrence Erlbaum, 2006.
Neimeyer, Robert A., Olga Herrero, and Luis Botella. "Chaos To Coherence: Psychotherapeutic Integration Of Traumatic Loss." *Journal of Constructivist Psychology* 19, no. 2 (2006): 127–145. 10.1080/10720530500508738
Neimeyer, Robert A., James W. Pennebaker, and Jessica G. van Dyke. "Narrative Medicine: Writing through Bereavement." In *Handbook of Psychiatry in Palliative Medicine*, edited by Harvey M. Chochinov and William Breitbart, 2nd ed. New York: Oxford University Press, 2009.
Neimeyer, Robert A. "Reconstructing the Self in the Wake of Loss: A Dialogical Contribution," In *Handbook on the Dialogical Self*, edited by H. Hermans and T. Gieser, Cambridge, UK: Cambridge University Press, 374–389, 2011.
Neisser, Ulric. "The Self Perceived." In *The Perceived Self. Ecological and Interpersonal Sources of Self-Knowledge (1993)*, edited by Ulric Neisser. Cambridge, UK: Cambridge University Press, 2006.
Ogden, T. H. "The Analytic Third: Working with Intersubjective Clinical Facts." *The International Journal of Psycho-Analysis* 75 (Pt 1), no. September 1993 (1994): 3–19.
Parsons, Michael. *The Dove That Returns, The Dove That Vanishes. Paradox and Creativity in Psychoanalysis*. London: Routledge, 2000.

Racker, H. "The Meanings and Uses of Countertransference." *Psychoanalytic Quarterly* 76, no. 3 (2007): 725–777.
Richards, J. Scott, Timothy R. Elliott, Richard M. Shewchuk, and Philip R. Fine. "Attribution of Responsibility for Onset of Spinal Cord Injury and Psychosocial Outcomes in the First Year Post-Injury." *Rehabilitation Psychology* 42, no. 2 (1997): 115–124.
Roos, Susan, and Robert A. Neimeyer. "Reauthoring the Self: Chronic Sorrow and Posttraumatic Stress Following the Onset of CID." In *Coping with Chronic Illness and Disability: Theoretical, Empirical, and Clinical Aspects*, edited by Erin Martz and Hanoch Livneh, foreword by Beatrice A. Wright. New York: Springer, 89–106, 2007.
Schafer, Roy. "Action Language and the Psychology of the Self." *Annu. Psychoanal* 8 (1980): 83–92.
Schafer, Roy. "Conflict: Conceptualization, Practice, Problems." *The Psychoanalytic Quarterly* 74 (2005): 47–63.
Schafer, Roy. "Narration in the Psychoanalytic Dialogue." *Critical Inquiry* 7, no. 1 (1980): 29–53. 10.1086/448087
Schafer, Roy. "The Reality Principle, Tragic Knots, and the Analytic Process." *Journal of the American Psychoanalytic Association* 55, no. 4 (2007): 1151–1168.
Segal, Orin. "'I Am Not Myself, but I Am Not an Other': Self-Dissolution Narrative in Medical Rehabilitation Psychotherapy." In *Memories and Monsters: Psychology, Trauma, and Narrative*, edited by Eric R. Severson and David M. Goodman. New York: Routledge, 2018.
Stern, Daniel N. *The Interpersonal World Of The Infant: A View From Psychoanalysis And Developmental Psychology*. New York: Basic Books, 2000.
Tremain, Shelley. *Foucault and the Government of Disability*. Ann Arbor: The University of Michigan Press, 2008.
Velde, Dominique Van de, Piet Bracke, Geert Van Hove, Staffan Josephsson, Ignaas Devisch, and Guy Vanderstraeten. "The Illusion and the Paradox of Being Autonomous, Experiences from Persons with Spinal Cord Injury in Their Transition Period from Hospital to Home." *Disability and Rehabilitation* 34, no. 6 (March 6, 2012): 491–502.
Wang, Katie, and John F. Dovidio. "Disability and Autonomy: Priming Alternative Identities." *Rehabilitation Psychology* 56, no. 2 (2011): 123–127.
Weingarten, Kaethe. "Making Sense of Illness Narratives: Braiding Theory, Practice and the Embodied Life (2001)." *International Journal of Narrative Therapy Community Work* 2006: 1–11. http://www.dulwichcentre.com.au/illness-narratives.html
Weiss, Mitchell G., Jayashree Ramakrishna, and Daryl Somma. "Health-Related Stigma: Rethinking Concepts and Interventions." *Psychology, Health and Medicine* 11, no. 3 (2006): 277–287.
White, Michael. "Working with People Who Are Suffering the Consequences of Multiple Trauma: A Narrative Perspective." *International Journal of Narrative Therapy & Community Work*, no. 1 (2004): 44–75.
White, Michael, and David Epston. *Narrative Means to Therapeutic Ends*. New York and London: W.W. Norton and Company, 1990.
Zilber, Tammar B., Rivka Tuval-Mashiach, and Amia Lieblich. "The Embedded Narrative. Navigating Through Multiple Contexts." *Qualitative Inquiry* 14, no. 6 (2008): 1047–1069.

Chapter 10

Language Games and Private Language, Wizards and Witches

How a Child with Autism Builds their Emotional World – A Psychoanalytic, Philosophical, and Literary View[1]

Irit Hagai

This chapter follows the processes of how children with autism build their emotional world, seeking to uncover how the emotional world of children with autism is created and constructed, as there is currently a lacuna in knowledge about this question.

The seminal and groundbreaking body of literature on autism, which brought attention to the condition and led the way in helping to understand it, is mainly psychoanalytic.[2] This literature focuses more on defensive and psychopathological processes and less on the processes of selfhood and the subjective world of children with autism.

In addition, the psychoanalytic literature is less inclined to address the linguistic difficulty of a child with autism and its impact on the child's processes of building a subjective world and the child's emotional experience. That is, most work in the field avoids addressing the question of how

---

1 This article appears as part of a PhD dissertation written under the supervision of Dr. Dorit Lemberger at the Program for Hermeneutics and Cultural Studies, Bar-Ilan University.
2 Alvarez, A (2005) Live Company: Psychoanalytic Psychotherapy with Autistic, Borderline, Deprived and Abused Children (Tel-Aviv tolaat sfarim 2005); Esther Bick, "The experience of the skin in early object-relation," *International Journal of Psychoanalysis* 49 (1968): 484–486; Donald Meltzer, John Bremer, Shirley Hoxter, Doreen Weddell, and Isca Wittenberg, *Explorations in Autism: A Psychoanalytical Study* (Strath Tay: Clunie, 1975); David Rosenfeld, "Understanding Varieties of Autistic Encapsulation: A Homage to Frances Tustin," in *Encounters with Autistic States,* eds. Theodore Mitrani and Judith L. Mitrani (New Jersey: Jason Aronson, 1997), 179–195; Frances Tustin, *Autism and Child Psychosis* (London: Hogarth Press, 1972); Frances Tustin, "Autistic Shapes," *International Journal of Psychoanalysis* 11, (1984): 279–290; Frances Tustin, *The Protective Shell in Children and Adults* (London: Karnac Books, 1990; Frances Tustin, "Reasons for Revision," *International Journal of Psychoanalysis,* 72 (1991): 585–591; Frances Tustin, "The Perpetuation of an Error," *Journal of Child Psychotherapy* 20 (1994a): 3–23; Frances Tustin, *Autistic States in Children,* trans. A. Bergstein and H. Aharoni, (Tel Aviv: Itab, 1994b).

DOI: 10.4324/9781003326588-10

the lack of language, or the limited ability to use verbal language, as well as the difficulty in using "emotional language," all influence the creation of the subjective emotional world.

In this chapter, I will demonstrate that linguistic difficulty is of considerable importance in building the subjective emotional world of children with autism of varying levels of functioning. As a result of this difficulty, these children create their emotional worlds using alternative means, namely, using non-verbal languages, or by using unique linguistic patterns they learn from their surrounding environment. These languages sound like an echo of sentences and words that these children internalize within their own mental framework and use to construct their emotional world.

In response to the fact that the literature dealing with autism has largely overlooked this issue of the linguistic elements of how a child with autism builds their inner world, this chapter applies an interdisciplinary approach in its analysis. Today, interdisciplinarity occupies an important place in the debate as to how knowledge is created.[3] In her article "Interdisciplinarity" in the book *Outside the Lines: Issues in Interdisciplinary Research* Liora Salter proposes different principles that she thinks should serve as a guide for adopting an interdisciplinary approach in research.[4] For Salter, an interdisciplinary approach is recommended when there is sense in the scientific community that a specific issue has been neglected over the years, or that the methodology or perspective of a certain research approach fails to answer the questions arising during the study. Salter further advises an interdisciplinary approach when scholars have long felt overly constrained, as she puts it, by the boundaries of their discipline or the study methods they use, and when they feel that these disciplinary boundaries limit their research direction or do not enable them to answer the study questions.

The study of autism would appear to be in a similar state to that described by Salter. Indeed, the effort to understand the inner world of a person with autism, and that person's selfhood and emotional experience, has been neglected over the years. Instead, emphasis has been given to the psychopathological processes characterizing the condition. The current approaches, mainly psychoanalytic and cognitive, constrain the scholars, in Salter's language, and do not enable them to expand their study into such areas as the creation of selfhood and the particular, subjective experience of the individual, which could shed light on the inner world of a child with autism, and thus help us also to understand that child and find

---

3 Julie Thompson Klein, *Interdisciplinarity: History, Theory, and Practice* (Michigan: Wayne State University Press, 1990).
4 Liora Salter and Alison Hearn, "Interdisciplinarity," in *Outside the Lines: Issues in Interdisciplinary Research*, eds. Liora Salter and Alison Hearn (Montreal: McGill-Queen's University Press, 1997), 26–43.

ways to enter this world and acquire greater knowledge and understanding.

This chapter is divided into two parts. The first part focuses focus on the processes of selfhood and the emotional world of a child with autism who has not developed verbal language and hardly uses verbal language for communicating with the environment. This discussion will refer to the philosophy of Ludwig Wittgenstein, who gave a lot of attention to the issue of selfhood and a person's emotional world, as well as to the place of language in these processes.

The second part of the chapter will deal with the creation of the inner world of children with autism who have developed a verbal language, but who face difficulty in using "emotional language," namely, to use language to express emotions and share their emotional inner world with others. For this analysis, I will draw from the discipline of literature, showing that children with autism who speak use literature in a unique manner that helps them construct their emotional world. The focus will be on examining the use these children make of the fairytale genre, a genre to which they are especially attracted. I seek to demonstrate that due to the unique characteristics of the fairytale, some of which exist also in the inner worlds of children with autism, these children are attracted to this genre, seeing within it an expression of their own inner worlds. In addition, I will show that autistic children find within the universal conflicts manifested in fairytales an expression of their own unique conflict.

"To Imagine a Language Means to Imagine a Form of Life" – Ludwig Wittgenstein's Contribution to Understanding the World of a Non-speaking Child with Autism

Drawing on the philosophy of Ludwig Wittgenstein, this section explores the process of how a child with autism, who has not developed a verbal language, constructs their emotional world. First, we begin with a discussion of what is referred to in the literature as the "Late Wittgenstein" period, to ascertain this particular school of thought's contribution to our understanding of how children with autism construct their subjective emotional world and their self.

One of the central themes in Wittgenstein's philosophy is language and its place in constructing an individual's consciousness. According to him, it is language, chiefly its use by people, that creates a form of life. The decision to apply Wittgenstein's philosophy to the question of the world of the non-speaking child with autism is directly connected both to the emphasis placed in his writing on language, dialog, and usage as the pillars for the construction of consciousness and the experience of selfhood and the world, and to the issues that preoccupied him, mainly in the periods referred to as "the

Late Wittgenstein Period" or the "Third Wittgenstein Period" – states of consciousness and the clarification of psychological terms reflecting the core of the inquiry in this chapter.

Rule and Use

The first time the subject of obeying a rule in *Philosophical Investigations*[5] appears when Wittgenstein writes about a series of numbers and asks what determines that the correct continuation of the series 2, 4, 6 is 8, or what determines that the rule here is to add 2 to each number? Numerous scholars, including Bar-Elli[6] and Kripke,[7] claim that this involves a material rather than a causative question. That is, the question is not how we know that the answer is 8 and not 10, for example, as in that case, the answer would be causative: if until now, on each occasion I have added 2 to the last number, then now, too, I should do so. Rather, the question is a material one and relates to a much more profound issue: What determines the actual establishment of the rule, the very act of obeying a rule? Or in the words of Wittgenstein: "But how can a rule show me what I have to do at this point?"[8]

Kripke[9] claims that at this point, Wittgenstein stresses the issue of the normativity of action that accords with the rule. For him, this is what determines an action as being correct, and in accordance with the rule, or as being incorrect and not in accordance with the rule. The rule creates a norm and determines future uses: "But I don't mean that what I do now ... determines the future use causally and as a matter of experience, but that in a queer way, the use itself is in some sense present."[10] In other words, there is a norm, a convention, that causes uses of the rule, a social convention that is common to the form of life of human beings.

Wittgenstein places tremendous emphasis on the link between **rule and use** and it appears that one inspires the other. For Wittgenstein, the rule is determined to a large extent by the meaning created when using it, and the use of the rule is what creates the meaning of the rule. In any event, this is a rule with social meaning. He emphasizes the issue of the correct social agreement also in relation to the rule: "So you are saying that human

---

5 Ludwig Wittgenstein, *Philosophical Investigations,* trans. Edna Ullmann-Margalit, ed. Jacob Golomb (Jerusalem: Magnes, 1999), paragraph 143.
6 Gilead Bar-Elli, *The Fathers of Analytic Philosophy, Vol. 3: Wittgenstein: Language, Mind, Reality* (Independent Publication, 2009).
7 Saul Kripke, *Naming and Necessity* (Cambridge: Harvard University Press, 1980).
8 Wittgenstein, *Philosophical Investigations*, paragraph 198.
9 Kripke, *Naming and Necessity*.
10 Wittgenstein, *Philosophical Investigations*, paragraph 195.

agreement decides what is true and what is false?" It is what human beings say that is true and false: however, they agree in the language they use. That is not agreement in opinions but in form of life."[11]

In this paragraph too, emphasis is placed on the agreement and the common form of life that enables the establishment of the rule. Therefore, Wittgenstein raises a question: "Is what we call "obeying a rule" something that it would be possible for only one man to do, and to do only once in his life? It is not possible that there should have been only one occasion on which someone obeyed a rule. It is not possible that there should have been only one occasion on which a report was made, an order given or understood; and so on. To obey a rule, to make a report, to give an order, to play a game of chess, are customs (uses, institutions)."[12] And he continues: "And hence also 'obeying a rule' is a practice. And to think one is obeying a rule is not to obey a rule. Hence it is not possible to obey a rule 'privately': otherwise thinking one was obeying a rule would be the same thing as obeying it."[13] Namely, an individual cannot obey a rule that only he or she can understand or obey a rule without relating to the world in which they are situated and without there being an external custom or criterion for readiness to obey.[14] As in the example of Wittgenstein: "As things are, I can, for example, invent a game that is never played by anyone. But would the following be possible too: mankind has never played any games; once, however, someone invented a game – which no one ever played?"[15] In other words, it is possible to invent a game even if nobody ever plays it, as mankind knows what a game is, is cognizant of the existing regularity of games, etc. In contrast, to invent a game in a given situation in which mankind does not know what a game is would be a pointless exercise, as the background, the form of life, lack the requisite regularity and order for such a game to have meaning.

This example illustrates the fact that in any given situation there can be no private rule and the rule must relate to the social form of life in which it exists. Even if we do not use the rule, but this rule takes into account this form of life and relates to its praxis, it may still be a rule, but not in a situation in which the form of life does not include this type of rule.

What, then, is the connection between a child with autism and following the rule? The term "rule" used by Wittgenstein can prove very enlightening when investigating autistic experience. Wittgenstein claims that obeying and

---

11 Wittgenstein, *Philosophical Investigations*, paragraph 241.
12 Wittgenstein, *Philosophical Investigations*, paragraph 199.
13 Wittgenstein, *Philosophical Investigations*, paragraph 202.
14 Bar-Elli, *Fathers of Analytic Philosophy*, 240.
15 Wittgenstein, *Philosophical Investigations*, paragraph 204.

following the rule are functions that guide human behavior. According to him, the use of a rule does not merely constitute obeying a social convention; rather, the very act of use attributes meaning to the rule. Use is what establishes the rule and creates its meaning so that a certain form of life is then made possible. Social rules are learned from the very beginning of life. A newly born baby is not yet familiar with the social rules, but gradually, its integration into the social environment and the very fact of its social orientation enables it to learn the rules.

Another term of Wittgenstein's relevant to our discussion is "**language games**," with the emphasis on language games being the interaction. Language is learned by interaction between people and during use. Namely, Wittgenstein claims that the basis for the development of verbal language is simple language games: the clear and transparent activity that we watch during primitive language games or games played among children. This is what will enable us to better understand the use of verbal expressions in the future. More complex forms of language are formed based on this.

Wittgenstein places great emphasis on the instinctive basis on which language is constructed, positing that non-verbal language games form the basis of what later develops into verbal language games, and therefore, they must be in harmony with each other. Wittgenstein explains that this involves the remnants of instinctive, primitive, and natural behavior whose sincerity and authenticity are beyond doubt, and this will help us later on to build more conventional linguistic behavior.

The concept of "language games" as we have seen is based on two central pillars and people with autism lack both of these. These pillars are the preverbal instinctive basis on which the verbal language games are based that will develop later on, and the social interaction that enables the language games to take place. These two factors either do not exist at all or are extremely uncommon among people with autism, and this is the main reason, according to Wittgenstein, why language games do not develop within a person with autism, or fewer language games will develop among them than among those who are ordinary. Consequently, according to this way of thinking, those with autism will encounter difficulty in conducting a form of life similar to that of ordinary children. Wittgenstein explains that this results from the fact that language games both enable and create forms of life. Social orientation is a necessity for language games to exist. There must be orientation toward the environment – and as we have seen, to a large extent, orientation is something lacking among people with autism.

Today, there is a strong body of evidence to support the proposition that from early infancy, children with autism encounter difficulty with simple, interactive games with their mothers. Those prelinguistic games to which Wittgenstein referred, such as games of turns, games of smiles, and shared gestures will not appear among them or will be much less common.[16]

One of the criteria today for diagnosis of autism from a very early age is the lack of the use of gestures, or what is referred to in professional jargon as a lack of prelinguistic communication. Early diagnosis of autism is to a large extent based on, among other things, the difficulty in using early gestures at a very young age, such as pointing and joint attention.[17] The ability to use gestures exists almost from birth, and the use of them is made immediately and instinctively, just as Wittgenstein mentioned many years earlier in his reference to non-verbal language games. It is thus apparent that language is not learned by a person with autism in the same way that language is learned by a person without autism, and it does not contain language games and a social context, and, as such, the language of a speaking person with autism is replete with quotes and repetitive patterns, lacking appropriate gestures and intonation. It is for precisely this reason that people with autism often tend to adopt an idiosyncratic language.

Wittgenstein refers to this issue in *Philosophical Investigations*: "Well, let's assume the child is a genius and itself invents a name for the sensation!— But then, of course, he couldn't make himself understood when he used the word ... what was its purpose? When one says, 'He gave a name to his sensation,' one forgets that a great deal of stage-setting in the language is presupposed if the mere act of naming is to make sense."[18]

And indeed, as we have already seen, people with autism have a tendency to adopt idiosyncratic language, and they tend to invent words and names that do not exist, and which are known only to them. The very fact that their parents are likely to understand them transforms this language into a language that is not private but is still idiosyncratic. It appears that the

---

16 Gregory S. Chasson, Gerald E. Harris, and Wendy J. Neely, "Cost Comparison of Early Intensive Behavioral Intervention and Special education for Children with Autism," *Journal of Child and Family Studies* 16, no. 3 (2007): 401–413; Sophia Mavropoulou, Eleni Papadopoulou, and Domna Kakana, "Effects of Task Organization on the Independent Play of Students with Autism Spectrum Disorders," *Journal of Autism and Developmental Disorders* 41, no. 7 (2011): 913–925; Petra Warreyn, Herbert Roeyers, Tine Oelbrandt, and Isabel De Groote, "'What are you looking at?' Joint Attention and Visual Perspective Taking in Young Children with Autism Spectrum Disorder," *Journal of Developmental and Physical Disabilities* 17, no. 1 (2005): 55–73. Stanley, G. C., & Konstantareas, M. M. (2007). Symbolic play in children with autism spectrum disorder. Journal of Autism and Developmental Disorders, 37(7), 1215–1223.
17 Nurit Yirmiya, Tammy Pilowsky, Sigal Tidhar, Lubov Nemanov, Larissa Altmark, and Richard P. Ebstein, "Family-based and Population Study of a Functional Promoter-region Monoamine Oxidase A Polymorphism in Autism: Possible Association with IQ," *American Journal of Medical Genetics Part A,* 114, no. 3 (2002): 284–287.
18 Wittgenstein, *Philosophical Investigations*, paragraph 257.

tendency to use idiosyncratic language is connected precisely to the lack indicated by Wittgenstein – that "stage-setting" that is connected to the language games, conventions, and norms regarding the language, and eventually the communication processes in which people with autism are less involved. The actual use of an idiosyncratic language underscores the fact that words in a language for people with autism are not necessarily intended for the purpose of communication and are not necessarily part of the existing language games among people without autism. This might also explain the specificity, the difficulty in understanding metaphors and humor that also characterize autistic language. The ability to understand all these is related to what Wittgenstein terms "stage-setting" in language, namely complex processes of language games through which the child learns and acquires the use of language, the nuances of the different words, the musicality of the language and the experience of its meaning. In the absence of all these, the reference to language is specific. The words express one limited picture, the reference is literal-verbal and there is difficulty in understanding the context in which the word is uttered or in which the use of humor is made.

Moreover, the preverbal instinctive capabilities are merely the first stage in the language games. These capabilities are only the first condition for establishing the language games and the accompanying form of life. Later, a more complex capacity for mutual interaction is required, one in which a person acquires the understanding of words, concepts, thoughts, and emotions – all via these games. Wittgenstein claims that within human experiences of all kinds, the emotional and social worlds are all learned using these games. Wittgenstein stresses that during the language games, it is not only the language itself that is learned but the entire human experience.

Indeed, when we begin investigating language acquisition among children with autism, we discover that a significant part of the language is learned by them passively by watching television series, movies, computer games, etc. Many children with autism spend hours upon hours exposed to all of these. They show less interest in interaction with other people, they are less involved in language games, and people are less of a subject of interest for them than screens; therefore, they learn the language in this manner rather than via language games. Consequently, as they tend to be blessed with a good memory, they often quote from the screens. They learn complete word patterns, often including the intonation and accent of the people to whom they have been exposed by viewing the screen. This is a rigid and repetitive language, predictable and lacking creativity, and its method of study does not involve language games or any interaction. As such, no understanding of the intention of meaning and learning form of life takes place. This is one of the key reasons why, if we use the terms and world view of Wittgenstein, the form of life of people with autism is so different from that of ordinary people.

Notwithstanding these behaviors, do people with autism play any language games? It seems that despite the rigidity and repetitiveness of the autistic language, it may be reasonable to assume that the use of quotes and of a patterned and repetitive language might be a type of language game unique to people with autism; possibly a less creative, flexible, and spontaneous language game compared with the language games of people without autism, but nevertheless, possibly in their own unique manner, people with autism might use quotes in a certain way that could be considered a type of language game.

Thus, for example, Matan, a three-year-old child with autism whom I was treating, and who hardly spoke, would quote a lot from a poem his mother used to read to him. He used to say, "Oh, how sorry I am sorry, Oh, how bitter, I am bitter." These statements that he would say sounded as though they were lacking any communicative intentions and were somewhat strange, but during the sessions, Matan's mother and I began to notice that he would utter this sentence in situations of hardship and frustration. We gained the impression that he was trying to say something, but as his language is not spontaneous and he is not able to use it in a communicative manner and play language games with it as other children do, he would use structured quotes he had acquired to express an idea of communicative meaning.

Observing this statement led to an insight that there is indeed a rule and there is a certain degree of repetition of this sentence, as mentioned above, mainly in relation to anger and frustration. Our response to this statement as a language game in which the child is in fact trying to tell us that he is sad or angry led to responses relating to the emotional experience. When Matan used to utter this quote, we would say: "Oh how sad you are," or "Oh, how angry you are," etc. Gradually, and after we repeatedly used these sentences relating to Matan's feelings and emotions, Matan learned to use these expressions himself. At the beginning, he would say, "How sad you are" and "How angry you are"; in other words, he used to repeat what we said echolalically, but later he learned to speak in the first person, too, in order to utter this sentence. Thus, once the response to Matan's statements was that of an interactive language game and the response to what was said was a statement of communicative meaning (precisely as a mother attributes communicative meaning to the utterances of her baby), this once structured and lifeless quote became a mutual language game.

Yehuda, a child from an ultra-Orthodox Jewish family who was diagnosed as suffering from autism, also used to quote from biblical sources: "Save us, we beseech you, O Lord!" (Psalms 118) all the time. He would also simply utter this expression, rather than using it as part of a mutual language game. But here too, Yehuda uttered this statement only in certain situations, mainly those of fear and anxiety. After the rule behind the use of this quote was understood, I began to relate to this saying as a type of language game and to respond to it as a language game. Gradually, Yehuda began to replace this patterned sentence with statements such as "I am afraid" or "I don't want Mommy to go," etc.

Even with regard to children with high-functioning autism, taking a close look at the "language games" of these children reveals that something in the interaction, the reciprocity, and the play itself, is lacking. Children with high-functioning autism find it difficult to conduct a two-way conversation. They mainly encounter difficulty with the pragmatic aspects of the conversation that are fundamentally so instinctive in nature, and which also exist in the non-verbal language games. They find it difficult to speak in turn, to shift from the position of the speaker to that of the listener, and they encounter difficulty using the appropriate language for their interlocutor and often use language that is too high or not appropriate. They also have difficulty talking about a topic of conversation that is also of interest to their interlocutor, tending to talk only about what interests them. Their body language and eye contact are not appropriate. They encounter difficulty playing language games and, in essence, their language games do not match the social environment in which they live and the form of life they conduct. Many people with autism refer to themselves as feeling, for example, like an anthropologist on Mars, as Temple Grandin put this,[19] as if they live on a different planet. Essentially, they are not familiar with the form of life on this planet and fail to understand it. In this context, the link between language games and the form of life of which Wittgenstein speaks becomes clearer. Due to their inability to play language games, people with autism experience difficulty in understanding the language and the nuances of the words, the correct use of words, the complexity of the experience, and the intended meaning of the words, and this hampers their ability to integrate in the form of life of their world.

What is the implication of these findings and insights for the purposes of treatment? It appears that above all, Wittgenstein's conceptualization of the language games teaches us just how important the spontaneous, daily context is in which these language games occur. Wittgenstein is really encouraging us to engage in mutual, spontaneous language games in social contexts, rather than learning the language in a technical and theoretical fashion. For the language game to be a game as such, it must be played in a social context as an interesting element common to both parties who seek to play that game. The language may be learned only in this manner, and it is only in this manner that children learn to use the various words in the correct manner. These words gradually accumulate and become charged with the relevant emotional meaning for the form of life of the environment

---

19 Oliver Sacks, *An Anthropologist on Mars,* trans. D. Levi (Tel Aviv: Maḥbarot le-Sifrut, 1996.

in which they live. According to this approach, any attempt to teach the language in a manner that is not part of a game, and does not involve interest and genuine reciprocity, is doomed to failure. It depletes the language of its emotional meaning and reinforces the behavioral pattern of relating to the words as objects and to the language as an object; this, then, is a tendency among people with autism as we have seen.

Little Mermaid and Peter Pan, Mowgli and Sleeping Beauty – How does the Child with Autism Construct their Emotional World Using Fairy Tales?

Up to this point, the discussion has centered mainly on the construction of selfhood and the subjective emotional world of the non-speaking child with autism. This section of the chapter will investigate how the speaking child with autism constructs its world through literature. The starting point of the discussion is that children with autism, mainly high-functioning children, tend to be captivated by certain literary genres, such as works of science fiction and fairy tales, and on occasion, works that combine a number of such genres.

The therapeutic effect of literary works has been well-known for a long time.[20] Early psychoanalytic approaches, led by Ernest Jones, as the successor of Freud in relating to literary work from a psychoanalytic point of view,[21] and later Bruno Bettelheim,[22] who created an orderly doctrine about the place of the fairy tales in a child's mental development, attributed a highly significant psychological role to stories and fairy tales in the construction of the child's emotional world.

If fairy tales do indeed have a primary psychological role to play in this context, then as far as the child with autism is concerned, this role assumes even greater importance. As "forbidden conflicts between secret wishes and the demands of society," as Bettelheim defines it, which have universal meaning and which according to him exist in every child, are of particular and unique meaning for the child with autism. The child with autism must contend not only with conflicts between the id and the ego, which are the fate of all children undergoing socialization processes. The profound and most difficult of all the conflicts, one accompanied by a threat of destruction, would appear to be the conflict between the desire to come into contact with the human world and that child's need to defend themselves from the

---

20 Adir Cohen, *Sippur Hanefesh* [Story of the Soul]. (Tel Aviv: Ach Books, 1990).
21 Ernest Jones, "Preface" in *I Could a Tale Unfold,* by P. M. Pickard (London: Tavistock Publications, 1961).
22 Bruno Bettelheim, *The Uses of Enchantment: The Meaning and Importance of Fairy Tales,* trans. N. Schleifman (Tel Aviv: Reshafim, 1980).

terrible dread, the fear of destruction and annihilation that threatens it, when it decides to relinquish the layers of defense that guard it from this world.

Autism, as observed by Tustin, one of the pioneers of research into the condition, "is a primal mechanism that operates as a response to the most primary terror, which derives from the sudden awareness of bodily separateness from a suckling mother ... which occurs before a baby has sufficient tools to contend with it."[23]

The conflict of the child with autism is thus a conflict of much more threatening intensity than the conflict of an "ordinary" child. The conflict holds the utmost significance for survival, and the threat the child with autism experiences is an existential threat. The fairy tale genre, which by nature appears to incline toward intensifying the conflicts and, on occasions, assign them a monstrous dimension, reflects the emotional experience of the child with autism. This might also be the reason why the fairy tale sometimes continues to accompany such a child even in those developmental stages when an ordinary child will abandon the fairy tale for more realistic stories. The fairy tale thus continues to reflect the profound inner conflict of the child with autism, sometimes for many years. It appears that the intensity of the anxieties on the one hand and the difficulty in gaining help from characters in the external world on the other, make the inner world of children with autism much more threatening than that of regular children; hence their considerable attraction to fairy tales.

Consider, for example, Hans Christian Andersen's fairy tale *The Little Mermaid*, which was adapted into a Disney movie.[24] This fairy tale recounts the story of the king of the sea's daughter who falls in love with a mortal, but who is unable to realize this love because she is not a mortal and has no legs. Left with no choice, she turns to the witch who agrees to prepare a potion for her that will turn her fishtail into a pair of legs, so that she might appear like any other human. However, the witch warns the mermaid that each step she takes will hurt "like walking on sharp knives." Moreover, in return for the potion, the witch asks for the mermaid's wonderful voice. The implication of this is that the mermaid will become a mute. The mermaid's father and family are opposed to taking this step, and even threaten to sever their ties with her, but the mermaid eventually consents to the witch's terms. As in any fairy tale, this one too has a happy ending: the prince falls in love with the mermaid after she turns into a human being and the mermaid makes peace with her father and receives her voice back.

---

23 Tustin, *Autistic States in Children*, p. 109.
24 Howard Ashman and John Musker, producers, and Ron Clements and John Musker, directors, *The Little Mermaid*. (Burbank: Walt Disney Studios, 1989).

It appears that this fairy tale, to a large extent, broaches issues related to adolescence, rebelling against a father figure, leaving the family nest, and the search for an independent life. In the spirit of the psychoanalytic approaches, these are the underlying unconscious conflicts in this fairy tale. However, from the point of view of the child with autism, there are additional components and other unconscious conflicts in this fairy tale that are particularly relevant, and it is no surprise that, as we shall see below, it is precisely this fairy tale that helped a child with low-functioning autism to start speaking.

In his book *Life Animate*,[25] which was adapted into a documentary film that was translated into Hebrew as *Hahayim-Seret Metsuyar* or *Life is an Animated Movie*, Ron Suskind talks about his son Walter. Walter, who was a child with autism, loved the movie *The Little Mermaid* and used to watch it time and again. When at a later stage he learned how to master the use of the video machine, he would rewind the movie back to the point where the witch demands that the mermaid give her voice to her. Only after constant listening, time after time, to this scene from the movie, did Walter's mother notice the similarity between the witch's words "Just your voice" and the word that Walter used to constantly repeat "Juicervose." And only after the mother repeated aloud the words "Just your voice" a number of times and witnessed Walter's ecstatic response and the immense joy he expressed due to the fact that his mother finally understood what he was saying, did the parents understand that this entire time, Walter had been trying to share with them his difficulty in speaking, his difficulty in sharing his voice with them.

Later on, the father describes how the use was made of this animated movie as a means of forging a connection between Walter and his parents: Walter's father, Ron, would speak in the voice of the characters from the movies, and Walter would then answer him in the voice of another character, and thus an initial dialog began to develop between them. One of the pinnacles of both the book and the documentary is when Walter, at a slightly older age, but at a stage when he is not yet talking, appears sad and withdrawn on his birthday. When his father tries to understand why he is sad, Walter succeeds in expressing a sentence: "I don't want to grow up, just like Peter Pan."

Walter's story would seem to be an inspiring illustration of just how fairy tales can help a child with autism to express their inner conflicts. Walter kept returning to that part in the fairy tale/movie that was clearly strongly connected to his own inner conflict, which at this stage he was completely unaware of. In a similar vein, the mermaid's dilemma of whether or not to give up her voice to obtain human legs that are not necessarily appropriate

---

25 Ron Suskind, *Life, Animated: A Story of Sidekicks, Heroes and Autism* (Glendale: Kingswell, 2014).

for her ("every step you take on land will be like walking on sharp knives") echoes the conflict: children with autism also have to contend with many painful efforts and concessions in order to adapt themselves to the world around them and the demands of society. This fairy tale does seem to symbolically reflect these difficulties: in order to become a human, the mermaid is required to leave behind her safe world under the sea, to leave her overly-protective father, and to face the sharp knives she will have to walk on. For a child with autism, this fairy tale may, to a significant extent, symbolize the anxiety involved in the process of separation and the dread of being cut off and having to cope with the world, which, according to Tustin lies at the heart of the autistic anxieties and defense mechanisms.

Namely, for the child with autism, this fairy tale might indeed reflect an unconscious inner conflict, not necessarily the universal conflict to which Bettelheim refers, but a particular, unique conflict of their own. By using the fairy tale and focusing on the repeated sentence, Walter tried to say something, without being able to do so directly, about the significance of the lack of a voice and the need for an inner voice. He used the fairy tale's voice for this purpose and, in this case, it truly functioned as his mouth in the literal sense of the word.

Another story in a similar fairy tale spirit, which also portrays a similar conflict and might also reflect the spirit of the psychoanalytic approach that relates to the fairy tale as an expression of unconscious conflicts, is the *Jungle Book*. The *Jungle Book* is not a classic fairy tale, nor is it part of a collection of fairy tales, such as that of the Brothers Grimm, Perrault, or Hans Christian Andersen, but it is replete with motifs that also appear in fairy tales. The story takes place in a remote and undefined location, in the jungle. In the story, unrealistic and imaginary events occur, such as animals who talk, dance, and sing, and a child who talks with animals, and throughout the tale there are constant battles between good and evil. Good defeats evil and the story concludes with a happy ending.

The protagonist in the fairy tale is Mowgli, a young boy who was raised in the jungle by animals and who faces many dangers that are represented by the character of the evil tiger Shere Khan, who constantly seeks to beleaguer him. He has two friends: an easygoing, cheerful, and goodhearted bear named Baloo, who teaches Mowgli the pleasures of the jungle, along with a constantly concerned and overly level-headed and cautious panther called Bagheera, who assumes the responsibility for returning Mowgli to the Man Village. Mowgli, who is not eager to return to human society, is captivated by the jolly bear Baloo, who is both full of joie de vivre but also highly irresponsible, and follows him around. Eventually, due to his love for his female mirror image, a young girl he sees in the Man Village, Mowgli agrees to return to the village. The height of the conflict occurs when Mowgli is torn between two worlds, as Baloo pulls him by the hand and tries to tempt him to return with him to the jungle, while the young girl uses her seductive charms to go after her until he finally chooses to return to life among people and follows the girl.

It appears that this fairy tale too, in a similar manner to the *Little Mermaid*, is one whose key material and profound issue for a child with autism is that of separation, giving up your inner world, exposure, and abandoning the layers of protection. To a large extent, Mowgli is a child with autism. He lives in the jungle with animals, communicates with them, but has no contact with humans. But the jungle is no safe place to be. It is a place swarming with dangers threatening Mowgli and his very existence, just like the dangers experienced by the child with autism. He does have friends who protect him, but as long as he is in the jungle, he will have to cope with daily, existential dangers. Mowgli must leave the jungle. He must leave his autistic and cut-off world and make contact with humans, but he finds this extremely difficult to do. The anxieties of the jungle are threatening, but the separation is no less threatening. Separation from the inner world involves threats, but this is familiar and known, and the effort to contend with the threatening and frightening human world, the separation from the characters who look after him but who perpetuate his existence as a helpless child, lies at the fundamental base of the particular conflict of the child with autism in this tale, more than, for example, the conflict between the super ego and the id, which are also echoed in this story tale. A conflict between the id and the super ego, however, tends to characterize normative development, and many children with autism have not yet reached the developmental stage, which is characterized by this conflict, and tend to be more, as defined by Tustin,[26] at a stage of conflict between withdrawal and avoidance of giving up protective layers and of going out into the world. This fairy tale might to a large extent reflect a particular conflict, despite its universal messages.

A further example is the story of Dean, which is somewhat similar to Walter's story mentioned above. Dean was a child diagnosed with autism at the age of two. When Dean was seven years old, he developed a strong attraction to the story of *Peter Pan*, as rendered in the Walt Disney movie.[27] At that time, Dean appeared younger than his actual age, as a toddler in a kindergarten, and his general conduct was that of a toddler. Although his verbal capabilities had noticeably improved since his diagnosis, and his communicative functioning appeared to have improved too, emotionally, Dean was rather naive and very childish, which did not correspond with his

---

26 Frances Tustin, *Autistic Barriers in Neurotic Patients*, ed. G. Gimpel, trans. M. Kaminer (Tel Aviv: Bookworm, 2008).
27 Walt Disney, producer, and Clyde Geronimi, Wilfred Jackson, and Hamilton Luske, directors, *Peter Pan* (Los Angeles: RKO Radio Pictures, 1953).

age. It is thus no surprise that Dean was highly attracted to the story of *Peter Pan*, the child who did not want to grow up.

Dean's mother recounted that she remembered the precise moment when Dean "understood" from the story of *Peter Pan* that it was possible to remain a child forever. From that moment, Dean began to show great interest in this story. At the same time, Dean also developed an obsession regarding ages. He became extremely interested in my age and the ages of the other family members and would constantly repeat questions on this issue in a repetitive and ceremonial manner. He would inquire as to the age of every person he met and would compare the age of one person to that of other people. At the exact same time, a regression occurred in his behavior. He began to ask for his pacifier again, which he had given up long ago, and asked to go back to sleeping in his baby bed. Dean's behavior was puzzling, the reason for this regression was not clear, nor was why he so obsessed with the issue of age, although from the outset, there did seem to be a slight connection between these two phenomena.

Only after it was understood that Dean had begun to develop an obsession with the movie of *Peter Pan*, and only after he began to ask his mother if he, too, like Peter Pan could remain a child forever and not grow up, did it become apparent that Dean was preoccupied with the question of age, as he was afraid of growing up, and the regression to earlier stages of development was a manifestation of this anxiety. Thus, this was not a regression following a traumatic incident, or stress and anxiety as is often the case. This was a practical expression of Dean's anxiety over separation and disconnection from his infancy and from the fusion with his mother, over giving up the autistic defensive mechanisms that swaddled him and shielded him from the world, and over breaking out of the autistic shell into the real world.

Only as a result of the understanding that Dean was attracted to the tale of *Peter Pan*, did both his mother and I as a therapist succeed in connecting between Dean's obsession with ages, his sudden regressive behavior, and the profound conflict he had to contend with, as manifested in this fairy tale. Thanks to this insight, and based on the use of this fairy-like tale, along with the characters and events in it, Dean received an appropriate response to this conflict and these anxieties during the treatment, and subsequently they began to subside significantly until they disappeared altogether and made way for other conflicts and anxieties.

It appears that in this tale too, alongside the fundamental universal element with which every child can identify – the fear of losing one's childhood, the need to cope with the adult world, giving up the joys of life, and satisfying the libidinal urges in favor of coping with daily life and the demands of the reality of the ego and the super ego – there is also a particular element to which Dean was magically attracted. The fear of growing up and maturing threatens the child with autism much more than it does the regular child. The threat to Dean of growing up was an issue of survival. Dean experienced this as a life-and-death struggle. To become an adult for him was almost equivalent to stopping living; therefore, he was so attracted to this tale, which gave him hope to remain a child. The attraction to the story of *Peter Pan* was thus not from the universal place, but from Dean's extremely personal and particular place.

Yet another example is the story of Sandra, a beautiful, delicate, and dreamy girl, who was also a child with autism. The encounter with Sandra was somewhat reminiscent of an encounter with a fairy – daydreaming, not at all realistic, touching yet not touching. Sandra would enter the treatment room and hardly make any contact with me as her therapist or with her mother. She loved to dress up the dolls, to change their clothes; she kept herself busy mainly by playing with dolls and their accessories, shoes, bags, earrings, combing them, and constantly changing their hair styles. The game tended not to develop much beyond this and throughout the sessions, she hardly spoke, initiated communication, or responded to communication, but was deeply immersed in her actions.

Sandra was particularly fond of Walt Disney movies and at the time, for a good reason, she was attracted to the movie *Sleeping Beauty*.[28] She even asked her mother if it were possible for somebody to get up after such a long sleep and open her eyes like the beauty in the story. Her mother, a nurse by profession, tried to talk to her about states of "getting up" and awakening, but Sandra constantly repeated the question in different variations and developed an obsession for watching the movie. She would focus the movie on the scene in which Sleeping Beauty is sound asleep, she would then slowly forward it to the scene in which she wakes up and would repeat the question again and again. Her mother stopped answering her as she understood that no answer would satisfy her.

In one of our conversations, when Sandra was not present, the mother herself gained the insight: "She is just like Sleeping Beauty, my daughter ... She sleeps all the time. It's like she is waiting for someone to wake her ... She herself is Sleeping Beauty ... She sleeps standing up ... Dreams ... When will she wake up?"

Sandra did indeed resemble Sleeping Beauty to some extent, and her identification with the fairy tale was by no means a coincidence. She regarded Sleeping Beauty as her mirror image. The movie gave expression to a profound conflict of Sandra herself. The desire "to sleep," to be cut off from the world, to withdraw within the shell and wrap herself in the autistic shell contrasted with the need to get up and get a hold of oneself. Similar to Dean and Walter who were afraid of growing up, of leaving behind their autistic world and being separated from it, Sandra was afraid of waking up forever.

---

28 Walt Disney, producer, and Clyde Geronimi, Les Clark, Eric Larson, and Wolfgang Reitherman, directors, *Sleeping Beauty* (Burbank: Walt Disney Studios, 1959).

The fairy tale she chose provided a precise expression of this conflict. This was a particular conflict for Sandra.

In summary, the psychoanalytic approach underscores the place of the unconscious conflicts that appear in the fairy tales and their therapeutic effect on children in general. With regard to children with autism too, the fairy tale would also seem to touch upon unconscious conflicts, but not necessarily the universal conflicts that other children experience from the fairy tales. The great significance of the fairy tale and one of the reasons why it constitutes such an attraction for children with autism might well lie in the fact that it also succeeds in touching on their own, extremely personal and particular conflicts, and above all, the basic conflict that is connected with giving up the rigid autistic defenses for breaking out into the external world. The various examples presented show that the fairy tales chosen by the children in the case studies to a large extent reflect this basic conflict, and the fairy tale tells the story of the children with autism, their narrative, in their language, in a manner that reflects and echoes their innermost, secret conflicts.

Summary

The objective of this chapter was to illustrate how applying disciplines from the philosophy of language and literature might be of help when exploring the inner world of the non-speaking child with autism, as well as children who have developed verbal language, but who despite having done so, encounter difficulty in using emotional language and communicating with the environment.

The basic premise of the chapter is that today there is a lacuna in the study of autism, mainly in the attempt to understand precisely who the child with autism is, and what is going on in that child's mind and inner world. This is accompanied by a gap in the literature, mainly the psychoanalytic literature, which deals less with the processes of selfhood and the subjective world of children with autism, and focuses more on defensive and psychopathological processes, despite its potential for contributing to the understanding autism and focusing attention on this world.

This chapter has applied interdisciplinary approaches in order to gain a better understanding of the inner world of the child with autism. It opened with examples of how the philosophy of Ludwig Wittgenstein, mainly the terms **rule, use, and language games**, might be able to offer insights into the world of the non-speaking child with autism and possibly even help therapists ascribe some tangibility to the child's inner experience, even without words.

Wittgenstein claimed that obeying the rule and following the rule are what guide human behavior and endow it with meaning. For him, use of a rule does not merely constitute obeying a social convention; rather, the very act of use is what attributes meaning to the rule, thus enabling the existence of a certain form of life.

This discussion has also suggested that due to their lack of social orientation and interest in the social surroundings, children with autism do not learn the social rules and therefore do not gain sufficient experience with rules and the use of rules. As a result, they fail to learn and understand the form of life of the society in which they live. Moreover, we found that due to the inability to play language games, children with autism have trouble understanding the nuances of words, the correct use of words, the complexity of the experience, and the intended meaning of words, and this has an adverse effect on their ability to understand and integrate in the form of life in the society in which they live.

These issues are of therapeutic significance due to the importance of the spontaneous, daily context in which obeying the rule, its use, and the language games occur. Wittgenstein is strongly encouraging us to engage in mutual, spontaneous language games in social contexts, rather than learning the language in a technical and theoretical fashion: for the language game to be as such, it must be played in a social context as an interesting part of common to both parties who seek to play that game. The language may only be learned in this manner, and it is only in this manner that children learn to use the various words in the correct manner, and the words become charged with the relevant emotional meaning for the form of life of the environment in which they live. According to this approach, any attempt to teach the language in a manner that is not within the framework of a game, and does not involve interest and genuine reciprocity, is doomed to failure. It empties the language of its emotional meaning and reinforces the behavioral pattern of relating to the words as objects and to the language as an object, which is a pronounced tendency among people with autism.

The second part of the chapter discussed efforts to investigate the emotional world of children with autism via the prism of fairy tales. Based on the premise that literature, and in this case fairy tales, should be able to help us understand what takes place in the inner world of a child with autism, this section explored the possibility that motifs from the fairy tales help that child to construct particular meaning in that child's inner experience. We tried to show that the fairy tales touch on the basic conflict that is related to relinquishing the rigid autistic defenses for breaking out into the world outside. The various examples presented illustrate how the attraction of various children to different fairy tales helped them, their parents, and their therapists better understand their profound inner conflict, as well as their secret anxieties and subjective experiences. This approach contrasts with that of simply viewing children with autism's attraction to fairy tales and their repeated viewing of the related movies as repetitive, useless behavior. By trying to understand the deep, underlying meaning of the fairy tale for that specific child, it was possible to gain insights into that child's world, often leading to a breakthrough in their therapy.

The chapter, examining two disciplines that have been applied less in the discussion on investigating and treating autism – philosophy and literature, and it tried to illustrate how specifically these disciplines might be able to shed light on those areas where there is a gap in the knowledge and understanding among the conventional disciplines about the true nature of the child with autism, thereby enabling us to understand just who the child in the room with us really is.

Chapter 11

Self-Constructive vs. Self-Destructive Mechanisms in the Writings of Anorexics[1]

Ruth Kaplan Zarchi[2]

Anorexia, a phenomenon that manifests throughout the human body, is one of the most bizarre and severe mental disorders. In spite of no other disturbances in thinking, beyond a distortion of body perception, intelligent individuals, mostly young women, starve themselves, sometimes to death.[3] Those afflicted with the eating disorder of anorexia experience distortions in body perception whereby, despite being underweight, they perceive themselves as overweight and have a fear of obesity.[4] They engage in behaviors such as reducing their food intake, excessive exercise, laxative use, and vomiting, until they become significantly, frighteningly underweight.

Anorexia, often perceived as contrary to human and evolutionary aspirations, is a mystifying act of self-starvation that may arouse revulsion and bewilderment among others. Another reason that anorexia is so difficult to understand is that it is rife with paradoxes, a primary one related to self-experience; although anorexia involves self-destructive behaviors, it also reflects an attempt at self-construction.[5]

This article first seeks to demonstrate that an interdisciplinary inquiry, combining psychoanalytic, philosophical-linguistic, and literary disciplines can make an important contribution to understanding the self-experience of anorexics, and, specifically, to understanding the paradoxical simultaneous presence of mechanisms of destruction and construction in the anorexic disorder. This will be followed by a linguistic-literary analysis of texts written by anorexics and an examination of the impact of different genres of

---

1 The article is based on a doctoral dissertation written under the supervision of Dr. Dorit Lemberger in the Hermeneutics and Cultural studies, Bar-Ilan University.
2 Clinical Psychologist, Eating Disorders Clinic, Director, Meuhedet HMO.
3 Eitan, Bachar, *Ha-pachad Litfos Makom [The Fear of Occupying Up Space: The Self-Psychology and the Treatment of Anorexia and Bulimia.]* (Jerusalem: Magnes Press, 2001), 11.
4 American Psychiatric Association, *DSM-5.* (Washington, DC: American Psychiatric Association, 2013), 340.
5 Hilde, Bruch, *The Golden Cage: The Enigma of Anorexia Nervosa* (Cambridge: Harvard University Press, 1978).

DOI: 10.4324/9781003326588-11

writing on the mechanisms of destruction and construction and the development of the anorexic self.

Anorexia Nervosa as a Disorder of the Self: Psychoanalytic Perspectives

Describing anorexia as a disorder of the self, Bruch writes that anorexics "... choose the road of self-starvation in their search for selfhood and self-directed identity."[6] They "cannot experience themselves as individuals ... entitled to lead their own lives. As anorexia develops, they feel that the disease is caused by a mysterious force ... that invades them and directs their behavior ... (They) speak of feeling as if they are divided, as if they are ... two people ... usually the secret but powerful part of the self is experienced as the personification of all who have tried to hide or deny due to being unacceptable to themselves or others."[7]

Bruch bases her work on Kohut's theory of the psychology of the self and Winnicott's theory of the false self. Kohut and Wolf, who coined the term "disorder of the self,"[8] describe patients with narcissistic disorder who exhibit a fundamental impairment in self-organization, sense of self, and self-esteem. Kohut and Wolf assert that the healthy self develops in an environment that enables three types of experiences of the "selfobject." The selfobject is one's experience of another person (object) as part of, rather than as separate and independent from the self, particularly when the object's actions affirm one's narcissistic well-being. The first type of experience pertains to "... those who respond to and confirm the child's innate sense of vigour, greatness and perfection."[9] The second type of experience involves powerful figures "to whom the child can look up and with whom he can merge as an image of calmness, infallibility and omnipotence."[10] The third type of experience is with a selfobject that evokes feelings of similarity between the child and him or herself. According to Kohut and Wolf, in the process of healthy development, the inflated images of the self and the other dissipate over time, and the person learns to adapt to the demands of reality. In contrast, people who have not had these experiences may develop a disorder of the self.[11]

---

6 Bruch, "Preconditions for the Development of Anorexia Nervosa." *The American Journal of Psychoanalysis* 40, no.2 (1980): 169.
7 Bruch, *The Golden Cage*, 58.
8 Heinz, Kohut and Ernest S. Wolf, "The Disorders of the Self and their Treatment: An Outline." International *Journal of Psychoanalysis* 59 (1978): 413.
9 Ibid., 414.
10 Ibid., 414.
11 Ibid., 414.

In addition to Bruch and Kohut, other writers from the "self school" argue that among anorexics, a traumatic and ongoing failure in the developmental stages of the selfobject leads to impairment of the development of the self and an impaired ability to preserve self-esteem and self-adaptive functions. As a result, the anorexic does not believe that she can rely on other people to fulfill her own needs; at the same time, she also erases and negates her inner needs.[12] Instead of relying on people to fulfill self-needs, she relies on food and physical activity.[13]

Winnicott sees the physical experience as the basis for building the self and the psyche-soma (body-mind) as one inseparable unit. According to him, starting at birth, a baby may lose touch with his body and its needs in response to environmental failure, and instead find refuge in mental function; in the mind. That is, if the mother is not "good enough," overactivity of mental function occurs, and a conflict is created between the mind and the psyche-soma. The mind becomes a substitute for maternal care, the center of life, and the source of creativity.[14] The psyche-soma, for Winnicott, corresponds to the existence of the true self, which includes the connection of the individual to physical sensations. He argues that impaired maternal function results in the creation of a false self that is not linked to the body and exists only as a mind.[15]

Bruch takes a slightly different approach, claiming that anorexics function through a "false self," and are unable to distinguish between their needs and those of their parents. Furthermore, the diachronic function of their selves is impaired. They do not sense their self as consistent over time, and this manifests as a shaky sense of self, low self-esteem, and difficulties with emotional regulation and interpersonal communication.[16] Recent findings

---

12 Richard A., Geist, "Self-Psychological Reflections on the Origins of Eating Disorders." *Journal of the American Academy of Psychoanalysis* 17, No.1 (1989): 5–27; Alan, Goodsitt, "Self-regulatory Disturbances in Eating Disorders." *International Journal of Eating Disorders* 2, no.3 (1983): 51–60.
13 Bachar, *Ha-pachad Litfos Makom*, 16–17.
14 Donald W., Winnicott, "Mind and its Relation to the Psyche-soma." *British Journal of Medical Psychology* 27, no.4 (1954): 201–209.
15 Donald W., Winnicott, "Ego Distortion in Terms of True and False Self." In *Maturational Processes and the Facilitating Environment: Studies in the Theory of Emotional Development*, ed. Donald Winnicott (London: Hogart Press Ltd, 1965) (Original work published 1960), 140–152.
16 Hilde, Bruch, "Anorexia Nervosa: Therapy and Theory." *The American Journal of Psychiatry* 139, no.12 (1982): 1531–1538.

correspond with Bruch's perspective, linking parental dysfunction in childhood with difficulty in recognizing emotions and integrating them into self-esteem.[17] Others show the link between "insecure attachment" in infancy and the development of anorexia later in life.[18]

Anorexia Nervosa: Self-Destruction or Self-Construction?

Anorexia embodies a paradox in that the same thoughts, actions, and habits that destroy the self and may lead to death, simultaneously reflect an attempt at self-survival or self-construction. That is, through the destruction of the body, the anorexic tries to save her soul and construct her self. Psychoanalytic conceptions offer a variety of explanations for this paradox. Some link anorexic self-destruction to the failure to succeed in the separation-individuation process. For example, Lane argues that the self-destruction of anorexia is a response to the lack of separation and boundaries between a mother and her daughter. The symbiosis between the anorexic and her mother does not allow her to direct aggression toward her mother, and so she subconsciously directs them toward her own body. Thus, the destructive behaviors of the anorexic are simultaneously an unconscious attack against her mother and herself (Lane, 2002).[19]

Malson complex view of anorexic as self-destruction posits that the condition embodies self-punishment resulting from the perception of the self as unclean, hated, without value, not worthy of nourishment, and therefore deserving of punishment and starvation. However, Malson also attributes to these behaviors a constructive quality, arguing that they express a process of "negative self-construction".[20] That is, they simultaneously reflect mechanisms of self-destruction and self-construction.

Malson draws on Bion's concept of paranoid-schizoid stage fragmentation[21] to describe self-extinction in anorexia. She describes a mechanism of

---

17 Antonella, Granieri and Adriano, Schimmenti, "Mind–body Splitting and Eating Disorders: A Psychoanalytic Perspective." *Psychoanalytic Psychotherapy* 28, no.1 (2014): 52–70.
18 Sidney J., Blatt and Rachel B., Blass, "Attachment and Separateness: A Dialectic Model of the Products and Processes of Development throughout the Life Cycle." *The Psychoanalytic Study of the Child* 45, no.1 (1990): 107–127; Giorgio A., Tasca and Louise Balfour. "Attachment and Eating Disorders: A Review of Current Research." *International Journal of Eating Disorders* 47, no.7 (2014): 710–717.
19 Robert C., Lane, "Anorexia, Masochism, Self-mutilation and Autoeroticism: The Spider Mother." *The Psychoanalytic Review* 89, no.1 (2002): 101–123.
20 Helen, Malson, *The Thin Woman: Feminism, Post-structuralism, and the Social Psychology of Anorexia Nervosa.* (Hove: Psychology Press, 1998), 161–162.
21 Wilferd. R., Bion, "Differentiation of the Psychotic from the Non-psychotic Personalities." *International Journal of Psycho-Analysis* 38, (1957): 266–275.

disintegration; by focusing on the minute details of life, the anorexic individual fragments difficult emotions into units so small that they lose their meaning. In this way, the person distances herself from experiences that threaten the self. Malson argues that anorexics' seemingly meaningless focus on details, such as calories or grams, can be seen as "an attempt to erase meaning from one's life, as an avoidance of any meaningful subjectivity."[22]

Another complexity is expressed in the perception of anorexic behaviors as defense mechanisms. Malson suggests that the softness and fluidity of body fat obscure e boundaries of the body and the separation between the self and the world; therefore, being fat represents the absence of self-definition and identity. In this way, anorexia can be seen as a defense mechanism against the experience of one's identity being blurred or "swallowed up." This perspective considers the anorexic's attempt to demarcate and enforce boundaries both as a defense mechanism and as an attempt to define identity; an attempt at self-construction.[23] "Anorexia becomes a way of coping. But this coping is achieved only through self-destruction, through obliterating all thoughts and feelings, becoming 'emotionally detached' and 'numb,' so that 'anorexia' becomes a means of coping through self-destruction".[24] Malson reaffirms that anorexic behavior is paradoxical, simultaneously reflecting an attempt at self-destruction and a desire for self-construction.[25]

As Malson summarizes this paradox: Anorexia "simultaneously reflects an identity that satisfies every need, as well as the absence of identity. "Without anorexia one would be devoid of identity, nameless because one is '[n]othing else but anorexia'. 'The self' is discursively produced as simultaneously having an 'all-consuming' ('anorexic') identity and obversely as otherwise lacking identity. Anorexia is 'something to be,' but without it the individual is 'nothing', a 'shell'".[26] While the mechanisms of self-destruction are clear (it is easy to see how ongoing starvation behaviors destroy the physical-mental self), the mechanisms of self-construction require special explanation. Anorexia evokes feelings of autonomy and individuality, thereby contributing to the development of the experience of the self. However, the mechanisms that evoke these feelings are not clear. This gives rise to the question of whether anorexia has unique characteristics and mechanisms that give a sense of identity and lead to self-construction.

Dewey's theory of self is proposed here as an explanation of the ways in which anorexic mechanisms are used for self-construction. Two main concepts in his theory contribute to this explanation:

---

22 Malson, *The Thin Woman*, 169.
23 Ibid., 148.
24 Ibid., 168.
25 Ibid., 142.
26 Ibid., 148.

1   Perception of physical habits as an integral part of the self.
2   Seeing human habits as inseparable from a social-environmental setting.

Physical Habits and the Anorexic Self

According to Dewey, physical embodiment is expressed through habits, which are an organism's acquired patterns of activity.[27] Dewey sees habit as a means of "building the self"[28] and a mode of communication between individuals and their world. Drawing on Dewey, Granger posits that the interaction people have with the world is through the "habitual body".[29] That is, adopting a new set of physical habits (destructive as they may be) is a process of construction whereby the "anorexic habitual body" and its intense bodily actions – vomiting, purging, fasting, etc. – reflect a process of organization and creation of personal meaning. Anorexic habits are not only defense mechanisms; in fact, the anorexic body becomes the self.

Dewey coined the term: "plasticity of the self,"[30] according to which the creation of the self is concerned with breaking old habits and creating new ones (Garrison, 1998).[31] In his words: "The ... evolving self ... meets new demands and situations along the way, and adapts and recreates itself. In this process ... the need to choose between the focus of interest of the old and the fluctuating and emerging self is repeated ... and exists in every ... period of life."[32] According to Granger, "although it is tempting to seek refuge in the habitual self when we encounter unsafe and unstable environments ... our ongoing existence inevitably throws us into situations that prevent us from activating our habits in their normal paths."[33] The process through which a person seeks to adopt new habits is made possible through the "plasticity of the self."

Anorexic individuals have often suffered from traumatic events and crises, such as sexual assault, parental divorce, etc., which their existing set of habits may not be able to address. Thus, the set of anorexic habits can be viewed as an attempt to construct a self that can cope with traumas, after the existing set of habits failed to do. As will be discussed in the next section, Dewey's philosophy contributes to the understanding of anorexics' self-construction through its conceptualization of the importance of bodily

---

27 John, Dewey, *Human Nature and Conduct.* (Southern Illinois: Carbondale, 1922), 21.
28 Ibid.
29 David, Granger, "Towards an Embodied Poetics of the Self: Personal Renewal in Dewey and Cavell." *Studies in Philosophy and Education* 20, no.2 (2001): 107–124.
30 Dewey, *Human Nature and Conduct*, 36.
31 Jim, Garrison, "Foucault, Dewey, and Self-creation." *Educational Philosophy and Theory* 30, no.2 (1998): 111–134.
32 Dewey, *Human Nature and Conduct*, 36.
33 Granger, "Towards an Embodied Poetics of the Self", 107–124.

habits for self-construction, as well as in its emphasis that the self develops through interaction with the social environment.

The Anorexic Social Self

Dewey asserts that habits are formed through an organism's interactions with its environment and that merging with its environment is so inherent to the organism's existence that its habits cannot be understood or addressed without the environmental context.[34] Individuals develop certain habits because they are rooted in the society and culture in which they live.[35]

Feminist writers have pointed to the influence of society on the development of anorexic habits, arguing that anorexia is a response of women to their place in a society that is dualistic and patriarchal in nature.[36] However, such feminist theories are one-sided, emphasizing the impact of the rule = society, on the individual = anorexic women, without addressing the ways in which the individual may influence the rule. As Dewey observed, while the influence of society on the individual is well-discussed, "the power (of the self) to change previous traditions" is often ignored.[37]

In this age of the internet, when every individual can present an agenda on blogs and social networks, it is important to examine how individuals affect their society. Thus, along with examining the mechanisms of constructing the anorexic self, how the self affects the environment must also be considered.

The proliferation of online communication in recent decades has led to anorexics no longer feeling alone and being perceived by their environment as ill and distorted, but rather as selves within an emerging community. This situation is unique with regard to anorexia, in that online communities of anorexics, often referred to as "pro-ana," feature content that helps members reach the anorexic ideal, from patents for weight loss to photographs and images that display the desired thinness. Like many communities, the pro-ana community promotes attributes and habits that community members are expected to assimilate and display, such as certain eating and fasting habits, reaching a target weight, etc. In addition, this society provides emotional support, as community members share emotional and personal difficulties and are listened to and encouraged by other members.

---

34 Dewey, *Human Nature and Conduct*, 15; John, Dewey, *The Later Works, 1925–1953*. Vol. 7. (SIU Press, 1985), 180.
35 Shannon, Sullivan, *Living Across and Through Skins: Transactional Bodies, Pragmatism, and Feminism*. (Bloomington: Indiana University Press, 2001).
36 Bordo, Susan, *Unbearable Weight: Feminism, Western Culture, and the Body*. (Oakland: University of California Press, 2004); Malson, *The Thin Woman*.
37 Dewey, *Human Nature and Conduct*, 46.

Following Dewey, Garrison coined the term "social self-creation."[38] With respect to anorexic disorder, this term indicates the existence of two parallel processes. In the first process, the individual anorexic self is formed through interaction with the wider environment (e.g., family, peer group, place of residence, etc.). In the second process, the anorexic influences the creation of a new and more limited community of anorexics. This self-creation, emerging from interaction with a community that encourages anorexic habits and gives them meaning, can help explain the difficulty anorexics face in giving up anorexic behaviors. This is, by renouncing anorexia, they would lose their sense of achievement and independence, along with losing the sense of belonging to a community that they perceive as strengthening and supportive.

In addition to seeing the self as evolving through the assimilation of habits and interactions with the social environment, Dewey views it as evolving through a process of reflection and self-criticism. He argues that as human beings, we are not witness to a completed cosmos, but, rather, are creative participants in an unfinished and incomplete work.[39] When existing habits fail, reflection is the only alternative to capriciousness and irrational freedom: "Thinking needs to be creative in order to set new goals."[40] Among people suffering from anorexia, the development of reflection and self-criticism can occur along two main axes:

1   Psychotherapy, in which an investigation of personal experiences and interpersonal relationships takes place.
2   Creative work, in which intensive writing activity takes place among those suffering from or recovering from anorexia.

The next section examines the mechanisms of construction and destruction in the writings of anorexics, as well as the implications of writing in various genres on the construction of the anorexic self.

Writing, Self-Understanding, and Self-Construction among Anorexics

People with anorexia write. They write blogs, autobiographies, prose, and sometimes poetry. To date, dozens of autobiographies by people with anorexia have been published in English alone. There are numerous blogs on the internet describing anorexic habits, as well as extensive writing on social media platforms. Writing poetry about anorexia is less common, but there

---

38 Garrison, "Foucault, Dewey, and Self-creation", 111–134.
39 Ibid.
40 Dewey, *The Later Works*, 185.

are a number of poets who suffered from anorexia and touch on the disease in their writing, among them Anne Sexton and Louise Glück.

The widespread expression of anorexia in the written language is an interesting phenomenon. This is because anorexics are often alexithymic; that is, they have difficulty expressing emotions through language. Interestingly, this widespread phenomenon of written expressions of anorexia rests primarily on the visual-physical dimension and is characterized by a great deal of concreteness. The gap between the difficulty anorexics experience in using language, and the widespread expression of anorexia in verbal media, makes the study of the linguistic use of anorexics a fascinating topic of study.

The Narrative Self: Autobiographies and Self-Construction among Anorexics

The stories people tell about their lives and the lives of others include a broad configuration of narratives through which individuals construct, interpret, and share experiences: "For we dream in narrative, daydream in narrative, remember, anticipate, hope ... by narrative."[41] The narrative structure contributes to the construction of the sense of self, to being an integral whole, with attributes of stability and continuity over time. "In the end, we become the autobiographical narratives by which we 'tell about' our lives."[42]

The prevailing position in narrative research regarding construction of the self supports Dewey's view of the relationship between the self and society. For example, Kerby explains that there is a pre-narrative social matrix of plots that serve as the basis for "our more explicit self-reflections [which] are formed along their narrative threads."[43] Kerby continues that the human self is not "behind the [narrative' acts, visible and fully formed at their inception; the self is rather a result of actions, something that actions imply."[44] That is, the language of narrative and of self-construction are intertwined and inseparable. Although Dewey's work paves the way for viewing the self and society as interrelated and inseparable, he hardly addresses the role of language in these relationships. Wittgenstein, on the other hand, places language at the center of mutual influence between the self and society.

---

41 Barbara, Hardy, "Towards a Poetics of Fiction: An Approach through Narrative." *Novel: A Forum on Fiction* 2, no.1 (1968): 5–14.
42 Jerome, Bruner, "Life as Narrative." *Social Research* 54, no.1 (1987): 11–32.
43 Anthony Paul, Kerby, *Narrative and the Self*. (Bloomington: Indiana University Press, 1991), 52–53.
44 Ibid., 56.

Wittgenstein proposes the term "language-play" to describe the ways in which words acquire their meaning.[45] According to Wittgenstein, the meaning of particular words or phrases is created from the actual use made of them and within the person's social context. To gain insights about a person's self, we must understand how that person uses language in the environment he or she inhabits.

Osgood describes the ways in which language enchants us[46] in relation to the anorexic image.[47] She cites Naomi Wolf's *The Beauty Myth,* in which Wolf describes the "perfect" anorexic: a ballerina dancer, who was an "anorexic ideal" and "left suddenly."[48] According to Osgood, these phrases produce an image of a "slow pirouette." "She did it," Wolf writes, "she eluded gravity."[49] Osgood argues that "Wolf's one very subtle mistake here is that while the tone may evoke pity, the image is a beautiful and invigorating one. Who doesn't want to fly?"[50] According to Osgood, "We attempt to debunk the myths of anorexic by couching its intricacies and impurities in pretty language that describes a graceful kind of suffering, a spiritual kind … ."[51]

Wittgenstein's claim of the "magic of language" is part of the concept of meaning as a dynamic and interactive process in which embodied agents respond to each other and to situations in the environment in a practical, vivid, and ongoing manner.[52] Thus, we do not seek an object that is long-lasting in nature,[53] but rather strive to understand the ways in which we construct the relationship between ourselves and our environment. We seek to reach a more complete understanding of the picture of our lives,[54] and we can achieve this if we trace how language operates.[55] Wittgenstein sees self-construction as a narrative process based on our ability to change how we

---

45 Ludwig, Wittgenstein, *Philosophical Investigations.* (Hoboken, NJ: John Wiley & Sons, 2010), §7.
46 Ibid., § 109.
47 Kelsey, Osgood, *How to Disappear Completely: On Modern Anorexia.* (New York: Abrams, 2014).
48 Naomi, Wolf, *The Beauty Myth: How Images of Beauty are Used Against Women.* (New York: HarperCollins, 2002), 206.
49 Osgood, *How to Disappear Completely*, 49.
50 Ibid.
51 Ibid.
52 John, Shotter, "Towards a Third Revolution in Psychology: from Inner Mental Representations to Dialogically-structured Social Practices." in *Jerome Bruner: Language, Culture, Self*, ed. David Bakhurst and Stuart Shanker (London: Sage Publications, 2001), 174.
53 Wittgenstein, *Philosophical Investigations*, §435.
54 Shotter, "Towards a Third Revolution in Psychology", 176.
55 Wittgenstein, *Philosophical Investigations*, §109.

view things,[56] and to describe the story of our lives. Thus, the narrative self is perceived as being in a state of ongoing, endless activity.

Wittgenstein's ideas about the importance of language in the process of constructing the self can be illustrated through an analysis of autobiographies written by anorexics. Osgood, for example, describes the first evening that she was hospitalized in an eating disorder ward: "When she [Christine, a patient] sat next to me, she circled her thigh with her hands and stared at mine. I lifted my feet off the floor to make the space between my legs look bigger (to make me look thinner). If I were older, and less captive to the system of comparisons offered by anorexia, I would have told her she is ridiculous."[57]

Osgood describes her behavior during her illness alongside her current point of view in relation to these actions. That is, she presents a change in her way of seeing things and creates a movement between the experience as her anorexic self and the experience of her present self, thus demonstrating how narrative writing creates meaning and changes the self-experience.

A similar shift in narrative can be found in Marya Hornbacher's autobiography *Wasted*:

> I appeared at dinner one night, sat down, looked at my mother, and watched her open her mouth and scream. What the hell? I said, and apologized. Jesus, my father said, staring at me as if I'd grown horns. WHAT? I said. Honey, what's wrong with your eyes? He reached toward me. I jerked away and toward the mirror that hung above the buffet. I looked: The lower half of the white of my eyes was deep red. My eyes looked as if they were welling with tears of blood. In fact, I had popped all the blood vessels while vomiting that afternoon, and the liquid red lay below the shimmery skin. I screamed and ran to my room. Looking back, I can say: There. My life split in half, finally and definitively, right there, seventh grade ... It felt more like a bad day, an embarrassing event, a too-close call—I almost got caught. I sometimes think about how different my life might have been if I'd done what I should have that day: I should have confessed ... I did not. I threw up again that night, half-afraid that my eyeballs would explode. But it was, by far, more important that I get rid of dinner.[58]

Hornbacher alternates between her present perspective and her previous perspective, examining possible alternate scenarios of her life story. This

---

56 Ibid., §144.
57 Osgood, *How to Disappear Completely*, 62.
58 Marya, Hornbacher, *Wasted: A Memoir of Anorexia and Bulimia*. (New York: Harper, 1998), 63–64.

movement expresses the place of language and narrative in the process of development and change in the experience of the self. These examples reveal the personal narrative as a dynamic and interactive agent in self-construction. In contrast to the emotional stagnation that characterizes the anorexic, a retrospectively written narrative is characterized by movement and continuity. While the anorexic is stuck in the present and halts her physical and emotional development, the language of the narrative leads to growth and development.

Following Wittgenstein, Donald Spence writes about the influence of the present on the perception of past events and links self-construction with the construction of a life story.[59] Spence calls this construction "narrative truth," meaning that the truth is embodied at the level of narrative and story, not necessarily at the level of history. He argues that no historical story stands in "one-to-one" conformity with the "facts" of the clinical encounter, and actually, it is a process of conversion of one story into another story, which is not devoid of context and theorizing.[60] Lemberger points to the similarity between Spence's and Wittgenstein's positions with respect to the possibility of interpretation according to a general rule. According to Wittgenstein, we do not have the ability to interpret a word or a sentence and the process that we call interpretation is, in fact, conversion: "It is appropriate to call 'interpretation' the conversion of one expression of the general rule into another."[61] That is, writing autobiographical narrative can be viewed as an ongoing process of conversion, in which past events are expressed from the present point of view, without being able to separate present perceptions and thoughts from the "facts" of the past.

Spence emphasizes the difficulty of relying on historical truths in the process of creating a life story.[62] An example of this is found in Raviv's autobiography, in which she tries to use her parents' memories to trace the first years of her life: "In the story of my life there is always my mother's wild imagination and hyperboles and my father's emotional detachment and rationale," "My mother says I was born a few days earlier, and my father

---

59 Dorit, Lemberger, "Bein ha'Ketunat v'ha'Pasim l'Sipor Haim: Chinun Atzmi b'emtzaut Debur." ["Between The Shirt and the Stripes and The Story of a Life: 'Self-establishment' through speech." in Esrim v'Arba Kreiyot b'Ketuvei Aharon Applefeld [Twenty-four Readings in Aharon Appelfeld's Literary Work], ed. Avidav Lipsker and Avi Sagi (Ramat Gan: Bar-Ilan University Press, 2010), 105.
60 Donald P., Spence, "Narrative Truth and Theoretical Truth." *The Psychoanalytic Quarterly* 51, no.1 (1982): 43–69.
61 Wittgenstein, *Philosophical Investigations*, §201; Lemberger, "Bein ha'Ketunat v'ha'Pasim l'Sipor Haim", 106.
62 Spence, "Narrative Truth and Theoretical Truth."

says I was born a few days later" (ibid.).[63] Her parents' conflicting interpretations are also described in relation to the crossed eyes (strabismus) with which she was born, which she links to eating difficulties in infancy: "She says she would put me in a high chair and lay down wall-to-wall plastic because as soon as the spoon came toward me I hit it away. She is convinced that because my squint was making me see double, a spoonful of food coming at me from different directions freaked me out. My father says it had nothing to do with my squint and that I had trouble swallowing and often regurgitated my food. He says there was never wall-to-wall plastic."[64] These examples illustrate the difficulty of relying on historical truth in creating the narrative of the self, and show how the simultaneous existence of contradictory "narrative truths" can lead to confusion and difficulty in the creation of the self, leading the anorexic adolescent to seek a defined and clear sense of self – a concrete self in which there are numbers, weights, and a clear goal to strive for; the "anorexic self."

Thus, anorexia is characterized by emotional stagnation, paralysis, and developmental problems, leading to the erasure of subjective aspects of the self-experience. Creating an autobiographical narrative allows anorexics to move between different time points and perspectives during the disease and contributes to understanding and the construction of the self.

Self-Construction of the Anorexic in Poetry: The Poems of Anne Sexton and Louise Glück

The current prevailing trend among scholars is to view writing poetry as a therapeutic act.[65] At the same time, there is a high prevalence of mental pathologies and self-destructive behaviors among writers, especially poets.[66] Bearing in mind the insight that a central paradox in the anorexic self-experience is that the same thoughts and habits that destroy the self coexist as an attempt at survival and self-construction, I will analyze the mechanisms of self-destruction and self-construction in the poetry of anorexics.

This analysis examines the following questions:

1 Does writing poetry lead to self-construction or does it reinforce the tendency to self-destruction among poets with anorexia?

---

63 Shani, Raviv, *Being Ana*. (Bloomington: iUniverse, 2010), 13.
64 Ibid., 13–14.
65 Adir, Cohen, *Sipur ha-Nefesh: Bibliyoterapia Halakha l'Ma'aseh, Helek A. [The Story of the Soul: Bibliotherapy in Practice - Part A.]* (Kiryat Bialik: Ach Publishing House, 1990), 183–187.
66 David, Lester and Rina, Terry, "Emotional Self-repair and Poetry." *OMEGA-Journal of Death and Dying* 28, no.1 (1994): 79–84.

2. What are the poetic features that express the mechanisms of destruction/construction in anorexic poetry?

The poetry of Anne Sexton and Louise Glück will be used to examine these questions.

Anne Sexton (1928–1974), was an American poet who committed suicide at the age of 46, and from her autobiographical background and poems, it seems that as a child she was sexually abused by her father. Sexton suffered from anorexia, depression, and extreme mood swings. She was among the group of confessional poets who worked in the second half of the twentieth century, writing about traumatic and pathological personal experiences, which until then had been considered taboo and inappropriate in poetry.[67]

Louise Glück (1943–) is an American poet who won the Nobel prize in literature in 2020. Although she belongs to the generation after Sexton, there is an overlap in the style and content of their writing; the poetry of both is personal and tormented, dealing extensively with the themes of madness and death. Critics have widely noted that their poetry reflects a sense of low self-esteem, submission, self-destruction, and self-loathing.[68] These qualities and characteristics are dominant in the anorexic's experience of self and are embodied, in a variety of ways, in the poetry of these two poets.

In their writings, Sexton and Glück use *ars poetica*[69] to express self-disintegration and self-destructive mechanisms. In the poem "The Inlet," Glück describes an unbearable experience of despair. She describes words as something she cannot hold on to, so words are described as failing her.[70]

Glück's words indicate that language and writing, which are often used for the holding of emotion, are unable to play this role in her current mental state. In this poem, the lack of control over words and language is as a metaphor for her experience of herself in the world: an experience of physical disintegration and lack of support.

In "The Silence," Sexton makes use of a similar metaphor. She describes the writing process as a miscarriage, or as words spreading out of her and attacking her back afterward.[71] In this poem, the experience of disintegration and lack of self-control is described as the loss of the most internal, personal type of creation; a miscarriage, in which "words" only describe passive disintegration, but also play an active role in destroying the body. The combination of body-directed attacks and uncontrollably disintegrating

---

67 Yael Gloverman, Epilog to, *Lessons in Hunger.* Trans, by Sexton, Ann. (Tel Aviv: Keshev Poetry, 2015), 175–177; 178–193.
68 Waltraud, Mitgutsch, "Women in Transition: The Poetry of Anne Sexton and Louise Glück." *AAA: Arbeiten aus Anglistik und Amerikanistik* 9, no.2 (1984): 131–145.
69 A term referring to a process of dealing with the creation of art, especially poetry.
70 Louise, Glück, *Poems 1962–2012.* (New York: Macmillan, 2012), 58.
71 Sexton, Anne, *Selected Poems of Anne Sexton.* (Houghton Mifflin Harcourt, 2000), 181.

bodies is consistent with the method of self-destructive behavior in anorexia. The anorexic actively attacks and breaks down her own body (through the use of laxatives, vomiting, etc.) for the purpose of weight loss, but also experiences unwanted physical breakdown as a result (e.g., weakness, hair loss, and more).

In Glück's poetry, feelings of disgust toward the body are described as a motive for the destruction of the self and the body. In "Dedication to Hunger," Glück describes how watching her body develop sexually as a teenager generated feelings of disgust and intrusiveness. In order to deal with these unbearable feelings she tries to erase and control that development. She describes how the need to be 'perfect' puts the anorexic girl in danger of death, while her body is portrayed as a grave.[72]

In this poem, the experience of disgust and repulsion regarding the body accompanies the anorexic longing for perfection and leads to the complete destruction of the self, to death.

Sexton and Glück's poetic styles embody destructive despair, morbidity, and an experience of self-disintegration. However, a number of questions remain:

1 Did writing about destruction and disintegration actually strengthen the mechanisms of self-destruction of these poets?
2 Does writing about difficult and traumatic events lead to being overwhelmed emotionally and self-destructive behavior, or does it evoke emotional processing mechanisms and thus contribute to constructing the self?

These questions have elicited differing and conflicting responses among theorists who study the interaction between psychology and literature. According to Horvath, the genre of confessional poetry was created as an attempt at self-construction, but it failed in its mission because many of the confessional poets, including Sexton, eventually committed suicide.[73] Horvath believes that the confessional poets relived past traumas by addressing them in their writing, and this led to their self-destruction.[74]

In contrast, others argue that confessional poets' suicides do not prove that poetry is what undermined their mental health. Lester and Terry assert that writing poetry provides poets with a beneficial catharsis and contributes to achieving a cognitive distance from internal conflicts. According to these authors, the high analytical capabilities required for writing poetry help

---

72 Glück, *Poems 1962–2012*, 141.
73 Horvath Rita, "Never Asking Why Build-Only Asking Which Tools": Confessional Poetry and the Construction of the Self. (PhD diss., Bar-Ilan University. 2002), 1–3.
74 Ibid., 11.

individuals observe and explore the self. Thus, they conclude that writing poetry helped these poets survive longer than would have been possible without it.[75] Support for this can be found in the poems themselves. For example, Sexton's "Double Portrait" demonstrates how the use of symbolic images serves as a communicative mechanism that contributes to self-creation. In this poem, presented as a letter to her daughter, Sexton describes an experience of self-awareness. She presents a memory, in which she and her daughter, were standing and watching yellow leaves falling and flapping in the winter rain. By describing this memory she transmits the enormous pain she experienced due to the forced separation from her daughter, following her hospitalization.[76]

The symbolic image of the shedding leaves is described as self-revelation, which she experiences as more accurate than any medical diagnosis she has ever received. The metaphor of the falling leaves illustrates the ability of a symbolic image to capture and organize the experience of self. In addition, the symbolic image contributes to construction of the self because it allows the transformation of an intrapsychic experience into an interpersonal experience. The image of falling autumn leaves can be imagined by almost anyone and is largely universal. Thus, one can see the use of this image as an attempt to create a shared dialog and understanding with a wide readership.

Another way in which the symbolic image is used to draw the reader closer to the poet's emotional experience is to create a spatial perspective. For example, the poem "Dedication to Hunger" presents a symbolic image of an anorexic girl lying prone on her bed and experiencing her body as invasive and disgusting. The reader can visualize the posture of the anorexic body and adopt her spatial point of view, thus empathically connecting to her emotional experience.

Consistent with Dewey's assertion that the ability to act in the world through dialog and interaction with the environment is essential for self-development, symbolic images that contribute to the dialog between an anorexic poet and her environment can be seen as a poetic device that contributes to her self-construction. Williams[77] describes anorexia as a "no-entry syndrome" characterized by the closure and obstructing attempts of approach from the environment. Therefore, the ability to produce interpersonal dialog is even more significant for poets suffering from anorexia. In contrast to the anorexic form, which arouses shock and resistance from the social environment, the use of poetic and symbolic tools allows the anorexic to create an alternative form that invites interpersonal dialog, thereby contributing to the development of a more flexible and healthy self.

---

75 Lester and Terry, "Emotional Self-repair and Poetry."
76 Sexton, *Selected Poems of Anne Sexton*, 28.
77 Gianna, Williams, *Internal Landscapes and Foreign Bodies: Eating Disorders and Other Pathologies*. (London: Karnac Books, 1997), 103.

Although writing poetry did not seem to lead to self-healing for Sexton and Glück, they nevertheless used it as a tool for self-construction, rather than self-destruction. Poetry contributes to self-construction because it strengthens the anorexic's ability to communicate with her environment. As Sewell wrote, "... while the clinical anorexic is inevitably on the side of silence ... poetry, like speech, moves beyond the confines of the body and the self, and through figure, theme and form, can articulate what the anorexic cannot say."[78]

The Anorexic on the Internet

The psychodynamic perspective interprets the diverse nature of cyberspace as a new dimension of human experience and an extension of the intrapsychic world.[79] There are a variety of online platforms for writing, such as blogs and websites, indicating how new technologies have changed the way people relate to reality and construct themselves.[80] There are dozens of online blogs, forums, and social media communities where anorexics write. These sites can be divided into two general types: pro-ana (pro-anorexia) sites and pro-recovery sites. This section will examine the ways in which writing on these sites activates mechanisms of self-destruction and/or self-construction.

Anorexia as Self-Destruction: "Pro-Ana"

Starting in the 1990s, a "pro-ana" community developed, and people began creating websites that present anorexia as a lifestyle choice, glorifying the anorexic identity, and denying the idea that anorexia is a disease involving suffering.[81] This community has sparked a heated discussion in the scientific community. The impact of pro-ana sites on the self-construction aspect of anorexia is controversial. Some argue they provide a platform for self-destructive behaviors among anorexics and can pose a danger to healthy girls and women exposed to these sites, as some argue that these sites have the power to trigger anorexia among vulnerable individuals.[82] Others clinical therapists see in these sites platforms for social and emotional support,[83]

---

78 Lisa, Sewell, "'In the End, the One Who has Nothing Wins': Louise Glück and the Poetics of Anorexia." *Literature Interpretation Theory* 17, no.1: (2006), 49–76.
79 Giorgia, Margherita, and Anna Gargiulo, "A Comparison between Pro-anorexia and Non-suicidal Self-injury Blogs: From Symptom-based Identity to Sharing of Emotions." *Psychodynamic Practice* 24, no.4: (2018), 346–363.
80 Ibid.
81 Ibid.
82 Heather, Ferguson, and Susan Klebanoff "The Enigma of Ana: Lost or Found in Cyberspace?." *Journal of Infant, Child, and Adolescent Psychotherapy* 13, no.3: (2014), 224–234.
83 Daphna, Yeshua-Katz, and Nicole Martins, "Communicating Stigma: The Pro-ana Paradox." *Health Communication* 28, no.5: (2013), 499–508.

thereby contributing to self-construction and identity acquisition by allowing anorexics to authentically express themselves in an accepting and non-judgmental environment.[84] Analysis of the characteristics of writings and use of language on pro-ana sites will serve as a platform for discussing this controversial issue.

This analysis shows that objectification of the body is a core mechanism of self-destruction, and is expressed in a number of ways:

1 Use of imperative and concrete language:

"Choose one food a day, such as an apple. Cut it into four pieces. Eat one for breakfast, one for lunch, another for dinner, and you have one piece left as a snack."

"Two tablespoons of vinegar before a meal helps to pump the fat out."

"Eat six small meals a day, spaced every three hours. Fifty calories each, six times a day, that comes out to only 300 calories."

According to Margherit and Gargiulo,[85] the widespread use of concrete terms and numbers relating to food and weight (calories, pounds, etc.) reflects the close link between anorexic identity and its symptoms. Such imperatives encourage the anorexic to treat her body as an object or as a number, leading to the objectification of the body. The anorexic is required to count, divide and cut until the body is no longer experienced as having needs and desires. She deals with splitting and disintegration until she identifies with the symptom, and erases the self.

2 Use of commandments aimed at punishing the body and arousing feelings of disgust and hatred towards it:

"Eat in front of the mirror naked, damn it, and see how much you want to eat then."

"Hit your stomach whenever it rumbles too loudly."

Some of the commandments are presented in the format of the Ten Commandments:

---

84 Carolina Figueras, Bates, "'I am a Waste of Breath, of Space, of Time': Metaphors of Self in a Pro-anorexia Group." *Qualitative Health Research* 25, no.2: (2015), 189–204; Martyn, Hammersley, and Peggy Treseder, "Identity as an Analytic Problem: Who's Who in Pro-ana Websites?" *Qualitative Research* 7 (3): (2007), 283–300.
85 Margherita, and Gargiulo, "A Comparison between Pro-anorexia and Non-suicidal Self-injury Blogs".

"Do not eat without feeling guilty."

"Do not eat fatty foods without punishing yourself later."

3   Attributing superior qualities to the identity of "ana"

Statements such as "I have always found something pure in 'ana'" or "I have always been the pure 'ana'" are common on these sites, as are statements with a religious tone, such as "I believe in wholeness and strive to achieve it" or "I believe in salvation through starvation." The use of words such as, "purity," "salvation," and "perfection" expresses the anorexic aspiration for being "superhuman." However, this aspiration detaches her body from its materiality and vulnerability and thus, from its humanity. Her body becomes an object; an object that can be "perfectly" controlled.

Analysis of the language use of pro-ana sites reveals that another way to build an ideal anorexic self is to create a hierarchy of eating disorders. Pro-ana sites reflect the belief that some members have higher moral foundations compared to others. Ana is represented as the ideal self, ranked in the upper tier. "Mia" (bulimia) is ranked next. Other eating disorders[86] are at the bottom of the hierarchy.[87]

The characteristics of language and discourse on pro-ana sites show that anorexics have a rigid and divided worldview, not only in relation to their bodies but also in relation to the people around them. In addition to the differentiation between and ranking of eating disorders, community members create rigid and impenetrable boundaries from those who are perceived as imposters and "wannabes."[88]

For example:

> "There's this girl ... that you can honestly say does NOT!!! have an eating disorder ... you can tell through ... her silly posts on the subject."
>
> Question: "Hey I'm new here ... Anna with tendencies to Mia ... trying to lose 20 pounds, need some tips ... I was thinking of going on a 'water fast' ... say every two weeks for two days ... is that okay? And if not? Please give me tips ..."
>
> Response: "If you were a real anorexic, then you would not need someone to tell you what to do ..."

---

86 The DSM-5 category Other specified feeding or eating disorder (OSFED).
87 David, Giles, "Constructing Identities in Cyberspace: The Case of Eating Disorders." *British Journal of Social Psychology* 45, no.3: (2006), 463–477.
88 This refers to the nickname "wannarexic" which describes girls who want to be anorexic and try to adopt anorexic habits and lifestyle, but do not meet the criteria of anorexia as a disorder. The term unifies into one word the desire to form an anorexic identity.

The dynamics between the identities of ana and wannarexic expresses the attempt to defend oneself against the "other," and to understand the self as hermetic. According to Giles,[89] the practice of determining who deserves to be called "ana is at the heart of being pro-ana."

Writing on pro-ana sites reflects an attempt to construct an individual self within a group, and to establish a collective online identity consisting of dozens or even hundreds of individuals. Although belonging to a social community is expected to strengthen one's ability to communicate with others, in the case of pro-ana groups, the same pathological mechanisms that make it difficult for the anorexic to communicate with her environment are also activated within online communication. The identification, categorizing, dichotomy, and aggressive condemnation of those who threaten ana's "pure" identity reflect schizoid-paranoid and primitive defense mechanisms of splitting and projection, generally attributed to early developmental stages.[90]

In addition, one can think of the social self that is reflected in pro-ana communities as an attempt at self-construction through enmeshment. Minuchin wrote about "enmeshed families" of anorexics in which family members have difficulty distinguishing between their personal needs and the needs of others.[91]

In this regard, the community is not composed of a group of individuals, but of "replicated selves." Members of the pro-ana community strive to be identical and work towards the same goal. There is no separation or distinction between them; they are one. Similar to the enmeshment within anorexic families, community members are unwilling to accept differentness among girls who wish to join the community, and thus any attempt to communicate with the "other" fails. Thus, although the enmeshment in these sites is mobilized as an attempt to build and strengthen the sense of self, it actually reinforces the rigidity and paranoid aspects of the anorexic experience, thus creating an obstacle along the path to self-construction.

Separation from Ana and Self-Construction

In recent years, members of the anorexic community have also been operating pro-recovery websites, revealing completely different dynamics from those presented on pro-ana sites in relation to self-definition and self-construction. In contrast to the imperative and concrete language used on

---

89 Giles, "Constructing Identities in Cyberspace: The Case of Eating Disorders."
90 Joshua Durban and Meirav Roth, introduction to *Ketavim Nevkharim, B [Selected Writings B]*, by Melanie Klein (Tel Aviv: Bookworm, 2013), 24–25.
91 Salvador, Minuchin, Lester Baker, and Bernice L. Rosman, *Psychosomatic Families: Anorexia Nervosa in Context*. (Cambridge: Harvard University Press, 1978).

pro-ana sites, on pro-recovery sites, references to self are characterized by abstract and metaphorical language that promotes processes of self-exploration and emotional contact. As one blogger writes: "Who am I? I am a young woman who has recovered from anorexia ... I feel so vulnerable and remember my feeling of shame ..." Another blogger uses metaphorical personification and describes anorexia as a male character: "Who am I without ED?[92] When I struggled with my eating disorder, this was a question that preoccupied me a lot."

Unlike pro-ana sites on which the anorexic self is "swallowed" by the body and there is no distinction between anorexia and the woman, pro-recovery sites present the separation from the anorexic identity as part of the healing process and self-construction. One way to do this is to make a distinction between the "diseased self" and the contemporary or "healthy self." As several bloggers write:

"Who am I? I am no longer the same lost girl. I am free."

"A key component in recovering from anorexia ... is the thought that your healthy self will cure the self with the eating disorder"

"I noticed that I have two parts of myself, during the struggle with anorexia ... a significant part of my recovery process was to identify them, and through an ongoing dialogue to strengthen the healthy self."

Another way to achieve separation from the disorder is the use of metaphors and personification, that is, externalizing anorexia and perceiving it as a different person. It should be noted that there is also personification on the pro-ana sites, through the presentation of the personified character of Ana. However, while on pro-ana sites, personification is used to create identification between the symptom and the self, in sites that promote recovery, anorexia is humanized as an external character, contributing to moving away from the disease. An example of this is referring to the eating disorder as Ed. One blogger presents Ed as an abusive lover from whom she must separate: "I have never married, but I am happily divorced. Ed was abusive ... and domineering ... I hated him, but I could not leave him. Ed convinced me that without him I was unimportant and inconsequential. He said he cared for me and worked for my personal good, but was always angry with me. He promised things that never existed. When I hit the bottom physically and mentally, I finally decided to divorce him ... Ed and I don't even talk anymore."

Another way to distance and separate oneself from anorexia is by conceptualizing it as an external entity that has taken over the self, as in these bloggers' words:

92 ED = eating disorder

"I am a survivor of an eating disorder ... I was enslaved to it for 25 years ... I was a prisoner of my own body..."

"... my mind was kidnapped. If you have never had the experience of being taken over by a mental illness, then it is impossible to understand ..."

Thus, the way in which the mechanisms of fragmentation and projection work on pro-ana sites is the opposite of how they work on sites that encourage recovery. On pro-ana sites, fragmentation and projection exist as schizoid-paranoid mechanisms leading to rigid separation between the self and the other, and to pathological identification between the symptom and the self. In contrast, pro-recovery sites allow the anorexic to look at both parts of the self as belonging to her, and to investigate their impact on her life in an introspective and integrative way.

The use of metaphorical and abstract language, which represents the development of symbolic ability,[93] and the transition from the perception of anorexia as an integral part of the self to one of a destructive "other," reflect the move from a paranoid-schizoid to a depressive state,[94] indicating that self-construction is occurring in pro-recovery websites.

In conclusion, while pro-ana sites attempt to construct a strong and glorified social self that is supposed to lead to self-construction, in practice they embody a variety of mechanisms that actually lead to self-destruction. On pro-recovery sites, however, a completely different picture emerges. The anorexic no longer experiences herself as persecuted and threatened, and manages to create a distinction between the self and the other, using symbolic mechanisms that contribute to self-development.

Conclusion

This article addresses the question of whether anorexia contributes to self-construction or leads to self-destruction. The psychoanalytic conception of anorexia is that of a paradoxical disorder that expresses a pathological attempt at self-construction, which in turn leads to self-destruction. However, psychoanalysis does not explain the mechanisms by which the anorexic tries to construct herself. This article has shown how an interdisciplinary investigation combining psychoanalytic, philosophical-linguistic, and literary analysis contributes to the elucidation of the mechanisms of destruction and construction in anorexic disorder while examining the impact of different types of writing on these mechanisms.

---

93 Hanna, Segal, *Klein*. (London: Karnac, 1979), 133.
94 Durban and Roth, Introduction to *Ketavim Nevkharim, B*, 23–24.

Dewey's self-theory contributes to the concept of anorexia as a unique phenomenon, simultaneously combining mechanisms of self-destruction and self-construction. His perception of human habits as being inseparable from the process of self-construction and from the social environment of the individual highlights the constructive mechanism of anorexic habits. While these lead to the destruction of the body and mind, they also reflect the attempt to define a self living in a particular society.

In addition, this article addressed the question of whether writing about anorexia leads to healing or reinforcement of the disorder. It has been suggested that while various genres of writing, such as narrative and poetry, contribute to anorexics' self-construction, online writings can influence self-construction in two opposing ways, depending on the type of website. Writing on pro-ana sites is characterized by the concretization and splitting that can contribute to self-destruction. Writing on pro-recovery sites, like artistic genres of writing, is symbolic and abstract, thus contributing to self-construction. Thus, an analysis of writing across the various genres shows that (apart from writing on pro-ana sites) writing promotes the ability for integration, symbolization, and mental flexibility, thus contributing to the self-construction of the anorexic individual.

Chapter 12

The Land of Shadows and Intuition

Bion's and Wittgenstein's Return to Plato's Cave[1]

Ronnie Carmeli

In reading Bion from a philosophical perspective, many obscurities arise. It is evident that Bion was significantly read in different philosophical writings. However, his usage of philosophical ideas is many a time particular to his own needs for clarifications, therefore being target to many criticisms, as to his lack of understanding basic philosophical ideas. In this chapter, I will try and clarify the paradoxical understandings of Bion, considering some philosophical epistemological questions. I will try to shed light, or shall I say, darken intensely enough,[2] on some philosophical ideas Bion makes use of, and how they aid in understanding the psychoanalytic action.

Bion's encounter with psychotic patients, who lack the ability to think and imagine non-sensual reality, leads him to basic questions already on philosophy's table: How does one understand the world and contact reality? How do reality and language interact? – Psychoanalysts have joined this puzzling table, very late on the meal some 2500 documented years after Parmenides and others set the table.

They were not always aware of the complexity and richness of the delicious dishes served before their arrival.

However, the psychoanalytic quest brings to the table dishes which entangle us with further confusions: For it is not the general question of Epistemology that is at stake – how one might know the truth of the *inanimate* world. Nor is it even solely the question of how one might know (?),

---

1 This chapter includes ideas about Wittgenstein from my PhD dissertation, "Paradox, Game, and Language in Wittgenstein, Lacan and Winnicott," under the supervision of Prof. Dorit Lemberger in the Culture and Hermeneutics Program at Bar-Ilan University. I am also in great gratitude to Avner Bergstein, for his sharp and generous contributions in reading the draft of this paper.
2 I am alluding to Bion's citation of Freud, in a letter to Lou Andreas Salomé: "The analyst must cast a beam of intense darkness into the interior of the patient's associations so that some object that has hitherto been obscured in the light can now glow in that darkness." In: James Grotstein, "Bion, the Pariah of 'O,'" *British Journal of Psychotherapy* (14)(1) (1997): 77–90.

be in touch with (?), experience (?) his own feelings or understand the *anima* of the *other*. For Bion, the question at stake is how one can understand the emotional reality in the analytic encounter of the session.

The question of perceiving and understanding the psychic movements of another human being, as well of one's own, engaged philosophical writings over the course of history. Wittgenstein writes:

> "*It is as though, although you can't tell me exactly what happens inside you, you can nevertheless tell me something general about it. By saying e. g. that you are having an impression which can't be described.*
>
> *As it were: There is something further about it, only you can't say it; you can only make the general statement.*
>
> *It is this idea which plays hell with us.*"[3]

In their psychoanalytic thinking, Freud, and later, Bion, like Plato, are also in the quest of truth and knowledge. However, they return to the darkness, to shadowland, as a method of noticing and observing unconscious psychic ideas, left behind in consequence of Plato's blinding by the dazzling light of his idea of 'Forms'.

Wittgenstein's development of the philosophy of language, and his turning from ideas of Logicism, echoes Plato's own development in his later dialogs, especially "Parmenides," and as I will try to demonstrate – Bion's delicate moves from his early writings toward his later epistemic understandings.

But let us first begin with Plato's idea of "Forms."

Plato's Cave and Theory of forms – the Epistemological Quest

In his work "Politea" (Republic), Plato[4] has tried to show us our way out of the cave, out of the world of shadows, of mere primitive sense impressions, into the light of conceptualization and the world of ideas. He gives an allegory of imprisoned slaves getting out of a dark cave with the help of a philosopher, as someone who is trying to free them from their narrow understanding of reality as concrete happenings, and guide them out to the ability of conceptualization, thinking, using, and knowing universals – which he called "Forms." This is an epistemological journey toward knowing the truth of existence.

Plato's "Theory of Forms" is developed in what is conventionally referred to as his "middle period dialogues," which include the *Republic*. In this

---

3 Ludwig Wittgenstein, "Notes for Lectures on "Private Experience" and "Sense Data," *The Philosophical Review* (77) (3) (July 1968), 275–320.
4 Plato, *The Republic*, https://www.gutenberg.org/files/1497/1497-h/1497-h.htm.

theory, Plato is attempting to answer the exact question bothering Wittgenstein: How one *can make sense* of mundane experience, sensual data, as well as inner feelings (e.g., in the *Symposium* he attempts to answer the question: "What is love?")? How and what can one *know* about his own private experience? Plato answers by means of understanding that these ever-flowing experiences of the world are glimpses of truth – they are shadows of the ontological objects which he names "Forms." Aristotle writes: "Socrates was the first to seek the universal in ethical matters but that he did not separate it. Plato, marrying Socrates' philosophy with that of Heraclitus, separated the universal, on the grounds that the sensible order, where Socrates had focused, was in flux."[5] Plato's theory of Forms is influenced by Parmenides as well: The idea of Forms derives from Parmenides' idea that what exists, the Ontic object, is eternal and unchanging. Motion and diversity imply the paradoxical idea of existence of that which does not. Thus, the ever-flowing experience of the human being must be bound to an ultimate, everlasting, unchangeable Form. The Form is the property or feature that different instances share. The Forms are "itself by itself," αὐτὸ καθ᾽ αὑτό. Following Parmenides – they are unmixed by the misguiding senses and can be reached by intellect alone[6].

In a manner of speaking, everything we experience "participates" in an eternal form. As an example, if a patient feels love for someone, he is participating in the Form of Love. The patient himself, entering the clinic, is only a passing shadow of the Form of "Man." This is of course a universal theory, and Plato does not speak of the psychoanalytic consulting room. I am giving these examples to already link Plato's theory to Bion's use of it.

Bion's Epistemology of the Psyche – the Grid and the Divided Line

Plato's famous Cave argument follows another section in the *Republic*, in which Plato introduces *The Divided Line.*[7] This analogy brings forth a Line which is divided between visible, sensible realm up to the portion of the line analogous to the realm of intelligibility. The lower portion also divides to the lowest – εἰκασία – imagination; and next πίστις – faith; the upper portion divides to the third part of the Line – διάνοια – thought, understanding – which is usually associated to the sciences; and the uppermost – νόησις – the understanding of the Forms. *This Line suspiciously reminds one of Bion's*

---

5 Allan Silverman, "Plato's Middle Period Metaphysics and Epistemology," *The Stanford Encyclopedia of Philosophy* (Fall 2014 Edition), Edward N. Zalta (ed.), URL= <https://plato.stanford.edu/archives/fall2014/entries/plato-metaphysics/>.
6 Plato, *Phaedo*, https://www.gutenberg.org/files/1658/1658-h/1658-h.htm, 65d4–66a.
7 Plato, *The Republic*, 509d–511e.

Grid and is indeed analogous to different stages in Plato's Cave metaphor, which Bion does mention: At first the slaves are bound to chairs, able to see only shadows of objects projected on the cave's wall, with the aid of a fire set behind them (εἰκασία). After they are released from their chairs, they are able to look around and see the object and fire which were the source of the shadows (πίστις). However, these objects were only imitations of the realm of the world outside. When they exit the cave, they are overwhelmed by the dazzling, blinding brightness of the world outside, and can look solely at shadows and reflections of real objects (διάνοια). Only after they accustom to the light, can they look and know the objects of the world in themselves (νόησις) – these represent the Forms.

The release of the slaves from their prison Cave, reminds one of another passage in Plato's writings, in which Socrates proves, by his method (*elenchos*) of interrogation of a slave about geometry, that given the right guidance, anyone can "recall" the Forms, which are innate but forgotten. This reminds one of the Jewish belief that every newborn is touched on his lips by an angel, resulting in his forgetting all he knows, which is everything.[8] It is also reminiscent of Bion's idea of preconception. Indeed, Bion sees Plato as one who believes in preconceptions, these are the innate Forms – thoughts without a thinker[9]. This idea is closely linked to Frege's concept of Logic as truth, and of language-seeking realism.

Bion speaks of Plato's Cave allegory in his discussion of the questions arising on the process of arriving to knowledge in psychoanalysis. He observes that most analysts are absorbed in the pursuit of knowledge in their work (e.g., knowledge about the patient's psyche, conflicts, drives, etc.), but they are not occupied by how this epistemic process work.[10] It is more surprising, according to Bion, that analysts act just like their fellow scientists do, and are not usually preoccupied with questions such as "How does one know? And how does one discern knowing from believing you know?". This is especially surprising since doubt is a major feature of psychoanalysis: That is partly why an analyst needs to undergo analysis as part of his training, as his initial interpretation of psychic reality is questioned. Moreover, "psychoanalysis is itself a technique for the investigation of the human mind."[11]

---

8 Bion cites this belief in Buber's version: "… in his mother's womb man knows the universe, and forgets it at birth." In: Wilfred R. Bion, "Caesura," *Two Papers "The Grid" and "Caesura,"* (Routledge, 1989 [1977]).
9 Wilfred R. Bion, *Transformations: Change from Learning to Growth*, (London: Tavistock, 1965), 106 footnote 2.
10 Wilfred R. Bion, *Cogitations*, (London: Karnac,1992), 151–152.
11 Bion, *Cogitations*, 152.

According to Bion, the psychoanalyst, just like the philosopher, guides the patient out of the cave,[12] letting go of his restriction to mere shadows of experience, and getting in touch with (emotional) truth. The analyst guides his patient towards better epistemic abilities, moving along the vertical column of the Grid – from shadowy beta elements, through alpha elements and dream thoughts (εἰκασία), then to preconceptions (πίστις – faith or belief), to conception, concepts and scientific deductive system (διάνοια) and finally strive, asymptotically, towards the (unachievable) ability of abstract thought and algebraic calculus (νόησις). This is roughly the parallel, although, to Plato, mathematics is most likely included in διάνοια and not in νόησις. For Plato, knowledge of the Forms is of higher ability. Unlike Plato's philosopher, Bion's analyst is of no desire, and rather observes the movements of the patient along the Line.

Although he does not mention the 'divided Line', Bion gives credit to Plato's 'Theory of Forms' in his different writings and admits that he is 'borrowing freely from Plato'. In *Transformations*, Bion introduces the concept of "O," which significance "derives from and inheres in the Platonic Form."[13]

Plato's Later Dialogs and Wittgenstein's Rule-Following Paradox

In his later dialogs, Plato had found fault in his "Theory of forms." This might be in consequence of his encounter with his bright student Aristotle, or it may be ideas he generated on his own. Probably both: as this is the work of potential space.[14]

In his dialog "Parmenides." Plato puts the words of this criticism in the mouth of an elderly Parmenides, meeting a young Socrates. This time, it is Socrates that is being interrogated by Parmenides, about the "Theory of Forms."[15] Parmenides gives plenty of arguments against the naïve Platonic idea of Forms. The most famous of these arguments is called "third person argument." A parallel argument can be found in Aristotle's *Metaphysics*, and is also referred to as "the problem of Universals"[16]:

---

12 In contrast to Plato's philosopher, Bion's analyst sets aside a desire to guide the patient out of the cave, and rather observes the movements throught the grid/divided line.
13 Bion, *Transformations*, 138.
14 Donald Winnicott, *Playing and Reality*, (London and NY: Routledge, 1971).
15 It seems that Plato's theory of Forms is his own development, although having roots in Socrates' thinking about Ethics. However, through the whole corpus of his writings, Plato puts his thoughts and opinions as Socratic teachings.
16 Aristotle, *Metaphysics Book VII*, (trans. W.D. Ross), http://classics.mit.edu/Aristotle/metaphysics.14.xiv.html.

Plato writes in "Parmenides":

"You see a number of great objects, and when you look at them there seems to you to be one and the same idea (or nature) in them all; hence you conceive of greatness as one.

Very true, said Socrates.

And if you go on and allow your mind in like manner to embrace in one view the idea of greatness and of great things which are not the idea, and to compare them, will not another greatness arise, which will appear to be the source of all these?

It would seem so.

Then another idea of greatness now comes into view over and above absolute greatness, and the individuals which partake of it; and then another, over and above all these, by virtue of which they will all be great, and so each idea instead of being one will be infinitely multiplied."[17]

The problem that Plato raises here is that the idea of "Forms,"[18] creates a problem of infinite regression: a need of linking "Forms" of infinitely higher orders. As an example: if the "Human" Form links Parmenides and Socrates, both sharing the same property, then what is it that links the Parmenides to this Form? What does it mean that Parmenides participates in this Form? Does the Form itself share a property of Humaneness, hence the affinity? If so, we need another Form now, that of "Humaneness" linking a private human being to the 'Human' Form. This solution means infinite regression and infinite dispersion of the world of Forms, instead of meaning gathering to the Form of "One"/"Good"/"Cosmos."

I wish to state here that this 'third man argument', is basically an ancient argument in *Philosophy of Language*. This argument resurfaced as relevant at the turn of the 20th century. In some respects, Plato's Forms come to solve the same problems as Gottlob Frege, founder of modern Logics, attempted to solve. How do different objects in the world share the same properties/predications as others? This is part of a much wider epistemological project, in which Frege attempts to base knowledge of the world on Logics, starting from Mathematics.[19] For the purpose of this paper, I will not go further into Frege's rich theory.

---

17 Plato, *Parmenides*, https://www.gutenberg.org/files/1687/1687-h/1687-h.htm. (132 a-b).
18 Note that the Greek word is translated here to "idea," and not to "form," which is the translation I am using, following Bion and many others.
19 Gotlobb Frege, *The Foundations of Mathematics*, Evanston, Illinois: Northwestern University Press, (1980 [1884]).

However, Frege's project of Logical Calculus, which reminds in some aspects of Cantor's "Set Theory," was found with a paradox: Bertrand Russell, a fellow philosopher and mathematician asked, "whether the set of all sets not containing themselves, contains itself," hence revealing a fallacy in Frege's predicate calculus[20]. "A set not containing itself" is a well-defined concept according to Frege's logical method. However, Russell's question leads to a paradox, for if the set contains itself, it does not contain itself. But if the set does not contain itself, it does.

Frege's idea of the concept is somewhat reminiscent of Plato's forms. Russell solved his paradox, with his own "Theory of Types": He proposes not to mix between "Types" of a different order. A set cannot contain or not contain itself, because it is of a different order than the sets which it consists of. This is parallel to the solution that one cannot attribute participation in being "Human" to the "Human" Form, for it is in a different (mathematical) order.

One can see that Russell's "Theory of Types" solution to his own paradox, leads to the "third person" problem, once again. Meaning is dispersed to infinity.

Wittgenstein, who was a student of Frege and of Russell, formulates his "Rule-following Paradox" to elucidate the problem. In his early *"Tractatus,"* Wittgenstein *writes: "The limits of my language mean the limits of my world."*[21] In this he is stating that one cannot describe language and its rules, outside of language itself. This is a position opposite to that of Plato's, which gives linguistic utterances (e.g., "Socrates is a man") its validity based on Ontological Forms outside language.

Later, in "Philosophical Investigations" Wittgenstein formulates the "Rule-Following paradox," as he speaks of "following a rule" in language:[22]

> *"This was our paradox: no course of action could be determined by a rule, because every course of action can be made out to accord with the rule. The answer was: if everything can be made out to accord with the rule, then it can also be made out to conflict with it. And so there would be neither accord nor conflict here."*[23]

---

20 Bertrand Russell, (1902) "Letter to Frege," in: Jean van Heijenoort, *From Frege to Gödel*, Cambridge, Mass.: Harvard University Press, (1967 [1902]), 124–125.
21 Ludwig Wittgenstein, *Tractatus Logico-Philosophicus*, (1921), https://www.gutenberg.org/files/5740/5740-pdf.pdf, 5.6.
22 For the purpose of this paper, consider "rule-following" as analogous to deciding whether an experience one encounters (object, sensuous experience, action) meets the criteria of participating in a certain Platonic Form. Whether one is conceptualizing truth or else forming a misconception, leading to -K.
23 Ludwig Wittgenstein, *Philosophical Investigations*, Oxford UK & Cambridge USA: Blackwell, 4th ed., (2009 [1953]), §201.

According to Wittgenstein, that meaning is determined within the language itself results in paradox. One cannot go out of language to determine its rules. But the problem remains – how does meaning evolve? If the rule is not outside the language (neither in "Types" nor in "Forms"), then the rule should be inside the language and have no outside anchor as to its validity. Paradox is inherent. One can only choose between the "Rule-Following Paradox" or else remain with the "Third Man" argument.

Wittgenstein's "Rule-following" paradox is closely linked to another question he raises[24] – whether it is possible for a subject to have a "private language" he cannot communicate to others[25]:

> "... But is it also conceivable that there be a language in which a person could write down or give voice to his inner experiences – his feelings, moods, and so on – for his own use? – Well, can't we do so in our ordinary language? – But that is not what I mean. The words of this language are to refer to what only the speaker can know – to his immediate private sensations. So, another person cannot understand the language."[26]

Again, we encounter the problem of validity: How can one know he is applying the rule of his own private language, correctly? How can he guarantee that this minute's sensation has the very same properties of an experience he had last month?

We return to the psychoanalytic question, that preoccupied Bion quite a lot – How can we make sense of the non-verbal sensuous and psychic experiences of our patients?

But what have we Forgotten in the Cave? Bion on Intuition and "O"

Bion mentions Wittgenstein's ideas only once, in a 1955 paper "Language and the Schizophrenic."[27] In this early paper, Bion attempts to show how disturbance in verbal thought plays a central part in psychotic functioning. Already in this paper, Bion marks Freud's paper on "Formulations regarding the Two Principles in Mental Functioning," as seminal to his own developments, as he will later use some of Freud's functions as the horizontal titles of his Grid. He describes the schizophrenic patient as having

---

24 Saul Kripke, *Wittgenstein on Rules and Private Language*, Cambridge Mass.: Harvard University Press, (1982).
25 The "private language" argument can also be seen in the Wittgenstein citation at the beginning of this paper.
26 Wittgenstein, *Philosophical Investigations*, §243.
27 Take notice that this is only two years after Wittgenstein's "Philosophical Investigations" was published.

little capacity for these mental functions and as lacking in his usage of language. For this reason, the psychotic patient brings Wittgenstein's question of a private language, and of rules for communicating private experience, to its extreme. Eventually, the study of the psychotic mind will be expanded by Bion, to understand the psychotic part of the personality of any patient.

Bion accepts Wittgenstein's criticism of Augustine's description of the child's purchase of a language,[28] as simplistic. For Augustine, a child learns language when the adult shows him the usage of words (e.g., "This is an apple.") According to Wittgenstein, language is not acquired by simple ostensive definitions. Ostensivity of language is a bypass to the problem presented at the beginning of this paper – that of communicating what cannot be shown. "In *ordinary speech,*" writes Bion "the meaning of any given word, and still more the meaning of the sum total of what a man says, depends upon the synthesis of a complex variety of elements; sounds have to be combined to form words, and words, sentences."[29] (my italics). In this early paper, in which Bion describes the lack of linguistic tools in the language of the schizophrenic patient, he describes how the analyst, not unlike Plato's philosopher in the Cave, should gather sense data of the session, in order to help the patient, verbalize his emotion.[30]

Bion speaks of "*ordinary speech,*" whereas Wittgenstein is an "*ordinary language*" philosopher of language: In his later writings, he rejects the reduction of natural language to logical formulations and regards language as a complex system consisting of different "language games" of varying complexities. A "language game" is a game one plays according to a set of rules determining the correct usage. These rules set the meanings of articulations in the language game. We have already seen that the question of meaning (rule-following) consists of paradox.

However, prior to Wittgenstein becoming an "*ordinary language*" philosopher, his thought was influenced by Frege's positivistic logic. Frege believed that sentences have meaning only if one can define the truth conditions which satisfy them, the "matters in the world" that occur and make the sentences true. Grammatically speaking, these are propositions in indicative modes.[31]

---

28 Wittgenstein, *Philosophical Investigations*§1; Wilfred, R. Bion, "Language and the Schizophrenic," in: Melanie Klein, Paula Heiman and Roger Money-Kyrle (eds.), *New Directions in Psycho-Analysis*, (London: Tavistock Press,1955), 226–7.
29 Bion, "language and the Schizophrenic," 227.
30 Avner Bergstein, "'Truth Shall Spring out of the Earth ...': The Analyst as Gatherer of Sense Impressions," *International Journal of Psychoanalysis*, (in print).
31 Ronnie Carmeli, "The Grammar of Paradox," *International Journal of Psychoanalysis*, (in print).

But what have we forgotten in the Cave that the psychotic part of the mind might help us find?

Bion writes that psychotic patients will tend to say, "It seems that ...," where non-psychotic patients will say "I believe that ...," using an *irrealis* form of speech[32] as opposed to the psychotic one.[33]

According to White, in his early period, Bion's "scientific deductive system" and his search for mathematical precision in psychoanalysis, are influenced by positivistic ideas, such as Frege's. However, like Wittgenstein, Bion abandoned the idea of "constructing a perfectly logical theory," and adopted a "transcendent position," in which the unknown and ineffable experiences are recognized.[34]

Bion begins "Attention and Interpretation" with these words:

> *"I doubt if anyone but a practising psycho-analyst can understand this book although I have done my best to make it simple. Any psycho-analyst who is can grasp my meaning because he, unlike those who only read or hear practicing psycho-analysis, has the opportunity to experience for himself what I in this book can only represent by words and about verbal formulations designed for a different task."*[35]

Bion regards understanding as rooted in experience: meaning is in practice and so, solely words are not sufficient for playing *any* "language-game," and perhaps *even more so*, the psychoanalytic one. Moreover, writing a book about psychoanalysis is playing a different language game altogether than the game played in practicing psychoanalysis.

This idea is in close affinity, and probably influenced by Wittgenstein idea that "meaning is in use" – the meaning of a linguistic articulation is in the way one uses it in the language game that one has learnt. Words are like tools of this game (i.e., one does not use a fork to spoon his soup. Only someone, a small child, who hasn't yet learnt to use his cutlery might do a thing like that). Thus, one can see that for Wittgenstein, as well, meaning is in practice. Once again, we are faced with the problem of *communicating*

---

32 As opposed to the indicative mode, indicating objective facts and their negation, the *irrealis* modes of linguistic utterances (e.g., the optative mode) take into account the subjective position of the speaker as part of meaning.
33 Wilfred R. Bion, "Attacks on Linking," *International Journal of Psychoanalysis*, 40 (1959): 308–315.
34 Robert S. White, "Bion and Mysticism: The Western Tradition," *American Imago* (68) (2011), 213–240, 234.
35 Wilfred R., Bion, *Attention and Interpretation: A Scientific Approach to Insight in Psycho-Analysis and Groups*, (London: Tavistock, 1970), 1.

private experiences, which neither Wittgenstein nor Bion strongly deny, although I will return to clarify this point.

In *"Transformations"* Bion introduces a new concept – "O": "It can be represented by terms such as ultimate reality or truth."[36] Bion's new concept, throws confusion and bewilderment as to his intentions. I will try to show that this confusion might do with the concept being inherently paradoxical, which does not cancel its significance and contribution to psychoanalysis. Nevertheless, there is an additional reason for the rejection and confusion, in certain quarters, of Bion's later writings and the concept of "O," which I believe to be Bion's lack of philosophical clarity, leading this concept to an obscure fate. Unlike Winnicott, Bion does not hold the idea of the inherent paradox in psychoanalysis, with the persistence that is called for. This might be, at times, in light of Bion's initial rejection (following Gödel and the Intuitionists) of the law of excluded middle and relevance of the term "paradox" to the human mind,[37] and at times in light of his own human lack of precision.

In 'Attention and Interpretation', Bion writes: "I shall use the sign O to denote that which is the ultimate reality represented by terms such as ultimate reality, absolute truth, the godhead, the infinite, the thing-in-itself."[38] Bion states that one "cannot know O" but can only become "O," be one with "O." He writes: "The point at issue is how to pass from 'knowing' phenomenon to 'being' that which is 'real.'"[39] Grotstein[40] writes, that in this concept, Bion is attempting to explain Freud's notion of the id as a "seething cauldron," in an even more profound and metaphysical way.

However, in his idea of O, Bion is consistent with Kant's idea of "thing-in-itself," as it is something that cannot be spoken of but still holds metaphysical existence. Grotstein writes: "O is both immanent and transcendent."[41] So, this is an "absolute truth," one can know nothing about? – Emotional, or proto-emotional, experience. The realm from which emotional flux flows. The source of all links detected in the analytic session. Then how on earth is an analyst supposed to *intuit* that which obviously cannot be communicated to him by means of *knowledge*?

What seems to hold the paradox in Bion's writings, is that **"O," "the thing-in-itself," is both the flux of emotional experience,[42] but also the Form, the idea, the unalterable ultimate truth. It exceeds both ends of Plato's divided line, of the grid, in a manner of speaking – rounding the line.** It is the underlying Heraclitan river glimpsing in the dark of the cave from the sensible

---

36 Bion, *Transformations*, 139–170.
37 Wilfred R. Bion, *The Italian Seminars* (London: Karnac, 2005), 14.
38 Bion, *Attention and Interpretation*, 26.
39 Bion, *Transformations*, 148.
40 Grotstein, "Bion, the Pariah of 'O,'" *British Journal of Psychotherapy*, 84.
41 Grotstein, "Bion, the Pariah of 'O,'" *British Journal of Psychotherapy*, 85.
42 Bion, *Attention and Interpretation*, 5.

world of shadows, a river that cannot be entered (not even once), but also the Parmenidean unalterable, bare, and devoid of predicates "being," the ultimate Form, shown by the "way of truth" (ἀλήθεια) – both becoming and existence.

Bion's allusion to Meister Eckhart's *mysticism*, in his analogy of O as Godhead, brings forth once again the question of communicating the experience. He writes: "Eckhart considers Godhead to contain all distinctions yet undeveloped and to be Darkness and Formlessness."[43] God is distinct from Godhead as "Heaven is from Earth." Eckhart was accused (and acquitted) of heresy, following his radical thoughts: the soul must go beyond identity with God, which is finite. It must abandon all things, and seek nothing, not even God. Eckhart calls "Godhead" the origin of all things which are beyond God, while God is what the soul engenders: The Son/Soul becomes the Father. It detaches itself beyond God. This is what Eckhart names "Godhead," which cannot be spoken.

Bion speaks of the Mystic in the analyst.[44] If the analyst blinds himself and speaks not (no memory and no desire) then the analyst can become O, and can intuit the emotional truth of the session from that which is unspoken. He may sense beyond sensible data and see beyond the abstraction of Forms. He may find that which has been abandoned, or forgotten, in the Cave. He becomes Tiresias, the ultimate Mystic, or Oedipus towards the end of Sophocles' play.

Wittgenstein concludes his *Tractatus* with the famous proposition 7: "Whereof one cannot speak, thereof one must be silent.[45] "– this statement is conventionally interpreted as positivistic –" Frege line of thinking. However, taking a second look at this phrase, I would like to propose another (quite radical) interpretation to this text, leaning on the etymology of the concept of the "Mystic" – Muw, -ein: to shut the mouth, and to shut the eyes. Used in Attic Greek to indicate shutting one's mouth about the secrets of the Mysticism of sacred rituals.[46]

In this sentence, Wittgenstein might be attempting to better understand the puzzle that has been at philosophy's table ever since Parmenides was told by the goddess[47]: "I hold thee back from this way of inquiry, and from the other also, upon which mortals knowing naught wander two faced." *He is stating that one "must be silent," perhaps as a Mystic should be, about what one cannot speak*. In this interpretation, one should be silent about that which one cannot speak of, not because it has no meaning, no sense, as the positivistic mind might hold, but rather because it is the "thing-in-itself" that

---

43 Bion, *Transformations*, 162.
44 Avner Bergstein, "The Ineffable," *Bion and Meltzer's Expeditions into Unmapped Mental Life*, (NY: Routledge, 2019).
45 Wittgenstein, *Tractatus Logico-Philosophicus*, 7.
46 Henry G. Liddel & Robert Scott, *An Intermediate Greek-English Lexicon*, (Oxford: Clarendon Press, 1994).
47 Unnamed goddess usually recognized as Dikh or Persephone.

cannot be known, but only sensed.[48] This accords with Wittgenstein's interpreters who find him a Kantian[49] – as Kant's somewhat religious antinomies appear in this sentence.

With his concept of the analyst's "intuition," Bion attempts to go beyond proposition no. 7 in Wittgenstein's Tractatus.[50] What cannot be spoken of; what cannot be known, may still be sensed, intuited. But not only Bion, but Wittgenstein himself also goes beyond his own proposition no. 7, not being able to hold his mouth shut, his tongue still, and his pen frozen, regarding that which cannot be known.

Wittgenstein's drafts of his thoughts regarding this issue, prior to "Philosophical Investigations" are abundant, but finally in 1953 he formulates:

"The paradox disappears only if we make a radical break with the idea that language always functions in one way, always serves the same purpose: to convey thoughts – which may be about houses, pains, good and evil, or whatever."[51]

Wittgenstein returns to the Cave via grammar: Language may bewitch us into presuming that everything we articulate is in the sphere of knowledge[52] – "conveying thoughts," which are propositions about matters in the world. But in fact, language does much more than articulate facts – true or false.

According to Wittgenstein: "Essence is expressed in grammar."[53] And although Wittgenstein doesn't give details of grammatical modes, linguistics can tell us that grammar gives us much more than the indicative mode of the verb. As an example, grammar uses the optative mode – the mode Freud referred to as the grammar of wishes, in his theory of dreams.[54]

Wittgenstein begins "Philosophy of Psychology – A Fragment," which is the second part of "Philosophical Investigations":

"Can only those hope who can talk? Only those who have mastered the

---

48 It is an intriguing fact of language, how to some philosophies, the sensible became nonsense.
49 Newton Garver, *This Complicated Form of Life*, (Chicago and La Salle, Illinois: Open Court, 1994).
50 Christina Wieland, "Freud's Influence on Bion's Thought," in: Nuno Torres & Robert D. Hinshelwood, Bion's Sources, (London & NY: Routledge, 2013), 104–123, 118.
51 Wittgenstein, *Philosophical Investigations* §304.
52 Wittgenstein, *Philosophical Investigations* §109.
53 Wittgenstein, *Philosophical Investigations* §371.
54 Sigmund Freud, "On Dreams," *The Standard Edition of the Complete Psychological Works of Sigmund Freud, Vol V*, (London: Hogarth Press, 1955 [1901]); Carmeli, "The Grammar of Paradox," *International Journal of Psychoanalysis*.

use of language. That is to say, the manifestations of hope are modifications of this complicated form of life."[55]

One can see that this statement is closely linked to Bion's mention of Wittgenstein's philosophy: The psychotic patient has not mastered the use of language and is not able to manifest hope in this complicated form of life.[56]

None of This is Possible Without Kant

Wittgenstein objects to his reading as a behaviorist,[57] and in many ways is a follower of Kantian ideas.[58] I'd like to propose that Kant's idea of "*synthetic – a-priori*" knowledge is not only a breakthrough in philosophical thinking, regarding the question of epistemic knowledge, but a necessary precursor to Wittgenstein's ideas, as well as Bion's.

It is Kant that has prepared the way for different grammatical possibilities in seeking philosophical truths and widening epistemological pathways. Prior to Kant, there was controversy regarding the way to assert epistemic knowledge, and 17th- and 18th-century philosophers have divided to the Rationalistic school and the Empiricist one. To put it roughly, the Empiricist school argued that human beings were born "*Tabula Rasa*" (a clear slate – a term used by John Locke), with no preconceptions or any innate tools for knowledge. According to them, knowledge was acquired solely by experience-sense impressions. The Rationalists, on the contrary, argued that sense impressions may be misleading (e.g., Descartes's malicious demon) and that only innate logical capacities allow us to reach any epistemic knowledge about the world.

In his "Critique of Pure Reason," Emmanuel Kant states that reason, trying to "take refuge in principles that overstep all possible use in experience," is bound to fall into "obscurity and contradictions."[59] Kant suggests a third route to epistemic knowledge: There are *a priori* cognitions, usually attributed to pure reason, denying experimental or intuitive data. These cognitions are reached via *analytic* method – analyzing the concepts in

---

55 Ludwig Wittgenstein, *Philosophy of Psychology – A Fragment*, (Oxford UK & Cambridge USA: Blackwell, 4th ed., 2009 [1953]), i 1.
56 When Wittgenstein uses the term "form of life," he is probably referring to another sentence in the beginning of PI: "And to imagine a language means to imagine a form of life." In: Wittgenstein, *Philosophical Investigations*, §19. The psychotic patient has not gained mastery of complex and complicated language-games that allow the articulation and practice of hoping, dreaming, and wishing.
57 Wittgenstein, *Philosophical Investigations* §§307–308.
58 Garver, *This Complicated Form of Life*.
59 Emanuel Kant, *Critique of Pure Reason*, 2nd ed., (1787 [1781]), https://www.gutenberg.org/files/4280/4280-h/4280-h.htm, 99. A viii.

question (e.g., Descartes's "Cogito" argument is simply an analysis of the articulation "I think" as containing within it the assumption of existence). There are also *a posteriori* cognitions, which are empirical, contingent, and derive from experience.[60] "Judgements of experience, as such, are all synthetic."[61] Kant calls a proposition "synthetic," when the proposition is not a simple analysis of the concept in question, but rather adds new information/predicate on the concept concerned. *"Analytic a priori"* propositions are characteristic to the Rationalistic school, while *"synthetic a posteriori"* to the Empiricists.

Kant suggests a third type of proposition: *"synthetic a priori"* propositions. These are cognitions acquired not by experience but are completely *a priori*. However, they are not tautologies but add epistemic knowledge to the concept in question. Kant gives as examples to this kind of propositions, the entire subject of Mathematics, judgments, and principles in Physics, and propositions in Metaphysics.[62]

Kant's revolution in philosophy, was a necessary link, for many ideas promoted by Wittgenstein[63]: First and foremost, with his combination of *"synthetic a priori,"* Kant expanded the ways in which epistemic language may function, an idea that sowed the seeds of Wittgenstein's statement that language functions in many ways, and not only in propositions about the world. Moreover, Kant's combination of intuition and concepts, Empiricism and Rationalism, gave way to Wittgenstein's idea of meaning in practice.

But not only Wittgenstein. Bion's writings are Kantian in essence, even though he usually does not explicitly state Kant's influence on his thought. Grotstein writes: "Bion was able to fashion an epistemophilic instrument for psychoanalysis which integrated *empiricism* (*'K'*) with *intuition* (*'O'*)."[64] But is Bion only an empiricist guided by intuition towards sense data?

Kant opposes *intuition* to *concept*: a *"concept"* is a mediated representation (A68/B93) (i.e., *Rationalism*) while an *"intuition"* is an immediate representation (B41), such as space and time (pure intuitions) or empirical intuitions such as an immediate perception of a physical object (i.e., *Empiricism*). Bion's interest lies in the immediate perception of an emotional experience of the analytic hour.

---

60 "... experience, which is itself a synthetic combination of intuition." Says Kant, *Critique of Pure Reason*, 142.
61 Kant, *Critique of Pure Reason*, 142. A viii.
62 Kant, *Critique of Pure Reason*, 143–146.
63 No philosopher after Kant could disregard his ideas. I believe that prior to Wittgenstein, Frege's distinction between "sense" and "reference" would not be possible as well, without Kant's contributions.
64 Grotstein, "Bion, the Pariah of 'O,'" *British Journal of Psychotherapy*, 82.

However, it seems that Bion, following Kant, as well as Plato, combines in his thought both the Empiricist and Rationalist traditions. He is seeking O, not only as intuition, but also as the ultimate concept, ultimate Form, and he is also following the long tradition of innate ideas, with his own version of "pre-conceptions." Bion writes: "The realization of the breast provides an emotional experience. This experience corresponds to Kant's secondary and primary qualities of a phenomenon."[65] – as the innate rationalistic pre-conceptions, encounter the *secondary and primary qualities* of the experience of phenomena, that Kant borrowed from Locke's Empiricist theory.

Bion is certainly taking Kant's distinction between the phenomenological world and the thing-in-itself into account. Kant takes the stand that nothing could be said about the thing-in-itself (like in mysticism, like in Wittgenstein "... thereof one must be silent.").

One might understand Wittgenstein's famous "Beetle in a box" metaphor of the existence of the private "mind" as an object in the world, as following Kant's idea that nothing can be said about the "thing-in-itself" – it contributes no additional sense or meaning:

> "... Suppose that everyone had a box with something in it which we call a "beetle." No one can ever look into anyone else's box, and everyone says he knows what a beetle is only by looking at his beetle. – Here it would be quite possible for everyone to have something different in his box. One might even imagine such a thing constantly changing. – But what if these people's word "beetle" had a use nonetheless? – If so, it would not be as the name of a thing. The thing in the box doesn't belong to the language-game at all; not even as a Something: for the box might even be empty."[66]

For Wittgenstein, there is no *sense* in the persistence of speech on the ever-changing "beetle," one can say nothing of. We can only acquire epistemic knowledge about the phenomenological world. But does Bion follow Kant here as well?

Bion departs from the Kantian priority of phenomena over noumena: He is moving from O to K and vice versa – he is giving no priority to either phenomena or noumena, as "the raw sense data of emotional experience seem to be linked by Bion to these things-in-themselves."[67]

"Bion, ..., mistakenly equates Kant's "thing-in-itself" with the Platonic Forms because Kant does not attribute objectivity to noumena, as Plato does to the Forms,"[68] writes White. In a similar manner, Noel Smith

---

65 Wilfred R. Bion, *Learning from Experience*, (London: Tavistock, 1962), 69.
66 Wittgenstein, *Philosophical Investigations* §293.
67 Grotstein, "Bion, the Pariah of 'O,'" *British Journal of Psychotherapy*, 82.
68 White, "Bion and Mysticism: The Western Tradition," *American Imago*, 229.

understands Bion's O as an example of "pure reason" as opposed to Kant's "thing-in-itself."[69] It is true that Forms are immaterial, non-spatial, and atemporal, just like Kant's thing-in-itself. Nonetheless, as opposed to Kant's thing-in-itself, which nothing can be said of – Plato says quite a lot about Forms.

It is interesting to note that according to López-Corvo, Bion regards the clinical material of the session as the phenomenon, which is the container of the contained noumena. This is a reversal of the idea that the noumena is analogous to Plato's Forms, in regard to which is the container and which is the contained. López-Corvo writes: "... while the phenomenon varies, the noumenon, the 'thing-in-itself' or original meaning, remains, representing an unconscious chain of events that structure a penumbra of painful emotions surrounding the pre-conceptual trauma."[70]

Bion writes: "Phenomena, the term being used as Kant might use it, are transformed into representations, T β. T β may then be regarded as a representation of the individual's experience O, but the significance of O derives from and inheres in the Platonic Form." This is Bion's paradoxical understanding of O, as both rooted in the Forms, and in the raw noumena of ineffable sensuous experience.

For Bion, it seems that O is both subjective and holds objectivity of "truth," *emotional truth*, just as Plato's Forms hold. But if one takes a closer look, Bion's use of the word *"truth"* as well as the allusion to Plato's epistemic theory, has a mere "family resemblance," to use Wittgenstein's words,[71] to the *"truth"* of philosophers. For Bion agrees with Kant that **O cannot be known.** However, coming from Bion, who has fought jargon in psychoanalysis, the use of the philosophically jargonish, saturated concept of *'truth'* is at best unfortunate.

Although distancing his philosophical ideas about language, from Frege's "meaning in truth" theory, Wittgenstein himself mentions the word *"truth,"* in a context very similar to Bion's usage:

> "When longing makes me exclaim "Oh, if only he'd come!", the feeling gives the words "meaning." But does it give the individual words their meanings?

---

69 Kelly Noel Smith, "Thoughts, Thinking, and the Thinker," in: Nuno Torres & Robert D. Hinshelwood, Bion's Sources, (London & NY: Routledge, 2013), 124–136, 129.
70 Rafael E. López-Corvo, "Plato's Theory of "Forms" and Homoemorphic Transformation of Pre-Conceptual Traumas, Using Bion's model of Container-Contained," *The Psychoanalytic Review (99)(6)* (Dec 2012): 877–898, 881.
71 Wittgenstein writes that words have "family resemblance" in the way one can use them, in different language games. A word's meaning doesn't have an essential feature or criterion one must meet in order to use it correctly, but one can recognize the familial affinity of different uses of a word.

But here one could also say that the feeling gave the words *truth*."[72]

Perhaps Wittgenstein here is using the word "*truth*" in closer familial affinity to Bion's use, than to the historical use of the word in philosophy, beginning with Parmenides "Way of truth" up to Frege's "meaning in truth." "*Truth*" here, breaks away from the idea of objective *knowledge*, and links to the idea of *meaning* – subjective meaning. For Wittgenstein, I remind, language functions not only to state propositions about the world, but to articulate subjective experiences as well.

We do not "know" what we sense of feel, but rather we just sense of feel it. Wittgenstein writes that: "… as a matter of fact we are wont to use the word 'to know'"[73] – even when it has no sense. For Wittgenstein, sensations are private by definition, but this privacy has nothing to do with first-person knowledge:

"Well, only I can know whether I am really in pain; another person can only surmise it," says Wittgenstein's imaginary interlocuter, as he immediately answers: "– In one way this is false, and in another nonsense. … It can't be said of me at all (except perhaps as a joke) that I *know* I'm in pain. What is it supposed to mean – except perhaps that I *am* in pain?"[74] – experiences, sensations, and feelings are not something we "know," but simply something we "have." Only another person can know how I feel (without absolute certainty, but with the usual usage of the word "know"), by observing my behavior. Garver adds: "That is to say, it can be said of me *neither* that I know I am in pain *nor* that I don't know I am in pain."[75]

Wittgenstein explains that one can "know" that another person is in pain, but it is not false, but meaningless to say of another person: "I feel his pain."[76] This, perhaps, is the difference between Bion's K and Bion's O: "Transformations in K may be described loosely as akin to 'knowing about' something whereas Transformations in O are related to becoming or being O or to being 'become' by O."[77] You cannot feel another person's experience but you can simply share an experience.

Returning to the Cave – Embryonic Sight

Plato, Wittgenstein, and Bion begin their journey seeking the truth in the world of "Forms" and logics, attempting to find an absolute logical

---

72 Wittgenstein, *Philosophical Investigations* §544.
73 Wittgenstein, "Notes for Lectures on 'Private Experience' and 'Sense Data,'" *The Philosophical Review*, 278.
74 Wittgenstein, *Philosophical Investigations* §246.
75 Garver, *This Complicated Form of Life*, 173 (original italics).
76 Wittgenstein, "Notes for Lectures on 'Private Experience' and 'Sense Data,'" *The Philosophical Review*, 277.
77 Bion, *Transformations*, 163.

mathematical method to lean on. All three come to question this *"way of truth"* and all three present hints of their later ideas already in early papers. As an example, one can find seeds of Bion's later thought already in his *early* 1958 paper where he cites Wittgenstein's *later* work.

Bion and Wittgenstein return to Plato's cave. For the shadows of εικασία and πίστις, are not of less importance to human experience than the brightness of νόησις.

Included in the many citations Bion uses as a preface to his paper "Caesura," Bion quotes Freud: "I know that in writing I have to blind myself artificially in order to focus all the light on one dark spot."[78] It is interesting to note the difference between this quotation and Bion's earlier reference to this idea in 1973:

"Instead of trying to bring a brilliant, intelligent, knowledgeable light to bear on obscure problems, I suggest we bring to bear a diminution of the light – a penetrating beam of darkness; a reciprocal of the searchlight. ... The darkness would be so absolute that it would achieve a luminous, absolute vacuum. So that, if any object existed, however faint, it would show up very clearly."[79]

Bion's analyst needs to blind himself to the dazzling light of knowledge, of "Forms," and to use primitive sight and immature senses to intuit and gather sense data of the analytic hour.[80]

These slip-sliding glimpses of such obscure sights, at peripheral zones of the mind, are subjects of Wittgenstein's investigations as well. One might call these zones "preconscious." As an example, Wittgenstein gives the case of someone being interrupted in the middle of a sentence (and is this not a miniature example of a minor trauma, and the investigation of archeological ruins?[81] – perhaps that is why an analyst must remain silent and uninterrupting, as long as he has nothing to contribute). Wittgenstein writes:

"When I continue the interrupted sentence and say that *this* was how I had been going to continue it, this is similar to elaborating a train of thought from brief notes.

---

78 Sigmund Freud, " Letter of 25th May to Lou Andreas-Salomé" in: *Letters of Sigmund Freud*, Selected and Edited by E. L. Freud. (New York: Dover, 1992 [1916]). 312–313.
79 Wilfred R. Bion, *Brazilian Lectures*, (London: Karnac, 2008), 20.
80 Bergstein, "Truth Shall Spring out of the Earth ...": The Analyst as Gatherer of Sense Impressions," *International Journal of Psychoanalysis*.
81 Wilfred R. Bion, "On Arrogance," *International Journal of Psychoanalysis* (39) (1958), 145.

Then don't I *interpret* the notes? Was only *one* continuation possible in these circumstances? Of course not. But I didn't *choose* between these interpretations. I *remembered* that I was going to say this."[82]

But does one remember? The interpretation has not yet been formed. Words are coming out from the formless darkness. Wittgenstein continues:

"It is as if a snapshot of a scene had been taken, but only a few scattered details of it were to be seen: here a hand, there a bit of a face, or a hat a the rest is dark. And now it is as if I knew quite certainly what the whole picture represented. As if I could read the darkness."[83]

What is yet unconscious and resides in the peripheral zone of attention, and in fact, never arrived to be consciously thought of and spoken, can only be interpreted by hints of 'scattered details' noticed by the analyst. Noticed by his trained ability to see in the dark: "O ... is darkness and formless but it can enter the domain K [Knowledge] when it has evolved to a point where it can be known."[84], writes Bion.

Plato's slaves in the cave, undoubtedly see the changing shadows of the cave with much more clarity, or at least with much more ease, than the philosopher does – as their sight is accustomed to darkness. The philosopher is, after all, not omnipotent in his sight.

It seems that Bion's return to the cave is at its extreme, in "Caesura." Bion writes: "Is there any part of the human mind which still betrays signs of an 'embryological' intuition, either visual or auditory?"[85]

Bion speaks of embryological optic pits, preceding the development of the mature eye. These pits allow the developing embryo some sensing of his surroundings, prior to the caesura of birth and to the ability to see clearly in the light of the world outside the mother's womb. Bion speaks of the parallel embryological mental intuition.

Perhaps the parallel could be taken further, adding the fact that in the optic sensory system of the fetus, "rods" develop first, and only then "cones" develop. Rod cells are photoreceptor cells in the peripheral zone of the retina which function better in darkness. They are sensitive to movement and are responsible for night vision. These are the photoreceptors needed in Plato's cave. Cone cells develop in the center of the retina, later on in fetal development. These cells are sensitive to color and precision of contour – they are responsible for day vision. The difference

---

82 Wittgenstein, *Philosophical Investigations* §634.
83 Wittgenstein, *Philosophical Investigations* §635.
84 Bion, *Attention and Interpretation*, 26.
85 Bion, "Caesura," in: *Two Papers:"The Grid"and "Caesura,"* 42.

between the types of photoreceptors, explains why one can see a glimpse of a distant star in the corner of the eye, but when turning to look (from the center of the retina) – the image disappears, for the cones are not sensitive to such faint images in the dark.

The analyst must have mature sight and knowledge of concepts if he is to make interpretations and advance understanding of the session's emotional reality. But, if he is to intuit the emotional happenings of the session, he must first use his mental-receptors parallel to rods, sensors characteristic to early fetal development, to the darkness of the womb and of the cave. This is done in the peripheral zone of his mind – the "penumbra of associations," to use Bion's terminology.

'Penumbra' is the space surrounding the light, or the dark spot. The shadowy surroundings of the object. "Umbra" means shadow in Latin. Note that Wittgenstein links the usage of the word "shadow" to "possibility"[86] – not a representation, not a picture, and not reality. But the possibility of movement – that which is parallel to dreaming and to the optative mode.

Afterthought – Parmenides' Prologue

But let us return to Parmenides. Parmenides' surviving fragments consist not only of the famous "Way of Truth," but also of a very mystical "Proem" in which he is taken by chariot to the Goddess, residing in the mythological space where night and day meet. She will teach him of things – the way of *truth* (ἀλήθεια) and the way of *belief* (δόξα).

It is illuminating to note that Parmenides' fragments do not end with the static "Way of truth," but continue to the human way of believing, distinguishing between light and night,[87] making up the illusory world of cosmology and science, and continuing to Eros and sexual interest:

> *"In the midst of these is the divinity that directs the course of all things, for she is the beginner of the painful birth and all begetting, driving the female to embrace the male, and the male to that of the female.*
>
> *First of all the gods she contrived Eros."*[88]

And indeed, it is Eros (Freud's) that contests the immobile, Thanatos-driven way of Truth. "Wherefore all these things are but names which mortals have

---

86 Wittgenstein, *Philosophical Investigations,* §194.
87 Note the similarity to Genesis 1a, and gods first words. And the darkness in the initial chaos.
88 Parmenides, "On Nature," in: John Burnet, *Early Greek Philosophy, 3rd ed.*, (London: Black, 1920). http://www.platonic-philosophy.org/files/Parmenides%20-%20Poem.pdf

given, believing them to be true—coming into being and passing away, being and not being, change of place and alteration of bright colour," says Parmenides. Nonetheless, the goddess urges Parmenides to "learn the beliefs of mortals, giving ear to the deceptive ordering of my words."

Not much of Parmenides's Fragments on "the way of belief" survived. Evidence shows that only a tenth of this part of the poem is known to us, as Parmenides dealt with the need to understand, among other things, both cosmology and physiology of human reproduction, as hinted in the remains of his verses.

The idea that Parmenides was an extreme Monist is rooted in the influence of Guthrie's *A History of Greek Philosophy*. However, after Guthrie's other interpretations to Parmenides's poem appeared, e.g., with some resemblance to Guthrie's ideas, Russel found Parmenides's text occupied with the same question's Logicism dealt with. However, both these interpretations do not explain the lengthy description Parmenides gives to the "way of belief."[89]

Perhaps Bion's ideas may shed light on the paradoxical thought of Parmenides and his two ways to human understanding: Perhaps Parmenides was the first to distinguish between K and O, concept and intuition, pure reason, and sensual data. As the goddess urges: "Meet it is that thou shouldst learn all things, as well the unshaken heart of well-rounded truth, as the opinions of mortals in which is no true belief at all."[90]

---

89 John Palmer, "Parmenides," *The Stanford Encyclopedia of Philosophy* (Winter 2020 Edition), Edward N. Zalta (ed.), URL = <https://plato.stanford.edu/archives/win2020/entries/parmenides/>.
90 Parmenides, "On Nature," *Early Greek Philosophy*.

Chapter 13

Shades of Loneliness
A Psychoanalytic Study of Samuel Beckett's *Rockaby*

Tsiky Cohen

Introduction

Literature has played an important role in the evolution of the thinking and conceptualization of psychoanalysis since its inception. The literary medium is capable of articulating what is essentially muted and obscure, so Freud tended to resort to Greek tragedies and plays to formulate intuitions and analytical preconceptions. Although the entirety of literary genres expresses a gamut of human situations and intense emotions, Freud (1906) believed that drama, in particular, "seeks to explore emotional possibilities more deeply" and that "suffering of every kind is thus the subject-matter of drama."[1] The uniqueness of drama is expressed in its aesthetic constitution, which relies on a technique of "showing" rather than of "telling," that is to say, on a discourse in which the world tells itself as a story and the reader can become directly acquainted with the characters' actions and exchanges.[2]

The present chapter seeks to employ the fruitful and dialectical relations that exist between literature and psychoanalysis, in order to clarify and describe the phenomenon of loneliness in the sense of a phenomenological experience. Loneliness is one of the human phenomena that have been widely discussed in various disciplines including philosophy, sociology, psychology, and art. Nevertheless, the attempt to describe and conceptualize the feeling of loneliness remains an oxymoron, since loneliness is essentially

---

1 Sigmund Freud, "Psychopathic Characters on the Stage," in *The Standard Edition of the Complete Psychological Works of Sigmund Freud 7*, ed. James Strachey (1906; repr., 1942): 305–306.
2 The terms "telling" and "showing" are distinct forms of time representation in a story, as well as different modes of describing the world. The term "telling" relates to a situation in which the author presents the events that take place in the story through the filter of the "narrator figure", while the term "showing" relates to a situation in which there is no narrator figure, and the reader can acquaint themselves directly with the actions and exchanges of the characters. See: Percy Lubbock, *The Craft of Fiction* (London: J. Cape, 1954); Wayne C. Booth, *The Rhetoric of Fiction* (Chicago: Chicago University Press, 1983); Michael J. Toolan, *Narrative: A Critical Linguistic Introduction* (London: Routledge, 2001).

DOI: 10.4324/9781003326588-13

a private language, a monadic experience, muted, silent, and uncommunicable. Even in psychoanalysis, which *prima facie* has set itself the goal of describing the unutterable, loneliness was almost never discussed, and when it was, this is usually done from an etiological perspective that traces the causes of the feeling of loneliness, be it a product of mental mechanisms, developmental failures or traumatic distresses.

According to Sullivan, the fact that the fear of loneliness may motivate a person to overcome their inhibitions shows that loneliness is different from anxiety and that it is experienced as more fearful.[3] Fromm-Reichmann also argues that the feeling of loneliness probably plays a much more significant role in the dynamics of mental disorders than psychoanalysis is willing to acknowledge.[4] Nevertheless, the many manifestations of the phenomenon of loneliness (social, interpersonal, intrapersonal, existentialist, etc.), and the many words that exist to describe the experience of it (loneliness, solitude, separation, isolation, aloneness), relegated loneliness to one of the least adequately conceptualized and described phenomena in the psychoanalytic literature.

Freud himself hardly addressed the feeling of loneliness in his writings. The word "loneliness" does not appear at all in the index of the 23 volumes of his work, and the word solitude is mentioned there merely a few times. In the *Introductory Lectures*, where he discusses childhood phobias, Freud argues that the first phobias are those of darkness and loneliness. He assumes that at the root of these phobias lies the sense of absence of the loved one who cares for the child, i.e., his mother. He writes:

> While I was in the next room, I heard a child who was afraid of the dark call out: "Do speak to me, Auntie! I'm frightened!". "Why, what good would that do? You can't see me." To this the child replied: "If someone speaks, it gets lighter." Thus, a longing felt in the dark is transformed into a fear of the dark.[5]

Freud suggests that the longing felt in the dark becomes the fear of the dark, but one of the interesting points in his discussion is the implicit connection that exists between a sense of loneliness and a lack of light, words, and language. "When someone speaks, it becomes brighter," the child says, thus alluding to the complexity of the experience of loneliness as a sensory reality

---

3 Harry S. Sullivan, *The Interpersonal Theory of Psychiatry* (New York: Norton, 1953).
4 Frieda F. Reichmann, "On loneliness", *Contemporary Psychoanalysis 26* (1959; repr., 1990): 305–329.
5 Sigmund Freud, 'Introductory Lectures on Psychoanalyses [1916–1917],' in *The Standard Edition of the Complete Psychological Works of Sigmund Freud 16* (3), ed. James Strachey (1917; repr., London: Hogarth Press, 1963): 407.

preceding the symbolic and linguistic plane. Moreover, in Fromm-Reichmann's paper *On Loneliness*, she describes the experience of loneliness as paralyzing, freezing, uncommunicable, and therefore as located on the semiotic, pre-verbal, and pre-linguistic planes. Fromm-Reichmann describes an encounter with a catatonic patient with whom communication could not be established. When she tried to ask her about her unhappiness, she noticed that the patient was lifting her thumb up, hiding the rest of her fingers so that they could not be seen. To this she responded explicitly, "So lonely?", when suddenly the patient's facial expression transformed into gratitude, and her fingers spread. She began to talk about herself with her fingers, and slowly emerged from her isolation.[6]

In the present chapter I would like to focus on describing the phenomenology of the feeling of loneliness through a discussion of *Rockaby*, a play by Samuel Beckett.[7] I will try to demonstrate how the experience of loneliness has an effective quality of "nameless dread"[8] or of "unthinkable anxiety"[9] which allows it to be expressed not on the symbolic level but rather mainly on the semiotic, pre-verbal and pre-linguistic level.[10] I would like to argue that from a phenomenological and psychoanalytic point of view, the experience of loneliness is not a static event but a persistent struggle between life and death instincts, a continuous process of withdrawal, depletion, calcification, and finally mental annihilation. The uniqueness of *Rockaby* lies in Beckett's use of unique dramatic techniques that amplify the representations of the text's semiotic effect. The play allows the reader to

---

6 Fromm Reichmann, "On loneliness."
7 Samuel Beckett, "Rockaby," in *Collected Shorter Plays*, ed. Samuel Beckett (New York: Grove Press, 1984): 271–282.
8 Wilfred R. Bion, *Learning from experience* (London: Heinemann, 1962).
9 Donald W. Winnicott, "The Location of Cultural Experience". *Int. J. Psycho-Anal 48*, no 3 (1967): 368–372.
10 By the term "semiotic" (*semeion* in Greek means trace, sign, differentiation) I mean the distinction offered by the psychoanalyst Julia Kristeva (1984) between the symbolic representation dependent on the structure of grammar and the modes of symbol creation, and the semiotic representation that is related to the emotional affect and that contains mechanisms linked to drives, motions, rhythms, and tones. Unlike the symbolic representation involved in the acceptance of the social order and the Law of the Father, semiotic representation reverberates a mindset the logically and chronologically precedes the sign, the meaning, and the subject. Although the semiotic is not a language, it bursts into language and through language. Every meaning created is a product of the combination of the symbolic and the semiotic, where the symbolic provides the necessary structure for communication (without which we are left merely with sounds or murmuring), while the semiotic provides the physical motive for generating communication, and for the commencement of a process of meaning. See: Julia Kristeva, *Revolution in Poetic Language* (New York: Columbia University Press, 1984).

experience the feeling of loneliness "from within," as an "aesthetic feeling" in Meltzer's terminology, which arouses, generates, and motivates consciousness.[11]

Loneliness From a Psychoanalytic Point of View

Throughout the history of psychoanalysis, the phenomenon of loneliness has been described from different perspectives and in varied manners. While some thinkers have tended to regard it as an experience that is primarily monadic and intrapsychic, others have emphasized the contextual and environmental dimension within which the feeling of loneliness forms and emerges. Freud, as mentioned, hardly referred to the feeling of loneliness in his writings, and where he did refer to it, he linked it to the childish anxiety of separation and fear of losing the beloved object.[12] Loneliness, for Freud, is primarily an expression of a painful longing for a lost object, or for the object's love. It is a remnant of childhood anxiety that most of us struggle to leave behind.[13]

Klein, like Freud, also traced loneliness to the intrapsychic world of the individual, but she believed that the experience of loneliness stems from a constant human longing for a perfect, unattainable, inner state.[14] She ruled out the link between a feeling of loneliness and the lack of significant connections in a person's life and assumed that the foundations of loneliness are constituted against the background of the physical and mental separation that exists from the moment of birth. Loneliness, for Klein, is characterized by a variety of longings for merging that cannot be realized, such as a person's longing to return to an unattainable inner state; the longing for the confluence of the infant's unconscious and that of the mother; the longing for the experience of being whole with oneself; and so on. Because the human condition is inherently characterized by partiality, finiteness, separateness, and otherness, these deep longings for unification inevitably remain unfulfilled.

Klein distinguished between loneliness in the depressive-existentialist sense and an experience of loneliness in its schizoid-paranoid form. She

---

11 Donald Meltzer and Meg H. Williams, The *apprehension of beauty: The role of aesthetic conflict in development, art and violence* (New edition: Harris Meltzer Trust, 2008).
12 Freud, "Introductory Lectures on Psychoanalyses [1916–1917],"; Sigmund Freud, *The Uncanny* (1919; repr., London: Penguin Books, 2003): 123–163; Sigmund Freud, "Inhibitions, Symptoms, and Anxiety," in *The Standard Edition of the Complete Psychological Works of Sigmund Freud 20*, ed. James Strachey (1926; repr., London: Hogarth Press, 1959): 77–175.
13 Freud, *The Uncanny*, 252.
14 Melanie Klein, *On the sense of loneliness. Envy and gratitude and other works*, 1946–1963 (London: Hogarth Press, 1975): 300–314.

believed that a deep feeling of loneliness often belongs to the schizoid-paranoid position and is associated with a lack of ego formation, a high level of fragmentation, and overuse of projective identification. It is these psychic mechanisms that cause one to experience oneself as lonely and isolated in a hostile world. As part of the depressive position, schizoid isolation becomes an experience of existential loneliness, that is, ontological loneliness concerning the purview of man as a separate entity, from birth to death. The ability to sustain the experience of loneliness and act creatively out of it constitutes, so Klein assumes, one of the conditions for the ability to enjoy old age.

Erich Fromm, in his book *Escape from Freedom*, also referred to the experience of loneliness and suggested distinguishing it from physical isolation or from the actual absence of others.[15] He believed that one could live with people and feel a sense of complete loneliness, or alternately, live alone and feel connected to ideas, values, and social frameworks that give a sense of fraternity and belonging. Fromm linked the experience of loneliness to the processes of self-integration and to the dialectical nature of separation-individuation processes. He believed that the more a person frees himself from his initial connections, the more he begins to experience himself as distinct and unique. The person becomes more and more aware of being lonely and isolated, of being a separate entity from all other beings. The awareness of distinctness and separateness from the other is akin, so Fromm maintained, to the expulsion of man from paradise, as it destroys the primordial harmony with nature, mother, and environment, leaving man forlorn and lonely, feeling ashamed of his nakedness, helpless and frightened. While some people manage to reconnect with the human milieu through love, work, and positive freedom, others tend to give up their freedom and independence in order to overcome the pain involved in the experience of separation and distinctness.

Unlike Freud and Klein who grasped the experience of loneliness as a fundamental characteristic of the intrapsychic existence of humans as such, others believed that the experience of loneliness often echoes a real failure to meet a person's attachment and development needs. Sullivan, for example, argued that the human need for connection and intimate relationships is so fundamental to mental well-being that the feeling of loneliness can be seen as nothing less than an expression of the absence or loss of everything that sustains us as human beings.[16] He assumed that the feeling of loneliness is more frightening and paralyzing than a feeling of stress or anxiety since it threatens a person's survival and constitutes the core of the formation of psychotic symptoms.

---

15 Erich Fromm, *Escape from Freedom* (New York: Farrar and Rinehart, 1941).
16 Sullivan, *The Interpersonal Theory of Psychiatry*: 260–261.

Early childhood experiences often play an important role in the development of the experience of loneliness in adulthood. At the beginning of life, the need for contact and connection with the other is met through the baby's intimate proximity to the person caring for and attending to him or her, his mother. Injury at this stage would lead, as Sullivan claims, to a terrible feeling of loneliness and what René Spitz described as "anaclitic depression."[17] Later, the need for connection and intimacy is satisfied by the child's sense of acceptance and belonging to their peer group, and by the creation of intimate and sexual relationships in adulthood. A lone child, Sullivan writes, will struggle to distinguish between reality and fantasy, as he will attempt to make up for the lack of active human presence by phantasmatic satisfactions. His loneliness will deepen, if, despite the pressures of socialization and the environment, he does not learn to distinguish between real phenomena and the phantasmatic products of life, which will lead to a continuous withdrawal that will increase his social isolation.

Like Sullivan, Fromm-Reichmann also referred to the connection between the feeling of loneliness and the failure to meet the needs of attachment, but unlike him, she distinguished between "real loneliness," which she characterized as a paralyzing and indescribable experience and normative manifestations of loneliness that most people experience during their lives.[18] An experience of real loneliness, Fromm-Reichmann argues, is essentially different from the culturally determined loneliness of modern man that sociologists and philosophers have discussed in their writings. It is also dissimilar to the sense of solitude that arises when a person feels their small size vis-à-vis the infinity of nature, a feeling that Freud described by the expression "oceanic feelings." Real loneliness also differs from the feeling of loneliness that arises when a person experiences loss or heartbreak that cannot be shared with others; and it is also different from a state of loneliness in the sense of seclusion, since the latter sometimes leads to artistic or scientific products, and therefore can be seen as creative or constructive loneliness:

> The kind of loneliness I am discussing is nonconstructive if not disintegrative, and it shows in, or ultimately leads to, the development of psychotic states. It renders people who suffer it emotionally paralyzed and helpless."[19]

Fromm-Reichmann believed that in a state of "real loneliness," the fact that there were people in the preceding life is forgotten, and the possibility that

---

17 Rene Spitz and Katherine M. Wolf, "Anaclitic Depression", *Psychoanalytic Study of the Child* 2. no 1 (1946): 313–342.
18 Fromm Reichmann, "On loneliness".
19 Ibid., 309.

there may be interpersonal relationships in a future life is outside the realm of human expectation or imagination as well. It is such a frightening, crippling and catastrophic experience that it cannot be endured for long without becoming psychotic. Unlike other experiences that are not directly communicable but empathetically shareable with others, the experience of loneliness in its deepest sense also does not allow the other to approach one's distress and pain. Empathic attachment is often blocked by the terrifying anxiety that inheres in the contact of both parties with the feeling of loneliness, so that even a person who has suffered from loneliness in the past will find it difficult to connect with the memory of loneliness and will try to dissociate themselves from it.

Fromm-Reichman hypothesized that the sense of panic that often arises in the contact with a deep sense of loneliness is related to the subversion that this feeling creates of the validity, cohesion, and presence of the self. She believed that because the self knows, defines, and identifies itself solely in terms of its relationships with others, when we are isolated and alone over a period, we feel threatened by a potential loss of boundaries around the ability to distinguish between the subjective and the objective world. The Swiss philosopher Ludwig Binswanger described this situation effectively by the words "naked horror" and "naked existence."[20] He maintained that in situations of deep loneliness, the entire existence loses a sense of selfhood, which may even prompt a person to suicide.

Winnicott, as is well known, emphasized in his writings the idea of the permanent isolation of the individual and proposed to regard human beings as essentially isolated entities. He believed that there is a muted center of silence in the personality and that "each individual is an isolate, permanently noncommunicating, permanently unknown, in fact unfound."[21] Nevertheless, Winnicott proposed to differentiate an experience of loneliness in the ontological and existential sense, from an experience of loneliness that indicates a lack of the "capacity to be alone" in the presence of the mother or another significant person.[22] The experience of loneliness in the latter sense is

---

20 Ludwig Binswanger, *Grundformen und Erkenntnis Menschlichen Daseins* (Zurich: Niehans, 1942): 177–178.
21 Donald W. Winnicott, "communicating and Not Communicating Leading to a Study of Certain Opposites," in *The Maturational Processes and the Facilitating Environment: Studies in the Theory of Emotional Development,* ed Masud R. Khan (1963; repr., London: The Hogarth Press and the Institute of Psychoanalysis, 1965): 186.
22 Donald W. Winnicott, "The Capacity to be Alone," in *The Maturational Processes and the Facilitating Environment: Studies in the Theory of Emotional Development,* ed Masud R. Khan (1958; repr., London: The Hogarth Press and the Institute of Psychoanalysis, 1965): 29–36; Donald W. Winnicott, "Psychoanalysis and the Sense of Guilt," in *The Maturational Processes and the Facilitating Environment: Studies in the Theory of Emotional Development,* ed Masud R. Khan (1958; repr., London: The Hogarth Press and the Institute of Psychoanalysis, 1965): 14–28.

intolerable, according to Winnicott, since it is an expression of primary experiences of impingement, which were created due to a lack of "I-relatedness" experience with a mother capable of reliable attendance. While primary maternal preoccupation and a supportive environment allow a person to bear his or her existential loneliness in a living and creative way, initial harms lead the person to withdraw from their relationships with others in order to protect the true self from violation.

In his paper *Psychoanalysis and the Sense of Guilt*, Winnicott presents an example of a nine-year-old boy who used to steal from school under the suggestion of a sorcerer's voice, which commanded him what to do. He writes that the child "was of course unaware of the intolerable loneliness and emptiness that lay at the back of his illness, and which made him adopt the wizard in place of a more natural superego organization; this loneliness belonged to a time of separation from his family when he was five."[23] Only when, following psychiatric counseling, the child was permitted to stay home with his parents and become ill, did he begin to recover and a year later he returned to school.

In the next section I will focus on the phenomenology of the feeling of loneliness through a study of the play *Rockaby*. I will try to illustrate the manner in which the play elucidates the phenomenon of loneliness both as an inherent, inescapable, element in human existence and as a formative experience of the self, which in some situations becomes a central mode of being that affects a person's mode of existence with himself and with others.

The Phenomenology of Loneliness – A Study of Samuel Beckett's *Rockaby*

> *going to and fro*
> *all eyes*
> *all sides*
> *high and low*
> *for another*
> *another like herself*
> *another creature like herself*

Rockaby is a short play written in English in 1980 and translated into French by Beckett himself in 1981. It premiered in 1981 in Buffalo, New York, starring Billie Whitelaw and directed by Alan Schneider. At the center of the play is an old woman sitting on a rocking chair as she listens to a recording of her monotonous, expressionless voice playing in the background. The woman hardly speaks throughout the play, but from her recorded voice we

---

23 Ibid., 27.

understand that she has searched her entire life for *"another creature like herself,"* a creature who can dispel her loneliness and validate her existence, but in vain. In the director's notes, Beckett emphasizes that apart from the woman and the chair there are no other props or additional sets on stage. The woman should look like a prematurely old woman, gray and unkempt, her eyes huge and her face white and expressionless. He describes her dress as an extravagant and inappropriate lace dress, which implies that the woman is in a precarious condition in which she is unaware of or does not care about her dress. He adds that the woman's posture remains unaltered throughout the play and that her eyes are *"now closed, now open, in unblinking gaze"*.

The name *Rockaby* consists of three signifiers of meaning: a baby crib, a rocking chair, and a familiar lullaby (Rock-A-Bye, Baby on the treetop./ When the wind blows, the cradle will rock;/When the bough breaks the cradle will fall,/and down tumbles baby, cradle and all). Moreover, the name of the play in French, *Berceuse*, also situates it in the context of lullabies with which mothers put their children to sleep.[24] Similar to a baby whose mother's gentle voice and the rocking of the crib lull him to sleep, so too the name of the play invites the reader to imagine an image of a mother on a rocking chair with her baby as she sings a lullaby.

However, once the play begins and the curtain goes up, the fantasized image is forcibly contradicted by the gloomy image of an old woman, swaying alone in the dark against a backdrop of a tinny-voiced recitation, and whose body and gaze form a hybrid creature merging the living and the dead. The sharp contrast between the innocent title and the dark stage involuntarily evokes a sense of *Unheimlichkeit*, facing the sense of alienation that infuses the intimate and the *heimlich*.[25] The reader finds himself activated, from the outset, by what I would like to define as "poetic projective identification," in which he experiences and feels – against his will – the inner

---

24 It is interesting to note that also Winnicott, in his well-known paper *Hate in the Countertransference*, used the song *Rock-A-Bye, Baby* to describe the mother's repressed hate toward her baby. He stressed the way the melodic character of the song puts the baby to sleep but at the same time enables the mother to express murderous-impulse thoughts by means of the somber words ("When the bough breaks the cradle will fall,/and down tumbles baby, cradle and all"). See: Donald W. Winnicott, "Hate in the counter transference", *International Journal of Psychoanalysis* 30 (1949): 69–74.

25 In his paper on the *Unheimlich (The Uncanny)*, Freud argues that the *unheimlich* is an affect that arises in moments when the known, the familiar and the *heimlich* are suddenly experienced as menacing, other and alien (*unheimlich*). He maintained that the *unheimlich* is not identical with the other and the unknown, but rather it symbolizes the feeling of alienness and otherness that is inherent in the known and the familiar. In the literary context it could be added the *unheimlich* also echoes what surpasses the boundaries of the signifier and its meaning, in contrast to the defamiliarization technique, which violates the ordinary relation to the object by making it alien. See: Sigmund Freud, *The Uncanny* (1919; repr., London: Penguin Books, 2003): 123–163.

world of the woman inside herself. The woman's loneliness is not something he can move away from, observe from the outside, or even understand or conceptualize. Instead, loneliness is experienced as "nameless horror," in Bion's terms, as a sensory entity preceding the symbolic representation and evoking the feeling of loneliness in its raw and preconceptual form.

According to Anzieu, Beckett's plays were inspired philosophically by the empiricist school, which regarded sensation and sensory experience as the fundamental given of psychic life. He even looked to present the objects of his inquiry through presentation, in which the object presents itself in its immediacy and haphazardness.[26] Esslin, too, thought that Beckett's work should be regarded as an ongoing search for a sensory reality that is beyond mere arguments in conceptual terms.[27] The empiricist school stresses a return from abstraction to sensation, from organization to association, from complexity to simple units, and from formal relations to sensory qualities. Anzieu finely expresses this when he writes: "This is showing and not presentation since the emphasis is no longer on representation, which is a rather restrained distancing. [...] The meaning of this feeling is emergence, bursting, breaching. It awes and shocks the mind. It enamors and terrifies it."[28]

Indeed, throughout the play it can be seen that Beckett seeks to present the experience of loneliness in a sensory and unmediated manner, as an aesthetic feeling that evokes, generates, and motivates the consciousness. He uses a variety of techniques that involve sound, lighting, and performance, in order to amplify the representations of the effect, which logically and chronologically precede the sign, the meaning, and the subject.[29] The *unheimlich* image of the woman, and the correlation between the rhythm of the rocking chair and the metallic voice played in the background, are what propel the play metronomically through four textual sections, each of which opens, according to the director's instructions, with a long intermission, during which not a single action, movement or word occur on stage. Each part of the play seems thematically and aesthetically as telling the same story, yet narrative development can be discerned in the consecutive recitations and especially in the last stanza. The protracted pauses between the four parts are interrupted solely by the

---

26 Didier Anzieu and Michèle Monnjauze, *Francis Bacon ou Le portrait de l'homme désespécé* (Paris: Seuil/Archimbaud, 2004).
27 Martin Esslin, *The Theatre of the Absurd* (London: Bloomsbury Publishing, 1985).
28 Anzieu, *Francis Bacon ou Le portrait de l'homme désespécé,* 48–49.
29 See: Reiko Taniue, "The Dying Woman in Beckett's Rockaby", *Journal of Irish Studies* 20 (2005): 86–98; Ruby Cohn, Just Play: Beckett's Theater (New Jersey: Princeton Press, 1980); Charles R. Lyons, "Perceiving Rockaby-As a Text, As a Text by Samuel Beckett, As a Text for Performance". Comparative Drama 16. no 4 (1983): 297–311.

woman's call for "more", which resumes the rocking of the chair and her voice in the background.

till the end
the day came
in the end came
close of a long day
when she said
to herself
whom else
time she stopped
time she stopped

The first part of the play seemingly opens with a dramatic moment of *caesura*, in which the woman decides to stop going to and fro, in search for another creature like her, "another living soul [...] another like her, a bit like her". We do not know what preceded her decision or what led to her experience of loneliness – does she suffer from some physical ailment or isolation, cognitive weakness of dementia, extreme age, or traumatic childhood? Her character remains empty and enigmatic throughout the play, but the word "till" alludes to the long time during which she searched in vain for another creature like her. Her hungry eyes, wandering sideways, high and low, inform us that her loneliness is experienced within her as something forced on her from the outside and against her will, as an egodystonic experience alien to herself. Her decision to stop looking for another creature like her does not indicate a voluntary action of an active and vibrant subject but rather a passive and helpless stance vis-à-vis the feeling of loneliness.

Beckett forces the reader to feel the rejection and helplessness that engulf the woman's inner world through the dense and compulsive repetition of the text and through the breaking of the theatrical convention of the perception of time. He does not allow the decision to stop looking for another creature to be conceived as a temporally unique action, or as a metonymic fragment from which a coherent and continuous narrative can be constructed.[30] Instead, the readers find themselves trapped in a frozen and repetitive time experience, as if in a loop that has neither beginning nor end. This part is made up of a rhythmic pattern of three sub-stanzas, which are repeated again and again, and which are almost identical syntactically, thematically,

---

30 Lyons, "Perceiving Rockaby-As a Text, As a Text by Samuel Beckett, As a Text for Performance."

and linguistically. Each stanza begins with the phrase "till in the end" and ends with the phrase "time she stopped."

The use of the same words, sentences, and syllables, which blend into one another and are recited monotonously and repeatedly to the sound of a rocking chair, turn the speech heard in the background into a hypnotic recitation that is part autistic, part psychotic. Language loses its capacity as a means of communication, and instead, it attacks thinking and does not allow the reader to escape the compulsive repetitiveness of the text. Already at this point it is clear that any attempt to delineate a coherent or linear narrative in the play is problematic. Instead of narrative development and adherence to the traditional Aristotelian structure – which is organized around a plot, with a beginning, middle, and end – the readers find themselves, like the woman in the play, trapped in a repetition compulsion, imprisoned in the present-static state of depersonalization, disintegration, and derealization. They are required to roam "all sides, high and low," in search of a meaning that transcends the experience of loneliness in the sense of "a conditional being."[31]

According to Antonio Ferreira, one of the specific characteristics that distinguishes the experience of loneliness from experiences of aloneness is the tendency of the subject to experience loneliness as a phenomenon imposed on them from the outside against their will and efforts.[32] Unlike the experience of aloneness, in which the person is aware of their active role in the formation of the situation they are in, in loneliness the person feels that they are separated and isolated from others by forces that are outside them. They feel despair, passivity, and rejection because they feel there is no significant other with whom to have a relationship. Ferreira likens this to the feeling of a person locked inside a shell or a vault that is not of his own making. He writes:

> There are no roads to rebuild for there is no place where they could lead. There are no bridges to reinstate, for there are no obstacles to cross. The situation is perceived as final, as the ultimate step into the Void, as the dissolution of Being into Non-Being, as Nothingness.[33]

Indeed, Beckett's choice to reduce the entire particular history of the woman to the act of searching and to the purified moment of a being of absence indicates the way the experience of loneliness affects the subject's sense of time and space, turning it into an experience of "duration," in which there is no perception of past or future, no modalities of time and space, but only

---

31 Viktor Frankl, *Man's search for meaning* (New York: Simon and Schuster, 1985).
32 Antonio J, Ferreira, "Loneliness and psychopathology", *American Journal of Psychoanalysis* 22, no.2. (1962): 201–207.
33 Ibid., 202.

eternal, frozen, and static present. It is in fact also the same frozen, ritual, and stereotypical experience of time and space that sometimes characterizes mental states in which an autistic experiential "pocket" is prominent.[34] Like an unsatisfied urge that acts as a vexing stimulus until it is satisfied, so the experience of loneliness slowly takes over a person's whole being ("*she is **all eyes***") and acts within them as a kind of "black hole" that sucks in and reduces the totality of consciousness into the very feeling of absence and nothingness. The subjective sense of time becomes an affect in itself, as it stands at the center of the experience as a distinct entity and even dominates the experiential world.[35] It reverberates the way in which loneliness constitutes the experience of the self and gradually becomes a kind of mode of being, which affects the way a person exists with themselves and with others.

> *so in the end*
> *close of a long day*
> *in the end went and sat*
> *went back in and sat*
> *at her window*
> *let up the blind and sat*
> *quiet at her window*
> *only window*
> *facing other windows*
> *other only windows*

The second part of the play returns once again to the woman's decision to stop going to and fro in search of "another living soul," but it adds the next stage of her conduct: withdrawal into the interior of the house and sitting by her window waiting for another creature like her. The concrete and metaphorical withdrawal into the interior of the house intensifies as the play progresses, and it hints at Beckett's unique perception of the feeling of loneliness as a formative experience that is not a static event but an ongoing process of withdrawal, convergence, depletion, and mental petrification. In the first part of the play, the woman's wandering eyes actively operated in the outside world, and they echoed her desperate and protracted struggle to find "another like her." Now, she is still longing and looking for the other's gaze, but the window and the house's interior already differentiate her from the outside. The window is an ambiguous representation because it serves as a threshold and limen between inside and outside, between openness and

---

34 Alina Schellekes, "When time stood still: Thoughts about time in primitive mental states" *British Journal of Psychotherapy* 33, no 3 (2017): 328–345.
35 Ibid.

closure, between being a protective wall against the outside world and an opening and aperture through which the outside world can penetrate. Accordingly, the window motif also refers associatively both to the familiar image of "*the eyes as a window to the soul,*" as well as to Leibniz's gloomy description of man as a "*windowless monad.*"

In this part, Beckett employs the archetypal figure of the individual person looking out through his window in order to reflect the way in which prolonged loneliness is gradually experienced in the intrapsychic world as a rupture, alienation, and disconnect from the social world as a whole. Like Fromm-Reichmann's claim that in a state of "real loneliness," the presence of people in the preceding life is forgotten, and the possibility of future interpersonal relationships also slips outside the person's expectation or imagination, so the feeling of loneliness at this stage seems to be identified with the idea of social alienation. This is no longer merely "dyadic loneliness" qua of lack or absence of I-Thou encounters with a particular other, but "triadic loneliness" in which the person experiences alienation and distance from the Big Other, and from the very belonging to the other.

Using Britton's descriptions of the sides of the Oedipal triangle, one can liken the feeling of loneliness at this point to a situation where one feels destined to assume a position outside the Oedipal equation, outside the group, as a rejected "third" relegated to observe "from outside" the relationship between the two.[36] Beckett hints at this direction as he expands the metaphor of the window beyond the particularity of the woman. He writes that her single window faces other single windows (quiet at her window/only window/facing other windows/other only windows), thereby seemingly indicating how a feeling of loneliness paints the internalized object relations and evokes the experience of being in a Kafkaesque, foreign and alienated world. The other as a whole is now experienced as an opaque, closed, and exclusionary entity, that is to say, as a windowless monad.

The woman's hiding behind her window may also indicate the defensive forms of attachment evoked by the experience of loneliness. The ongoing harm that loneliness inflicts on a person's sense of ontological security renders the self-fragile, fragmentary, and flimsy. To protect and preserve oneself, one retreats into one's inner world with the help of unique forms of attachment, which can be described, in the spirit of the play, as "windowed defenses," such as Winnicott's "false self" concept (1960); Steiner's "psychic retreat" (1993); Tustin's "autistic enclosure" (1990), etc. What these defenses

---

36 Ronald Britton, "The Missing Link: Parental Sexuality on the Oedipus complex," in *The Oedipus Complex Today: Clinical Implications*, ed. Ronald Britton, Michael Feldman, and Edna O'Shaughnessy (London: Karnac, 1989), pp. 83–101.

have in common is that they form a buffer between the person and the other, a protective shell in Tustin's terms, which does not allow direct or intimate contact with the other.[37] The true self is in hiding, which seemingly lends them a sense of cover and protection, but at the cost of stagnation, reduction, and distancing from real life.

Winnicott for example described the defensive role of the false self in concealing and protecting the true self.[38] He believed that while the true self comes from the vitality of the body tissues and the bodily functions, the false self leads to the splitting of the psyche-soma, creating a sense of lack of spontaneity, unreality, and futility. In the play, too, the split between the physical body and the consciousness of the woman represented by her voice in the background hints at the experience of fragmentation she has and is even underscored by her tendency to speak of herself in the third person ("she") instead of in first person ("I"). Nonetheless, her decision to raise the curtain of her window ("let up the blind and sat") in the hope of finding another like her, implies, as Winnicott claims, a possible recognition of the true self as a potential that is still allowed a secret life. Her eyes, eager for recognition and validity, are now hiding behind her window, but they keep seeking here and there another creature like her.

Steiner's "psychic retreat" also expresses a similar mental move, which in addition to involving withdrawal and retraction, preserves the dialectical fragility that exists between the life and death instincts.[39] Steiner proposed the term "psychic retreat" as an image of a unique mindset in which a person disconnects from the other and from real relationships and draws back to a kind of shelter or mental retreat that gives them a partial sense of protection and relief. Although the hideout compels its occupant to avoid dealing with what their psyche seeks to shield itself against, and in this sense the former has the characteristics of a death instinct, it is also characterized by a dash of life instinct because of its allowing the psyche to preserve itself until it can face internal and external reality. The relief provided by the hiding place is actually achieved at the cost of isolation, stagnation, and lack of real relationships.

all eyes
all sides
high and low
for a blind up
one blind up
no more

---

37 Frances Tustin, *The protective shell in children and adults* (London: Routledge, 2018).
38 Winnicott, "Ego Distortion in Terms of True and False Self."
39 John Steiner, *Psychic retreats: Pathological organizations in psychotic, neurotic, and borderline patients* (London: Routledge, 2003).

never mind a face
behind the pane
famished eyes
like hers
to see
be seen

The woman's withdrawal to her inner world continues in the third part of the play, but unlike the previous part in which she sought a creature like her while hiding behind the window, she now settles for a blind-up as evidence of the existence of a living human presence. Resorting to the concrete sign of the blind up as evidence for the existence of the Other's presence hints at the way in which the absence of spontaneous and creative relations with the social world gradually leads to deep regression and the dashing into smithereens of thought, self, and other. Unlike the previous part where the woman's withdrawal expressed a distancing from a relation to the object in order to preserve the self (i.e., retreat in the sense of withdrawal), now the withdrawal expresses fragmentation, an assault on thinking and a return to earlier developmental stages (i.e., retreat in the sense of regression). It points at the way in which lasting loneliness creates a sense of depletion and inner void since a selfhood that feeds solely on itself gradually becomes unrealistic, that is to say, an intangible and transcendent selfhood.[40]

This part is imbued with a sense of catastrophic horror that stems from the realization that, for the woman, the windows and houses in themselves no longer signify and attest to human life. Unlike the previous part, where the closed windows represented the alienated other and the way in which the feeling of loneliness creates a rift and disconnect between the person and the other, now the woman feels trapped within a solipsistic and apocalyptic world devoid of the presence of civilization. Her horror echoes the way in which a prolonged experience of loneliness nullifies and disintegrates the representations of the self and the other, thereby evoking intense feelings of terror that cannot be endured for long without becoming psychotic. This, in fact, is precisely the sense of panic that Fromm-Reichmann described in her paper on the feeling of loneliness, and which is well exemplified in a poem written by a patient of hers, named Eithne Tabor:[41]

And is there anyone at all?
And is There anyone at all?
I am knocking at the oaken door ...

---

40 Ronald Laing, *The Divided Self: An Existential Study in Sanity and Madness* (London: Penguin Modern Classics, 1965).
41 Eithne Tabor, 1950. Quoted in Fromm Reichmann, "On loneliness": 320.

And will it open
Never now no more?
I am calling, calling to you—
Do not you hear?
And is there anyone near?
And does this empty silence have to be?
And is there no-one at all to answer me?
I do not know the road—
I fear to fall.
And is there anyone
At all?

One of the interesting things that happen in the reading experience of this part of the play is the deceptive and disturbing gap between the terrifying and nightmarish world in which the woman is supposed to be and the flat and apathetic affect the reader feels as a consequence of the text's repetition compulsion and the monotonously reciting voice in the background. Like Green's descriptions of the characteristics of *"white psychosis,"*[42] it also seems that the white aesthetics of loneliness in the sense of a semiotic representation of emptiness, void, and absence does not allow the reader to emotionally connect to the experience of horror and annihilation of loneliness. It stands in contradiction to the catastrophic premonition and annihilation anxiety evoked by the feeling of loneliness, thus perhaps also hinting at the way in which loneliness presents itself dissociatively on two planes and in two parallel modalities of existence: *void existence* and *annihilation existence.*[43]

On one level, which externalizes itself mainly on the symbolic plane of the play, the feeling of loneliness constitutes what Irit Valdarsky referred to as "annihilation existence," i.e., existence in a punctured and leaky two-dimensional world, with shallow or partial object- and self-representations, which trigger acute distress and anxieties of obliteration and annihilation.[44] This existence has a catastrophic and paranoid-schizoid quality, as being on the verge of the inorganic or non-life. It evokes anxieties of disintegration, dissolution, and extinction facing an infinite inner abyss. Yet on another level, which is externalized mainly through the semiotic representations of the play – in the sense of sound, movement, lighting, and rhythm – loneliness is actually experienced as an apathetic and one-dimensional experience of

---

42 André Green, "The dead mother" *Psyche 47*, no 3 (1993): 205–240.
43 Irit Valdarsky, "Void existence as against annihilation existence: differentiating two qualities in primitive mental states," *International Journal of Psychoanalysis* 96, no.5 (2015): 1213–1233.
44 Ibid.

"annihilation existence." It externalizes itself as an intrapsychic experience of desolation, loss of sensation, and existence in a static space devoid of real objects and living representations. Unlike the first layer in which the dominant experience is the fear of annihilation and disintegration, in the second layer the dominant experience is of calcification and stagnation. It's a form of psychic death in which "there is neither subject nor object. There is neither being nor nothing. There is neither a sense of disconnection from a thing nor attraction to a thing. Existence is not punctured, but it is the puncture itself."[45]

The rocking chair is perhaps the play's main signifier of the layer of void existence of loneliness since in its monotonous, mechanical, and repetitive movement it captures the way the experience of loneliness calcifies the psyche and turns the person into a kind of *Muselmann*, neither alive nor dead, neither loving nor hating, but mostly apathetic, fossilized, frozen in a mental void. Symbolically, a rocking chair associatively refers to signifiers of vitality and sexuality such as fertility, childbirth, and breast-feeding; mother-baby relationship; intergenerational transmission by mothers and grandmothers, etc. The rhythm and sound of the rocking chair are also unconsciously charged with erotic connotations, as they not only mimic the rhythm of lullabies but also the rhythm of a pounding bed during sexual intercourse, which is brought to the fore in the play by the woman's calling "more" at the beginning of each stanza.[46]

In *Rockaby*, however, the rocking chair sways back and forth mechanically and repetitively, by the force of inertia rather than by the woman's will and desire. Beckett explicitly emphasizes in his director's instructions that the rocking chair is "mechanically controlled," and that the chair must move automatically without assistance from the woman. He transforms the living motion of the chair into a mechanical, frozen, and petrified movement until the very last stanza, in which the chair's motion ceases completely and death prevails. Making the living chair an autistic object implies that the shell of the death instinct in a deep experience of loneliness is not by necessity expressed phenomenologically in lively and turbulent processes, characterized by a continuous internal assault or intense emotions, but rather quite the opposite: the person may feel apathy, detachment, indifference, and a resigned acceptance of their condition.

A patient of Fromm-Reichmann described this aspect well when she equated her loneliness to being in a frozen hell: "I do not know why people think of hell as a place where there is heat and where fires are burning. That

---

45 Ibid., 117.
46 Laura Jones, *Alan Schneider's Direction of Selected Monologue Works by Samuel Beckett* (Michigan: UMI, 1989); Taniue, "The Dying Woman in Beckett's Rockaby."

is not hell. Hell is if you are frozen in isolation into a block of ice."[47] Irit Valdarsky also maintains that the uniqueness of void existence lies in the self's being subject to a kind of continued annihilation, but without pain and without annihilation anxieties.[48] In the extreme form of loneliness, it becomes an experience without mentalization, and therefore, as Bolas claims in his descriptions of the *fragile self*, it also does not grasp the fiery power of hatred, envy, contempt, and cynicism that generally characterize personalities that reside in the hell of the death drive.[49]

> *so in the end*
> *close of a long day*
> *went down*
> *in the end went down*
> *down the steep stair*
> *let down the blind and down*
> *right down*
> *into the old rocker*
> *mother rocker*
> *where mother rocked*
> *all the years*
> *all in black*
> *best black*
> *sat and rocked*
> *rocked*

The concluding part of the play represents the woman's final withdrawal from her inner world while forgoing the possibility of communication and contact with another human being. After having found no evidence of a human sign, the woman lowers her blind and descends a steep stair "into the rocking chair, mother's rocking chair." She gives up her search for a human connection and becomes "another of herself, another living soul of herself." Her eyes, which for so long had sought to see and be seen, are now shut. This part is perhaps the most personal and narrative part of the play due to its linking of the feeling of loneliness with a diachronic-developmental perspective, that is, with the woman's depressive mother, who sat all her life in the rocking chair, "all black, the best of black" until she became insane. The reader understands that the rocking chair is "mother's rocking chair"

---

47 Fromm Reichmann, "On loneliness", 319.
48 Irit Valdarsky, "Void existence as against annihilation existence: differentiating two qualities in primitive mental states."
49 Christopher Bolas, *Catch them before they fall: The psychoanalysis of breakdown* (New York: Routledge, 2013).

and that its mechanical, petrified, and inanimate body represents the hollow and empty psychic body of both mother and daughter ("the same arms at last"). The woman's doubt as to whether her mother died during the day or at night implies that it was a mother who had been mentally dead for many years before her physical death.

The last part actually sheds new light on the previous three parts as well, as it allows us to understand in retrospect that the woman's longing eyes, and her constant search time after time for another creature like her, are directly related to the lack of response to primary needs of attachment and to a prolonged feeling of privation. Like the words of the *Rockaby* lullaby describe, by a pleasant rhythm, the baby crib falling from the top of the tree, so too the woman's experience of loneliness is now elucidated as associated with the experience of primary omission, collapse, and intense impingement. The morbid depiction of the mother, associatively referring to the description of the "*dead mother*" by Andre Green's, implies that the woman's thirst for the other's gaze, and for a human face that can evoke and validate her concreteness, stems from the fact that her mother never reflected her daughter's self back to her through her gaze. The opaque windows and the closed blind are actually the echoes of the mother's opaque, shut, and hollow face.

However, I would like to suggest, from a phenomenological point of view, that the uniqueness of the play *Rockaby* does not lie in the connection Beckett proposed between the particular history of a person and their experience of loneliness, but in the way he moves throughout the entire play between the different shades of loneliness – be it loneliness in the sense of social, interpersonal, intrapsychic alienation, existential loneliness, etc. He illuminates the phenomenon of loneliness both as an inherent element of human existence that is inescapable and as a formative experience of the self that in some situations becomes a central mode of being that affects a person's mode of existence with themselves and others. The choice to end the play by linking the woman's feeling of loneliness with an experience of inner otherness ("was the other of herself, another living soul of herself") indicates how the experience of loneliness also involves a deep sense of psychic alienation that exceeds the boundaries of the signifier and its meaning. The other in this case is not the other in the sense of a different consciousness, nor is it the Big Other in the sense as an absolute otherness. Rather, it is an *unheimlich* other that represents the sense of alienation and otherness inherent to the intimate, the familiar, and the known.

Freud, in his paper on the *unheimlich*, also linked loneliness with the feeling of *Unheimlichkeit*, but he reduced the meaning of *Unheimlichkeit* to the castration anxiety and the return of the repressed.[50] He believed that the

---

50 Freud, The Uncanny.

eyes motif and the anxiety of blindness in Hoffmann's *Sandman* story are filled with meaning only once the father substitutes for the Sandman, "the same father we expect him to castrate."[51] In the *Sandman* story, however, the eyes motif is also powerfully reflected through the wax face of Olimpia, the doll, which deceives the protagonist into thinking she is a living creature, except in moments when he looks into her frozen, lifeless eyes. The doll's hollow gaze, reminiscent of the empty gaze of the woman in Beckett's play, also evokes a sense of *unheimlich* horror, but not because it originates in the symbolic plane and the Law of the Father, but because it annihilates the purpose of the human gaze – to indicate the existence of consciousness, perception, expression, presence, vitality, and communication.

Loneliness in this sense can thus be elucidated as the experience of horror that involves being unknown in one's being, being devoid of a validating and presenting gaze of your own self, as Hegel, Levinas, Buber, Winnicott, Kohut, and many others have suggested. In severe cases, it can undermine a person's perception of themselves and their humanity and push them to the realm of psychosis, as Fromm-Reichmann argued, since existence in which the self exists without relation to the other, "I without Thou" in Buber's words, evokes a strong sense of terror and ontological insecurity. It deprives a person of everything that makes them human and makes them a stranger to themselves, a human emptied of his humanity, in the words of Anzieu.[52]

---

51 Ibid., 61.
52 Anzieu, *Francis Bacon ou Le portrait de l'homme désespécé*.

Index

Page numbers followed by "n" indicate a note on the corresponding page.

acquired chronic medical conditions (ACMC) 174–194; complementarity and tragic knots following 179–191; relational complementarities and 179–180; self-dissolution following 175–177; self-illness narrative model 177–178
Aeschylus 50, 51n59, 54n69
Agamemnon 51–53
alienation 10, 12; from nature 13–16
Allport, Gordon 7
Alvarez, A 105n37, 198n2
Amir, Dana 56n8
Analysis of the Self, The 90
Andersen, Hans Christian 209
Angel, Ernest 2
anorexic on the internet 234–239; ana and self-construction, separation from 237–239; commandments use 235; imperative and concrete language use 235; "pro-ana" community 234–237; self-destruction, core mechanism of 235
anorexics/anorexia nervosa 218–240; autobiographies and self-construction among 226–230; defense mechanisms 222; as a disorder of the self 219–221; Kohut's theory of 219; "language-play" in 227; physical habits and 223–224; psyche-soma (body-mind) 220; psychoanalytic perspectives 219–221; self-construction of the anorexic in poetry 230–234; self-constructive vs. self-destructive mechanisms in 218–240; as self-destruction 234–237; self-destruction or self-construction 221–225; writing, self-understanding, and self-construction among 225–226
anorexic social self 224–225
anxiety 10, 13, 41, 52
Anzieu, Didier 272, 272nn26, 28, 283n52
Aron, Lewis 179n16, 180, 184n32, 191, 191n43, 192nn44, 45
Ashkenazy, Yoav 162n69
Ashman, Howard 209n24
Atwood, George E 186, 186n38
Augustine, Saint 58–62, 59n19
Autism children's emotional world 198–217; *Jungle Book* 211; *Little Mermaid* 208–215; *Mowgli* 208–215; non-speaking child 200–201; *Peter Pan* 208–215; *Sleeping Beauty* 208–215; using fairy tales 208–215

Bakhtin, Mikhail 134n6
Bar-Elli, Gilead 201, 201n6, 202n14
Bearn, Gordon C. F. 59, 60n21, 63, 63n32, 67n51
Beauty Myth, The 227
Becker, Ernest 72, 72n65
Beckett, Samuel 263–283; psychoanalytic study of 263–283; *Rockaby* 263–283; *see also* loneliness
"Beetle in a box" metaphor 256
Being and Time 31
Bell, David 38, 38n24
Benjamin, Jessica 174, 177n9, 179, 180nn21–22, 183, 183n31, 191
Bergman, Shmuel Hugo 78n13
Bergstein, Avner 249n30, 252n44, 259n80
Bettelheim, Bruno 208, 208n22

Beyond the Pleasure Principle 153
Billig, Michael 64n38
Binswanger, Ludwig 2–3, 3n2, 269n20
Bion, Wilfred R. 65n45, 86, 86n65, 96, 96n12, 241–262, 244nn8–11, 245n13, 249n29, 250nn33, 35, 251nn36–39, 42, 252n43, 256n65, 258n77, 259n79, 259n81, 265n8
Blidstein, Jacob 22, 22n63
Bolas, Christopher 56n5, 281n49
Bonanno, George A 133n4
Bonomi, Carlo 95n7, 106n44
Borbely, Antal. F. 105n40, 106n43
Bouveresse, Jacques 65n42
Brandchaft, Bernard 56n6
Brentano, Franz 84
Breuer, Joseph 84
Britton, Ronald 105n38, 276n36
Bruch, Hilde 218n5, 219nn6–7, 219–220, 220n16
Bruner, Jerome 226n42
Buber, Martin 3, 22
Burnham, John 7n11
Butler, Judith 178n14, 185, 193n48
Buytendijk, Frederik J. J. 2, 15

Carmeli, Ronnie 249n31
Cavell, Stanley 67n50
Celan, Paul 115
Chasson, Gregory S. 204n16
Cheophoroe 51
Cohen, Adir 208n20
collective existence 22–24
compartmentalization 24
complementarity and tragic knots 177, 180–182; following acquired chronic medical conditions 179–191; freeing the dyad from a 191
Concept of Anxiety, The 69
conceptual investigations 33–55; depression 50–55; empty space of infantile anxiety 37–43; guilt 50–55; interpretation of 33–55; literary fiction as 33–55; projective identification and wish to be another person 43–45; suffering 50–55; superego 50–55; Wittgenstein on 33–37
Concluding Unscientific Postscript 69
Confessions 59
constructivists 177–178
creativity concept 43
Csigó, Katalin 57n13

Dar, Reuven 61n25
Davidson, Michael 186n39
Davis, Lennard J 185n34, 186nn40, 41, 193n47
death instinct 154
depression 50–55
developmental semiotics 100
Dewey, John 7, 223–225, 223nn27, 30, 32, 224n37, 240
Divided Line, The 243
Donald W. 220nn14, 15
Durban, Joshua 86n62, 237n90, 239n94

Eckhart, Meister 252
ego 213
Eigen, Michael 113, 113n4
Ellenberger, Henry 2
Emergence of Ethical Man, The 14
empty sign 108–109
empty space of infantile anxiety 37–43
Erel, Osnat 87n69
Erikson, Erik H. 144n52
Erlich, Shmuel 156n25, 157–158, 158n35, 169, 169n82
Escape from Freedom 267
Esman, Aaron H. 57n10
Esslin, Martin 272, 272n27
Eumenides 52
existence 2–3, 19–26; compartmentalization 24; *existential facts* 19; fact and action 19–21; personal and collective existence 22–24; repression 24–26; separation 24
Existence 5, 7nn10, 13, 23n65, 27n86
Existence: A New Dimension in Psychiatry and Psychology 2
existentialist psychotherapy and eponymous philosophy link 2

Fairbairn, Ronald W. D. 155, 155n11
Farrante, Elena 134n5, 145n54
from fear to creativity 33–55
Feldman, Michael 47
Ferreira, Antonio J. 274, 274n32
Fichte, Johann Gottlieb 80n31
Figueras, Carolina 235n84
Fiurama, Corradi 107n46
Forster, E. M. 44n40
Frank, Arthur W. 185n36
Frankiel, Rita V. 149n62
Frankl, Victor 2, 114n6, 115, 115n10, 274n31

Frege, Gotlobb 123n51, 246n19, 247, 250
Freud, Anna 56n3
Freud, Sigmund 37n21, 38n23, 40n28, 51, 56n2, 64, 65nn39–41, 82, 82nn38–45, 94n3, 99n22, 114n9, 136–138, 137nn18–21, 138n22, 144, 144n49, 153–154, 153n3, 154nn6, 9, 157n33, 165, 165n74, 166nn77, 78, 167n79, 168n81, 253n54, 259n78, 263, 263n1, 264n5, 266–267, 266nn12, 13
Fromm, Erich 85n59, 267, 267n15

Gabbard, Glen O. 57n11
Gadamer, Hans-Georg 77, 77nn8–10, 92
Garver, Newton 253n49, 254n58, 258n75
Giles, David 237n89
Glück, Louise 230–234
Gordon, Baker 142n40
Grandin, Temple 100
Granger, David 223, 223nn29, 33
gravitational field of meaning 163
Green, Andre 104, 104n35, 279n42
Green, Julian 44
Grotstein, James 251nn40, 41, 255n64, 256n67
guilt 50–55
Gunn, Jane M. 176n7
Guthrie 262
Gutting, Gary 160n51
Gyler, Louise 111n55

Hacker, Peter Michael Stephan 141n39
Hagit, Ahorioni 148n61
Hahayim-Seret Metsuyar 210
Halliday, Michael A. K. 127n71
Hardy, Barbara 226n41
Hearn, Alison 199n4
Heaton, John M. 143, 143n44, 46–47, 151n66
Hegel, Georg W. F. 158–160, 158nn36, 39, 160n46, 165n73, 166n76, 171n93
Hegelian phenomenology 160
Heidegger, Martin 3, 13n27, 31
Heinze, Hans-Jochen 219, 219n8
Helen E. Herrman 221n20
Heraclitus 134, 134n8
Herzog, Patricia 84n52
History of Greek Philosophy, A 262
Hoffman, Louis 114n8
homelessness 12–13; alienation 12; anxiety 13; lack of authenticity 13

Hommel, Bernhard 61, 61n27
Hornbacher, Marya 228, 228n58
"hubris" concept 51
Hughes, John 68nn52, 55

icon 99
iconic malfunction, symbolic equation 105–106
If I Were You 44, 50
"I" in Steiner's unitive approach 80–81
Imagination 35nn13, 14
index 99
indexical malfunction 107
infantile anxiety 41
Inhibitions, Symptoms and Anxiety 154
internal states 61
interpretant 100
interpretation 114
Investigations 123, 125

Jackobson, Roman 106n42
James, William 7
Jastrow, Joseph 62n30, 170n88
Jones, Ernest 94n4, 208, 208n21
Jones, Laura 280n46
Joseph, Betty 46, 47n52, 156n19

Kant, Emanuel 253–258, 254n59, 255nn61–62
Kant, Immanuel 78, 79n19, 80n30
Keinanen, Matti 101, 101n27
Kierkegaard, Søren 68–69, 69nn56–59, 120, 120n33
Kitron, David 157–158, 157n28, 158n34, 166n75
Klein, Julie Thompson 199n3
Klein, Melanie 33–55, 39nn26, 27, 40nn29, 30, 42nn34, 35, 43nn36, 38, 44nn42, 43, 46n49, 48n55, 49nn56, 57, 50n58, 51nn60, 61, 52n62, 54n67, 65n43, 86, 94, 94n5, 103, 103n30, 136, 136n16, 138n26, 139, 139nn27, 28, 144, 181n27, 266–267, 266n14
Kohut, Heinz 89nn87–89, 90n93, 91, 91nn94–95, 219–220, 219n8
Kol Dodi Dofek 20, 21n61, 22n62
Kripke, Saul 201, 201nn7, 9, 248n24
Kristeva, Julia 140n32
Kuhn, Roland 2
Kulka, Ra'anan 87n68
Kuusela, Oskari 34n9

Laing, Ronald 278n40
language game and separations 133–151, 161–163; and "dawning" of an aspect 141–144; language as system of activities 142; *see also* separation experience
language games and private language 198–217; non-speaking child with autism, Wittgenstein's contribution to 200–201; preverbal instinctive capabilities 205; rule and use 201–208; "stage-setting" in language 205
Laplanche, Jean 152n2
Lawrence, Nathaniel 15, 15n39
Lazar, Rina 156n25, 157–158, 158n35, 169, 169n82
Lemberger, Dorit 98n16, 103, 103n31, 123n50, 136n17, 229n59
Lester, David 230n66, 232, 233n75
Lev, Gideon 83nn50–51
Levinson, Daniel J. 144n53
Levi, Primo 115
Liddel, Henry G. 252n46
Liebersohn, Harry 22n64
Life Animate 210
Life is an Animated Movie 210
Little Mermaid, The 209–210
Livneh, Hanoch 176n8
Loewald, Hans W. 96, 156, 156n22
loneliness 4–19, 263–283; "aloneness" and, distinction 10; being misunderstood as a reason for 5–9; *fragile self* 281; phenomenology of 270–283; from a psychoanalytic point of view 266–270; Samuel Beckett's Rockaby study 270–283; as singularity 16–19; in a social setting 9–13; white psychosis 279; *see also* alienation; existence
On Loneliness 265
Lonely Crowd, The 11
Lonely Man of Faith, The 10, 4–5, 9, 12n25, 18, 25, 25n77
Lopez-Corvo, Rafael E. 257, 257n70
love 26–30; love of God 29–30; parental love 29; privacy 27
Love and Will 30
Lurie, Yuval 120n39, 122n47

malfunctions in symbolic space 93–112; *see also* psychoanalytic-semiotic integrative model; symbolic malfunctions in psychoanalysis
Malkiel, Eliezer 126n66
Man's Search for Himself 2, 5, 8, 11
Man's Search for Meaning 115
Mansfield, Nick 138n24
Margherita, Giorgia 235n85
Martz, Erin 176n8
May, Rollo 1–32, 3n3, 5n4, 7n12, 9n17, 14n33, 27nn84, 85, 28n88, 30n95
McColl, Mary Ann 189
McGinn, Marie 68n53
McKay, Dean 56n9
meaning in life through language 113–131; limits of the inquiry 116–122; meaning as choice 127–131; ordinary language use 122–127
Meaning of Anxiety, The 2
Meltzer, Donald 266n11
Merrell, Floyd 107n47
Meyer, Victor 66n47
Michaelis, Karin 41
Mills, Jon 83n48
Minkovski, Eugene 2, 15
Mitchell, Stephen A. 177n10, 179n15
monism of thought 79–80; projective identification and 85
monistic philosophy, Rudolf Steiner's 76–92; contribution to psychoanalytic conceptualization 76–92; as a foundation for psychoanalytic conceptualization 85–91; "I" in 80–81; monism of thought 79–80; objective idealism 78; Philosophy of Unity 77–81; projective identification and 85; psychoanalytic thinking and, dialogue between 81–91; "self-object" and "selfobject", monism of thought and 89–91; self, the subject, and the object, relationship 90; subjectivity 89; transitional space and 87–89; unique encounter between 83–85
Monnjauze, Michèle 272n26
Moyal-Sharrock, Daniele 135nn11, 13
Mulhall, Stephen 170n91
Muller, John. P. 99n24, 100, 100n25
Murray, Gilbert 51
Musker, John 209n24
mysticism 252

Nanton, Veronica 180n23
narrative self among anorexics 226–230

narrativists 177–178
Neimeyer, Robert A. 177nn11, 12, 180n24, 192n46
New Revised Standard Version (NRSV) 152n1

object 100
objective idealism 78
obsessive- compulsive disorder (OCD) 56–72; Augustinian picture 58–62; internal states in 61; Paradox of Rules 62–64; "pictures" of reality 58
O'Connor, Daniel 15, 15n39
O'Connor, John 56n7
Oedipus complex 40–41
Ofir, Adi 126n67
Ogden, C. K. 98n21, 105, 105n39, 106n41
Ogden, Thomas H. 56n4, 63, 63n34, 85, 86n60, 96, 96n10
Orange, Donna M. 83n49
Oresteia, The 50, 52–53
Osgood, Kelsey 227, 227nn47, 49, 228, 228n57

Palmer, John 262n89
Paradox of Rules 62–64, 66
Parmenides 243–246, 261–262, 261n88, 262n90
Peirce, C. S. 93, 93n2, 98, 98nn17, 18, 99n23, 101, 102n29, 105, 109, 109n52
personal existence 22–24
Philips, James 101, 101n28, 109, 109n51
Philosophical Investigations 58–59, 62, 67–68, 115, 121–123, 126, 170, 201, 204
Philosophical Remarks 34n7, 35n12
Philosophy of Existence, The 24
Philosophy of Language 246
Philosophy of Unity 77–81
physical habits and anorexic self 223–224
Plato's Cave and Theory of forms, Bion's and Wittgenstein's return to 242–262; Bion on intuition and "O" 248–254; Bion's epistemology of the psyche 243–245; embryonic sight 258–261; epistemological quest 242–243; Kantian ideas, importance 254–258; Parmenides' prologue 261–262

Plato's later dialogs and Wittgenstein's rule-following paradox 245–248
Pontalis, Jean-Bertrand 152n2
Precht, Richard David 141nn35, 38
privacy 27
projective identification 43–50; Klein's interpretation 45–50
pseudo-sign 108–109
psychoanalysis and OCD 56–72; chronology of impasse 56–58; "the real discovery" 67–69; therapy duration 70–72; truth and commitment 69–70; unconscious, in search of 64–67; *see also* obsessive-compulsive disorder (OCD)
psychoanalytic-semiotic integrative model 102–110; confusing levels of symbolization 108; empty sign 108–109; iconic malfunction, symbolic equation 105–106; indexical malfunction 107; sign and object, connection between, rejecting 106–107
psychoanalytic thinking and Steiner's thinking, dialogue between 81–91; philosophy, spiritual doctrines and, relationship 81–83; Steiner's monism of thought as a foundation for 85–91
psychosemiosis 101
psychotherapy and philosophy 1–32; *see also* existence; loneliness; love

Readings in Existential Phenomenology 15
Reichmann, Fromm 264–265, 264n4, 265n6
relational complementarities 179–180; acquired chronic medical conditions and 179–180
relational perspective in psychotherapy 174–194
repetition compulsion 152–154, 165–167; from the standpoint of contemporary theories 154–158; and transparent prison of language 167–169
repression 24–26
Restoration of the Self, The 90
Rice, Emanuel 57n12
Riesman, David 11n23
Rita, Horvath 232n73
Robert C. 221n19
Rockaby study 270–283

Roos, Susan 177n11
Rosenfeld, Herbert 46, 46n51
Rosenzweig, Franz 3
Roth, Meirav 86n62
rule and use 201–208
Rule-Following Paradox 247–248
Russell, Bertrand 247–248, 247n20

Sacks, Oliver 100, 207n19
Sagi, Avi 13n31
Salter, Liora 199n4
Sandler, Joseph 157, 157n30
Sartre, Jean-Paul 3
Sato, Atsushi 61n26
Saussure, Ferdinand 98n19
Sayers, Janet 37n19, 42n32
Schafer, Roy 104n34, 174, 174n3, 180–182, 181n26, 182n28, 184n33
Scheler, Max 5
Schellekes, Alina 275n34
Schopenhauer, Arthur 79, 79n22
Schwartz, Dov 5n5, 13n28, 26n82
Segal, Hanna 42n33, 94, 94n6
Segal, Orin 98, 98n20, 174n2, 176n6
self-constructive vs. self-destructive mechanisms 218–240; *see also* anorexics/anorexia nervosa
self-illness narrative model 177–178; role of the other in 192–193
"self-object" and "selfobject", monism of thought and 89–91
Self Psychology and the Humanities 91
separation experience 24, 133–151; case studies 145–148; change and permanency 134–136; lifetime changes compared to object relations 144–145; Psychoanalytic-Philosophical View about 133–151; in psychoanalytic theories of Freud, Klein, and Winnicott 137–140; Wittgenstein's contribution to 140–144
Set Theory 247
Sexton, Anne 230–234
Shiner, Roger A. 135n10
Shkedi, Asher 125n60
Shotter, John 227n54
Sidney J. 221n18
sign 100
Silverman, Allan 243n5
singularity, loneliness as 16–19
Smith, Kelly Noel 257n69

Soloveitchik, Joseph B. 1–32, 6nn6–8, 9n16, 12n25, 13nn29, 30, 15n40, 16nn42, 43, 18nn49, 50, 20, 20n57, 23, 25n74, 26n80, 27n83, 28n89
Sovran, Tamar 126nn63, 65, 141n34
Spence, Donald 229, 229n62
Spillius, Elizabeth 46, 46n50, 144n50
Spitz, Rene 268n17
splitting 52
"stage-setting" in language 205
Steiner, John 277n39
Steiner, Riccardo 110, 110n53, 111n54
Steiner, Rudolf 76–92, 76nn2–3, 78nn12, 14–16, 79nn17–18, 20–21, 23–24, 80nn25–30, 32–33, 81nn34–37, 84nn53, 57–58, 87nn71, 72, 88, 88n80, 89n83, 90nn90–93; *see also* monistic philosophy, Rudolf Steiner's
Stolorow, Robert D 84n56
Storr, Anthony 138n25
Strauss, Irwin 15
subject's unhappiness 158–160
suffering 50–55
Sullivan, Harry S. 264, 264n3, 267n16, 268
super ego 213
superego 41, 50–55
Suskind, Ron 210, 210n25
symbol 99
symbol externalization malfunction 109–110
symbolic malfunctions in psychoanalysis 93–112; applying the model to clinical work 110–111; as destruction of the connection 95; as difficulty in creating defense 94–95; icon 99; index 99; interpretant 100; object 100; semiotics contribution for 98–102; sign 100; symbol 99; *see also* psychoanalytic-semiotic integrative model
synthetic-a-priori 254–255

Tabor, Eithne 278, 278n41
Tabula Rasa 254
Tauber, Alfred I. 83nn46–47
Terry, Rina 232, 233n75
Theory of forms 242–243
Theory of Types 247
Tillich, Paul 13
Tönnies, Ferdinand 22
Tractatus 252

tragic knots 174–194; being victimized vs. gaining a sense of agency 182–184; complementarities and 178, 180–182; complementarity, freeing the dyad from 191; following ACMC 179–191; interaction in, interpreting 187–191; maintaining privacy vs. belonging and dependency 184–187; *see also* acquired chronic medical conditions (ACMC)
Transformations 251
transitional space, monism of thought and 87–89
translation 114
triadic theory 98
Truth and Knowledge 78
Tustin, Frances 209, 209n23, 212n26, 277n37

Ulman-Margalit 121nn43, 44
Uncanny Essay, The 165
unhappy-certainty 152–172; death instinct 154; to extricate oneself from 169–171; gravitational field of meaning 163; limits of language and 161–163; lord-slave (subject–object) split 159, 160–161; manifestations in a person's life 164; paradox of repetition compulsion 163–167; repetition compulsion under 152–154, 165–167; from standpoint of contemporary theories 154–158; subject's unhappiness 158–160
unhappy consciousness 160–161

Valdarsky, Irit 279n43, 281, 281n48
von Gebsattel, Viktor E. 63, 64n36

Wahl, Jean 160, 160nn50, 52
Warnock, Mary 35nn13, 14
Wasted 228
Weingarten, Kaethe 178n13, 179n17

White, Robert S. 250n34, 256n68
Wieland, Christina 253n50
Wilferd. R. 221n21
Wimsatt, W. K. Jr. 134n7
Winnicott, Donald W. 65n44, 87, 87nn66, 67, 70, 73, 74, 88, 88nn75–79, 81, 89nn84–86, 95, 95nn8, 9, 96, 100, 103, 103nn32, 33, 107n45, 108, 136, 139nn29–30, 140nn31, 33, 144, 155, 155n17, 156, 245n14, 265n9, 269–270, 269nn21–22, 277n38
Wittgenstein, Ludwig 33–37, 34n7, 35n12, 44nn44, 45, 57, 58nn16–18, 59n20, 60nn22–24, 62, 62nn28, 29, 31, 63n33, 64n37, 66n46, 66–68, 67nn48–50, 68n54, 69n60, 70nn61–64, 77nn5, 7, 115–124, 115n11, 116nn12, 13, 120n36, 121n40, 123n52, 124nn57, 58, 125nn61–62, 64, 126nn62, 64, 127n68, 133n2, 135nn9, 14, 136n15, 141nn36, 37, 142–143, 142nn41, 43, 143n48, 149n63, 151n64, 161–163, 161nn54, 56, 58–59, 162, 162nn60, 68, 163nn70–71, 167, 168n80, 169n83, 170nn86, 89, 92, 200–201, 201nn5, 8, 10, 202nn11–13, 15, 204n18, 207, 227–229, 227nn53, 55, 229n61, 241–262, 245n14, 247nn21, 23, 248n26, 249n28, 252n45, 253nn51–53, 254nn55, 57, 256n66, 257n71, 258, 258nn72–74, 76, 261n86
Wittgensteinian-existential perspective 56–72
Wolf, Ernest S. 219, 219n8
Wolf, Katherine M. 268n17
Wolf, Naomi 227, 227n48
Wright, Kenneth 109, 109n49

Yalom, Irvin David 2, 113n3
Yirmiya, Nurit 204n17

For Product Safety Concerns and Information please contact our EU
representative GPSR@taylorandfrancis.com
Taylor & Francis Verlag GmbH, Kaufingerstraße 24, 80331 München, Germany

www.ingramcontent.com/pod-product-compliance
Lightning Source LLC
Chambersburg PA
CBHW052013290426
44112CB00014B/2229